The Cana Sanctuary

The Cana Sanctuary

History, Diplomacy, and Black Catholic Marriage in Antebellum St. Augustine, Florida

Frank Marotti

THE UNIVERSITY OF ALABAMA PRESS
Tuscaloosa

Typeface: AGaramond

Cover photograph: Wedding in St. Augustine, Florida, ca. 1923–24. Photograph by Richard Aloysius Twine. Courtesy of the St. Augustine Historical Society.

Cover design: Gary Gore

∞

The paper on which this book is printed meets the minimum requirements of American National Standard for Information Sciences—Permanence of Paper for Printed Library Materials, ANSI Z39.48-1984.

Library of Congress Cataloging-in-Publication Data

Marotti, Frank, 1954–
The Cana sanctuary : history, diplomacy, and Black Catholic marriage in antebellum St. Augustine, Florida / Frank Marotti.
p. cm.
Includes bibliographical references and index.
ISBN 978-0-8173-1747-8 (trade cloth : alk. paper) — ISBN 978-0-8173-8606-1 (electronic) 1. Fugitive slaves—Florida—Saint Augustine—History. 2. African Americans—Civil rights—Florida—Saint Augustine—History. 3. African Americans—Florida—Saint Augustine—Politics and government. 4. Diplomacy—Social aspects—Florida—Saint Augustine—History. 5. African American Catholics—Florida—Saint Augustine—History. 6. African Americans—Marriage—Florida—Saint Augustine—History. 7. Catholic Church—Florida—Saint Augustine—History. 8. Saint Augustine (Fla.)—Race relations—History. 9. Saint Augustine (Fla.)—Church history. 10. Florida—History—1821-1865. I. Title.
F319.S2M37 2012
305.8009759'18—dc23

2011042575

Dis ting inside Cana town, Galilee side, dis da first time Jesus wen do someting awesome. He wen show how awesome he stay, an da guys he teaching wen trus him.

—John 2:11, *Da Jesus Book: Hawaii Pidgin New Testament*

Contents

Acknowledgments

A major source for this study was the Patriot War claims located at the National Archives in College Park, Maryland. Grants from the National Endowment for the Humanities and the Pennsylvania State System of Higher Education enabled me to spend several months in College Park locating and taking notes on the claims. I could not have found these documents without the generous assistance of archivist Wayne De Cesar. Dr. W. Clinton Pettus, formerly the president of Cheyney University, and the late Dr. Anne S. Jenkins, the ex-chair of that university's Department of Social and Behavioral Sciences, made possible my academic career and encouraged my research, giving me valuable time away from my teaching duties.

Historians of the South Dr. Idus A. Newby, professor emeritus at the University of Hawai'i, and Dr. Whittington B. Johnson, professor emeritus at the University of Miami, were constant sources of inspiration. Charles Tingley of the St. Augustine Historical Society Research Library always responded promptly to my requests for information and assistance. Dr. D. Gail Saunders and her staff at the Department of Archives in Nassau, Bahamas, eased my way through unfamiliar sources. Dr. Mark T. McNally of the University of Hawai'i came to my rescue in the final stages of this project. Daniel J. J. Ross and Daniel Waterman took a chance on me at The University of Alabama Press.

Christopher and Eileen Cortese, along with Margaret Paletta, provided me with much hospitality during the writing process, as did my mother, cancer-survivor Catherine Marotti. The spirit of my father, Frank Marotti Sr., urged me to hurdle numerous obstacles. Ultimately, I wrote this book for the voiceless antebellum African Americans of St. Augustine, Florida, and silent unborn children everywhere.

Introduction
Sanctuary

This study of African American diplomacy in antebellum St. Augustine, Florida, is an intellectual history that explores the roots of a campaign by black Catholics to protect their families from the United States slave society that had solidified by the early 1840s. Because of the economic importance of history to the inhabitants of the former Spanish capital, blacks succeeded in using the past to better secure their present. I argue that significant numbers of white St. Augustinians remembered Spain's rule as a golden age of prosperity and promise that Washington shattered forever. Local black Catholic militiamen stood out in white antebellum memories as heroic defenders of this noble regime. African Americans in St. Augustine, during the last two decades before the Civil War, exploited these memories to negotiate their freedom. By doing so, they were practicing an art that stretched back to 1687.

Around that time, an "embassy" from the Protestant English colony of Carolina reached St. Augustine. The party arrived well prepared. They understood the geopolitics of the Southeast. Immediately, the "diplomats" commenced negotiations that would infuriate Carolina's governor and England's monarch. The agreement that they hammered out with the Spaniards reverberated for nearly two centuries. Two fugitives were anonymous women—one of which was nursing an infant. Their eight male comrades were Cambo, Conano, Dicque, Jacque, Jessie, Gran Domingo, Mingo, and Robi. They had paddled a commandeered canoe, and Mingo had committed homicide, so that his wife and baby could accompany him. Their owners would want them extradited. In need of a sanctuary, they asked for a sacrament—Catholic baptism.[1] It was a brilliant gambit, for by doing so, they had placed Governor Diego de Quiroga's immortal soul in jeopardy. Thus began their liberation.

Oral traditions regarding Catholicism and intelligence gathered from the tongues of black troops participating in Spanish raids in Carolina likely inspired the embassy. When Governor Quiroga refused to extradite the refugees, a wonderfully effective black "grapevine" encouraged others to journey to Florida. Eventually, these fugitives moved the Spanish Crown to make an important foreign policy pronouncement in 1693, when Charles II proclaimed the "liberty" of all of the runaways.[2] In this way, a tradition of coopting whites to speak on behalf of black freedom developed. This constitutes a key theme of my study.

One significant consequence of Charles II's decree was the establishment, in 1738, of Gracia Real de Santa Teresa de Mose, a free black settlement about two miles north of St. Augustine. In the famous Stono Revolt of 1739, the presumed destination of the uprising's Afro-Carolinian participants was the Ancient City. When Spain ceded Florida to the British in 1763, Mose's settlers, along with the vast majority of the colony's inhabitants, evacuated to Cuba. An oral tradition regarding the black settlement went with them. The memory of Mose also survived in British East Florida. Francisco Xavier Sánchez, a prominent cattle rancher who remained behind, along with his slaves, would have remembered it. Since the British had attacked Mose during previous efforts to wrest Florida from Spain, they, too, would not have forgotten the settlement.[3]

Spain's reacquisition of the colony in 1784 reinvigorated historical traditions associated with Mose, since a number of black fugitives from departing English owners invoked the incoming regime's religious sanctuary policy in negotiations for their liberty. These successful diplomats constituted the core of East Florida's free black population during the Second Spanish Period (1784–1821). After more runaways, this time from the United States, parlayed for their freedom under the policy, the Crown, in 1790, bowed to Washington's demands to abrogate it.[4] Nevertheless, memories of the black negotiations conducted under the sanctuary policy remained imbedded in East Floridians' popular historical consciousness.

Black diplomacy was bound inextricably to Catholicism. The "basis of [black] freedom [at Mose]," in the historian Jane Landers's analysis, was "religious conversion, and it behooved [blacks] to be as public as possible about it." Catholicism functioned as a critical "vehicle for African assimilation," as well as for "social acceptance and advancement in Spanish communities. . . . It was the one true equalizer."[5] Thus, Afro–East Floridians, when they attended Mass and received the sacraments, engaged in diplomacy.

Under U.S. rule, as Protestant preachers poured into East Florida starting in 1821, Catholic power waned, and over the years, the number of blacks initiated into the Spaniards' creed declined. Paradoxically, however, between 1821 and

1862, more and more of the region's African American couples asked Catholic priests to bless their marriages.[6] One reason for this development was that Holy Matrimony provided a sanctuary. In the New Testament, at a wedding in Cana, the Virgin Mary convinced Jesus to miraculously transform common water into extraordinary wine. In antebellum East Florida, enslaved negotiators asked the Catholic Church for a miracle: turning what civil authorities regarded as sham nuptials into sacred unions recognized under canon law and duly recorded in writing by an international body exercising moral suasion over their masters.

If they officially sanctioned slave marriages, antebellum southern legislatures believed they would undermine owners' property rights, thereby corroding the chattel principle that supported the "peculiar institution." Historians, in their analyses of why individual slaveholders consented to these nuptials, have pointed to motivations such as paternalism, the need to quell servile resentment through "inversion rituals," the use of Christianity as a social control mechanism, the self-serving promotion of community stability, the assuagement of white guilt, and even a perverse desire to mock their human property. Scholars also have acknowledged the diplomacy, open and hidden, inherent in slaves' wedding ceremonies. Slaves used weddings to underscore the importance that they attached to family life. They appropriated symbols from the dominant culture to proclaim their dignity. Their weddings, in short, carried meanings that helped to protect families buffeted by a slave society. Although the meanings that whites and blacks attached to slave marriages differed, researchers such as Thomas Will have stressed that, practically speaking, even the most elaborate nuptials "posed no serious threat to [the masters'] rule."[7]

Contrary to this assertion, I contend that in antebellum St. Augustine, "an island of Catholicism in a spreading sea of Protestantism,"[8] sacramental slave weddings posed an insidious threat to chattel slavery. Historians have described how the religious beliefs of some masters caused them to confront the "inherent conflict between Divine Law and Southern Law." In 1808, for instance, North Carolina's Sandy Creek Baptist Association validated slave marriages by recommending that owners not break the conjugal ties of their bondsmen. Although this was "less a mandate than a suggestion,"[9] a similar pronouncement emanating from the hierarchical Catholic Church would carry much greater authority among that faith's devout slaveholding adherents. It also should be noted that many slaves deeply embraced Catholicism. Herman Bennett, for example, found that in Mexico, "[t]hroughout the colonial period," the dread of mortal sin and its consequence, "eternal hell," drove "numerous [black] couples" to abandon "common-law arrangements" by having their long-standing relationships "solemnized" within the church.[10]

Catholic masters or priests who, by their indifference, sloth, or obstinacy, refused to afford slaves a sanctified marriage risked their own damnation. Bond persons in antebellum St. Augustine who requested sacramental unions, therefore, engaged in the same patterns of diplomacy that their forebears had practiced in East Florida during the seventeenth and eighteenth centuries. Southern lawmakers, in short, recognized that legalized slave marriages would open a Pandora's box of freedom. East Florida's Catholic slaves aimed to loosen the lid.

Mark Smith, in his study of the Stono Revolt, depicted a "powerful, residual Afro-Catholicism."[11] Antebellum black East Floridians harnessed this force to gently erode a legal foundation of the slave society. Other blacks had done the same. Slaves in colonial Mexico had utilized Catholic marriages both to forge ties to those who lorded over them and to craft ethnic identities for themselves. In a similar vein, throughout the antebellum era, along the Gulf of Mexico, as Virginia Gould discovered, the "overwhelming majority" of people descended from Spanish subjects of color "adhered to Catholicism which in turn reinforced their group identity and thus their status" after the United States acquired the region.[12]

According to the terms of the treaty by which Spain ceded Florida to the United States, all former Spanish subjects, which included free blacks, were to receive American citizenship and presumably enjoy the rights thereof. This provision was contrary to the laws of slave states in the Union, a fact that soon became apparent when the U.S. regime began enacting a series of measures relegating free people of African descent to the margins of society.[13] Still, some black East Floridians were able to summon their "treaty status" to protect their land, property, and social status. Significantly, blacks were not the only "old inhabitants" that the Americans had aggrieved. Plenty of white holdovers, as well, disliked the consequences of U.S. rule. Catholicism tied antebellum African Americans, both free and enslaved, to the Spanish regime, a government that many of their white neighbors remembered as having presided over East Florida's golden age.

Moreover, it was in the financial interest of many of these "old inhabitants" and their descendants to keep anti-American memories part of the public discourse. In 1812, invaders from Georgia, supported by federal troops, sought to foment a revolution that would replace monarchy with a republic that would request annexation to the United States. From Washington's perspective, East Florida was, in modern parlance, a "failed state" that created numerous security threats. Its bustling entrepôt of Fernandina, on Amelia Island, harbored those desiring to profit from punitive American commercial policies aimed at disrespectful European powers. Other men used the free port to evade the recent U.S. prohibition of the international slave trade. Seminole warriors raided the Georgia frontier with impunity. Runaway slaves gravitated south to Seminole sanctuaries. East Florida's military depended upon free black soldiers. Loyalist planters prospered. And, if Britain were to seize or acquire East Florida, the United States would face a dire threat to its independence. Finally, the Spaniards controlled an abundant reservoir of rich cotton land, timber, and cattle.[14]

Washington had acquired territory in West Florida in 1810 after American filibusterers inspired a "republican revolution" and an annexation petition. Why not, President James Madison thought, try this tactic again? The United States, at a low cost in blood and treasure, could tighten its security while maintaining the image of an innocent bystander who was only complying with the will of the people in a neighboring fledgling republic. In prosperous East Florida, however, Georgia filibusterers failed to attract much voluntary support. To make matters worse, besieged St. Augustine refused to capitulate. Then, Seminoles and blacks embarrassed U.S. forces by breaking the siege. For a few more years, East Florida remained Spanish, but it did not regain its prosperity. The scorched earth policy of the retreating invaders did much to ensure the colony's poverty.[15]

East Floridians of all classes and ethnicities long remembered the devastating, life-shattering events of this "Patriot War" of 1812–1813. These nightmarish memories provided leverage for antebellum African American diplomats. When Spain formally ceded Florida to the United States in 1821, the latter pledged to compensate Spanish subjects for damages caused "by the late operations of the American Army in Florida." Congress implemented this provision in an act of 3 March 1823, authorizing federal judges in Florida to adjudicate claims and make awards. The secretary of the treasury then was to review the awards and pay those that he found "just and equitable." But the only damages covered under this law were those occurring during U.S. military incursions in 1817–1818. Not until 1834, did Congress declare that "losses occasioned in East Florida, by troops in the service of the United States in 1812 and 1813," also fell under the 1823 act. For "more than half a century," the historian Rembert Patrick wrote, "claims for losses cluttered courts of the United States."[16] In the meantime, the adjudication process generated a rich historical record that documented the lives of white and black East Floridians at the outbreak of the Patriot War, during the conflict itself, and in the years beyond.

While conducting research at the National Archives under grants from the National Endowment for the Humanities and the Pennsylvania State System of Higher Education in 2000, I rediscovered approximately two hundred Patriot War claims cases.[17] The vast majority of these cases had not been examined by historians because the documents were thought to have perished in a nineteenth-century fire at the Treasury Department. Many times, the archival staff had to break the red wax seals that bound the cases' pages together, so that I could read them. In this study, my concern is not with the veracity of the testimony in relation to the actual events of the Patriot War. Rather, I am interested in what witnesses said that they remembered. That is, my focus is on what can be learned about East Florida under U.S. rule, even though witnesses, on the surface, were discussing the latter years of the Second Spanish Period. The testimony that supported these lawsuits, besides being a popular history of the Patriot War, also constitutes an antebellum intellectual history of everyday people who had been engulfed by an expanding American empire. In particular, the pages of the claims cases bring to life voices of African Americans, Hispanics, females, the elderly, youths, and the impoverished, as they protested U.S. foreign policy.

The litigants' primary goal was to obtain as much monetary compensation from the United States as possible. Protest, therefore, is an integral part of their petitions. But, because a great many of the witnesses offered testimony between the mid-1830s and the mid-1840s, when they were reeling from the twin blows of the Second Seminole War and economic depression, the legal proceedings furnished East Floridians with a dais from which to register their displeasure with the vagaries that had followed the Stars and Stripes. Furthermore, East Florida's respected elders could contrast the Spanish colonial government's efficiency in providing relief from a destructive hurricane that struck in 1811[18] with Washington's dilatory tactics and byzantine judicial rulings. These hearings in East Florida's federal court reopened wounds that had festered for a generation or more. Consequently, a certain solidarity transcending age, class, ethnicity, gender, and race was reborn. African American claimants came to share common interests with white neighbors, and such unity had been the bedrock of black diplomacy.

Taking advantage of their treaty status, free persons of color who had been Spanish subjects filed claims. In doing so, blacks acted as diplomats. They seized a unique opportunity to publicly chastise the United States for constraining their liberty and stifling their human potential.[19] Blacks coopted white witnesses who agreed to provide testimony in their cases. At the same time, evidence suggests that whites found it necessary to gather essential information from free blacks and slaves. The entire Patriot War claims adjudication process constituted a multiethnic project that solidified African American ties with whites, which, in turn, provided diplomatic leverage for protecting black freedom. Significantly, court testimony cast the Americans as barbarous villains who had plundered (and were plundering) East Florida of its wealth under the guise of pledges of political stability, republicanism, and economic opportunity. A resultant longing for the good old days of Spanish (Catholic) rule armed African American folk diplomats with a sword.

And, history could be used as a shield. The claims cases reminded whites of black achievements during East Florida's glory days. They demonstrate that antebellum African Americans circulated stories of the exploits of Spanish-era free blacks and slaves. These tales fueled hope and pride in a beleaguered community fending off American attacks on its freedom. Moreover, because of the social upheaval that the Patriot War generated, Afro–East Floridians who lived through it had viewed the carnival-like spectacle of white masters being fed bitter doses of humiliation normally reserved only for people of color. Such incidents would have been the seeds for humorous barbs secretly directed at slave owners. Humor, along with heroes, helped to make black life more bearable. Conversely, sensitive or thoughtful masters, as a result of the "enslavement" that they had endured during the Patriot War, and the black bravery that they witnessed, subconsciously viewed African Americans with Spanish ties more sympathetically than those people of color who lacked these linkages. Thus, black diplomats enjoyed more "wiggle room."

The Second Seminole War (1835–1842), perhaps the largest slave rebellion in United States history,[20] provided African Americans with a new generation of heroes. Heroes most likely weaned on tales from Spanish days. Many of them were diplomats serving as intermediaries between the Seminoles and the United States.[21] Since the Patriot War, Spanish East Florida's slaves increasingly fled to the interior for sanctuary among the Seminoles. Black fugitives from the United States joined them. During the chaotic aftermath of the Patriot invasion, the British, too, had promised sanctuary to runaway slaves. Accordingly, from Seminole havens, some Afro–East Floridians made their way to the Bahamas. On Andros Island, British authorities opted to respect the liberty of Florida fugitives. To this day, their descendants have preserved stories of their peninsular origins.[22]

The freedom saga of Andrew Gué illustrates how East Florida's tradition of African American diplomacy aimed at sanctuary was alive and well after the Second Seminole War. Gué, weaned during the Patriot War's upheaval, had attained notoriety among whites (and fame among blacks) as a consequence of his bold support of the Seminole cause during the late 1830s. By 1843, his youthful anger appeared to have subsided. He embraced Catholicism, started a family, and was working to purchase his liberty. In the summer of that year, nevertheless, he mimicked the actions of seventeenth-century black diplomats from Carolina. With several enslaved companions, Gué seized a seaworthy vessel from St. Augustine's harbor and sailed for a sanctuary. His destination was not Spanish territory. Instead, the black grapevine directed him to the British Bahamas, where slavery had been abolished. On their voyage, the fugitives killed a settler while foraging for supplies. Newspapers breathlessly reported their daring. When the British refused to extradite them, an international diplomatic furor ensued.[23] Once again, black diplomats were able to enlist white formulators of foreign policy to defend their aspirations.

Nearly two decades later, Gué's erstwhile African American community in St. Augustine compelled another member of the white elite to be the official spokesperson for their liberty. These black diplomats of the antebellum statehood era directed their efforts toward ameliorating two long-standing problems in East Florida—the breakup of enslaved families and the sexual abuse of women of color, problems that had worsened as the U.S. administration took root.[24] Their diplomacy produced a surprising advocate. He was Jean-Pierre Augustin Mercellin Verot, a Frenchman who had become the shepherd of East Florida's Catholic flock in 1858. Verot's 1861 sermon in St. Augustine's eighteenth-century cathedral defending the Confederate cause earned him the sobriquet "the Rebel Bishop."[25] The prelate's homily, like slave weddings, contained layers of meaning. I contend that skillful negotiations informed his message. That is, the Frenchman's words reflected black diplomacy that had been forged in a 170-year-old crucible.

My first five chapters are based mainly on the Patriot War claims cases. The vast majority of testimony in these chapters comes from white witnesses, although there are some black voices that illuminate an African American version of the conflict. I agree with historians such as John B. Boles, W. Fitzhugh Brundage, and Eugene Genovese, who contend that one cannot separate slaves' histories from those of slaveholders. Furthermore, following Lawrence Levine's *Black Culture and Black Consciousness,* I allow witnesses to speak for themselves to a great extent, so that readers might absorb more directly the memories of antebellum East Floridians.[26] The last two chapters are case studies demonstrating how black diplomats utilized this history in order to negotiate their freedom. Mindful of the "hubris" of historians "who work in quiet libraries . . . and believe . . . that they can reconstruct the life of a slave from a few marks on a page,"[27] I have striven to illuminate a veiled history, for even when my sources record black voices, they have been muffled by white hands.

I
"The Good Old Flag of Spain"

Three years after the Civil War's end, and nearly five decades after Old Glory first had been hoisted over St. Augustine, Eliza M. Whitwell finally was coming home. She had been a young bride when her neighbors exiled her from the Ancient City in 1842. Now, as a physician's widow, she was returning to East Florida because of a sense of duty, rather than for sentimental reasons. Mrs. Whitwell announced her intentions in a bitter letter to Dr. John Peck, the scion of one of the town's most distinguished families. She complained about the injustices that had made her life hard. These troubles had plundered her beauty. She feared that people who had known her in her youth would no longer recognize her. Nevertheless, she still found room in her heart to praise the flag—but not the Stars and Stripes. Instead, she reserved her tribute for "the good old Flag of Spain" that "enslaved none but the slaves giving equal rights & privileges to all as her subjects without distinction." To be sure, the coming of United States rule had not brought her family the blessings of democracy. Instead, America's "bad Laws . . . drove us away from our homes & prevented us from returning . . . to see to our property."[1]

That property was substantial. George J. F. Clarke, Whitwell's grandfather, had been an "intimate friend and trusted adviser of the Spanish governors." Clarke had succored his sovereign as East Florida's surveyor general, in addition to functioning at various times as a militia officer, timber agent, interpreter, justice of the peace, police chief, deputy governor, engineer, and diplomat. The Crown reciprocated, making him "one of the largest landowners in Florida." He was well connected, both socially and politically. His prestige survived long after his death in 1836. On 30 December 1845, federal judge Isaac H. Bronson, who in his official capacity had heard and read hundreds of eyewitness accounts describing life in Spanish East Florida, concluded that the Clarke family had been one "of some wealth and consideration."[2] Whitwell still was able to bask in the glory of her grandfather's achievements a half century after Judge Bronson's assessment.

A St. Augustine newspaper article published in 1894 recounted Clarke's role in the "lowering of the Spanish flag . . . on the 10th of July, 1821, at noon." It described him as the royal colony's "Lieutenant-Governor" who was "at the time acting consul at St. Marys, Ga., an important shipping point for Florida." The governor had summoned his consul home in order to participate in the ceremony marking East Florida's cession. Indeed, the "flag of Spain fell and the stars and stripes were unfurled by [Clarke's] hands." The article then informed its readers that one of his granddaughters, Mrs. Eliza M. Whitwell, "still lives in this city, and although 81 years of age, has a wonderful command of language, an excellent memory, recounting the story of her life with wonderful pathos." Due to a leg injury, she was being looked after "gratuitously" by a "prominent physician" and the "King's Daughters." She derived additional comfort from "a picture of her grandfather, in the dress of a Spanish officer."[3]

Whitwell also had preserved a treasure trove of family documents. In a follow-up letter to Dr. Peck in 1868, she scolded the physician for attempting to circumvent her during a looming land dispute, reminding him that she, rather than her male relatives, was "to be consulted in the affairs of my Father's property." "I am," Mrs. Whitwell wrote, "his eldest child & well known to all his affairs & my Grand Father's, as well." At the time of her death, she was eulogized as a woman "constantly going to the post office, never without a large bag of papers, which would confirm her titles to numerous landed estates in and about St. Augustine, this property having belonged to her grandfather Clarke."[4] His Patriot War claims, which she surely had access to, besides more fully explaining why Clarke's octogenarian grandchild cherished Spanish rule, boasted of East Florida's booming economy at a time when Washington considered the province a "failed state" in need of American redemption.

The roots of the Spanish colony's prosperity lay largely in the United States quest for national security. At a time of international conflict between Great Britain and France, the young nation had aimed to stay neutral and create a windfall by trading with both belligerents. Thus, not only would it preserve its resources and independence, it would grow its economy. When the British and French thwarted this strategy by refusing to respect America's neutral rights, President Thomas Jefferson, in 1807, moved Congress to approve the Embargo Act. Jefferson's plan to bring the British and French to their knees by forbidding American ships from trading abroad backfired. After the U.S. economy went into a tailspin, the Non-Intercourse Act replaced the embargo in 1809. This measure singled out Britain and France, prohibiting commerce only with these battling superpowers. Once more, however, America's economic warfare failed. By 1812, the politically divided and economically depressed fledgling republic found itself fighting mighty Great Britain.[5]

The contrast between the bustling economy in the royal domain south of the St. Marys River and the stagnating one of the United States is striking. Francis R. Sánchez recalled that in 1812, East Florida had been "tranquil and prosperous for ten years." Sánchez added that there were "no taxes—no oppressive duties to perform." A "good deal of wealth," Mary Smith stressed, resided there. Zephaniah Kingsley and Dr. James Hall wholeheartedly seconded her opinion. Matthew Long remembered a colony in "a flourishing condition . . . and the people comfortably situated." Charles W. Clarke agreed that the "country was in a thriving state." Likewise, his brother, George J. F. Clarke, contended that the "condition of the country was most prosperous—every man was making his fortune, hand over hand, as fast as he could." Mrs. Sarah Acosta concurred, asserting that in those days, there was a "great deal of comfort and independence."[6]

Jeffersonian foreign policy inadvertently had created a healthy demand for Spanish Florida's timber and cotton. Eager to cash in on a bonanza, George J. F. Clarke had relocated his family in 1808 from St. Augustine to Fernandina, which suddenly emerged as East Florida's "commercial center." Boasting a fine harbor and easily accessible location on Amelia Island's north end, nine miles from St. Marys, Georgia, the entrepôt attracted merchants and smugglers. The end of the U.S. participation in the international slave trade also drew them. Fernandina's mushrooming streets "abounded" with boards and scantling intended for local construction, so much so that there was no place to secure it. Governor Enrique White eventually called upon Clarke, who lived in a "very fine frame dwelling house," to reconfigure the boom town's disorderly layout. The port's population soon surpassed that of hoary St. Augustine. By 1815, four out of ten Floridians resided in the urban upstart. As Clarke explained, "in consequence of the restrictive measures of the American Government, the trade of the United States with all the world except Spain centred at Fernandina." Joseph M. Hernández recalled that the settlement "had just sprung up . . . buildings were multiplying" and "150 square rigged vessels from all nations at one time" anchored "in the Harbor." Brisk trade meant that "money was plenty."[7] The Spaniards had trumped Washington's designs to profiteer from European quarrels.

Spain's search for security likewise spawned Clarke's cheery financial prospects. To bolster their frontier with the United States, the financially strapped Spaniards took the calculated risk of attempting to buffer East Florida by opening its borders to American and other foreign settlers. Beginning in 1790, the

Spanish offered immigrants liberal land grants in proportion to the number of family members and slaves that they brought into the province. In order to attract more capital, the Crown fueled "a rage for lumbering in consequence of certain privileges and inducements offered to the Inhabitants." Only Spanish subjects were permitted to cut timber in East Florida. Those immigrants who swore a loyalty oath could fell trees on public land "free from any cost or charge." On the Georgia side of the St. Marys River, lumbermen paid a fee of twenty-five cents per tree. In 1812, according to Zephaniah Kingsley, "one Hundred sail of vessels," mostly foreign, were waiting at Fernandina to load lumber, and almost everyone in the province was cutting it."[8]

Clarke counted himself a member of this crowd. As the colony's surveyor general, he was entitled to a portion of its timber exports for his salary. Consequently, he amassed copious amounts of this valuable commodity. He acquired more lumber privately. Some was purchased, but most came from his own "establishment." He cut trees at six locations near the St. Marys and St. Johns Rivers. In order to carry on these logging operations, he invested significant funds. Horses, oxen, wagons, carts, chains, harnesses, as well as an assortment of tools and boats were required. He needed lumberjacks and teamsters, so he employed slaves, whites, and free blacks. Clarke supplied each worker with an iron pot and an axe, housed the men in clapboard cabins, and fed them with corn, rice, and pork. Matthew Long recalled that "it is well known that [Clarke] had everything in first-rate order" and that the buildings, provisions, utensils, furniture, and implements in his lumber camp "must have been very considerable."[9]

Just before the American invasion of 1812, Clarke anticipated earning $1,470 from twenty piles of white oak barrel staves, each pile eight feet high, that sat in the "Swamp" of the Little St. Marys River. The purchasing power of this sum can be gleaned from witnesses who remembered the yearly wages of a lumber worker as being anywhere from $144 to $300. Elsewhere, John (Juan) Leonardy had helped to cut "a good many cords" of pine and had "arranged the greater part of it" on the banks of Pigeon Creek. Clarke estimated that this lathwood was worth $285. At other spots on the St. Marys and its tributaries, the surveyor general had cut "a large quantity" of good-quality yellow pine ranging timber that he valued at approximately $3,300. To the south, a mile from the mouth of Julington Creek, which empties into the St. Johns River near modern-day Jacksonville, Clarke's men had collected red cedar, which they had cut, hauled to the water's edge, and prepared for market. Its price at that remote location was $5,615. This figure would double once the cedar reached Fernandina.[10]

Because "it was the time of the American Embargo and lumber was very high," Clarke logged year round. John Moses Bowden and Peter Pons remembered sizable rafts of Clarke's timber frequently floating down the St. Marys.

Clarke's cedar was rafted to Fernandina via the St. Johns. Pedro Rodríguez, in 1838, could visualize the rafted logs "piled up and down the water side" of the port. In addition to the "large quantity of lumber on the Beach in front of the city," Pons had observed a "great deal" more sitting near Clarke's dwelling house and horse-powered sawmill on Egan's Creek. When Joseph Lourcey would converse with Clarke's slaves whom he encountered going back and forth from the "maine to Amelia," they told him that they were engaged in harvesting timber. The surveyor general's expectations for 1812 were high. Clarke built boats of his own, and in 1811, he had two carts "suited to the lumber business" shipped to Amelia Island. They were "fitted with chains and harness complete." John Leonardy opined that Clarke "was well known as the most enterprising of all others carrying on the lumber business."[11]

Other "old inhabitants" might bestow this title on the already wealthy John Houston McIntosh, a "shrewd and hard-nosed businessman" whose lust for mammon drove him to forsake the U.S. republic for the Spanish monarchy. In 1803, McIntosh left Georgia with his family, established residency in East Florida, and pledged his allegiance to a distant sovereign. By 1812, he had garnered a lucrative lumber contract that annually earned him thirty-six thousand dollars above his expenses. Gabriel Priest, his "first rate" timber manager, strained to deliver three hundred thousand feet of pine ranging timber each month for three years to an agent for a Liverpool firm. British ships at Fernandina "were loading all the time with this timber." Approximately sixty "strong and able" male slaves, eight to ten white men, twenty-six yoke of oxen, and twenty horses labored under Priest's direction on the St. Marys. All were part of the "very extensive and systematic arrangements" that McIntosh made to fulfill the terms of his "immense" contract.[12]

McIntosh also invested heavily in the second pillar of East Florida's prosperity—Sea Island cotton. He fixed his "principal place of residence" at his Fort George plantation, which he constructed on a barrier island three miles long and half as wide, at the mouth of the St. Johns River, some forty miles south of Fernandina. The overseer, John G. Rushing, supervised between 160 and 170 slaves. This "splendid" plantation's 70 to 80 "able bodied working hands" were either women, or men too weak to join their comrades toiling in the forests under Gabriel Priest. Of the island's 600 acres of "planting land," 250 to 300 acres were devoted to cotton. Provisions—corn, peas, and sweet potatoes—were raised, too. McIntosh claimed to have cleared seventeen thousand dollars each year from this estate's cotton production. Thirty miles away, on the west bank of the St. Johns, at the mouth of McGirt's Creek, he cultivated a second plantation, "Ortega." Here again, the 30 to 40 field hands were mostly females. They looked after 120 to 130 acres of cotton, along with 60 to 70 acres of provisions. William

Broadnax described Ortega as "extensive" and "well improved," though not as large as Fort George. McIntosh, in his lumber and cotton concerns, Joseph M. Hernández sniffed, "was enjoying every advantage." He was "almost coining money."[13]

Zephaniah Kingsley and John Fraser were even more systematic cotton planters than McIntosh. They sank their funds into the large-scale introduction of "picked" slaves directly from Africa. Kingsley had come to East Florida in 1803. "Laurel Grove," the center of his plantation complex, was six miles from Ortega, on the west bank of the St. Johns at the mouth of Doctors Lake. A mile from Laurel Grove stood "Springfield," and five or six miles away, Kingsley established "Canefield," also known as "Elm Spring." These three plantations, still "very good cotton and provision lands" in 1843, "might in fact be considered as one, as they were all contiguous to each other." He planted two hundred acres of cotton in 1812, and he anticipated earning twenty thousand dollars from this source alone. Seymour Pickett explained that the reason for Kingsley's "division of his negroes into different fields, was that he might cultivate the most choice lands." Over a hundred slaves wrested wealth from the soil. Kingsley had chosen "principally young, full grown African Negroes," so compared to most cotton plantations, the percentage "of old put out & infants was unusually small." The "greater part" of these Africans were men.[14]

Fraser, who arrived in East Florida around 1808, "selected & brought" African slaves into East Florida on a more massive scale than Kingsley. Perhaps he had been encouraged by the latter's agribusiness, where half of the crop amounted to pure profit. Francis Richard Jr., Fraser's overseer at the Greenfield plantation from 1810 to 1812, worked 206 "picked young negroes" who were "introduced but a few years before from the Coast of Africa." Greenfield was situated on the west side of Pablo Creek, three miles from the mouth of the St. Johns. It was "first rate Hammock Land well calculated for cotton." Richard's charges planted eight hundred acres of cotton with an estimated worth of $80,000. To the north, on the St. Marys at the Great Cut Off plantation, 60 to 70 additional "picked hands" cultivated a large rice field for Fraser's benefit. The "ditching and dams" that they constructed "took in" five hundred acres. Judge Isaac H. Bronson ruled that Fraser would have earned $11,600 from this rice plantation in 1812.[15]

A number of East Florida's cotton planters were women. As in the cases of McIntosh, Kingsley, and Fraser, Mrs. Catherine Baker maximized her workforce by dividing it. She owned three plantations and over one hundred slaves. Her main cotton plantation, the Orange Grove of San Pablo, was built on the St. Johns River, just south of Fort George Island. She expected to realize $17,500 from this single crop in 1812. Mrs. Baker, a South Carolinian, had acquired this estate from her first husband, Andrew Dewees, who died in 1794. Baker's next two husbands, the last of whom had died in 1808 or 1809, had contributed no additional land or slaves. According to Spain's precepts, the holdings that a woman brought into her marriage were not transferred to her husband's control. In Spanish times, acceded a somewhat befuddled Judge Bronson, "such things could well be." By the treaty that ceded Florida to the United States, American officials were bound to recognize "all the immunities" of the king's former subjects. Rather than being grounded in English common law, these immunities were based on the *Siete Partidas* of the thirteenth-century Castilian monarch Alfonso X.[16]

This financial independence seemed to generate respect for the abilities of women planters. Although Mrs. Baker was an "unprotected widow," she was admired as a "woman of property" who lived in "affluence and plenty" on a "planting interest that was drove ahead." Several of George J. F. Clarke's neighbors were female cotton entrepreneurs. The "lone widow" Lucy Fitzgerald, who cultivated the staple on Amelia Island and owned forty slaves, "lived very independently & was always reputed to make large & valuable crops." She augmented her labor force by cutting live oak, using the proceeds to acquire more slaves. Her neighbors believed that her deceased husband had "married her on account of her property." Mary E. Saunders also grew cotton on Amelia Island, utilizing land and capital "not subject to the control of her husband." Mrs. Saunders enjoyed "comfortable" circumstances "with a prospect of Early wealth." Her "successful and prosperous sister," Margaret Starrat, kept a "fine bunch" of twenty to thirty slaves at Seymour's Point, near the Nassau River's mouth, on the mainland, just opposite of the island's midsection. Thomas Suárez remembered her as a "good planter" whose skills were reflected in her "elegant" dwelling house. Samuel Russell recalled that she "was alone interested in this property." Her father had given it to her, and Thomas J. Andrew stressed that under "Spanish Law it was hers, and is so now."[17]

Fifty-four miles south of St. Augustine, Mrs. Ann Maria Williams, whose husband had died in 1811, leaving her with four children, ran Orange Grove, a 3,200-acre estate on the Halifax River. Samuel Williams, in the year of his death, owned fifty to sixty slaves on this plantation, and the same number on Watling Island, in the Bahamas. Regarding Orange Grove in 1812, Philip Weedman Sr. remembered that she "controlled and managed it all." Mrs. Williams counted on earning $10,230 from her 136 acres planted in cotton. A mile to her north, another widow, Mrs. Frances Kerr, raised $7,200 worth of cotton on 96 acres, with a labor force of twenty-four to thirty slaves. She was esteemed as an "intelligent," "industrious woman" and "skilful manager," who was "well versed in the business of planting." In the same general vicinity, along Tomoka Creek, a third widow, Mrs. James Ormond, with thirty to forty enslaved hands, made forty to fifty bales of cotton per year that brought her $6,750. Her acquaintance, the former Mrs. Williams, testified that Mrs. Ormond had been a "thrifty planter" and a "good manager."[18] Eliza Whitwell's independence, assertiveness, and business sense was derived partly from the ambience that Spanish law and successful female planters had engendered in East Florida.

She also could credit her grandfather Clarke with passing these traits to her. He realized that if he could somehow plant a stake in the cotton boom, he could tap into a vast reservoir of local wealth. One historian has calculated that commodity prices in nineteenth-century East Florida should be multiplied by about thirty-five in order to approximate their dollar value for the year 2000. Using this criterion, Fraser's annual cotton earnings would be $2.8 million; Kingsley's, $700,000; Baker's, $612,500; Williams's, $358,050; Kerr's, $252,000; and Ormond's, $236,250. Unlike these planters, however, the surveyor general owned only ten adult working slaves. Of the four women, one tended to Clarke's domestic needs, while the others were hired out as laundresses or house servants. The six men mostly labored, alongside rented slaves and free wage-earners, in his lumber business, where he concentrated his resources. Clarke participated in commercial agriculture as a middle man who earned a commission by buying his neighbors' crops, storing them at Fernandina, and selling them for export. In fact, he "was in the habit of buying and selling a great many kind of goods, he had a great deal to do, with the shipping in Port," and he had a "good deal of cotton in store."[19]

Clarke claimed that in 1812, his warehouse contained fifty-eight bales of Sea Island cotton averaging 375 pounds each, worth $10,870, or about $380,450 in modern currency. Lorenzo Gracesqui (Lawrence Graceski), almost thirty years later, recounted how, two or three days before the Americans invaded, he had been working for him in a warehouse near Clarke's residence on the creek east of Fernandina's fort, repairing the bales, patching them, and "setting the negroes to pick over cotton." Clarke also claimed fifty additional bales that were the property of the firm of Clarke & Garvin. Shortly after moving to Fernandina, he entered into a business partnership with William Garvin, who would become Eliza M. Whitwell's father. Garvin was remembered as "an ingenious and industrious man" who "improved every thing that came into his hands." The import-export firm purchased cotton, lumber, and "other staples." The majority of its trade involved cotton, but its "business was to buy and sell any kind of goods." Pedro Rodríguez remembered that "the association of Clarke and Garvin commenced with the embargo." As in the case of lumber, George J. F. Clarke was scrambling to take advantage of international geopolitics. A controversy concerning the quantity of bales on hand in 1812, and whether or not they belonged to Clarke individually or to the partnership, would embroil Whitwell, her family, and the federal government into the twentieth century.[20]

According to one witness, Clarke also grew cotton "on a small scale." If he did, it must have been for family use, because there is no indication that he derived significant cash from it. In any case, he was not a member of the planter class. The surveyor general and his brother Charles did inherit a three-hundred-acre Spanish grant from their mother, Mrs. Honoria Clarke. This tract was on the south side of Moses Creek at its mouth, along the Matanzas River. George occupied the northern end and Charles lived on the southerly portion. St. Augustine stood twelve miles to the north. The brothers cut and sawed a good deal of timber in their neighborhood. They also gathered oyster shells for their lime kilns. The Clarkes floated the wood and lime to town on their flatboats, since the government required shingles for public buildings, and the outside walls of houses were kept clean by whitewashing them with lime. Charles cultivated twenty-five to thirty acres of a forty- to fifty-acre fenced field. George planted a little more—forty to fifty acres. Both men raised corn, peas, sweet potatoes, pumpkins, and other vegetables. They probably sent their surpluses to market. Each had formerly resided on their Matanzas plantation, but because they busied themselves in government service, the timber industry, and mercantile concerns, and had moved their slaves and families with them to Fernandina, they hired some free men of color to work their acreage.[21]

One could fashion a comfortable life by supplying foodstuffs to St. Augustine. "[V]egitables sold better then than now," Esteban (Estevan) Arnow mused wistfully, because the city's population was larger and the demand was greater. Consequently, the prices of green corn, Irish and sweet potatoes, pumpkins, cucumbers, melons, peas, beans, cabbages, turnips, onions, carrots, radishes, tomatoes, okra, squash, peppers, garlic, and other garden vegetables were "very dear" in 1812. Joseph Baya surmised that St. Augustine's population was twice as high then as it would be twenty-five years later. Baya remembered as many as 1,200 to 1,500 Spanish troops being stationed in town. Andreas Pacetty Sr. could specify ten companies of white soldiers. These infantry, grenadier, dragoon, and artillery units hailed from Cuba, as well as from Málaga and Catalonia in Spain. He pointedly mentioned that "four Companies of blacks" and "one Company of mulattoes," all from Havana, also had contributed to the Ancient City's defense and prosperity. Other soldiers required rations—three companies of white Florida volunteer militia, each containing sixty men, and "one Company of blacks raised in Florida under the Command of Capt: Prince . . . which was eighty strong." Thanks to St. Augustine's importance as a military garrison and East Florida's thriving economy, Mateo Lorenzo recalled, there was "plenty of money in circulation."[22]

Vegetable farming, therefore, could be quite profitable. Pablo Sabate, a "merchant of St. Augustine," was the proprietor of "Casacola," a plantation five miles north of town on the west side of the North River, worked by ten slaves. It contained, within its five hundred to six hundred acres enclosed by a pine rail fence, "a good piece of Land and of good dimensions" devoted to a "garden." The "large and valuable vegetable Garden, from which the St. Augustine market was Supplied," provided Sabate with "an annual large income." Cabbages, garlic, peas, beans, tomatoes, pumpkins, watermelons, and abundant quantities of onions were some of the moneymakers from this "very fine" garden. In addition, his field hands tended two hundred acres of corn planted with peas, and fifteen to twenty acres of sweet potatoes. Judge Isaac H. Bronson calculated that Sabate cleared $1,118 each year from Casacola's vegetables and provisions, making his profits in the 31 to 36 percent range.[23] As noted above, grand cotton planters like Zephaniah Kingsley derived greater profits, but Sabate's income from his farming business was well over three times that of the highest-paid skilled lumberjack.

The widow Margarita Acosta earned almost twice the income from her vegetable business as Sabate from his. She, like him, lived in town, where her enslaved servants Rose, a "good cook," and Madalina, a "prime" "washerwoman," attended to her housework. A pair of "trusty" female slaves vended "vegitables in the morning at the market." During the rest of the day, they constantly "carried [produce] about and through the City, and sold [it] from their baskets." Acosta also owned two "very comfortable" houses beyond St. Augustine's gates. One was located a half a mile away, along the east side of the road leading from town. Here she attested that she tilled sixteen acres. The other house sat perhaps a half mile distant from the first, on the opposite side of the king's highway. At this site, the widow swore that eighteen acres were under cultivation. Andreas Pacetty Sr. regarded Mrs. Acosta's grounds as "extensive." Pacetty noted that the crops required "a great deal of labour and care." Her force of seven bond persons, by their assiduous hoeing and weeding, enabled their mistress to feed all of her dependents, with more than two thousand dollars left over in profits. George Acosta, who died in 1811, had passed the two farms to his wife, Margarita. Joseph Baya reported that in 1812, they were considered to be Mrs. Acosta's property, and that afterward, they were sold by "her alone."[24]

A person approaching St. Augustine would, from a distance of 1,500 yards from its gates, between the St. Sebastian River and Matanzas Bay, pass through a "bountiful" and "well cultivated" plain that "looked like a garden." Esteban

Arnow recounted how nearly forty of these "*garden-farms,*" ranging from four to forty acres, checkerboarded the Ancient City's northern fringe. Joseph Baya, speaking through an interpreter in the mid-1830s, placed the acreage limit at a maximum of twenty. For purposes of defense, the government cautioned farmers not to plant corn, trees, or other tall growth, in order to give troops "a full and fair view" of an approaching enemy. If farmers failed to heed this warning, it was at their own risk and the authorities absolved themselves of any responsibility if the military judged it necessary to destroy such plants. Half of the garden farms contained dwellings. Some were "good houses," that were "plainly but comfortably furnished," and others were "not so good." John Lawrence's "small Palmetto house" was worth under ten dollars and provided only a rudimentary shelter from the rain and sun. Lawrence was being an obedient subject. His security-minded governor had decreed that none but palmetto houses should be built. Arnow remembered that "this was often evaded." A "good House of Plank and boards was erected, and then covered over with Palmetto in Such a manner as to deceive the eye." He also recalled how the cultivators of "the Plain" shared the ownership of their fencing. Only the panels fronting the road belonged to individuals.[25]

The cultural patterns of garden farming on the Ancient City's northern plain had migrated from the islands of the Mediterranean. In 1768, 1,403 indentured servants from Greece, Italy, Corsica, and Minorca left their homelands to work on Dr. Andrew Turnbull's indigo plantation at New Smyrna, seventy miles south of St. Augustine. The vast majority of these laborers, one thousand, hailed from Minorca. Four years later, only six hundred recruits had survived the voyage to East Florida and the subsequent starvation, withering work regimen, physical abuse, psychological dislocations, and malarial fevers that "seasoned" them. The survivors "coalesced into a closely interacting community." These "Minorcans" eventually sought deliverance from their "death-camp like existence" by embarking on an "exodus" to St. Augustine, where in the summer of 1777, the English governor granted them small parcels of land near the city gates. They remained after Great Britain departed, becoming the "core of the Hispanic population." The Minorcans carried with them to East Florida a zest for urban living, strong communal ties, and the practice of spending their days tending to crops with family members on outlying tracts, and returning to their homes in the evening to socialize with their neighbors.[26]

Because of their mores of sociability, the Minorcans were well apprised of one another's material circumstances. And, their oral traditions painted the days of Spanish rule with warm, glowing colors. They proudly displayed their prized household objects where their neighbors might easily see them. Andreas Pacetty noted that "intercourse by visiting is [still] frequent among the people, and they often talk of their furniture and other possessions." He added that the Minorcans in 1812 emphasized the spoken word, even in business dealings. "They were an honest people," Pacetty nostalgically reflected, "and stood by their bargains without writing." Bennet Seguí reminisced that garden farmers "supported themselves comfortably and were able to lay up money every year."[27]

A small, five-acre plot could provide for a sizable family. Christopher López owned such a plot. His city-dwelling family consisted of his wife, her mother and sister, two children, and a free black farmhand. The mother-in-law sold the farm's produce in the market each day. López and his black employee, both of whom were considered to be "industrious," along with one other family member, grew vegetables in his "flourishing and well cultivated" field a half mile beyond the city gates. A "Palmetto Hut" and fifteen panels of a cypress post-and-rail fence also belonged to him. Gardening, along with occasional fishing and stints as an oarsman on a pilot boat, constituted his sole means of support. Mateo Lorenzo surmised that López earned $500 yearly from vegetables and that it cost $350 to maintain the family. Bartolo Pons agreed with this income figure, but he believed that López could support his dependents on only $200 to $300. Esteban Arnow placed the latter sum at $300.[28] Clearly, these neighbors acknowledged that López was keeping his head above water. Thus, the Clarkes' Matanzas provision farm represented a nest egg worth keeping for a financial safety net.

While visitors entering St. Augustine through its northern gates feasted their eyes on a pleasing patchwork of tidy Minorcan-owned garden farms, those arriving by sea inhaled the welcoming Mediterranean fragrance of orange blossoms. Jack Smith, writing after the Civil War, still reveled in memories of the scent that greeted him as his ship approached his new home in May 1817. The port seemed like one huge orange grove punctuated by rooftops glistening in the sunshine. On the town's western margins, a parade of groves perfumed the air with the smell of money. A single tree could yield five thousand to six thousand oranges worth fifty to sixty dollars. John M. Bowden refused an offer of one hundred dollars for one of his trees. "It was a rare thing," he recalled, "for a man to sell a full grown bearing orange tree." Orange groves were not confined to St. Augustine. On the St. Johns River, fifty miles from its mouth, Francis P. Fatio sported a legendary grove at his "New Switzerland" plantation. Zephaniah Kingsley, who cultivated a fabulous orchard of his own nine miles below New Switzerland, marveled at the "very extensive Orange Grove" from which Fatio "derived a large income." George Petty called it "a most splendid Orange Grove." Fatio's one thousand bearing trees produced five thousand gallons of juice. He even operated a "Cooperage" at his plantation to fashion juice casks. His overseer reported that in 1811, Fatio made one thousand dollars from the juice and another one thousand to two thousand dollars from the fruit.[29]

Indeed, money grew on trees for numerous rural East Floridians. Andrew Atkinson estimated the value of the orange grove on his St. Johns River plantation at three thousand dollars. Hence, it is easy to imagine why Zephaniah Kingsley surrounded his nine-acre grove with a "Cypress Stockade picket nine feet in height." At Laurel Grove, Kingsley protected seven hundred trees, many bearing or "just ready." He also plowed resources into a "large nursery of thrifty young Orange trees." On Drayton Island, "in the mouth of Lake George," far to the south of his core plantation, Kingsley experimented with oranges, as well as "outlandish plants" such as coffee. José Peso de Burgos, like Kingsley and many others, was expanding his fruit business. Just west of St. Augustine, Peso de Burgos owned one hundred bearing trees that produced between fifteen and sixteen thousand oranges. The grove also contained one hundred and fifty maturing trees. He recently had stocked his "Guana Creek" plantation, eleven miles north of town, with trees from St. Augustine. In 1812, Guana Creek contained three hundred to four hundred young orange trees standing six to seven feet tall. Similarly, Edward M. Wanton was hoping to alchemize fruit into gold—and also good will. His neighbor, William Bardin, recalled that Wanton had planted orange and lemon trees "in considerable numbers" at various places around the "Chancery" and on an adjacent island. Bardin reckoned that between five hundred and six hundred young trees grew on this plantation near the Spanish military post at Picolata. Some already-bearing trees earned Wanton a hundred dollars per year. Since he was "a very liberal man," he "gave much of the fruit away."[30]

The planting of orange nurseries symbolizes the optimism that East Floridians felt for their futures. One could smell dreams in the breezes. One could also hear them in the sounds of hammers constructing new homes. George J. F. Clarke made no claims for damages to orange trees, although his diverse businesses and his acumen for exploiting the local economy suggest that he would be unlikely to neglect the fruit's earning potential. Other migrants to Fernandina, and probably Clarke as well, were planting citrus on their town lots. The slave trader James Dusman English, for example, had vegetables and a dozen four- to five-year-old "China Orange Trees" growing at his Fernandina home in 1812. English also maintained a nursery of two thousand trees about half as mature. Under the Americans, Clarke kept a similar nursery at his town house in St. Augustine.[31]

Regardless, at his Matanzas plantation just prior to the Patriot War, he was, like many of his neighbors, building a bigger and better dwelling. On a fishing trip in 1811, John and Bartolomé Leonardy spent most of the day at Clarke's plantation. The brothers described the old dwelling as a two-story framed and weatherboarded structure, "lined or ceiled inside," measuring thirty to thirty-five feet by twenty to twenty-five feet. It had a porch and the lower floor contained a hallway that separated two rooms. They estimated that it was worth between nine hundred and one thousand dollars. Tony Primus called it a "pretty good decent house." It was less than ten years old, because in 1802, the Seminoles had torched all of Clarke's buildings. Unlike the vast majority of rural East Florida homes, it featured glass windows. Rather than being made of logs, it had been built of sawed wood. Framed homes were "considered to be more elegant," so most people aspired to own them. Yet, Clarke, even though his family no longer lived there, had decided to upgrade. His new two-story dwelling was forty by thirty feet. Its frame had been raised and weatherboarding covered a portion of it. The roof and chimneys were missing. Boards, shingles, lime, stone, and other materials transported there to finish the structure sat nearby. A new detached kitchen also was being completed.[32]

José Peso de Burgos was another of the numerous East Floridians with the funds and optimism to improve his country residence. Previously, at Guana Creek, he had contented himself with a one-and-a-half-story dwelling painted red and green, with "plain and substantial" shutters and doors. This twenty-five by fifteen foot house featured four inside apartments; a porch and porch room; sashed and glazed windows; a plastered, tabby-floored lower story; and an unplastered, pine-floored upper story. It was worth between seven hundred and eight hundred dollars. His "new and costly," "Hart Pine" dwelling measured forty-five by twenty feet. The upper half-story had been completed. Peso de Burgos already was sleeping there in order to avoid mosquitoes. The floor had been laid on the lower story. Its doors and shutters were done, but the windows had yet to be sashed, and the chimney was only partially built. This home would be worth two thousand dollars. About three miles to the north, also on Guana Creek, Pedro Cocifacio owned a "well built" plantation house with "good work on it" that was similar in size and amenities to Peso de Burgos's older home. Cocifacio, a "very particular" man who "had everything comfortable," like his neighbor, was an affluent Minorcan merchant-planter. He opted to upgrade other structures, rather than his estate's main dwelling. Recently, Cocifacio had improved his slave cabins and he was erecting a new storehouse.[33]

Arbina Follis and Levin Gunby joined Cocifacio and other Spanish subjects in making capital improvements. They were partners in a "first rate water saw mill with two saws" that they had raised on Sweetwater Branch, a half a mile from the king's highway, twenty-five miles north of town. Their efforts to establish the mill had been strenuous, a reflection of the earning potential of lumber exports as well as the province's construction boom. The mill's dam, a "heavy and expensive piece of work," had demanded a great deal of attention. Joseph Lourcey, a millwright and carpenter, thought it was worth three to four thousand dollars. The dam stood eight feet high, twenty feet wide at the top, and fifty to sixty feet wide at its base. Its central floodgate was "well secured with spiling and a double set of posts and beams." Many witnesses recalled that the earthen dam broke several times before Follis and Gunby finally stabilized it. The mill's machinery was also costly because "all the iron work was brought from the North." The mill house measured forty to fifty feet by twenty-five to thirty feet and was "built in a substantial manner." The complex included "quite an expensive" dwelling priced at $1,200 to $1,500. Lourcey judged the enterprise's buildings, dam, and machinery as having a value of $10,000. He added that the mill had just been "thoroughly repaired," so that in early 1812, it was "better than she was 6 months after she was built."[34]

Those familiar with the "very prosperous" and "well to do" Follis and Gunby esteemed them as "money making men," but even less admired, simpler folk took part in East Florida's building spree. Bennet Seguí owned twenty to thirty-five acres on the "river Macriz," a quarter of a mile beyond St. Augustine's northern "plain of 1500 yards," east of the king's road. He, his two daughters, and, sometimes, hired help worked the place. Seguí's crops matched those of other garden farmers, but he was especially remembered because, "his whole yard was in Pumpkins." On this "little farm," he was constructing a twenty-five by sixteen feet, one-story, "good frame House," with two porches. It still needed to be shingled, so it was not quite finished, but the materials to complete the three-hundred- to four-hundred-dollar home had been brought to the property.[35]

Seguí's contemporaries considered his home much more desirable than that of Robert Hutchinson, a Protestant native of the "County of Darry," Ireland, who swore allegiance to Spain on 11 July 1811. He brought his wife, six children, four slaves, three horses, and six black cattle into Florida with the intention to farm. At Hobkirk's Bluff, two miles from the St. Marys River's mouth, he put up a "tolerable log house" worth between $50 and $60, in addition to three other log buildings that were not deemed very valuable. Still, James R. Woodland remarked that "they were as comfortable as were usually put up by common farmers." Samuel Swearingen added that "altho they were common, they were large and made of heavy timber." The fencing that surrounded Hutchinson's ten-acre field and his "large ox lot" was considered, at $150, equal in value to his four buildings, because he had to haul its rails from nearly a mile away. He was "doing very well getting out lumber" and grew only provisions on his farm.[36]

Hutchinson, like so many other East Floridians, had plunged head first into the timber rush. Putting up a frame house was more expensive than constructing a log one, and doubtless, he intended to improve his buildings with his profits. In his new life, Hutchinson surely aimed to rise above the station of a "common farmer." The height of his expectation that lumbering in the Spanish colony would allow him to realize the "American dream" can be measured in the small size of his planting concern and the spartan characteristics of his dwelling. According to John Broward, a witness whose testimony Judge Isaac H. Bronson respected as "reliable," the "cheapest kind of a log building in which a white family could or would live in those days would have cost as much as one hundred dollars."[37]

Lewis Christopher, who was beginning a new life as a married man, did not have to endure such austerity in his pursuit of material success. His father, Spicer Christopher, a "great planter and a very wealthy and independent man," owned one hundred "taskables" who planted cotton and provisions on Talbot Island, just north of John Houston McIntosh's Fort George plantation. William Houston explained that "very few" of Spicer Christopher's slaves were not taskables because the great planter "had bought all his hands and it was his rule to purchase all grown hands." Before his death in July 1811, Spicer gave Lewis a wedding present. It was St. Charles plantation, twelve miles from the mouth of the St. Johns, on its north bank. The plantation was "almost ready to occupy" in early 1812. Its "fine new two story house," forty-four by forty-four feet, was "nearly finished." The elder Christopher had promised to pay a contractor $2,600 for the completed dwelling. He also built two outbuildings for his son, each worth $150.[38]

Spicer Christopher had procured part of the money to pay for his son's plantation from raising cattle. As with timber, cotton, vegetables, and oranges, there was a "considerable" demand for beef. In St. Augustine, for example, the government "consumed a great deal." John D. Braddock supervised Christopher's cattle, but Samuel Russell, Braddock's employee, was the one who personally tended them "for years." The herd of more than six hundred contained, said Russell, "many fat beeves and fine steers." Christopher was not alone in his bovine predilection. In 1812, the entire colony was "abounding in cattle" and "every one of any property" owned them. Each plantation was stocked with the animals. And, not only rural settlers desired them. James Green recalled that "it was usual for Every man to have a bunch of cattle when he could possibly get them." It is easy to account for this cattle-mania. According to Zephaniah Kingsley, beef cattle fetched sixteen to eighteen dollars per head. Joseph M. Hernández and Bartolo Solana placed the figure a little lower, at fifteen dollars per "beeve." Moreover, Francis R. Sánchez noted that a good herd would reproduce a third of its number in calves each year.[39] By owning cattle, a person's fortunes could multiply rapidly.

For twenty-five years before 1812, Joseph Hughes had been the stock keeper for several cattlemen on the Matanzas Range, south of St. Augustine. He received every third new calf from each man's herd. Consequently, Hughes came to own a "very extensive Stock of cattle himself"—450 head. In Spanish East Florida, Joseph M. Hernández explained, a herd of 200 to 400 was considered a "large stock." A number of people, like Spicer Christopher, possessed a great deal more. The partnership of Fernando de la Maza Arredondo Sr. and Antonio Huertas, for instance, owned at least 1,500 of the beasts. Manuel Solana could count over 1,000 in his herds. The Seminoles also controlled significant supplies of the four-legged wealth. In fact, Arredondo, Huertas, and Solana had purchased much stock from the Indians.[40] Hughes's experience demonstrates why many parents in the colony would lovingly present cattle to their children. It was a gift that would keep on giving.

The cases of Samuel Sauls and John Black provide interesting illustrations of this custom. In Georgia, Sauls eloped with David Davis's daughter. This so incensed Davis that he "threatened to kill Sauls." Eventually, "the matter was made up" and Davis, "a large stock owner," bestowed a "bunch of cattle" upon the couple as a peace offering. The Sauls took the sixty cattle with them to Florida. Mrs. Cynthia Sweeney, when pressed to explain how John Black could possibly have a legitimate claim for personal property damage when he was only twelve years of age during the Patriot War, retorted that parents commonly gave young children a cow and calf and let them keep the "increase." In this manner, Master Black accumulated "quite a smart bunch of Cattle." At the outbreak of the Patriot War, the lad owned twenty-five to thirty, in addition to two horses that his father had given him in exchange for part of his herd.[41]

The most illustrious cattle baron in Spanish East Florida was Francisco Xavier Sánchez. Sánchez's father, Joseph Sánchez de Ortigosa, moved to St. Augustine from Cuba, married into a long-established local clan, and received a land grant on the Diego Plains, twenty miles north of the city. Francisco, born in 1736, was the youngest of his eight children. Francisco's brother's marriage into the prestigious Espinosa family, who ranched on the Diego Plains, cemented a powerful dynasty. When Britain gained Florida in 1763, Francisco remained as his family's property manager. Under the British, he won government contracts to furnish fuel and beef, and he accumulated a thousand acres and eight hundred to nine hundred cattle on the Diego Plains. When the Spaniards returned in 1784, he successfully competed to retain his contracts. Sánchez also derived wealth as a merchant, lumberman, and planter.[42]

In 1787, when Sánchez was fifty-one, he married María del Carmen Hill, who was not yet eighteen. She became the mother of eight of his children. On 3 October 1807, Sánchez died, leaving nine plantations, an equal number of houses in St. Augustine, numerous slaves, extensive mercantile interests, and vast herds of cattle. Spanish law did not award a widow all of her husband's property. The children received a portion of it. In 1812, however, the Sánchez estate remained in María del Carmen's hands. Like her widowed sister, who continued to manage Samuel Williams's plantation on the Halifax River, she had not yet divided her deceased spouse's holdings among her children. John Masters believed that nearly 1,000 of the estate's bovine stock grazed on the Diego Plains, "a famous range for cattle." Esteban Arnow thought that 700 roamed on this "most excellent range." Her sister, the former Mrs. Williams, surmised that if Sánchez's cattle on various ranges were assembled, they would total between 1,500 and 2,000. Mrs. Sánchez's son, Francis Román, estimated the total as 1,250.[43]

Not surprisingly, George J. F. Clarke counted cattle among his possessions, but their numbers pale in comparison to Sánchez's: only thirty to forty. His brother Charles's fifty to seventy-five cattle grazed on the Matanzas Range, which "commenced" sixteen miles south of the Clarkes' plantation and "extended principally South and west and as much as 10 or 15 miles." This grazing land reputedly hosted between five thousand and thirteen thousand cattle in early 1812. Dr. James Hall reminisced that the years 1807–12 had been "favorable to stock." Eliza M. Whitwell's father, William Garvin, saw opportunity in this good fortune. He established a tannery in Fernandina and used the province's abundant raw cowhides to make leather.[44] Garvin's and the Clarke brothers' stakes in the ranching industry demonstrate both the ubiquity of cattle ownership in Spanish East Florida and the presence of large herds that enriched the province.

Although skeptics might dismiss old inhabitants' descriptions of their creole Elysium as a fictitious stew of nostalgia for lost youth, time-corroded memories, and a conspiratorial plot to hoodwink the U.S. Treasury Department, contemporary federal officials were convinced of the general veracity of the portrait that witnesses painted of Spanish East Florida in 1812. On 15 March of that year, Winslow Foster commanded one of the five American gunboats in the flotilla that supported the Patriot invaders when they took Fernandina. The "highly prosperous" state of the province's agriculture impressed Captain Foster. He especially noted the "flourishing" cotton trade and the "good price" that the commodity commanded. Judge Robert R. Reid extolled the "flourishing condition of the country around St. Augustine." The market in the Ancient City for the produce of nearby farms was "high and steady." In fact, said Reid, the entire province was "very prosperous." Plantations along the St. Johns River were well cultivated, "flourishing," and "gradually attaining to opulence." The staples were cotton and lumber, he informed the secretary of the treasury, and prices for them were high, especially in Fernandina. Large herds of cattle populated the plains and woods. Not since British times had East Florida experienced such a period of peace and prosperity. His successor, Isaac H. Bronson, acknowledged that this was a time of "great prosperity" in the colony, and that all agricultural products, in addition to timber, brought high prices. The industrious, Bronson admitted, were accumulating wealth rapidly.[45]

After reviewing between one hundred and two hundred Patriot War claims cases, Judge Bronson was most impressed by the testimonies of Zephaniah Kingsley, Joseph M. Hernández, Francis Richard, Gabriel Priest, and George J. F. Clarke. These men obviously took pride in Spanish East Florida and in the role that they had played in building it. Rebecca E. Read's emotions demonstrate the powerful lingering attachment that the region's "old inhabitants" felt for the days when the Spaniards reigned supreme. She was Rebecca Richard in 1812, and she fondly memorialized her father-in-law, Francis Richard Sr. The widow with four "little children" ran a "small farm" on the west side of the St. Johns River. William Munroe (or Monroe), a sailor serving on an invading American gunboat, lauded her as a "pretty good planter and a thriving and industrious woman." On the east side of the St. Johns, nearly opposite her farm, she could see Richard's Isabella plantation. Read greatly admired this "first rate planter" who "in every time of life was so esteemed." She recalled Isabella as being "an elegant place well filled up and under high improvement." "Frequently," she mistily reminisced, "the old Gentleman would take her by the hand and lead her into the field to witness his improvements and works of industry." Only recently have scholars in the United States come to recognize the veracity of the oral history that Judges Reid and Bronson had come to accept by the 1830s and 1840s.[46]

By elegizing the "good old Flag of Spain," Eliza M. Whitwell, like Mrs. Read and other "old inhabitants" of East Florida, shared an identity that transcended ethnicity, social class, and gender. This identity was a valuable asset for Mrs. Whitwell, for she, like all of George J. F. Clarke's heirs, was a person of color—the descendant of an ex-slave. Under U.S. rule, antebellum African American folk diplomats strove both to foster identification with the Spanish regime and to exploit this identity. In the same manner, Mrs. Whitwell, after the Civil War, crafted an identity based on St. Augustine's Spanish past in order to protect herself from the raging hurricane of Jim Crow segregation that buffeted the South in the 1890s. During the 1910s in the United States, an "enthusiasm for things Spanish" was in full bloom. This "romanticization of the Hispanic past" had appeared much earlier in certain areas of the Southeast. In fact, David Weber concluded, "[n]o southern community celebrated its Spanish past more enthusiastically than St. Augustine."[47] Thus, as Afro–East Floridians had done for generations, Whitwell used history, whites' economic interests (in this case tourism), and the paternalistic desire of oppressors to feel good about themselves to negotiate her freedom. She became a local celebrity whom whites publicly praised and assisted, despite her efforts to undermine white supremacy by fighting for family lands stolen by East Florida elites. Moreover, she manipulated her condescending oppressors into heralding African American history. Thus, she masterfully exercised a black diplomatic tradition that stretched back to the very origins of Spanish colonization in the sixteenth century.

In her old age, Eliza M. Whitwell mourned the day that her grandfather had hauled down Spain's colors for the last time. East Florida had been prospering under the Spaniards in 1812. This prosperity had thrust her family into the spotlight. The clan's material wealth strode hand-in-hand with its growing prestige. Government service, lumbering, and the cotton trade promised to make its future bright. The legal heirs of the provincial luminaries John Fraser and Zephaniah Kingsley also shared African blood with Whitwell. So did the children of Francisco Xavier Sánchez's first family. In short, under the Spanish monarchy, Eliza M. Whitwell could look forward to occupying the upper middle ground of a tri-racial social structure that offered her greater opportunities for self-realization than did the American republic.[48] As a woman, she could anticipate a life of financial independence and the opportunity to earn the respect of her male neighbors for her business acumen.

But what of the province's slaves? That is, the one group that Mrs. Whitwell placed outside the circle of Spanish-led prosperity. Certainly the opportunities for success that free blacks enjoyed gave slaves hope. But, change was on the way. In St. Augustine, while the economy boomed, it seemed as if Catholic prayers offered in a cathedral filled with incense and sacred ornaments were being answered. The piety of townspeople who commonly doffed their hats when passing the cathedral, and who immediately stopped what they were doing to pause in prayer when its bell sounded at 7 P.M., apparently was being rewarded. Moreover, the saints seemed to be smiling upon a populace whose numerous celebrations honored them, at the same time that they transformed the sweet-smelling Ancient City into a joyous place. Daniel L. Schafer posited that the province was in the process of transformation. It was on the road to becoming another Cuba: a colony characterized by "massive slave imports, brutal use of enslaved Africans, and a sharp decline in the status of free people of color." "At which point," in the words of John Lewis Gaddis, "God, or at least His agents, intervened."[49]

2
"Jackasses of the Lion"

God's agents who invaded Spanish East Florida in March of 1812 were Americans. Perhaps some saw themselves on a divine mission to spread the blessings of democracy. None came to undermine the institution of slavery in the colony. But the invaders did exactly that, illustrating that Providence does indeed work in strange ways. Thomas Suárez, in 1838, using a metaphor that evoked an angry deity, compared the troops to a "raging storm" that was "smashing everything."[1] Such disasters give societies pause to take stock of themselves. The invasion enabled white men and women of all socioeconomic classes to suffer splinters from the cross of enslavement. It presented them with the opportunity to consider the burdens that involuntary servitude placed on the bond persons who produced the province's wealth. It called them to repentance. It portended both the Second Seminole War, when large numbers of African Americans deserted their masters,[2] and the Civil War, when the region's slave owners would lose their human chattel permanently. Thus the howling winds from Georgia prophesied.

For many white antebellum witnesses, the invasion, which essentially introduced United States rule to East Florida, had suddenly and permanently quashed their dreams for a happy future. The Patriot War claims cases presented them with a dais from which to voice their displeasure with a republican regime whose promises of security and economic prosperity had, up to that point, proved to have been chimerical. Couched in the language of popular history and voiced within the context of financial gain, the testimonies of "old inhabitants" collectively protested the American takeover, implicitly bemoaning the passing of the monarchical Spanish colonial government that the United States had fatally wounded more than a generation earlier. In keeping with their local diplomatic traditions, African Americans would harness this divisive undercurrent to their advantage.

Witnesses did not mince words with Washington regarding the deleterious impact of its foreign policy upon their homeland. Mrs. Sarah Acosta reminded federal officials that there had been "a great deal of Comfort and independence" in the colony prior to the Patriot War and "had they been left alone those inhabitants would have become rich." Esteban Arnow added that "many who had lived comfortably died in poverty." John Egan remembered that the invaders "had broken up everybody." William Monroe, who had served in the U.S. naval flotilla during the conflict, admitted that the province was in "excellent circumstances" in early 1812, but that afterward, it was "reduced very much in circumstances." Samuel Swearingen spoke more bluntly. The American assault, he swore, "ruined East Florida." Zephaniah Kingsley agreed, recalling how troops had pillaged the lumber and cotton exports that had caused it to flourish, leaving the land "a perfect desert."[3]

Memories of these depredations impelled the catastrophe's survivors to grieve over the passing of Spanish times. Many of them had abandoned any hope that they or their offspring ever would live as well under the United States. In 1838, John Bowden mourned a region that still had not "recovered its former prosperity." The following year, Abraham Daniels lamented that East Florida "never did recover the shock." Mrs. Mary Smith testified in 1841 that it had not, before or since the invasion, been so prosperous and "happy." Esteban Arnow concurred, doubting that he ever would see the return of halcyon days. A depressed Matthew Long bemoaned both his father's sudden and miserable death in 1812 and his family's subsequent "life of poverty and blasted prosperity" under the American regime.[4]

While some old inhabitants focused their thoughts on economic losses or dashed dreams, others offered testimony that reveals a more deeply seated fear. Their memories brimmed with tales of social upheaval, that in turn hinted of the nightmare of seeing themselves enslaved. Mateo Lorenzo expressed this horrifying prospect by employing the phrase "the world turned upside down." In such a world, masters would become slaves. Similarly, Rebecca Read invoked the Haitian Revolution when she referred to the U.S. invasion as "the reign of terror to East Florida." The names of her beloved father-in-law's bond persons indicate that he, Francis Richard Sr., had fled from the chaos of St. Domingue's version of the French Revolution. In poignant human imagery, Gabriel Priest, a former overseer for the wealthy planter John Houston McIntosh, expressed the relationship between the Patriot War and white enslavement. The Americans, Priest wailed, "stripped us of nearly all that we possessed, and left ourselves, our wives, and children to the cold charity of the world."[5]

In the process of stripping East Florida's population of their wealth and dreams, the invaders seemingly perverted the forces of nature by their profligate use of fire. John Bowden explained that normally in April and May the woods would ignite. Sometimes a "thunder storm" would set them ablaze. At other times, ranchers started fires to make "fresh burns for cattle." But under the Americans, the forests were "burning at all times." Joseph Lourcey recollected how "wherever they went, the Troops made fires, using fence rails or anything else that could be had for that purpose." Typically, they would "shoot Beeves & make fire from rails—cooking what was needed for present hunger—and then leaving the carcasses and fences without further attention." If the frightened proprietors had abandoned their places, as frequently happened, the conflagrations "often occasioned great injury." Unfortunately, James Pellicer noted, the filibusterers had arrived at the right time of the year for spreading fires.[6]

Indeed, the invaders' reckless abuse of fire seared old inhabitants' memories. William Black, as a teenager, observed fifteen to twenty American mounted men ride up to Francis Richard Jr.'s plantation, where they set fire to the nearby woods. Before the soldiers left his yard, the flames had spread to the fences and soon the entire estate was burning. Black wistfully recalled how Richard, so that he might "[s]ecure them from the ravages of the American troops," had "by himself" emptied his dwelling of valuables, vainly hiding them in combustible bushes before he fled. Paul Masters, when he was around twelve years of age, witnessed U.S. troops torching Pedro Cocifacio's recently abandoned property. On the "large Savannah" adjoining its west side, "there was a party of them coming across the grass and they set fire to it to see it burn." Enoch Daniels shamefully recounted how, as he and his Patriot comrades dug potatoes at night on the absent John Dixon's farm, they had set a building on fire just to "make a light." Adding insult to injury, they roasted Dixon's hogs with some timber that he had cut for export.[7]

When a plantation's owner or overseer was present, matters could and did get ugly. James Mattair was about Paul Masters's age when he gazed wide-eyed upon a hellish scene on Horatio Low's premises. As the crackling and smoking woods consumed Low's prized timber prepared for market, the flames leapt to the plantation's buildings. At the same time, U.S. regulars were butchering squealing hogs. In the midst of this surreal inferno, Mattair saw Low vehemently arguing with Colonel Thomas Smith. When the commanding officer had enough of these angry words, he ordered Low to "hold his tongue." Likewise, young Masters observed American soldiers humiliate John Moill, Pedro Cocifacio's overseer. When Moill attempted to prevent the troops from taking Cocifacio's household furniture, they threatened to "tie him up and whip him." They later burned the barn. The emasculated Moill henceforth would sleep at Masters's mother's farm.[8] Significantly, the invaders had addressed Low and Moill in language that planters and overseers might use with their slaves, thus giving the two men a taste of their own medicine.

Whites thus learned what their slaves already knew: "remonstrance was dangerous." To be sure, it was "not safe to forbid [the Patriots] as they always did worse." The Americans "even extended that rule to the relations" of their opponents. Francis Richard Sr. had spoken "freely and loudly . . . against [the Americans]—call[ing] them marauders and robbers—invaders of his country for the purpose of plunder." Early in the summer, occasional scouting parties had foraged their horses on his crops. At autumn's approach, soldiers drove cattle onto his fields to fatten them for slaughter. Soon, gunboats were "lying off the place." Each day, "troops and marines were . . . rummaging & plundering & destroying." Finally, Richard ran away, taking his slaves with him "by stratagem." His daughter-in-law, Rebecca Read, remained, "relying upon her sex & providence for protection." Although she and her "little children" felt "uncomfortable," the invaders tolerated them. Then, one morning in 1813, a Patriot band arrived, boasting of their "express purpose" to not "leave the old rascal [Richard] . . . an inch of house or board." Despite Read's plea to desist from "burn[ing] her & her children out of their house," when darkness enveloped Isabella plantation, its outbuildings went up in flames.[9]

Besides terrorizing the inhabitants, Washington's minions utilized fire to destroy the lumber industry, one of the twin pillars upon which East Florida's prosperity rested. In the opening months of 1812, the province's "brisk and profitable" timber business hummed. Between August and February, "hands were generally employed in getting Lumber for market." Even with a hundred ships waiting at Fernandina, timber "could not be exported as fast as cut," so the forests were "full of it." Since the Americans "constantly fired" the woods, the consequences proved disastrous for the economy as well as for inhabitants' lives and independence. The timber fortunate enough to escape the flames "rot[ted] to pieces." As James Green explained, this export commodity "required personal attention." "[O]ne summers exposure," William McCullough added, "will ruin any stock of timber." Loggers commonly rafted their harvest to market, but the Patriot War "compelled the labourers to quit the rafts—and they all went adrift."[10]

Lives, too, went adrift. In 1838, James Woodland somberly considered how Stephen Vanzandt "seemed to have lost his courage with his hopes in 1812 & 1813." He was characterized as a "noted man for industry and driving his business surprisingly." Vanzandt and his family lived in a "snug comfortable loghouse." He was "fast-adding to his property" and if the United States had not invaded, he would have become "a rich planter." The invaders burned his dwelling, along with his outbuildings, which were those of a "smart planter." The destruction of his fortunes went on "continually." He owned a large quantity of lumber, most of which sat at his river landing, ready to be rafted to market. It, too, was burned. In fact, as late as 1838, "some of the refuse of it" haunted Vanzandt and his neighbors. After the war, "though he labored hard and drove business he never prospered much and never seemed to be successful." Ultimately, he "died in low circumstances."[11] Vanzandt's story struck a chord with East Florida's elders, for to them, it symbolized the region's fate under the United States.

The destruction of the timber harvest profoundly impacted even small entrepreneurs like Samuel Sauls, who strove to quickly boost his social standing by cashing in on the province's booming export market for forest products. Although Sauls cultivated a "little patch for vegetables," he "did not pretend to plant." Instead, he turned his "whole attention" to lumbering. The ambitious Sauls had convinced an Amelia Island merchant to grant him a contract to supply one hundred thousand feet of logs for shipment to England. Sauls then proceeded to hire "a good many men" to do the cutting. When the United States invaded, he had two hundred "sticks" or sixty thousand feet of pine on hand. "Most all the timber which was lying in the woods cut down & hewed was destroyed, sometimes Wantonly and wilfully, & Sometimes by the Woods being set on fire and no persons being near to 'out it.'" In 1847, James Green stressed that this arson had constituted a "severe loss to Sauls, as it broke him up completely in his works." After the Patriot War, he was "very poorly off."[12]

Robert Hutchinson, like Sauls, based his prospects on logging. The Protestant Irishman arrived in East Florida in 1811, along with his wife, six children, three horses, and six black cattle. He told the Spanish authorities that he intended to farm. The opportunity to "get rich quick" changed his mind. On his land along the St. Marys River, he erected four buildings "of a common kind," and enclosed his ten-acre provision plot "with good fencing." Hutchinson also penned a few cows and calves for milk. Then, he devoted himself to cutting down trees by investing in a "first rate timber cart," as well as "some as fine oxen as were ever 'hitched.'" To protect them, he laboriously constructed a "very high" and sturdy fence around his "large ox lot." In 1812, he was "doing very well getting out lumber." Over one hundred "sticks" were piled at his landing and more logs were ready to be hauled to the riverbank. Samuel Swearingen, who "did not like" Hutchinson, admitted in 1846 that it was "fine large timber." This thriving enterprise, like so many others, met with an untimely demise. Before burning his "sticks," U.S. troops seized Hutchinson's oxen to haul cannons. Hence, the year 1813 found him "living in a very common way & in poverty." Moreover, psychological wounds brutalized him, for "[h]e suffered a great deal in consequence of being broken up besides what he actually lost." By 1815, Hutchinson was dead.[13]

So was East Florida's timber business. After the United States took Fernandina, the numerous ships waiting in its harbor departed, and commerce was "paralised." For a long period after the Americans evacuated in 1813, trade remained "stagnant." Lumbering no longer brought invigorating profits. Out in the woods, expensive, "bulky" timber carts had been reduced to ashes, while their iron wheels, gearing, hooks, and "large heavy and costly chains" rusted. Axes, tools, saws, and the remains of laborers' huts littered the forest floor. The oxen, horses, and mules that had helped power the operations were gone. Huge contracts, such as the one that the provincial firm of Hibberson & Yonge held for $665,000, lay unfulfilled forever. The ruins of charred sawmills rotted in the blazing sun, while otters and alligators burrowed into their earthen dams.[14] Subsequently, antebellum East Floridians would associate the United States with the demise of an extractive industry that had promised to rapidly make even poor men wealthy.

What especially frustrated many of the old inhabitants was that they had almost succeeded in shipping their logs to market. When U.S. forces attacked Fernandina, George J. F. Clarke was measuring Hibberson & Yonge's timber, which was about to be loaded onto a waiting British ship "of the largest class." He had to desist immediately, and the six-hundred- to seven-hundred-ton vessel set sail without the cargo. Clarke's business associate, William Garvin, was rafting his valuable cedar down the St. Johns River when an American gunboat ordered him ashore. He was not able to recover it, despite his frantic appeal to the American authorities. In some cases, the Patriots confiscated timber, sold it, and kept the money for themselves. On other occasions, the invaders mocked East Floridians by burning their sylvan gold as firewood. Particularly galling were memories of soldiers who maliciously set dreams ablaze, without even using the timber for fuel. Henry Sweeney remembered the American troops lighting huge bonfires of hewed wood. The still-livid children of George Fleming (who "had entered into a large contract" to deliver timber bound for British vessels and whose logs were piled "mostly on the waters' edge" at the time of the invasion) excoriated the "Jackasses of the Lion" in 1834, for "wantonly" burning "every stick" of their father's treasure.[15]

This being said, those who invested in lumbering typically exploited slave labor. During the pre-invasion boom times, enslaved lumberjacks continually saw themselves deprived of the riches that their sweat had created. Now, the Americans had turned the tables on the slave's masters. Indeed, during the troubles commencing in 1812, God's American agents offered whites ample opportunities to experience firsthand the anguish of seeing others feast on the fruits of their toil. Jeremiah Wingate recollected how the "country was nothing but a camp, and negroes nor white men were safe or able to pursue their agricultural labors." What enraged witnesses was the fact that if the Americans had not invaded, their husbandry would have reaped abundant harvests. Numerous elders emphasized how nature was smiling upon them while the invaders rampaged through the province. They remembered milder winters and richer land in those days. As James Plummer deposed in 1841, "the spring seasons were more forward in this country." Because of the fertile soil and favorable climate, according to Wingate, "the difficulty of making crops in those years was but trifling compared to the present time."[16]

On top of these advantages, in the old inhabitants' minds, the 1812 and 1813 growing seasons reigned as wondrous and potentially bountiful. This, in turn, made the U.S. attack more criminal. Regarding the 1812 harvest, crowed Joseph Lourcey, "the prospect was beatiful." John M. Bowden also remembered that year as being "very favorable for crops." It was more than that, waxed John D. Braddock, it was "extraordinarily luxuriant." Dr. James Hall recollected seeing John Crichton's cotton and corn that summer, when they "looked remarkably well." Hall's observation bolsters James Pellicer's recollection of a "remarkably fine season for corn" and Francis Richard Jr.'s assertion that 1812 was "uncommonly" favorable for cotton. James Plummer added potatoes to the horn of plenty, which also included, according to Joseph Manucy, garden vegetables. Richard, who had worked as an overseer for the wealthy planter John Fraser, reminded the court that in both 1812 and 1813, "the seasons were good & no gales—crops would have been excellent." James Mattair called them "unusually good" crop years. They were, Harry Hartley swore, "remarkably productive." William Braddock characterized them as "excellent."[17]

It is possible, however, that recurring nightmares of the "severe gale" that pummeled East Florida in 1811, along with the agricultural hard times of the late 1830s, may have brightened their memories. Rebecca Read, for example, qualified these men's narratives by stating, in reference to 1812, that it was "not so good in the Early part of it but towards the latter part of it the season was very favorable." Francis Pellicer classified 1813, with its cold spring, as only an average year.[18] Nevertheless, it is significant that various witnesses stated under oath that they believed that in addition to driving East Florida's exorbitantly lucrative lumber industry to extinction, the United States had squelched its agricultural productivity at the very time when it should have fully blossomed. As in the case of fire, the Americans had perverted nature.

Sea Island cotton cultivation, an agricultural activity that differentiated the Spanish colony from the United States, constituted a key casualty of the invasion. The mild climate of East Florida (and Georgia's proximate barrier islands) offered an ideal setting for raising a commodity that "[b]ecause of its length and luster . . . was used to manufacture delicate laces and cloth of remarkable silkiness." This "long staple" cotton, whose "price functioned largely independent of the vagaries of the short-staple variety" common to the United States, "sold very high" in 1812. So high, in fact, that planters "very scantily raised" food crops. As Joseph Hernández explained, they preferred to purchase provisions in order to maximize production. Recognizing this trend, one shrewd farmer, Lodovic Ashley, who also ran a boardinghouse and ferry, in addition to a logging concern, grew only corn, cowpeas, rice, sweet potatoes, and garden vegetables. Ashley thought it "more profitable to raise provisions" than to grow cotton.[19] A scarcity of food crops would drive up their prices, and hence the profits of those who could harvest more than they required for their own families, slaves, and livestock. In light of the American attack, Ashley's strategy proved uncannily astute, for one could not eat cotton. Due to the increasing acreage devoted to it, if its markets suddenly vanished, the specter of famine loomed large.

And vanish these markets did, along with the cotton itself. When the Americans reached Amelia Island, in mid-March, the crops "required immediate labor." Planters generally began to prepare their fields in February before planting in March. Cotton in its earliest stages, Matthew Long explained, is a "very delicate plant and is soon overrun by the grass if it is not well attended to." A field should be "gone over with the hoe" at least once, preferably twice each month. Otherwise, the "cotton fields were wasted and choked with cockspurs." Around the first of April, it had to be "thinned." By mid-September, when the pods began to open and the "fields were white," slaves hastened to the harvest. If they tarried, the cotton fell from the pods and was lost. Clearly then, when the invaders interrupted this routine, the province's most profitable agricultural export drowned among the weeds. Thus, when the Patriots forced Lewis Christopher to join them, his twenty-five-acre cotton field "suffer[ed] for proper attention." Similarly, but on a much grander scale, cotton production at Zephaniah Kingsley's Laurel Grove plantation ceased because of the "operations & conduct of the Troops" who occupied it. In the spring, on Kingsley's two hundred acres, the staple "was coming up well." By July, after the Americans had ensconced themselves at Laurel Grove, it was "entirely ruined from want of work."[20]

In addition to the disruption of work regimens, soldiers ruined cotton production by destroying its infrastructure. When occupying forces' fires charred fences, the fragile crop succumbed to trampling livestock. Even when they escaped the flames, fences frequently fell victim to troops for whom "gates were not much looked for." Samuel Swearingen denounced the Americans for habitually and thoughtlessly pulling them down. He remembered how they had turned their horses on Daniel Hogan's cotton field after demolishing his fencing. At John Crichton's plantation, fifty U.S. regulars encamped for a week, destroying one thousand rails of his "good inside fences." The troops also burned his two miles of "good and extensive" outside rail fence. William Bardin estimated that this fencing was worth four hundred dollars—one hundred dollars more than the dwelling house. Crichton devoted only twenty to thirty acres to cotton.[21] Large-scale planters required much more fencing. When the invaders ruined it, they stabbed the cotton industry with a double-edged sword, for not only did planters lose their incoming profits, but they also were obliged to outlay significant money, time, and labor before they could even begin another season's sowing.

The capital for essential fencing diminished markedly when soldiers' fires enveloped barns. As with fences, "cotton houses" represented sizable investments. Mrs. Ann Maria Hernández asserted that planters constructed them almost as carefully as they built their own family homes. For example, Jesse Long and John M. Bowden assigned a value of four hundred dollars to George Fleming's "large and good" log dwelling house, while they felt that his "very good" cotton house "built of sawed lumber" was worth five hundred dollars. John Uptegrove described Francis Richard Sr.'s storehouse as a "framed building and quite substantial, an excellent building." Pedro Rodríguez admired the "Large Dimentions" of Manuel Romero's seventy-five by twenty-five foot structure. The two forty by fifty foot cotton houses on Fort George Island had cost John H. McIntosh five hundred dollars each, claimed his overseer, John G. Rushing. At Ortega, McIntosh's other estate, the invaders did not burn the cotton house. Instead, they brazenly stripped off its roof, transporting the lumber away to "make camp."[22] Therefore, besides having to erect new fences to protect their growing crop, ravaged planters faced the considerable expense of constructing sizable, secure buildings where they could safely store and process their harvest.

This processing involved removing the seed from the cotton. Kingsley B. Gibbs reported that it took a thousand pounds of cotton "in the seed" to produce three hundred pounds of "clean cotton." Joseph M. Hernández and Paul Masters fixed the ratio at 3:1. Masters estimated that at a time "when hands are not wanted in the field," fifteen slaves working with picked cotton could produce fifteen to twenty bales in three weeks. Thus, as Dr. James Hall explained, cotton plantations required gins. Joseph Floyd's foot gins were worth $6 each, while George Fleming's would fetch more than double this price. Unfortunately, they were moveable. When the Patriots discovered that John Bunch's "spacious" cotton house could serve as "a look out on all sides," they "removed [his foot gins] to the waterside," so they could "use [the house] with the greatest convenience." Once outdoors, the gins were "ruined by the weather." The Americans absconded with sixty of John H. McIntosh's essential devices. The hefty double gin that the soldiers could not transport perished when they burned McIntosh's cotton house. Large gins were expensive. William Walker charged Domingo

Fernández $210 to build his. Henry Yonge paid $300 for a "first rate new" one. Francis P. Fatio's cost $500, and Samuel Williams's "Eaves Patent Roller Gin carried by wind Sails" set him back $800. George Gianopoli itemized John Fraser's horse-powered contraption, which was hacked to pieces, at a whopping $1,200 to $1,500.[23] By targeting cotton gins, the invaders further crippled East Florida's capacity to reconstruct its post-invasion economy.

The Americans saddled Spanish subjects with additional burdens by pillaging the colony's transportation infrastructure. Planters along the St. Johns River enjoyed a reputation for producing cotton "of superior value," because "it could be shipped directly" to Fernandina. To do so required boats, which the invaders needed to move men and materiel throughout the province. Therefore, they kept their eyes peeled for sizable river-going vessels. Francis P. Fatio's New Switzerland plantation, fifty miles from the St. Johns's mouth, was "abundantly supplied" with boats useful to the invaders. A large new canoe boat or "*peroiague,*" generally used to take provisions to Amelia Island, stood out in the memory of the former overseer, John Leonardy. It had cost $250. Zephaniah Kingsley's Laurel Grove spread also contained all the accouterments that a "well-supplied plantation could offer," including a quantity of boats. Hence, throughout the province's cotton-producing zones, U.S. forces used and abused plantation vessels. At Talbot Island, for instance, they encountered Spicer Christopher's *Lord Nelson,* an "immense" cotton boat worth between $400 and $500, that could carry forty to fifty bales. William Houston saw at least sixty-five troops traveling in it at one time. He later recognized a piece of its wreckage. Lucy Fitzgerald's "noble boat," the *Blacksnake,* for which one planter had offered $600, was even more valuable. Thomas Suárez recollected how his father would borrow it to transport his cotton. A Patriot detachment loaded the *Blacksnake* with a portion of Fitzgerald's property, before heading north to the border. After another party stole some of her horses and mules, they "chopped a piece out of" James Cashen's "large flat," so that they could load the animals on board with "greater Convenience."[24]

Due to the Patriot War, planters not only lost their growing cotton crops, fences, storage buildings, gins, and boats, but also the capacity to market their staple for export. Upon Fernandina's surrender to the Patriots, foreign vessels weighed anchor. Large flatboats were seized to carry men and supplies. Consequently, resident merchants like George J. F. Clarke could neither sell the cotton that planters had shipped there nor move it out of the province. Witnesses estimated that a combined one hundred to two hundred bales sat in Clarke's three warehouses. Each bale averaged 280 pounds. Since cotton sold for fifty cents per pound, the bales were worth at least fourteen thousand dollars. Moreover, from the guardroom where the invaders had imprisoned him, his brother,

Charles W. Clarke, "rebuked" the "wives of the U.S. Soldiers tearing away the weather boarding from the sides of [one of George's] warehouse[s]." He subsequently saw soldiers returning several times from the building "in the twilight" with more "convenient" wood for "guard and garrison fires." This vandalism occurred "from time to time according to the whim of the Troops." All of the entrepôt's warehouses for the reception of cotton shared the same fate. Decades later, a resentful Charles W. Clarke suggested that the slothful Americans could have fetched firewood out on the island, just as the locals did.[25]

The exact fate of the stored cotton remained hazy in its details. United States military personnel, Peter Pons boldly declared, destroyed much of Fernandina's warehoused staple "by opening the bales and scattering the cotton, as also carrying a great deal of it, in the night to the American side" of the St. Marys River. The invaders, he growled, "acted as they thought proper, carrying devastation wherever they pleased. . . . The Troops done what they pleased and no property was secure." Nevertheless, although the former U.S. navy midshipman John J. Abernathy noticed cotton "loosely scattered about the Town from bales which had been ripped open," he saw none of it used for any purpose. Likewise, Bartolo Ponce acknowledged that the staple had disappeared, but he did not actually see any soldiers "meddle" with it. Nor did Joseph Lourcey, Lorenzo Gracesqui, or Charles W. Clarke. Yet, since the invaders stationed guards throughout Fernandina "so that folks should not run off to St. Augustine," and American gunboats, ships, and a "Revenue cutter" frequented the harbor, circumstances convicted the occupiers.[26]

American conduct in other parts of East Florida lent credence to these suspicions. As with timber shipping and the cotton planting cycle, the invasion could not have come at a worse time for those who exported the crop. Planters typically shipped their cotton in "two parcels." The first shipment took place in December, before Christmas. In return, growers like Mrs. Frances Kerr received provisions "for the support of their families through the year, the use of slaves, and as presents for the Indians." James Smith, for instance, sent a portion of his annual forty to fifty bales to John Forbes & Company to pay for supplies. The second shipment occurred in the spring. John Chevalier recalled how his sloop brimmed with cotton bound for Savannah when, on the invasion's eve in Georgia, the U.S. forces asked him to help transport troops. Meanwhile, in East Florida, William Berrie's cotton house contained three thousand to four thousand pounds ready for market. Zephaniah Kingsley had fifty to sixty bales from the 1810 and 1811 seasons on hand. At Don Justo López's estate, where a hundred acres of the commodity grew, "clean cotton of the long Staple culture" was piled thirty-five feet high in the "large" forty by fourteen foot "house." Some planters, like Pedro Cocifacio, had not yet baled or even ginned all of their crop. Catherine Taylor remembered that Philip Dewees neither had sold nor shipped to market any of his 1811 cotton.[27]

Under the unexpected travesty of the U.S. assault, this situation proved to be a recipe for disaster. Robert McHardy, who lost seven bales, always suspected that "the d—d Rebels had stolen his cotton." The invaders, Philip Weedman speculated, may have carried it off in a "coasting Vessel or Gunboat," or perhaps in McHardy's own "large Cotton Boat." On Fort George Island, there was no doubt about it. The overseer, John G. Rushing, saw three hundred American regulars and Patriots load forty to fifty bales of John H. McIntosh's 1811 cotton onto boats as they evacuated East Florida in 1813. The thirty to forty thousand pounds of seed cotton that perished when the soldiers burned the plantation's two cotton houses was from the 1812 crop, the best one that Rushing had ever seen. The 1813 cotton was being cultivated when the Americans destroyed the estate. At McIntosh's sister property, Ortega, John M. Bowden witnessed the Patriots gradually take away all of the 1811 crop, the equivalent of sixty bales of clean cotton, during the summer of 1812. In a scene reminiscent of Fernandina, they took "large quantities" and "spread it about in places in the yard and use[d] it as beds to sleep upon." The remainder rotted and was only fit to be spread on the fields as fertilizer.[28]

Although the destruction of the timber and cotton industries at the hands of U.S. forces permanently maimed the provincial economy, the plundering of its foodstuffs seemed to evoke greater anger from victims who survived into antebellum times. This perhaps reflects the deprivation that they had suffered at the most fundamental human level. It also stems from the gross humiliation that accompanied this deprivation. That is, the Americans treated those whose crops they plundered like slaves. Paul Masters reminded federal officials in 1840 that when the invaders visited a property, they always stayed to eat at least one meal. Their practice was to kill, eat, and carry off property. They also routinely terrorized their reluctant hosts psychologically. For example, when troops appeared on the seriously ailing William Dewees's plantation, they would eat until they were full, punctuating their feasting by "break[ing] up something—tables or dishes." Indeed, Joseph A. Mattair angrily recollected, the Patriots "were in the habit of makeing people use their furniture and houses for the benefit of themselves. It was a usual thing for a detachment to demand of the master of the house, that a meal be provided for them."[29]

Such abuse sapped even the toughest planters' resolve because it forced them to play the role of slaves in a horrifying drama that struck the raw nerve of their deepest fears of a world turned upside down. Lucy Fitzgerald's case is illustrative. Because her husband had died sometime in 1805 or 1806, a neighbor described her as "altogether unprotected." But, she was by no means impoverished. With her overseer and thirty working slaves, Mrs. Fitzgerald cultivated eighty acres of cotton, forty-five to fifty acres of corn, and eight to ten acres of potatoes on "as good land for crops as any in the country." During her marriage, as Spanish law permitted, she had owned her plantation and slaves as separate property. The widow's estate, "Black Hammock," stood on Amelia Island, "immediately upon the waters" near a strategic crossing point to the mainland. Seymour Pickett remembered her as very independent, with a reputation for making "large & valuable crops." Consequently, this "fine old lady" lived in "considerable fashion," in a "rather better style than the common people in the Country."[30]

With the arrival of American troops, this affluent existence slowly unraveled. Margaret Starrat recalled how the Patriots would come to Mrs. Fitzgerald's, turn their horses into her corn, and "do as they pleased" with her property. Although Maria Hogans "was a woman and could not see much," she was "continually hearing of the mischief done to [Fitzgerald's] property." Her brothers, Thomas, Peter, and William Suárez, saw the invaders butcher the elderly widow's 250 cattle. Hogans herself observed a "quarrel" that broke out when the feisty Fitzgerald "made a great Effort to save" her favorite horse, "Bolds," from marauding soldiers. Other military units "ordered the old Lady to have dinner got for them & she dared not do any other way." Sarah B. McDonnell reflected on how U.S. forces would "frequently burst into [Fitzgerald's] yard & not only use her property as they pleased, but insult her besides—she was Extremely ill at one time from the alarm & Excitement occasioned by these visits." Fitzgerald's overseer, Joseph Crews, during one such raid, cowered in fear "behind a stack of fodder." McDonnell advised Fitzgerald to leave, but optimistically hoping that matters would improve, she remained "longer than it was thought prudent by those who were Engaged in resisting those invaders," Finally, after Crews fled to Georgia and raiders carried off some of her slaves, the stubborn female planter abandoned Black Hammock, just when her crop was "nearly made."[31]

To be sure, the Americans taunted and tormented East Floridians mercilessly. Foraging parties, "upon one or more occasions . . . enquired of Mr. [William] Bardin what he was going to do with his crops, saying that he might as well give it to them to feed their horses." They told John J. Lowe that "he might as well hold his tongue, and still his complaints, for they should take just what they pleased." Seymour Pickett noted that their "habit was to ride up to a man's place and take what they wanted." According to Stephen Williamson, they were "arbitrary" men who "would be rash & unreasonable though you gave them all you had." John Jones also remembered them as being "very arbitrary and brutal." They drove William O'Neil from his plantation "out of sheer spite." Likewise, "insults and abuse," "hostile and rude conduct," and "rash acts," impelled James

Dell, David S. H. Miller, and William Nelson to abandon their homes. To Henry Sweeney, "it appeared as if [the Americans] could not do bad enough." On one scouting foray, George Petty's squad approached Mrs. Manuel Romero's establishment and "went up to the house or to the yard & kitchen where [they] got some supper." Although she served the Patriots graciously, one "ruffianly fellow," who had been a "privateersman," along with another rogue, were "insolent or abusive to her." A "female was not safe where these marauders were lawless and profligate as they behaved," a disgusted James E. Mattair recalled. All in all, John Bowden bitterly reminisced, the "object seemed to be to destroy as much property—do as much mischief and produce as much distress as possible."[32]

Indeed, in 1841, more than a generation after the Patriot War, Thomas Suárez railed that the "[i]nvaders were determined to prevent all the Citizens of Florida from doing any good for themselves." Samuel Russell explained that the Americans destroyed what they did not immediately need, in order "to weaken the loyal party." The wastefulness of this policy vividly stood out in the minds of scores of witnesses. Samuel Swearingen once watched twenty cavalrymen as they plundered Joseph Higginbotham's farm. The corn house had been broken open. Some men dug potatoes. Others skinned a hog. Another group chased poultry, as the remainder made preparations to cook. Meanwhile, horses gorged themselves on corn. "[T]here appeared to be a general waste of every thing," Swearingen complained. "[I]t was the character of these people," he added, "to leave everything a waste." In fact, they "generally acted more like madmen than sober, intelligent human beings." Similarly, twenty-five years after the fact, a seething Catherine Taylor scolded the Americans for having used stored corn (which the local populace depended upon for sustenance until the autumn harvest) "with the greatest extravagance & prodigality feeding it out in heaps to their horses without the slightest regard to economy." What was not eaten was left on the ground to spoil. Rafael Olivares observed soldiers taking maize for their mounts from Fernando Fulany's fields. When they departed, they left unconsumed ears "wantonly strewed about" the farm.[33]

Yet, there was a method to the Patriots' madness. As with lumber and cotton, the invaders made sure that it would be difficult to resume the cultivation of provisions. They burned corn houses. They broke corn mills after they finished with them, and such mills were "scarce and dear." In James Pellicer's words, "they were not delicate about using anything." While grinding the elderly Robert Gilbert's harvested corn in his mill, the invaders mutilated his growing crop by throwing down his fences and turning into his field the very horses that they had stolen from him. Once foraging parties destroyed these costly barriers, they subjected any ungathered crops to damage from a plantation's own livestock and from those on neighboring properties. In this manner, John Crichton's orange trees and William Hart's "fine peach orchard" sustained injuries. On George Morrison's place, hogs rooted up his potatoes. After the invaders evacuated from East Florida, Mateo Lorenzo found two "very large Hogs" that had grown "fat" on Francis Pellicer's plantation because the Patriots had demolished fencing. Furthermore, as Matthew Long pointed out, even though many horses refused to eat growing corn, especially if abundant grass grew nearby, they would "trample it greatly" in the absence of fences. Still, some corn would remain, but a field's multiple exposure to mounted parties' visits would result in "no crop whatever."[34]

In addition to targeting the barns, corn mills, and fences necessary to preserve, process, and protect provision crops, U.S. forces attacked East Florida's agricultural infrastructure by destroying its rural orange groves. Old Robert Gilbert could count himself fortunate because even though soldiers "acted while on [his] place as if everything belonged to them," and thus gathered and ate oranges from the forty to forty-five "very full" trees that surrounded his dwelling, they did not kill them. Others were not so lucky. George Fleming's one hundred young citrus trees succumbed to invaders' fires because nobody was present to prevent weeds and vegetation from springing up near the plants. On the St. Johns River's opposite bank, troops "ruined by fire & the axe" Francis P. Fatio's magnificent grove worth an estimated ten thousand dollars. Further down the St. Johns, Francis Richard Sr.'s hundred or more bearing orange trees went up in flames. Joseph Summerall counted only about twenty immature orange trees on his small farm, but foraging parties refused to spare them. Edward M. Wanton made a hobby of cultivating citrus, which he shared with his neighbors. William Bardin recounted how Wanton had planted five hundred to six hundred orange and lemon trees in various locations on his plantation and on an adjacent island. A few already had been yielding fruit. Wanton also possessed twelve peach trees, along with a nursery of two hundred to three hundred more. Patriot fires destroyed all.[35]

When groves vanished in the wafting smoke, part of East Florida's unique Anglo-Mediterranean culture dissipated with them. Furthermore, victims realized that just as orange trees could not be resurrected overnight, neither could their fortunes. The destruction of the province's cattle herds induced an even greater sense of malaise because the populace "prided themselves as ranchers." An examination of witnesses' memories of this troubling aspect of the Patriot War becomes especially useful due to "[c]attle's ubiquity throughout the society," which, in the historian Susan Parker's analysis, "allows us to touch upon the histories of all sorts of persons."[36] Stockholders large and small united in expressing, during their testimonies in the antebellum claims cases, a long-simmering, angry sorrow over the wanton slaughter that took place under the aegis of the

United States. Indeed, in one sense, American policy toward the Spanish colony's bovine wealth bears an eerie resemblance to Washington's post–Civil War strategy of exterminating the buffalo upon which the Plains Indians depended. That is, the United States meant to demoralize as well as starve those whom it perceived as threats to its national security.

The years between 1807 and 1812, Dr. James Hall recalled, had been "favorable to stock." Consequently, ranchers like Manuel Solana, Fernando de la Maza Arredondo Sr., Antonio Huertas, and the Francisco Xavier Sánchez estate had accumulated "immense" herds. Since "every one of any property owned cattle," and there were "good stocks in the country," almost all free persons enjoyed a share of the province's rapidly multiplying bovine wealth. With the eruption of the Patriot War, however, these widely available utilitarian status symbols disappeared into the stomachs of men and vermin. "The plunder of . . . Cattle," Thomas J. Andrew thundered, "was the constant practice the martial law of the invading army countenanced this conduct because they never checked it & they hushed into Silence all other law." What was not "used or wantonly destroyed [was] taken to Georgia to replenish the stores of the *crackers* of that state who were engaged in the revolution."[37] Thus, East Florida's communal memories of the Spanish-era cattle industry, along with oral accounts of the provincial economy's forestry, cotton, and comestibles sectors, tarred the Americans as deviants who had subverted a bountiful natural order. Moreover, since a flourishing ranching tradition had existed under the Spaniards as far back as the seventeenth century,[38] the invaders had targeted the very core of the colony's economic essence.

In this respect, United States forces once again turned East Florida upside down. And they did so with a remarkable, though chaotic, efficiency. "[A]fter a diligent search" in 1816 of the Matanzas Range, some twenty-eight miles south of St. Augustine, ranchers located only 20 to 30 of the several thousand cattle that had grazed there. To the north and west of town, the firm of Arredondo & Huertas, which boasted possibly the biggest herd in the province, lost all of their 1,500 to 2,000 head. Manuel Solana's drove of at least 1,000 to 1,200 in the same general area also disappeared, with "Buzzards Dogs and wolves" devouring many of his "large steers." On the historically significant Diego Plains, "a famous range for cattle" about twenty miles north of the Ancient City, where reputedly the best beeves in the country roamed, all of the 1,400 beasts belonging to Francisco Xavier Sánchez's estate were driven off, "with the exception of a few that went wild from neglect and from the constant use of firearms among them." These hardy survivors, however, could not be "recovered for use," so they were shot "by those who chose to hunt them." Sánchez's son estimated that in 1813, merely 200 cattle remained in the entire stretch of territory between St. Augustine and Georgia. Elsewhere, two of his cousins remarked that "all was *desolate* and *gone*." In fact, when Charles W. Clarke went out to round up cattle, he found "not even a track of one."[39]

Under these devastating circumstances, even more modest cattle owners saw their stocks vanish. John D. Braddock's herd included 200 of his own animals, and 600 belonging to the estate of his deceased father-in-law, Spicer Christopher Sr. These "first rate prime cattle," which grazed on an "excellent range," featured more than the usual numbers of "fine beeves" and "fat bullocks." For this reason, James Woodland considered them "among the very best in the Country." Like other ranchers, Braddock lost them all and in 1813 he had to "Commence his Stock" all over again, even though "there was hardly a hoof in the Country to commence with." At John H. McIntosh's Ortega plantation, Allen Brazil "devoted all his time to taking care of" over 300 of the fattest cattle that John M. Bowden ever had seen in Florida. The troops at nearby Camp New Hope regularly came over in boats to harvest this ready supply of beef. None of Stephen Vanzandt's 250 cattle remained after the U.S. evacuation. Nathaniel Wilds managed to save 20 to 25 of his 150 to 200 head by taking them to Georgia. After William Dell was killed in the early months of the Patriot War, his family, a year later, found 20 cattle out of his pre-invasion stock of more than 100. William Bardin and his brother John thought that they had outwitted the Americans when "they made kind of a party" to drive the "remnant" of their herds northward from Picolata to Mandarin. William's stock totaled over 100 head, while his sibling's herd totaled 75 to 80. After a successful drive, however, the Bardins still ended up losing them to various raiders.[40]

Because the Americans especially targeted the "cattle of the faithful Spaniards," some East Floridians actually joined the invaders in the hope of protecting their herds. Those who adopted this strategy saw themselves duped, for as Gabriel Priest pointed out, the Patriots' pledges proved intrinsically false, because they had to take food and forage where they found it. Consequently, even "the Cattle of men under arms [were] brought up, and shot before their faces." Stock owners fighting with the Patriots, along with their royalist neighbors, with very few exceptions, could not sell their livestock nor attend to them. Samuel Sauls discovered this the hard way. "Sauls run away with a daughter of David Davis of Georgia," recollected Samuel Swearingen, "and for a long time Davis threatened to kill Sauls, but after a while the matter was made up," and "Davis, who was a large stock owner, then gave Sauls a bunch of cattle," some sixty, which the latter brought to Florida. In the early days of the U.S. invasion, Sauls initially fled to Georgia. Then, hoping to save his cherished herd, which he had placed with a caretaker near St. Augustine, he joined a Patriot unit. Nevertheless, since his cattle were the "handiest" to his comrades' camp, they, despite knowing full well that the animals belonged to Sauls, butchered all of them bit by bit. Sauls was "as mad as he could be." He insisted that Swearingen accompany him to look at five cattle that the troops had shot that morning. Patriot promises notwithstanding, Sauls never received a lick of compensation.[41]

Indeed, as William Daniels observed, "the troops paid no respect to persons. . . . They roamed about as they pleased and did as they pleased." Not only did they force Francis R. Sánchez to drive his own small herd into their camp, they also ordered him to plunder his legendary father's cattle on the Diego Plains, promising compensation to his prestigious widowed mother, but never keeping their word. By such disrespect, the Patriots forged a memory-chain of suffering linking scions like Sánchez to East Floridians from much humbler circumstances. Cornelius Griffith lost all of his "very pretty bunch" of sixty to seventy cattle except for "one 'cow beast.'" Emanuel Mott remembered the time when his uncle, John Ashton, who owned forty "good cattle," anxiously informed soldiers that the animals that they were rounding up were his. They replied that they did not care whose they were. The septuagenarian Jeremiah Wingate, still fuming in 1838, recounted how his son John "lost every hide and hair" of his "small choice stock" of thirty-one to thirty-two cattle. A month before the invasion, Peter Trope made the unfortunate decision to move his twenty-five "Picked; that is to Say: the best of Cattle," seven miles, from St. Augustine to the "Casacola range," near one of the Sánchez family's plantations. Here they fell prey to the Americans. A mere five hundred yards from the city gates, Joseph Baya's six milk cows vanished.[42]

Women and minors also comprised a portion of the memory-chain connected to plundered cattle. When United States troops stole William Nelson's twenty-five "very fine" cattle, they left his "five little children" and wife "very distressed." Soldiers robbed twelve-year-old John Black of his small herd of ten to twelve cattle. Everybody, Mrs. Cynthia Sweeney swore in 1841, knew that they were "Johnnys." "Whatever they wanted," U.S. regulars and Patriots "took without hesitation" on each of their frequent visits to the farm of Jane Lane, a widow with two boys. This included all but fifteen to twenty of her eighty to one hundred "very good cattle." They would stop at her place and shoot them even before she deserted the premises. Mrs. Francis Pellicer also fell victim to sadistic cruelty. While her husband and three oldest sons were engaged in Spanish military service, she and her offspring, "some of them quite young," came face to face with a Patriot foraging party on her Matanzas plantation. The leader of the party quickly arrested her fear by "profess[ing] a desire to serve" her. He "humanely requested that her little son might be sent to point out the milch cows she wished to keep, assuring her that they should not be touched." After the lad identified them, "they were the first driven off by the Patriot officer."[43]

To make matters worse, the invaders completed their cattle genocide with a nauseating flourish of cruelty. The stench of their actions still sickened antebellum witnesses. In order to force St. Augustine's surrender, officers ordered troops to deliver all of the cattle that they could to "the Stockade," a military camp of six hundred to seven hundred men, located four miles from town. There, under herdsmen's watchful eyes, the four-legged plunder awaited their demise "in a pen" where, Francis R. Sánchez related with disdain, "every man was his own quartermaster and killed as he thought fit." Since the beasts "cost nothing but the trouble of driving them in from the country," John M. Bowden scornfully noted, the Americans "were never particular about how many they killed so long as they killed enough." Sánchez recalled a soldier who slew three beeves "before he found one to his liking," and then used only thirty pounds of the choicest meat. On one occasion, Bowden saw "so many cattle killed that two of them were left dead in the pen, no knife was ever put to them." The besiegers, Sánchez estimated, actually consumed only 10 percent of the animals that they drove to camp. The remainder, they simply shot. After the U.S. forces evacuated, they left behind abundant physical evidence of their malfeasance. John Leonardy, John Geiger, and Papy Rose, after searching through a stack of rotted hides at the abandoned cow pen, identified some of the ranchers that the Patriots had victimized by the still-discernible brands on two hundred of the freshest skins.[44]

If it was not feasible to drive cattle to the stockade, foraging parties were instructed to kill them where they found them. The consequences of this policy greased the angry wheels of memory in numerous Patriot War survivors. Thus, Felipe Solana, a member of one of East Florida's most eminent ranching families, recounted his continuing inner vision of the living nightmare that he had experienced as he traveled through the East Florida countryside: "carcasses of cattle lying dead in all directions along the road." About twenty miles south of St. Augustine stood Little Bar Island, just beyond the range of Fort Matanzas's cannons. On this speck of *tierra firme* measuring one mile long and half as wide, the Patriots "behaved wantonly and outrageously." Using guns, bayonets, and swords, they massacred or maimed an estimated seventy to one hundred unruly cattle that balked at traversing a shallow, shell-bottomed exit route. More perished while the American forces drove them to the mainland. The remains of shot, "cut and hacked," or drowned cattle, according to eyewitness James Pellicer, "were strewed upon the shore for miles." Much smaller slaughters, however, also raised the hackles of the region's old inhabitants. The American practice of shooting ranging cattle "for sport" and "killing a beef when they only wanted a small piece," irked Robert Hodges, Thomas Suárez, John M. Bowden, William Daniels, and Sarah Acosta alike.[45]

Ranchers required horses for handling their herds, as well as for farm work and personal transportation. Unfortunately, the Patriots were horse thieves, as well as cattle rustlers. "People were very much afraid of the Georgians at that time," Philip Weedman mused, "and would not trust them further than they could see them." This proved especially true regarding horses, which were scarce and very expensive in 1812, and according to Pablo Masters, superior to those that East Floridians owned in antebellum times. Moreover, as Isaac Wingate groused, U.S. troops took all of the horses that they could find. And, as in the cases of timber, cotton, provisions, oranges, and cattle, the invaders were no respecters of persons in this regard. They did not hesitate to press the hapless pre-teen Johnny Black's two horses to carry supplies. When the Americans captured Masters and held him briefly as a prisoner, they attempted to con the boy into surrendering his mount. Soldiers also tried to relieve Dr. James Hall of his horse while he was doing them the favor of attending to one of their wounded comrades. The widow Prudence Plummer's confiscated "fine mare" ended up as supper for Colonel Daniel Newnan's men after the Seminoles killed it during a battle at Alachua Prairie. Mrs. Eliza Crews, Francis P. Fatio's daughter, undoubtedly shocked her listeners in 1846 when she recounted how, as a young teenager some thirty-three years earlier, she had spotted a Patriot riding her pony in St. Marys, Georgia.[46]

A number of the horses that the Americans stole represented either their victims' lofty positions in provincial society, or their aspirations to achieve such positions. Elites like Zephaniah Kingsley, who favored "high-bred white chargers," and Francisco Xavier Sánchez, "the richest man in the country," were "fond of horses" and "raised many of fine blood." Fernandina's commandant, Don Justo López, owned a "splendid blooded" gelding racehorse worth $300, at a time when "a good plough Horse would sell for $100." Witnesses raved about John D. Braddock's "very fine first rate Stallion," for which he paid $500. "Such a horse is rarely Seen," Jeremiah Wingate gushed. "I have traveled a great deal to many parts and do not think I have Seen his Superior." Felipe Solana, who was "fond of good Horses and of riding," adorned his favorite mount with "a double reined and double bitted, handsome, silver plated bridle." More than a generation removed from the Patriot War, the names of these magnificent creatures survived. The "Arabian" had cost Spicer Christopher $750. William Dewees owned "Stockings," a cream-colored horse with "four bright white feet," and he called his bay mare "Widow." Michael Ledwith referred to his "noble horse" as "Bluebuck." "Flatheels" belonged to Lewis Mattair, "Bonapart" to Fernando D. McDonnell, "Speculator" to James Pelot, and "Hallowell" to Seymour Pickett. Francis R. Sánchez's "very fine fast horse" was "the Reindeer," and "Backus" was his "very good Saddle horse."[47]

Accordingly, the loss of cherished steeds filled many East Floridians with unrelenting grief. Samuel S. Christopher, who "would not own a poor or Mean horse," saw the invaders take his "beautiful English mare," along with his "capital" saddle horse, and a "common horse," not "first rate" or "blooded," but still "sarvisable." Christopher often spoke of them after the war. When Americans grabbed Frederick Hartley's "valuable young stud," he sought to dissuade them by warning that the animal would be difficult to handle. They replied that they would "cool him." Hartley, George Petty sadly noted, "grieved much about him." The manner in which others' horses died infuriated witnesses. James A. Rogers and Joseph Haddock remembered that "a picket guard" near St. Augustine killed one of Lodovic Ashley's best horses by "stabbing him in his flank with a bayonet." A U.S. rifleman sent a "ball Shot through" John D. Vaughan's "fine" stallion, Thomas Suárez and Ephraim Harrison recalled. William O'Neil's "chesnut sorel mare," William Braddock and Samuel Russell deposed, was "wornout" in the enemy's service. The waste of this favored livestock surely imbedded indelible rage into their owners' memories as well. Despite James Dell's vehement protests, the invaders seized his horse, which subsequently died "while rode on an express." Dell likely was voicing his own angst and that of numerous neighbors when he testified that John Dixon often complained about losing a "good horse" to the invaders, that "he thought much of." Finally, even the disappearance of inexpensive equine property cast a lingering cloud of gloom upon the region's elders. Thus, one of James Falany's thirty-dollar colts "t'was a fine little animal," according to Francis Marín.[48]

By employing phrases such as "fine pacing . . . large gray Indian Pony" or "beautiful bay mare young and likely" to describe horses that perished during the United States–sponsored "revolution," antebellum witnesses expressed their affectionate nostalgia for Spanish times. In contrast, when they disparagingly referred to the invaders as "U. States Highwaymen" or "Jackasses of the Lion,"[49] they were protesting both Washington's expansionist policy of 1812 and the calamities that its contemporary rule had thrust upon them. Afro–East Floridians long had exploited rifts in the white community to protect and promote their freedom. Therefore, the Patriot War and its aftermath armed them with another weapon of diplomacy—a boiling resentment among local whites toward the Americans for having dared to "enslave" them. The invasion also furnished blacks with a second, more subtle means to leverage liberty; namely, a dim, barely discernible subconscious sympathy in whites' memories for persons of African descent who had shared the experience of Patriot War victimization. This common cross-racial identity can best be plumbed by examining memories of the plight of the province's free people of color during the "troubles."

3
Barbarians at the Gates

Robert R. Reid was a "thoughtful, introspective man with an affection for biblical study and the classics." This native Georgian, who had graduated from South Carolina College and served in Congress from 1819 to 1823, had come to Florida in 1832 as a federal district judge. He would rise to occupy the governor's mansion in Tallahassee. The final day of August 1836 found Reid anxiously mulling over the events of the Patriot War. Initially, he had found it difficult to believe traumatized witnesses as they testified in their neighbors' lawsuits against the United States. He hypothesized that time had failed to erase the mental "state of excitement and agitation" that exaggerated their losses. The Second Seminole War's outbreak, however, tempered his skepticism, as he saw with his own eyes the horrible violence that U.S. policies had engendered. The conflict with the Seminoles did not shock Mrs. Jane Redding so deeply. "People complain of the Indian War, and no doubt suffer much," she adamantly proclaimed, "but the suffering of the poor People during the Revolution of 12 and 13 was far greater." James Plummer, another "old inhabitant," voiced his assent. "[T]hose were sharp times," he laconically mused in 1840, "worse than these." Even persons whose familiarity with the Patriot War rested solely upon copies of claims cases forwarded to Washington from St. Augustine felt repulsed by the behavior of the invading forces. In 1852, one Treasury Department lawyer indignantly railed against the "monstrous atrocities committed by those unfeeling barbarians."[1]

The solicitor's evocation of uncivilized white American hordes running amok is telling, as is the fact that men of color stemmed the tide of this "barbarian" invasion. Nonwhites' valor turned racial hierarchy topsy-turvy. In accordance with a time-honored principle of folk diplomacy stretching back to the colony's foundation, Afro–East Floridians seized upon frontier turmoil to craft alternative identities that transcended the degradation of blackness. The martial traditions and intercultural skills that they exercised during the Patriot War ensconced them as heroes in local lore. Over a generation later, this exalted niche in white memories permitted veterans of African descent to gamely employ a legal loophole to lodge public protests against the American regime that had marginalized them. Their subtle jeremiads, like the apocalypse of 1812, presented whites with an opportunity to reconsider the wisdom of racial oppression and to remedy it. Enslaved diplomats as well would hitch popular history to the engine of their liberty.

According to Susan Parker's research, Francis Philip Fatio Sr., like scores of free black East Floridians, had mastered the art of benefiting from the "tumult of both in- and out-migration of people and governments." Thirty miles from St. Augustine, Fatio's ten-thousand-acre New Switzerland plantation lined the banks of the St. Johns River for twelve miles. Here he quartered eighty-six slaves, whose toil generated the wealth that enabled him to live in baronial splendor. Fatio was born in the francophone region of Switzerland and in 1743–48 joined the French in their struggle against England during the War of the Austrian Succession. After residing in Sardinia and Albion itself, he emigrated to British East Florida in 1771. During the American Revolution, he cast his lot with the former enemies of his Swiss youth. When Britain retroceded its peninsular colony as a consequence of defeat, Fatio, sensing an opportunity to "make himself nearly indispensable to the incoming Spanish," opted to remain. He subsequently prospered due to his knack for efficiently devoting his resources to diverse economic activities well suited to the frontier region's natural and political milieu. Fatio's thriving enterprises in ranching, forestry, and citrus cultivation demonstrated that the "country could support the material comfort of those who correctly analyzed what actions and adaptations were needed to succeed in that . . . environment."[2]

Magnificent holdings such as New Switzerland were microcosms of the colony's booming economy. Indeed, even East Floridians of modest means could engage in the ventures that had made Fatio rich. Moreover, as a man "noted for his fine library and love of learning," Fatio was no mere crass entrepreneur.[3] His New Switzerland mansion functioned as a bastion of western civilization in the midst of a wilderness. He personified the wealthy Renaissance man that the province's lesser inhabitants could become, thus fueling their dreams of upward mobility. Therefore, when the relentless clouds of Patriot War–induced doom descended upon provincial luminaries, their poisonous vapors sucked the very life out of commoners' aspirations. This sense of despair remained firmly fixed in Joseph Arnowe's memory. "Such was the depression of Spirits and circumstances produced by the Revolution," he recalled, "that few persons returned to their farms in 1813." Arnowe's dismal recollection illuminates the deeper meaning behind Samuel Swearingen's astute observation that the United States invasion "was the most onerous upon those who had large estates."[4] Similarly, the events transpiring at New Switzerland while U.S. forces possessed it reveal the disturbing images of white Americans that haunted antebellum East Floridians—nightmarish phantasmagorias that melded well with black folk diplomacy.

Lewis Fleming, Francis P. Fatio Sr.'s grandson, was a lad about fourteen years of age in 1812. His main pursuits consisted of "Riding about the Country, going to School etc. etc." He was well acquainted with New Switzerland, because he would stay "months there at a time." Although he admitted that he did not actually observe its "destruction," Fleming attempted to bolster his credibility as a witness by invoking the value of oral history. The entire sordid affair, he asserted in 1837, "is spoken of by the inhabitants of this country with as much confidence as the Battle of Bunker Hill was . . . in Massachusetts." During the previous year, Judge Robert R. Reid had alluded to such "certainty" (based upon deponents' knowledge of the community's vibrant historical traditions), when he informed the U.S. secretary of the treasury that testimony often was not what witnesses had seen for themselves. Rather, they frequently based their assertions on information that they did not doubt because they had heard it related to them so often. A decade later, in 1846, Reid's successor, Isaac H. Bronson, commented that "the history and traditions of the losses & sufferings of the Fatio family . . . are notorious in East Florida."[5] Those responsible for New Switzerland's demise, therefore, infamously resided in citizens' memories as territorial Florida entered the Union.

Significantly, in the midst of the Second Seminole War, witnesses emphasized that the chief vandals of New Switzerland wore white face. While it is true that the Seminoles were responsible for the surprise attack that drove the half-shaved Francis Fatio Jr. and his partially clad family to a small boat in which they "almost by a miracle" escaped with their lives, the raiders departed in a few hours. They only took away what they could conveniently carry—bedding, clothing, and an "Elegant Canoe" worth five hundred dollars that the Americans (who ultimately destroyed it) recovered just across the St. Johns River. Forty Fatio slaves also disappeared. It is likely that a goodly portion welcomed their "kidnappers." William Broadnax, a Georgia militia officer who arrived at the scene soon after the warriors had vanished, found "not very great" material damage. Only a few small outbuildings, slave cabins, were "then smoking." Fatio's major structures, including his "richly furnished" dwelling, which contained "a very valuable and extensive library," remained intact. The Seminoles harmed neither New Switzerland's storied orange grove nor its livestock.[6] The situation would change for the worse once U.S. forces set up camp.

At least ten whites resided on the estate when the Patriot War erupted, along with six house servants, fifty field hands, and twenty-four to thirty other slaves too young, old, or disabled to work. The Great House contained twelve rooms—a parlor, dining room, library, office, storeroom, and seven bedrooms. All of the "solid mahogany" furniture that filled these rooms had been transported from England. During family meals, a "great quantity" of the "best quality" china, silver plate, glassware, crockery, and eating utensils graced the dining room, along with the "Liquors, wines, tea, coffee, sugar & other family stores, usual & necessary for a gentleman of . . . fortune & living in the style [that Fatio] did." He "was in the habit of having & entertaining much company & people who were traveling frequently stopped there & were of course always entertained." If these visitors fell ill, medicines on hand in the plantation's apothecary shop might relieve their symptoms. At night, they reposed in feather beds covered with linen sheets. A "Back gammon board" and "chess-men" livened the parlor, while a "spy glass" and "mathematical instruments" amused the more scientifically inclined. Fatio owned tools for repairing his guests' watches and a "large Eight day clock" by which he marked the length of their stays. Tall "looking glasses" enabled boarders to ensure that they were presentable before they partook of the bounty of New Switzerland's flocks and fields.[7]

To be sure, the mansion dazzled wayfarers with its visual delights. Seven "valuable oil paintings" adorned its walls. Some were family portraits. One battle scene measured five feet by six feet long and two feet by three feet high. The two "as large as life" and "very costly" depictions of St. Cecilia and St. Jerome, which Fatio "highly valued," reached "from the ceiling to the chair railing of the room & [were] as much as 8 or 10 feet long." All of this artwork sported gilt frames. The Fatio women enhanced their beauty with gold chains, earrings, finger rings, and crosses encrusted with gemstones. The province's finest library, a "splendid & beautiful one," contained 1,200–1,500 "Choice books," many of them "very large," written in English, French, German, and Spanish. William E. Broadnax estimated the size of the room that housed this collection as being at least four hundred square feet. "[F]rom floor to ceiling," it was "completely filled with books besides several large trunks containing books and papers." In addition to shelves and tables, the library furniture featured a pair of mahogany stands, each supporting globes that symbolized the Fatio family's international outlook and interests.[8]

The Fatios particularly esteemed two objects in New Switzerland's treasure trove. One was a "silver gilt" quart tankard "very handsomely carved to represent a bunch of grapes and [Fatio's] coat of arms . . . was engraved upon it." It was used only on "extraordinary occasions." This "very old and valuable relic" had "been in the family for centuries." The tankard, along with its matching gold salt cellar, "had from time immemorial descended to the eldest son." Francis P. Fatio Sr.'s daughter, Mrs. Sophia Fleming, judged that the clan had followed this custom "for nearly three hundred years." It must have served as a source of comfort for a family who had lost its matriarch in 1810, and its patriarch the following year. In fact, just prior to the Patriot War, they had "left off" two years of mourning. The deceased patriarch's son, Francis P. Fatio Jr., marked the end of this period of sorrow by journeying to St. Marys, Georgia, where he spent a thousand dollars to clothe his entire white ten-person household with fresh wardrobes. He also purchased "an unusually large supply of provisions . . . & also table linen & bed linen."[9] Little did Fatio realize how fleeting would be his respite from grief.

A month after his return from St. Marys, the Seminole raid took place. On the Indians' heels, soldiers under Colonel Daniel Newnan's command set up camp. Newnan, a Georgia planter and militia general, was born in North Carolina. He was the son of a physician and he attended college prior to receiving a commission in the United States Army. Leading 250 volunteers, he crossed the St. Marys River into East Florida both to chasten the Indians for abetting fugitive slaves and to succor the struggling Patriots. Francis P. Fatio Jr. had not enamored himself to the latter. Prior to the New Switzerland attack, the invaders had forced Fatio to their camp. Soon, "his determined hostility" was causing desertions among admiring neighbors who had been coerced to the rebel cause, so he was released. Newnan's men came to hate the scion without ever meeting him. When they broke open his trunks and discovered that the absent Fatio had been a "Quarter-master" in the British army, they demonstrated their "considerable animosity" by constantly cursing him as a "damn'd old British officer on half pay." They extended their bile to his recently buried father. Dr. James Hall, who had fought in the Battle of Yorktown and was, in the 1830s, as the historians James Denham and Keith Huneycutt explained, "one of the most substantial citizens of East Florida," observed their sacrilegious manifestation of U.S. nationalism. In Hall's presence, some of Newnan's men "broke open the family vault and took out the body of Francis P. Fatio, Sen.[r] and left his bones scattered about."[10]

The U.S. invaders perpetrated additional abuses against the trappings of civilization at New Switzerland. Many of the estate's two hundred sheep were slaughtered for sport or spite. Their bloated carcasses, uneaten and unskinned, "lay . . . stinking about the yard, where they had been wantonly shot by the soldiers." The plantation bell, which the patriarch had imported from England, was hung in the "Market House" at St. Marys, Georgia. Lieutenant William

Broadnax "read many of the Books" in the library and recalled drinking from a cherished heirloom, which he described as a "curiously wrought silver Tankard." Doubtless, his comrades followed suit. After the library's collection was perused, its volumes were tossed about on the floor. Some tomes were pilfered, reappearing on Amelia Island. A U.S. Army officer stole board games, mathematical instruments, and a spyglass. Despite pleas from a conscientious Marine Corps counterpart, the commissioned thief refused to return them. From August–October 1812, the bivouacked Georgia militia, along with soldiers from nearby Patriot and U.S. posts, helped themselves to Fatio's provisions. When Newnan's charges abandoned New Switzerland, "hardly anything of account" remained, and "the whole place was a ruin." By early 1813, fire had consumed the plantation's once-opulent mansion. Farquhar Bethune vehemently asserted that the Indians did not burn it. The Americans were the culprits, and they torched the "very excellent library" in the process.[11]

Back in the United States, the public hailed Colonel Daniel Newnan as a "national hero," due to newspaper reports of his punitive expedition of 24 September to 11 October 1812. Although this campaign did halt the Indians' intervention in the Patriot War, American commanders in East Florida, the scholar James Cusick wrote, privately perceived it as a "near catastrophe saved by luck." The Seminoles had pinned Newnan's force down in the province's remote Alachua interior for a harrowing week. Then, the beleaguered Georgians saw themselves forced into a grueling retreat. Nevertheless, despite this courage under fire, antebellum witnesses in the Patriot War claims hearings remembered Newnan's soldiers primarily for pressing horses, wastefully slaughtering cattle, and making off with corn, potatoes, meat, bread, rice, flour, and whiskey, without asking for permission or offering payment. Dr. James Hall, one of the rare persons who lauded Newnan for "sav[ing] the country from Indian Ravage and destruction," was the same man who detailed the outrages that the colonel's soldiers had heaped upon the Fatio family. Elijah Higginbotham, unlike Hall, maintained that the Indians had defeated Newnan. Consequently, he swore in 1843, settlers on the Little St. Marys River "got alarmed" and fled to Georgia. It might be argued that the claims cases present a skewed view of Newnan, since their purpose was to prove damages taking place at the hands of the American invaders. A comment by Michael Sloan, however, hints at a deeper reason for old inhabitants' lack of praise. "It was the U.S. Troops & Patriots," Sloan complained, "that brought down the Indians upon us."[12] Sloan's barb, coming in 1841, during the Second Seminole War, constitutes a protest against Washington's handling of Indian affairs—past and present.

Similarly, testimony on Zephaniah Kingsley's behalf also reveals contemporary resentments rooted in the Patriot War. Laurel Grove plantation stood some nine to ten miles downriver from New Switzerland, on the opposite bank of the St. Johns. The Indians attacked it on 25 July 1812, about three weeks before they raided the Fatio estate. This assault proved more serious than the latter. Warriors burned almost all of Kingsley's buildings, killed or wounded one white man and three slaves, and led forty to fifty more bond persons to the interior. But, as Francis Richard and John M. Bowden acknowledged, they were acting as Spanish allies, rather than wild savages. Before the U.S. invasion, George Petty, John Houston, and Samuel Swearingen pointed out, the Seminoles' behavior toward East Floridians had been friendly. They burned Laurel Grove because its strategic location and extensive facilities were of "great importance" militarily. If the American forces had not come, the Indians would not have molested Kingsley. Hence, the United States bore ultimate responsibility for the destruction.[13] Like in the rape of New Switzerland, Anglo-Americans were portrayed as barbarians, even though the Second Seminole War raged around antebellum witnesses.

By the same token, old inhabitants' characterizations of Captain William Cone defy Patriot self-images as divinely anointed bearers of "Anglo-American civilization" to oppressed U.S. emigrants, Spanish royalists, recalcitrant Loyalists, savage Seminoles, and barbaric blacks. Moreover, East Floridians' memories vividly exemplify how history, even the unwritten variety, differs according to the perspectives and purposes of its proponents. Cone was the "son of a Revolutionary War hero." His own star rose after he was wounded during Newnan's famous Alachua campaign. He consolidated his position when the fading Patriot movement splintered into warlord-headed factions. Cone's renown grew at Waterman's Bluff, on 8 August 1813, because of his role in the retreating Patriots' face-saving victory in a skirmish with the Spaniards. Subsequently, he was prominent among the diehards who, in 1814, at Alachua, established Fort Mitchell as the capital of the rump Republic of East Florida. Washington's rebuff and the Spanish-induced assassination of Buckner Harris, the republic's magnetic "director," moved Cone to return to the United States, where, according to James Cusick, he "became a kind of Georgian version of Davy Crockett . . . the center of many tall tales." His status as a "local folk hero" blossomed when he battled the British and fought for Camden County in Georgia's legislature. Cone then moved back to Florida, where he served in the territory's legislative council, and, in 1854, the state senate. One scholar, Chris Monaco, has recently argued that Cone was a "solid citizen of the type who had made America great."[14]

In the version of history documented in the Patriot War claims cases, however, Captain Cone emerges from the mists of time as the heartless master of a band of brigands. Judge Isaac H. Bronson associated Cone with the notorious plunderers of the storied Fatio estate. Catherine Taylor held him responsible for the "prodigality" of feeding Philip Dewees's corn to horses and casting the leftovers to the ground to spoil. She added that his men drove Dewees's cattle into a pen and cruelly slaughtered them. These abuses drove the Dewees family to Fernandina "in a state of great anxiety and alarm." William Daniels also recalled Cone's utter disrespect for inhabitants' personal property. At Willoughby Hodges's place, Daniels swore, his troops "shot cattle for sport." Sarah B. McDonnell related how Cone had been with a squad who confiscated Lucy Fitzgerald's slaves, cotton boat, and other possessions. After a quarrel ensued over the division of these spoils, the plunderers stranded Cone and three other men on Amelia Island. Cone led the castaways to McDonnell's father's plantation, where, over the latter's protests, they seized a boat. Andrew Fullwood, testifying in 1847, accused Cone of shamefully stripping Fernandina merchant Ezekial Hudnall of his dry goods. Elsewhere, Joseph Simeon Sánchez linked Cone to the pointless and spiteful firing of the royalist planter George Atkinson's dwelling as the invaders were evacuating the colony in 1813. James R. Woodland blamed Cone for sacking James Erwin's plantation in August 1813, some three months after the evacuation.[15]

But it was Cone's involvement in the pillaging of James Cashen's "extensive" Erin Hall estate that sealed his villainous reputation in East Florida lore. Indeed, one prominent antebellum politician, David Levy (also known as David L. Yulee), called this incident "a *National Outrage.*" Erin Hall was located on Amelia Island, four miles from Fernandina. Thirty-six field hands cultivated a hundred acres of cotton, fifty acres of corn, and twenty acres of potatoes and peas, making their master the second-largest planter on the island. The "wealthy and respectable" Cashen served the Spaniards as a militia captain and judge. He counted Justo López, "the commandant of Amelia," as his friend. Susan, his wife, was "born and raised a Lady." In his "large fine house," which featured "costly" furniture "not common in Florida" and other "necessary articles of domestic luxury," he "lived in good style." His "table was a gentleman's table—well furnished with silver and plate." Cashen had earned a reputation as "a liberal gentleman" who "often supplied gratuitously those who were in want of Provisions." On 19 September 1812, at midnight, shortly before the harvest, at a season when the "fields were white with cotton," William Cone helped himself to Cashen's wealth.[16]

Cone led the party that broke into Cashen's dwelling, kidnapped its owner, and pulled the rings from "Mrs. Cashen's fingers." The Patriot raiders also appropriated the mistress's "very fine gold watch" and earrings. In addition, they stripped the house of its furniture, silverware, crockery, and table linen. Furthermore, the master lost his bedclothes, watch, chains, seals, and purse. From the plantation storehouse, Cone's men pilfered coffee, sugar, and all the valuables that they could find. Tragically, they made off with forty slaves, thus ensuring that Erin Hall's cotton crop never would be gathered. The commander of the company of U.S. regulars stationed at Fernandina, Captain Abraham Massias, claimed that it was "impossible" for him to protect property outside the "lines of [his] defenses" from "depredations." Nevertheless, as it turned out, the American military worked hand in hand with Cone, who had established a "strong hold" on the Florida side of the St. Marys River, "within a short stones throw" of Fort Pinckney, on the opposite bank, in Georgia. In fact, Zephaniah Kingsley opined, Cone never would have embarked upon his larcenous sprees if it were not for the "countenance" that the army post "afforded." Cone and his thirty to forty "banditti" engaged in "constant intercourse" with Fort Pinckney's commander, officers, and enlisted men, all of whom were scandalously present at the public sale of Cashen's stolen property.[17]

Captain Cone's thievery at Erin Hall, like Colonel Newnan's plundering of New Switzerland, endured in East Florida's communal memory of the Patriot War. Cone and Newnan certainly do not appear as folk heroes in antebellum testimony connected with compensation claims. Regarding Cashen, his suffering at the hands of the U.S. military did not end in 1812. The year 1818 found him still living at Erin Hall. Although the lack of an enslaved labor force meant that Cashen no longer planted cotton, his buildings and machinery had not yet been destroyed. This surviving infrastructure meant that in the future, he might again commence planting. Cashen's two-story, forty foot by twenty foot framed cotton house was worth $800 to $900. A large, "double horse gin," valued at $500, featuring "three wheels & a large band," was attached to the "outside of the building and protected from the weather by a separate frame about 15 feet square." The plantation's slave cabins, "small framed houses" valued at $80 to $100 each, remained livable. The old single-story, thirty foot by eighteen to twenty foot dwelling house continued to shelter Cashen, but he was investing $2,000 to construct a new two-story, forty foot by twenty-five foot one. In addition, he had upgraded his kitchen, abundantly supplying it with cooking utensils. Joseph Lourcey estimated that it had cost Cashen between $350 and $400. James Mattair recalled that the estate also contained stables, along with carriage, dairy, and pigeon houses.[18] Obviously, then, Cashen's hopes for a happy future had not been extinguished.

American troops, however, soon engulfed his dreams in flames. On 29 June 1817, Francisco Morales, the panic-stricken commandant of Fernandina, surrendered to Sir Gregor MacGregor, a Scotsman transplanted to Venezuela, who headed a force of 78 men, most of whom hailed from Georgia and South Carolina. MacGregor was acting under a commission issued by a Philadelphia-based "informal junta" representing the rebel governments of Mexico, Nueva Granada, and the United Provinces of Río de la Plata. His intention was to use the Florida port as a base from which to harass Spanish shipping, thus aiding the cause of Latin American independence. Nearly three months later, on 15 September, the Frenchman Louis Michel Aury, a "first rate privateer" in the service of the Republic of Mexico, took over for MacGregor. Subsequently, privateering became a "big business." Although Aury was a "legitimate independence fighter," who had established, by the beginning of November, a reasonably stable republican government on Amelia Island, the United States saw him as a threat to its own national security. Aury counted 130 Haitians among his force, men whose very presence was perceived as an incitement to servile uprisings. Washington also accused him of preying upon neutral shipping, smuggling, and illegally introducing slaves condemned as prizes of war into the United States. Under the guise of suppressing the international slave trade, 250 American troops, on 23 December 1817, captured Fernandina, placing it "in protective custody" for the Spaniards.[19]

MacGregor, cognizant of the "memory of the often disorderly conduct" of the American invaders in 1812–13, took pains to protect the inhabitants' property. He ordered his troops to purchase supplies rather than steal them. Despite his best efforts, nevertheless, MacGregor failed to prevent the soldiery from looting plantations outside of town. Aury, too, had discipline problems. On two occasions, the Frenchman imposed martial law and forced troublemakers from Amelia Island. While the men serving under MacGregor and Aury indubitably annoyed islanders, the actions of the United States forces that succeeded them were remembered as even more unruly. Domingo Acosta recalled how MacGregor had pledged publicly to protect private property. In contrast, the Americans, Joseph Lourcey complained, "were under no control whatever" and did "pretty much as they pleased." For example, Lourcey continued, MacGregor had used Henry Groves's Fernandina home as a hospital, but did not damage it. The "malicious" U.S. troops, however, stripped the building of its doors, floors, weather boarding, and window shutters. Furthermore, they appropriated Groves's pile of red cedar, which had sat unmolested for six to seven months before the U.S. Army arrived, as well as a hundred "Raw hides" that he was storing in a small "Blacksmith's shop." Seymour Pickett singled out the infantry as being "particularly . . . disorderly & theiving."[20]

The American soldiers had occupied Fernandina during the winter, making firewood a pressing necessity. Aury's men, in fact, had started to tear down the fencing surrounding the Groves lot. Also, the corsair's followers, for the most part, lived on their ships. The U.S. troops constructed barracks, which further increased the demand for lumber. They used a small portion of Groves's hides for "a sacking or bottom for their bunks." In addition, the soldiers were dissatisfied with their rations. This drove them to kill cows, sheep, hogs, and poultry belonging to Antonio Díaz. They told Díaz that they would continue to do the same "till better provisions were furnished to them." Still, their actions had a sadistic bent. After all, they simply destroyed 85 percent of Groves's hides. According to Díaz himself, they slaughtered a "pet cow" that "had been raised in my yard & fed by my daughter—I would not have taken any money for her, I always valued her so highly, her mother had been previously killed by the soldiers." Ynocencio Cardona, speaking of two sheep that ended up in soldiers' stomachs, recollected how the animals were "trained in a cart, & used to draw one of [Díaz's] daughters about the streets. These were valued highly by Mr. Dias—he would have taken no price for them." Andrew López added that Díaz was "in the habit of feeding" these "very tame sheep . . . at his door with ground corn or Hominy." Díaz discovered the "feathers & remains" of his poultry at the "quarters of a mess of soldiers" after the latter had left a taunting note daring "black Antonio" to "look for his fowls and be da—d." Ten of the fowls in question were an "excellent" breed of fighting cocks that Díaz had brought from the West Indies and "preserved with great care."[21]

It is within this context that James Cashen's Erin Hall plantation met with its final destruction. James Mattair remembered the incident well. On an August Saturday in 1818, one of Cashen's slaves came to Mattair's employer in Fernandina, bearing the news that U.S. soldiers were at Erin Hall and had ordered Susan Cashen off the premises. Mattair was quickly dispatched to the plantation. En route, he encountered a "very much alarmed" Mrs. Cashen, who told him that the Americans were destroying Erin Hall and had arrested its master. She implored Mattair to return to Fernandina that night with whatever additional information that he could gather. When he reached his destination, he found fifty troops under the command of a lieutenant. Mr. Cashen was in his house bound by chains. His captors were killing poultry and creating havoc. Mattair was permitted to speak to the imprisoned Cashen, who anxiously inquired about his wife's safety. Mattair then went outside and "had a great deal of altercation with the soldiers." Meanwhile, the cotton house and fodder stacks were torched. Forty-five minutes later, Cashen was released and told "to be off the best way he could." He rode Mattair's horse to town, while Mattair walked beside him. A week later, Mattair, along with the Cashens, returned to Erin Hall. All of its buildings were "in ashes."[22]

Overall, the unsavory behavior of U.S. regulars, militia, and Patriot "volunteers" in 1812–13 and 1818 entrenched them as highly disrespected louts in East Floridians' memories. These memories impressed federal district judge Isaac H. Bronson, who either heard or had access to transcripts of almost every claims case, as accurate. Writing in 1855, Bronson lambasted American officers for being "arbitrary and tyrannical towards the inhabitants." The soldiers, he continued, had committed "acts of even wanton aggression." Thus, "property of every description was indiscriminately plundered and destroyed." Almost twenty years earlier, Bronson's predecessor, Robert R. Reid, had described the consequences of this United States barbarism: many East Floridians who had been comfortable in 1812 were reduced to "extreme poverty" in the space of fourteen months. In the more than two decades since the Patriot War, Reid wrote in 1836, the region had not yet recovered from an invasion that had left it "desolate." Some ten years prior to Reid's analysis, his predecessor, Joseph L. Smith, had decried the "exercise of illegal power" by the U.S. commanders who held Fernandina in 1818. When Charles Seton, Farquhar Bethune, Charles W. Clarke, and George J. F. Clarke held Washington accountable for the Seminoles burning six thousand cubic feet of Charles F. Sibbald's valuable red cedar timber in 1818, Judge Smith concurred. The Indians, Smith explained, mistakenly thought that the cedar had belonged to Henry Yonge, whom they suspected of having joined Andrew Jackson's forces in attacks on the "principal towns" of "Mickasakee" and "Suwanee." The fact that the witnesses were "among the most intelligent and respectable Citizens of the territory" convinced Smith of Jackson's culpability.[23]

In short, although witnesses acknowledged in numerous cases that the Seminoles had killed and plundered during the "troubles" resulting from American invasions, they justified this "savagery" as a legitimate response to Washington's aggression. Moreover, even the comportment of the U.S. forces compared unfavorably to that of the Indians. Sarah Acosta was living at the garrisoned trading post of Picolata on 22 March 1812, when eighty Patriot volunteers seized it. "[T]hey were Foreigners," she emphasized—"not a Floridian among them." The Spanish troops stationed there, "a Sergeants guard of 10 or 12 men," had departed less than an hour previously. Although the Spaniards were vastly outnumbered, if they had remained, Mrs. Acosta surmised, they would probably have staved off the Patriots, "who came drunk and staggering from their boats, and who behaved neither like men nor soldiers." She did observe twenty to thirty Indians in the vicinity, but they did no damage, despite the notion that they were "supposed to be mischievously inclined." The Patriots handed Picolata over to United States regulars, who arrived two to three days later. By the end of the year, these regulars had burned the trading post.[24] Once again, white Americans were cast in the role of barbarians.

The old inhabitants strongly connected the invaders' abuse of alcohol to their abuse of East Floridians. For example, George J. F. Clarke, who chided one U.S. commander of Fernandina during the Patriot War, Captain Fiedler Ridgeway, for allowing soldiers to do whatever they pleased, added that the officer was "given to drink." To be sure, "Ridgeway had a long record of drunkenness and court-martial." Sometimes troops' alcohol consumption proved fortunate for property owners. In the waning hours of April 1813, Francis Román Sánchez lucked out during the invaders' retreat, when, in accordance with their scorched-earth policy, they were burning every plantation along the St. Johns River that they could find. Sánchez's place escaped this unhappy fate when the man ordered to torch it "got drunk and getting in the woods, could not find the house."[25] On an earlier occasion, fortune also had smiled upon the men in one thoroughly sloshed Patriot squad. Indeed, this drinking bout nearly resulted in their annihilation.

During the first week of April 1812, some twenty-two to twenty-five miles south of St. Augustine, twenty-one men calling themselves U.S. troops, but not wearing American uniforms, happened upon 70 to 125 puncheons of "superior Jamaica Rum." The puncheons were resting "under a shelter on the River," within five miles of Fort Matanzas and a mile from John B. Ferreira's plantation. Francis Pellicer's slaves had salvaged the rum and "hauled it" a distance of nine miles "from the sea-beach." It had been the cargo of a vessel sailing from the West Indies to Norfolk, which foundered offshore late in 1811. James Pellicer, about fifteen years of age, along with a slave, was guarding it. The Patriot party left three men to watch Pellicer and his companion. The other eighteen soldiers then proceeded to Little Bar Island, four miles away, where the Spaniards were keeping a herd of cattle intended to feed St. Augustine. After driving the cattle ashore, the Patriots returned to the rum that same day. They next "took a supply of grog" and camped on Gabriel W. Perpall's plantation for a night. The following afternoon, the squad rendezvoused at the puncheons, saddled their horses, and "cleared out."[26]

Subsequently, other squads from the camp near St. Augustine visited in search of cattle and liquor. Each time, "a great deal of Rum [was] carried off in Jugs, Bottles & Kegs." And, in their "drunken fits," they "destroyed . . . any other property they came across." On one such foray, the Patriots "had a great spree & drunken frolic . . . & had amused themselves by shooting Balls through the heads of the puncheons of Rum." Afterward, "the whole party became beastly drunk and were lying asleep in all directions." At this point, the slave stationed there with James Pellicer, "a mullatto man" and a "St. Domingo creole," saw a golden opportunity. Accordingly, he "proposed to his young master, to destroy them all. He said with a broad ax which he had he could kill them one by one as they were lying drunk and asleep." Then, "upon the horses they could make their way to St. Augustine." The thought of this massacre horrified Pellicer. Because he "was a boy," his elder brother later explained, he "did not countenance the proposition." Since the rum created such a discipline problem, the American commander at St. Augustine eventually ordered it destroyed.[27]

Significantly, by employing the trope of intoxication, witnesses testifying mainly during the Second Seminole War or its immediate aftermath reversed a racial stereotype with vivid verbal imagery that, once heard, was difficult to forget. That is, their colorful, chilling, and didactic tales of the dangers of demon rum, recited in the midst of a national temperance movement, painted oral pictures of inebriated, bestial whites, rather than "drunken Indians." Even slaves were depicted as more civilized and intelligent than a stupefied white soldiery, which, after pillaging the province, had biliously set the stage for its own destruction. Moreover, the Pellicer case served as a metaphor for the prospect of a bloody, Haitian-inspired slave rebellion that the American invasion might have sparked in East Florida. Fortunately, the case goes on to imply, the slaves sided with the Spaniards, thus remaining under white control. During the Second Seminole War, when Pellicer's claim was before the federal court in St. Augustine, whites also feared a servile uprising. Anxious slave owners could take a measure of comfort in the mulatto slave's loyalty to young James Pellicer. The United States, in short, according to the veiled protests of white witnesses, had subjected East Floridians to the twin terrors of Indian attack and black revolt in 1812–13, 1818, and 1835–42.

However, soldiers of African descent, like Seminole warriors, and unlike U.S. troops, were embedded in white memories as defenders of civilization in East Florida. To understand this phenomenon, it is necessary to examine the U.S. invaders' investment of St. Augustine. For many of the region's antebellum elders, the Patriot War had been the defining moment of their lives. The conflict marked the turning point of their dreams. After it ended, those who suffered through it were never the same psychologically. From the deepest recesses of their minds, memories of the invasion reminded them that they had passed the apogee of happiness. Within these smoldering recollections of the life-altering events of 1812–13, a segment of the victimized populace could point to the American siege of St. Augustine as the defining moment of the defining moment. It began "suddenly & unexpectedly," like the horrible events of 11 September 2001. Only this time, Washington was the terrorist. "Nobody knew of the approach of the enemy," recalled Bennet Seguí, "until the alarm Gun was fired and the Drums beat to Arms." Then, he continued, "men women and children rushed into the city." Witnesses used expressions such as "great haste," "great excitement," and "great confusion" to describe a frenzied dash to the gates accompanied by cannon fusillades from the Castillo de San Marcos, the venerable fortress that guarded the city.[28]

Some inhabitants of more distant areas, which, nevertheless, were only about ten miles from town, never reached the safety of the garrison. Fortunately for John Andrew, who lived eleven miles away, at Oyster Shell Bank, "one of the most beautiful situations on the North River," he successfully escaped in a vessel barely large enough to hold his family. Andrew Capella, who cultivated "Drunken-

Mans-Island," also on the North River, between five and nine miles from town, was not as lucky. The invaders surprised him and his family, captured them, and held them as prisoners of war for four days. When Capella promised to remain on his property, the Americans released him. "[I]mmediately" afterward, he piled his family into a boat and took refuge in the Spanish capital. Similarly, James Falany, whose homestead stood ten miles south of the Ancient City, on Moses Creek, saw himself forced to cram his loved ones into a "small two oared canoe boat" in order to avoid Capella's fate. Indeed, the Patriots "kept a sharp look out for stragglers." Thus, they seized Antonio Capo at nine o'clock in the evening, "at the 4 mile Road," as he was returning from a farm near the Twelve Mile Swamp. Capo remained a captive for the war's duration. Clearly, the environs of the Twelve Mile Swamp proved dangerous for refugees. Lewis Scofield and his wife were traveling to St. Augustine in a horsecart from "Pleasant Hill," their plantation near the swamp, when the invaders captured them. Not far away, they seized Mrs. Mary Weedman at her father's farm on the North River, nine miles from town. Like Antonio Capo, she, along with her father and children, suffered captivity under the Americans for the entire Patriot War. On the Saturday or Sunday that "the alarm drum was beaten," Mrs. Weedman's father, Anthony Hindsman, was in St. Augustine. The governor granted Hindsman permission to see to his family, but when he reached them, he, too, was seized by enemy troops.[29]

Those who lived farther from the capital found it very difficult, if not impossible, to flee to the Castillo's guns. Almost no settler along the St. Johns River made it to town. Still, some refugees from distant neighborhoods did reach St. Augustine. Lázaro Ortega, Ramón Sánchez, and Nicholas Sánchez, who ranched on the Diego Plains, more than twenty miles beyond the gates, arrived as many other Spanish subjects did—crammed into a small boat. The city also hosted refugees, including several female planters, from the Tomoka settlement, located some sixty miles to the south. Ironically, other southerners residing much closer to town experienced more tortuous journeys. George Long, who lived about as far south of the capital as the Diego Plains were north of it, never completed his trek to safety. When the Patriots "quite sudden[ly]" approached his premises, Long crossed the Matanzas River and "took shelter in the woods at Little Bar Island." There he soon died "from exposure and from *grief* for his ruin and the ruin of his family." Long's nearest neighbors, the Pellicers, also faced the elements. Francis Pellicer, accompanied by his three eldest sons and most of his slaves, went to St. Augustine by the governor's orders, while the rest of his family, "some of them quite young," remained behind for three or four months. Because of frequent harassment by the Patriots, "the only priviledged characters in the

Country South of St. Augustine," men who "paid no respect to age or sex" and who were attracted to the area by puncheons of salvaged rum, Mrs. Pellicer fled to Anastasia Island in a canoe too small to paddle to town. She camped in tents on the beach opposite Fort Matanzas for two months. Having brought only "one pot to cook in," and perhaps some bedding, she, her children, and slaves "suffered much" before they finally secured passage to the besieged capital.[30]

Certain inhabitants made daring escapes to St. Augustine from U.S.-occupied Fernandina. Those of Felipe Solana and James Arnowe were the stuff of legend. Solana, a prominent cattleman and brother-in-law of Don Justo López, Fernandina's commandant, left the port "at an hour's notice." He was a man who was "fond of good Horses and of riding." His mission was to bring St. Augustine "the news of the fall of Fernandina." After equipping George J. F. Clarke's horse with López's saddle and bridle, he dashed "to the south of the Island." Solana continued his Paul Revere–like journey by water, until he reached St. Johns Bluff, a Spanish military post consisting of a "commissary with a corporal's guard." Solana's heroism was such that had he returned to Fernandina, Charles W. Clarke asserted, the Americans "would have been glad to see him—to make him a present of a Bullet." Arnowe also won fame as the bearer of the commandant's dispatches. For the two crop seasons prior to the invasion, he had been the overseer at Pablo Sabate's Casacola plantation, which stood five miles north of St. Augustine. His wages consisted of a fifth of "the products of the Plantation." In 1812, he decided to "giv[e] up the charge" and strike out on his own. Arnowe proceeded to construct a four-hundred-dollar house at "Mackaree Creek," a little over a mile from the city gates. With his wife, three children, and slave, he raised corn, potatoes, and market vegetables on a thirteen-acre plot that was part of an enclosure in which other Minorcans planted. A couple of weeks before the invasion, Arnowe butchered two "very large" hogs. He turned their meat into "a great many Sausages" and "black puddings." In addition, he "Salted a full barrel of pork." With these chores done, he departed for Fernandina "on business." A fortnight after his arrival, the United States seized Fernandina.[31]

The occupation forces prohibited loyal Spanish subjects from leaving the port. And, James Arnowe was loyal. Pointedly equating the Americans with savages, he declared at the age of sixty that "So far from Joining the Patriots he would have run from them, as soon as from an Indian." The prospect of indefinitely languishing on Amelia Island, far from his family, did not suit him. Therefore, the day after Fernandina's capture, he and ten others asked Justo López for permission to take the latter's large six-oared boat in order to deliver the mail to St. Augustine. The commandant assented, instructing the loyalists to "drown the mail" if pursued. On the open ocean, they encountered rough weather that subjected them to "one day and a half of hard times." At last, however, the ten fugitives safely "arrived in St. Augustine." For the remainder of the Patriot War, Arnowe served as an "artillery-man" in his beloved Ancient City.[32]

Unlike the escapades of Solana and Arnowe, John Seguí's conduct during his voyage to safety in St. Augustine caused him "to be the Subject of Ridicule." He owned a hundred acres on the "Governor Grant Lands," which were "formed by the junction of the Guana Creek with the North River." In 1848, Antonio Masters, demonstrating the historical consciousness of the inhabitants of St. Augustine and its environs, explained that it was said that a mid-eighteenth-century English governor had lived there. The site of Seguí's farm was variously estimated at between seven and eleven miles north of town. He cultivated about thirteen acres of his grant, raising corn, sweet potatoes, Irish potatoes, pumpkins, watermelons, and a "flourishing" vegetable garden. Every other morning, he would travel to the city in order to sell his crops in the market. His agribusiness brought him four hundred to five hundred dollars annually. He kept a hundred poultry, no more than two hogs at a time, and "never owned a Horse in his life." Still, Seguí earned his peers' grudging admiration due to his skillful, hard-working, efficient, and frugal husbandry. Esteban Arnow remembered him as a "great hand to work with the Hoe" who never had to hire help. He was a "close[-fisted] man," Arnow ruefully added, "& never bought anything if he could help it—he usually made his provisions." In a similar vein, Andreas Pacetty characterized Seguí as "thriving" but also as "a curious man in relation to his money."[33]

Antonio and Paul Masters, who were respectively sixteen and fourteen years of age in 1812, lived eight miles north of Seguí. The teenagers were able to remain on their widowed mother's plantation for four or five months after the Patriots first appeared before St. Augustine, because the governor considered Paul too young and Antonio too "small and badly grown" to assist in the colony's defense. They observed the invaders crossing the North River to pilfer Seguí's "considerable quantity of provisions." After about five weeks, the American forces had transformed Seguí's houses and fences into ashes. Paul Masters emphasized that none of Seguí's losses could be attributed to the Indians, who "were never on the West side of the North River." Seguí kept three hundred to four hundred dollars on his place and the final fate of these funds remained open to question. "It was the custom of the old people in those days, to keep their money in their beds," Andreas Pacetty noted. According to Pacetty's recollection, Seguí had to leave these coins when he came to St. Augustine, where, Francis Triay explained, "So Soon a[s] Segui came to Town a musket was placed in his hands." Subsequently, "instead of having money to lend as formerly, [he] was in debt and obliged to go in debt for a tierce of rice and then work, to pay for it." Several years after the war, Pacetty continued, because Seguí used to mark his coins, he claimed that he recognized some of them in town. Esteban Arnow, however, remembered matters differently. Arnow asserted that before boarding the government launch sent up the North River to evacuate the inhabitants, Seguí "cried like a Child. . . . for permission to go and get his money which was concealed in a pile of Corn Stocks." His wailing garnered the commander's sympathy. Thus, during the siege, he was able to lend one Mr. López the sum of four hundred dollars.[34]

Regardless of which version of the tale of Seguí's treasure is true, the incident illustrates several facets of life within besieged St. Augustine. As Andreas Pacetty asserted, many refugees saw themselves "obliged to run in debt." Consequently, they emerged from the war "reduced to wretchedness." The unexpected materialization of the invaders contributed significantly to this sad state of affairs. That is, when the authorities suddenly sounded signals to abandon the fields, garden farmers like Joseph Baya "did not bring in the head of a pin." Those who came to town by boat, explained Diego Hernández and John Carreras in 1849, could carry very little with them other than clothes and bedding. Once they were safely inside the city gates, they encountered skyrocketing prices for foodstuffs. Mateo Lorenzo stated that under normal circumstances, the inhabitants would pay two dollars for a bushel of corn. During the siege, Lorenzo recollected, the going rate doubled. Even at this price, supplies were scarce. Sophia Fatio recalled the grain's price reaching five dollars per bushel. Although the government mustered all able-bodied free men into military service and "[s]upported [them] by rations issued from the public store," these rations barely could feed each individual soldier. Moreover, "[t]hose who were in Service received no pay or remuneration except a Blanket a piece which was charged at 12$ and deducted from the expected pay." In fact, the conscripts never received a bit of compensation after the war ended. To make matters worse, there were few employment opportunities for anyone other than the soldiery.[35] Thus, John Seguí was no fool when he wept for his money. He risked ridicule in order to feed his family. He sacrificed his "manhood" in order to be a man.

Under these desperate circumstances, Seguí and other men who possessed savings were able to preserve a degree of the personal independence associated with freedom, thus blunting the emasculating aspects of confinement inside the city gates. Albert Rogero, for example, had "a family quite large," but "he was fortunate in having some money by him" to use for their support. Likewise, John Triay, because he could do nothing for profit until the gates opened, "had some money by him, and was obliged upon that, to support his wife and his Slaves." Some refugees counted on the assistance of family members. When Bennet Seguí arrived in town, he had a small amount of funds, but not enough to avoid becoming a charge of his father. Others, like Joseph Baya and Christopher López, maintained their loved ones by tapping into multiple sources of sustenance. Baya "sold or bartered property" to supplement the "some little money" that he had with him. Despite being an "industrious man," he found it necessary to indebt himself to "Paow's store" for provisions. López, another "industrious" garden farmer, who, because of the sudden siege, never got "as much as a melon" from his plot, depended upon "the kindness of friends very much for the Support of his family." He, like numerous needy St. Augustinians, turned to "Mr. Paow," who was "very kind to the poor; he was a rich man with plenty around him; those who had the money to pay down he received it; but he credited those who had not." "Paow supported a good many," Esteban Arnow mused, adding that Fernando de la Maza Arredondo "was also kind to the distressed." In short, the Americans had transformed hard-working free men who "supported themselves comfortably and were able to lay up money every year" into debt-ridden draftees dependent upon, in the words of Bartolo Pons, "the aid of good persons and credit."[36]

War-induced anxieties regarding their future capacity to reestablish their financial independence ratcheted up refugees' psychological trauma. For security purposes, the governor required "a full and fair view" of enemy movements toward the Castillo de San Marcos, which commanded the northern approaches to St. Augustine. Therefore, Spanish troops could destroy whatever obstructed this view within 1,500 yards of the city defense lines, be it houses, fences, trees, or tall crops, without the owners receiving any compensation. Thus, the mere threat of an American assault meant that the garden farmers' fortunes were in jeopardy. Accordingly, the day after the government summoned the inhabitants to town, "a sally was made" to fire the obstructions dotting the Minorcan-cultivated plain adjacent to the gates. After the soldiers torched five or six buildings, however, the invaders repulsed them. Subsequently, almost every night, the Americans pillaged the garden farms, sometimes coming within 150 yards of the lines. To discourage this audacity, the Spaniards adopted several strategies. In the earliest stage of the siege, on the darkest nights, they sent out parties to build fires "about 100 yds from the fort." The governor discontinued this practice, however, after fifteen or twenty missions. A "body of Dragoons" was sent out the day after the people were ordered in, and it captured a Patriot. Whenever the investing forces came "very near the town," the governor dispatched troops who skirmished with them. Moreover, the Spaniards frequently shot at enemy plunderers with guns and cannons.[37]

Bennet Seguí recounted how on one night, when the Americans stalked near enough "to fire on the Lines," an exchange of volleys ensued. The invaders struck first, "and after 3. or 4. discharges the fire was returned from the Lines but nobody was killed." Another time, Esteban Arnow related, "a bomb Shell was thrown from the fort and bussted as it fell; [the Americans] were seen scattering from the Scrub in all directions." Indeed, as George J. F. Clarke also attested, the besiegers had good reason to be wary of Spanish cannons. When they initially "sat down before St. Augustine the artillerists of the Fort were desirous of testing their gunnery," Clarke began, so they aimed their weapon at the flag flying above the investors' fort. The "first shot nearly struck the staff," he continued. Then the gunners zeroed in—the second shot landed "still nearer, and half buried a little Drummer in the sand, from which he was extricated unhurt." Yet, the U.S. forces were "very often within reach of cannon shot, and were fired upon from the fort and from the lines." Southwest of the city, at the Spanish outpost on Solana's Ferry, Antonio Canovas and his comrades fired "a field piece and 12 pounder" at a Patriot squad, "and they dispersed." This artillery fire undoubtably destroyed loyalist property. Joseph Manucy, for instance, recollected how John Gianopoli's "little place" was demolished by cannonballs that the Spaniards aimed at the Americans who occupied it. Nevertheless, the king's militia continually observed their foes "with bags" for pillaging property. According to Mrs. Mary Weedman, when the besiegers were "on the 1500 yds" and took fire from the urban defenders, "they used to laugh a great deal about it," boasting that they would go to the "1500 yards Distance" to take what they wanted when they wanted it.[38]

Civilians and soldiers alike could observe the flames incinerating their property, track enemy troop movements with rooftop spyglasses, and listen to the rat-a-tat of American drums. Reports from those granted permission to reconnoiter outside of the city often confirmed their worst fears regarding the fate of their abandoned property. For Fernando Fulany, who cultivated twenty-five to thirty acres on Moultrie Creek, six miles south of town, the bad news came after he "sent out a negro & ascertained that his corn was destroyed & every thing on his plantation laid waste." John Masters would gather news of rural devastation on his periodic nighttime journeys fourteen miles up Guana Creek, in order to visit his mother and two younger brothers. After he and forty to forty-five comrades manning "two barges," each armed with an "Eight pounder," evacuated his family and a couple of others in August 1812, another Spanish party went out to investigate. It contained three barges and sixty men. After ascending the North River for nine miles, the party happened upon a house that Anthony Hindsman owned. The Americans "used [it] as a depot for property which they had plundered in the country." The loyalists found a great deal of corn, honey pots, hides, saddles, bridles, and two cauldrons that Pedro Cocifacio had used to make castor oil. Before they were stolen, the pots had been "set in an arch or stonework." All of this booty subsequently was transported back to St. Augustine, where the authorities auctioned it. The governor divided the proceeds among the expeditionary force that had retrieved this private property that had become the spoils of war.[39]

Refugees sequestered in St. Augustine, then, had much to worry about. Many saw their life savings quickly evaporate. Moreover, they likely witnessed the ruin of the sources of their livelihood or learned of it second hand. In addition, they fretted about the safety of their male friends and relatives who were performing military duties. Engagements beyond the city's defense could be especially harrowing. Colonel Ignacio Salems, an artillery officer, Esteban Arnow related, commanded three vessels armed with cannons and 150 men, to an American post located approximately three miles up the North River, on a tributary creek a mile from where it emptied into the river. Two of Salem's vessels ventured up the creek until they reached a house containing "loop or port holes" designed so that riflemen could pick off assailants making their way from the creek's landing, which was a little less than a mile away. A "centinel" wearing the uniform of a United States regular paced atop the flat roof. When the two vessels opened fire, the guard shot back before jumping to the ground to join his comrades inside the house. The ensuing gunfire proved "pretty Sharp on both sides." Suddenly, a cannonball from the "18 pounder" on the third Spanish vessel, a schooner anchored in the North River, "passed directly through the House," causing the U.S. troops to "hastily" retreat to their main camp. The Spaniards proceeded to occupy the house before the schooner signaled for them to withdraw. Triumphantly, the victors carried with them to St. Augustine "the Cap of an American Soldier which he had left on his flight," as well as a canteen with the "Letters U.S. upon it."[40]

The social tensions resulting from overcrowding exacerbated the debilitating effects of anxieties raised to a fever pitch. Enemy parties surrounded St. Augustine's land sides. Furthermore, the United States "closely blockaded" the city. Offshore, James Pellicer reminisced, two U.S. vessels, the "Saucy Jack" and the "Victory," cruised, bringing commerce to a standstill. The American navy also interrupted the mail boat service to Havana, forcing the governor to send messages "in canoes." These conditions made it dangerous to leave town. Francis Marín marveled retrospectively that "even the Fisherman were taken Prisoners." Bartolo Pons specifically recalled an instance when "fisherman were taken on the outside of the city—they had ventured to fish at the mouth of the north river." Understandably, then, after "the Inhabitants flocked into the city," the Spanish authorities decreed that they "were not permitted to go out." To prevent unauthorized departures, they stationed gunboats in the Matanzas River. This policy caused disgruntlement among the garden farmers who believed that they could have salvaged much of their movable property if the governor would have agreed to their pleas to do so. Those who dared to defy the ban faced "severe" punishment. One rebellious soul "was put by the authorities into the Fort for it." Fragmentary evidence suggests that being "shut up" in the city caused close relationships to fray. Mrs. William Williams stayed only two months with her sister, Mrs. Francisco Xavier Sánchez, before moving to Father Miguel Crosby's house. After the same length of time, Mrs. John Bunch succeeded in relocating to the Bahamas subsequent to persuading the governor that she would be unmolested on her Tomoka estate. Her neighbor, Mrs. Frances Kerr, "a fearless old lady," also was granted permission to return to Tomoka.[41]

Empty stomachs surely manifested themselves in unsettled minds. The United States aimed to secure St. Augustine's surrender by strangling its sources of nourishment. Although "no comer was ever rejected, because the numbers in the city were too great or a famine prevailed," the governor advised the Tomoka planters to remain on their estates in order to try to protect their property (and to lessen the number of mouths to feed). This perhaps explains why Mrs. Williams and Mrs. Kerr were allowed to depart from town. What is certain is that the two aristocratic women, like their fellow refugees, were "suffering a great many calamities." The people, Sophia Fatio asserted, "were in a state of starvation." At the beginning of the siege, each soldier received sixteen ounces of bread and six or seven ounces of fresh meat daily. Mateo Lorenzo disparagingly referred to this allotment as "Rations Such as were allowed to negro troops." In time, this "very Slender allowance" plunged to a pint of "bad corn" per diem. Because of the inadequacy of this diet, off-duty troops were permitted to fish at night. They also ate "Such oysters & other articles of food as [they] could pick up." Eventually, however, "even the oysters became scarce upon the Shore." Civilians as well shared the nightmare of hunger. They had no salt, butter, lard, or fresh pork. Lorenzo Gracesqui recalled them "fry[ing] their fish with beef tallow." "Those who had provisions," Esteban Arnow remembered, "concealed them, least the Government should seize them to Supply the general wants." Moreover, the Americans detained or destroyed two ships in Fernandina loaded with provisions bound for the Ancient City. To put an end to their agony, the people wanted to go out to fight the invaders, but the governor would not agree "though often urged upon that point." By 25 July 1812, St. Augustine was on the verge of capitulation.[42]

The city's saviors wore war paint and sported black faces. In a world turned upside down, where white barbarians assaulted civilization in East Florida and white civilizers cowered in the province's only remaining outpost of urbanism, Seminoles and fighting men of African descent valiantly came to the rescue. Their attacks repelled the onslaught of American empire, sending the United States invaders scurrying to the Georgia frontier. Thus, they enshrined themselves in whites' memories as heroes of a bygone Hispanic age of happiness and prosperity. One militia unit, Prince's Black Company, was singled out for special acclaim. In the antebellum Patriot War claims cases, international law set the stage for a white recounting of Afro–East Floridian valor. Black folk diplomats, in turn, harnessed this same international agreement to register a poignant protest against the U.S. racial policies that strove to demean them into irrelevance. Black Patriot War veterans refused to be erased from history. In St. Augustine's federal courtroom, they hung a Sword of Damocles over their oppressors' heads. Their words emboldened the enslaved, providing them with a weapon with which to defend their humanity against latter-day barbarians. And so we turn our thoughts to an extraordinary man—Prince Juan Bautista Witten.

4
Prince's Black Company

In 1946, the undefeated Ken High Red Raiders was the best scholastic football team in western Pennsylvania. The squad's fame spread far beyond the Pittsburgh area, and consequently, it was selected to play a Texas school in Miami's Orange Bowl. The invitation must have thrilled the players from the cold, grimy industrial boomtown along the banks of the Allegheny River. Nevertheless, they refused to travel to Florida. Less than a month before the contest, the Red Raiders learned that because of the Sunshine State's segregation statutes, no African Americans could take the field with whites. As a result, Ken High's sophomore star, Willie Thrower, was barred from competing. Vince Pisano, one of Thrower's talented teammates, speaking nearly fifty years later, explained that "[w]e voted not to go. . . . [i]f he couldn't go, we would not go." Thrower went on to lead Ken High to another western Pennsylvania championship the following season and to earn All-America honors his senior year. After graduation, he played for Michigan State University, which, by 1950, had ten former Red Raiders on its football team.[1]

At MSU, Thrower lettered as a backup quarterback (the first black to play the position in the Big Ten Conference) on the undefeated 1952 team that won the national championship. He later played briefly for the Chicago Bears, becoming the National Football League's first African American quarterback. Hometown area whites did not hesitate to effusively praise Thrower in their recollections. "Willie would compare with the best players today," Pisano asserted. "He could be right there with the [Dan] Marinos and [Joe] Montanas," two western Pennsylvania quarterbacks elected to the NFL's Hall of Fame. "Willie was the greatest," proclaimed Ed Modzelewski, a high-school opponent who later garnered

All-America honors at the University of Maryland and played professionally for the Pittsburgh Steelers and Cleveland Browns during the 1950s. Ex–high school and college teammate Bill Horrell called Thrower "probably the greatest passer I have ever seen. . . . [h]e could throw 60 yards falling backward and still hit the mark." The 111-year-old *Valley News Dispatch* announced Thrower's death on 20 February 2002 by a front-page headline. Sportswriter George Guido eulogized him in a column that mentioned Thrower's white schoolboy comrades' decision to forego a trip to Florida on his behalf. A year before his passing, ABC television had publicized his achievements and travails to a nationwide audience. In 2006, a statue was erected in his honor next to the New Kensington gridiron on which he rose to stardom.[2]

The laudatory comments of Thrower's local white former teammates and opponents somewhat cryptically protested his treatment by the football establishment. They beg the question of why, if Thrower was so talented, did he not play more in the National Football League? Stories about the segregated contest at the Orange Bowl suggest an answer. Thrower himself was more direct. Referring to the time after his senior season when he was designated the captain of an all-star team that was slated to play in Corpus Christi, Texas, Thrower recounted how, "[w]hen they found out I was black, they said I couldn't play in the game." Regarding his abbreviated NFL career, he criticized the Chicago Bears for denying him a fair opportunity to prove himself. "I was a hell of a passer," he noted. "If yesterday was like today, I would have been there. Having a professional black quarterback was unheard of." These statements assume greater significance considering the comments of his white Ken High teammate George France: "From the very beginning, you knew Willie was something special. . . . [he] had lots of reasons to have a big ego, but he never did." Similarly, upon hearing of Thrower's death, his high school coach's aged widow compared his demise to "'losing a member of the family' because she and her husband 'liked Willie so much.'"[3]

Willie Thrower often told his youngest son Melvin that "the only way to make it is to be a giant . . . [y]ou got to be a giant in everything you do." At his funeral in New Kensington's Mount Calvary Missionary Baptist Church, the Reverend Mildred C. Taylor, before 150 mourners, which included an NFL representative (from the Pittsburgh Steelers rather than the Chicago Bears), eulogized him by reading the story of David and Goliath.[4] Statements by blacks and whites regarding Thrower and his career can be understood on a number of levels. On the surface, friends, relatives, and acquaintances were paying homage to a great athlete and a beloved person. Their reminiscences also can be seen as protesting a bygone era that used racism to squelch human potential. At the same time, Thrower's son and pastor hinted that today's society still limits black achievement. Newspaper accounts of past racial injustices, by focusing on those that took place in communities distant both spatially and temporally, can make local whites feel good about themselves in the present. Moreover, especially in the cases of the NFL and ABC television, publicizing historical injustices is not only politically correct, but potentially profitable. In the chapters that follow, whites, particularly "ethnic" elders (along with some African Americans), will discuss black "giants" because of a variety of overlapping and underlying motivations. While digesting their testimony, it is instructive to keep in mind the example of Willie Thrower.

Communal memories of the valor of Prince Witten and his military charges united East Floridians divided by class and ethnicity in an antebellum social setting characterized by a rigidifying racial milieu. Besides revering Felipe Solana, a locally born Hispanic whom Francis Román Sánchez lauded as "the terror of the American troops," white "old inhabitants" and their descendants also admired Witten, a black man whose courage, intelligence, skill, physical presence, and loquaciousness commanded respect. Witten seized the opportunity for fame that imperialism furnished him, starring on the battlefield by serving his sovereign under arms in 1794–95, 1800–1803, and 1812–13. Moreover, he was a man willing to speak out against injustice. When the planter Jayme McGirtt tried to illegally force Witten's wife into the role of a field hand, he sued McGirtt. Witten worked hard to assist free black Anglophone subjects of the king of Spain. In 1795, he petitioned the governor for acreage so that he could establish a small free black settlement beyond St. Augustine's gates. The high regard in which his countrymen of color held him is reflected in the Ancient City's Catholic parish records. These ecclesiastical documents reveal that Witten sponsored twenty-three children for baptism.[5]

Prince Witten also displayed a keen eye for international diplomacy as well as a strong family orientation. The African-born Witten, his "smart, active" creole spouse Judy, and their two children entered the province seeking freedom under the Crown's sanctuary policy. As mentioned previously, Mingo, one of the original canoe-load of fugitives whose request for Catholic baptism in 1687 impelled Spain's king to issue a decree encouraging other English slaves to abscond, had fled in order to keep his family together. Witten's motivation, some hundred years later, was the same. His master advertised that Witten wished "to avoid a separation from his family to which he is much attached." This was typical of runaways to East Florida, who "sought to maintain family and friendship ties even in flight." Accordingly, in the scholar Jane Landers's analysis, to comply with a major requisite for the family's freedom and integrity, "shortly after presenting themselves to Spanish authorities," the fugitive couple, in 1788, insisted that their children receive the waters of baptism. Four years later, Prince and Judy themselves were initiated into the religion of the Spaniards. The Wittens then moved to further ensure that their family remained inviolate. They formalized their union of twenty-one years by partaking in the Catholic sacrament of Holy Matrimony. Furthermore, they made sure that their children wedded in St. Augustine's cathedral.[6]

Consequently, the nuptials of the Witten clan were recorded in parish registers, official records of an international entity whose reach extended to the earth's distant corners. Should there later be any doubt regarding the clan's legitimacy, the written word would dispel it. Thus, in addition to baptism in Spanish East Florida, the Wittens utilized a second haven, Roman Catholic marriage—the Cana Sanctuary.

Witten earned his immortality in an event that took place during the waning days of the summer of 1812, northwest of St. Augustine, in the Twelve Mile Swamp, which the historian Joseph Alexander described as a "thick dense hammock several miles in extent . . . well adopted to Indian warfare." United States Marine Corps captain John Williams recounted what took place there in a report that he authored on 15 September 1812: "On the night of the 11th Instant as I was marching with a command of about twenty men with two waggons from the Camp [near St. Augustine] to this place [Davis Creek Blockhouse], I was at about ten miles from this on the dusk of the evening attacked by a party of Indians and negroes, who fired upon us, and it being dark, we Commenced Battle which continued nearly as long as a man of my command had a Cartridge, during which time I Received Eight wounds." Alexander has characterized the attack as "intelligently planned and well-executed" and as "a masterful ambush," in which the troops under Prince Witten's command "executed perfect fire discipline, waiting to spring the trap." Captain Williams, who was "literally shot to pieces," and "in a dreadful Situation," listed the wounds from which he hoped to recover "in a few months": "my right Leg is Broke, my right hand Shot through with three Balls, my left arm broken my left leg shot through, a Ball in my left thigh near the Groin, another through the Bottom of my Belly, which renders me altogether helpless." Two weeks after the forty-seven-year-old Williams dictated this report, his anguish ended in death. Moreover, the supply lines of the American invaders had been severed. Consequently, the invaders ended their five-month siege of St. Augustine.[7]

Ironically, of all of the members of the United States armed forces and their Patriot allies that occupied Spanish East Florida in 1812–13, Captain Williams is the only person who elicited positive commentary from antebellum witnesses in the Patriot War claims cases. George J. F. Clarke testified that shortly after the invaders captured Fernandina, Williams was in charge of the port for two months and was "very popular with the Inhabitants." Clarke remembered him as a "mild, kind and obliging man." Robert Harrison added that during Williams's brief command, the occupying troops were "civil." One of his successors, Captain Abraham Massias, in contrast, was "rough, ungentlemanly abusive and in some instances oppressive after using in his intercourse, the harshest terms." Moreover, Massias "sometimes confin[ed] the people of the island in the stocks, and at others [put] them in close prison." Margaret Starrat corroborated Harrison's complaints, while at the same time praising Williams for humanely permitting Amelia Islanders to continue cultivating their crops. She further lauded him for restraining the Patriots. Mrs. Starrat's neighbor, Thomas Suárez, recalled that Williams was "well liked." Massias, on the contrary, said Suárez, was "hated." Charles W. Clarke also contrasted the Marine Corps officer's "kind" treatment of the inhabitants with the unkind behavior of his two successors.[8] Thus, it is safe to assume that Captain John Williams was the American military man whom East Floridians least desired to be slain.

Nevertheless, despite the respect that Captain Williams had garnered, his death did not diminish whites' esteem for Prince Witten, even in an antebellum era during which free people of color increasingly were finding their liberty and property under assault. What whites neglected to say about the ambush at Twelve Mile Swamp is significant. They failed to mention that one white soldier was scalped and stripped. Nor did they express disdain for the tactic of ambuscade. Thus, they took care not to portray Witten and his men as barbarians. Although they paid homage to Williams, they stressed the ultimate beneficial outcome of Witten's attack. For example, George J. F. Clarke, in the 1830s, acknowledged that "Williams was killed fighting bravely," but he added that "immediately afterward the Patriots and United States Troops fell back upon the St. Johns where they remained until . . . they left the country." Zephaniah Kingsley's commentary parallels Clarke's, except that initially, he was more direct in his praise of the black company. In 1823, he recounted how "about 50 coloured militia inhabitants of this then Province saved by their Bravery and fidelity the City of St. Augustine from being taken & Plundered." By the 1830s, however, the cagey Kingsley, like Clarke, had muted his language to fit more racially oppressive times. "Capt: Williams a meritorious American who was escorting the supplies for the army," Kingsley carefully explained, "fell about that time into an ambuscade of Provincial Blacks and Indians and was killed." Kingsley now avoided crediting Witten's troops with breaking the siege of the Ancient City. Instead, he more generally attributed it to the Spaniards' decision to "let loose" the Indians on plantations lining the St. Johns River.[9]

Clarke and Kingsley had good reasons to be circumspect during the 1830s, since both men had fathered large families of mixed-race children. Hence, they understandably hesitated to make statements that might cast their free-colored progeny as potential military foes of the United States. Still, other St. Johns

County residents with less intimately vested interests kept alive the saga of the ambush at Twelve Mile Swamp. Dr. James Hall, who tended to Captain Williams's wounds, admitted that "medical aid could avail him not." Hall was present at Williams's burial, which was conducted "with military honors." The prominent physician noted that the marine's squadron had been "completely routed" by a "detachment of Black Troops from St. Augustine" in a "skirmish" at Twelve Mile Swamp. Hall went on to credit Witten's victory with causing the invaders to retreat from their position before St. Augustine. In the midst of the Second Seminole War, certain whites actually drew comfort from the communal memory of Prince's Black company. On 31 August 1836, St. Augustine's *Florida Herald* reported that Ben Wiggins and two other free men of color had seen "numerous signs" of Seminole activity in the Twelve Mile Swamp. The newspaper article reminded its readers that the swamp "is the place where Capt. John Williams of the U.S. Army was attacked and repulsed by a party of Indians and negroes about 50 in number. . . . Capt. W. was mortally wounded. . . . The father in law of Ben Wiggins and we have heard Ben himself figured conspicuously in this action."[10] The *Florida Herald* strongly implied that during the Second Seminole War, as in the Patriot War a generation earlier, whites could count upon the martial skills and active loyalty of the city's free black men.

To be sure, during the Patriot War, black troops earned a reputation for a ferocity that gripped the invaders in a vise of fear. Part of this fear originated in whites' visceral trepidation of facing a St. Domingue–style "race war." On this point, Governor Sebastián Kindelán had to walk a diplomatic tightrope. When he reached St. Augustine in June 1812, Governor Kindelán commenced a series of delicate maneuvers to "pressure the United States to abandon the rebel cause." The 270 free-colored Cuban reinforcements that arrived in the Ancient City in the summer of 1812, Kindelán ascertained, might actually provoke more U.S. support of the Patriots if Washington were to perceive the Afro-Cubans as serious threats to its domestic tranquility. Yet, black soldiers inherently brought a psychological dimension to combat that was absent when white Spanish forces tangled with the enemy. Kindelán's solution was to use his provincial free men of color, along with the Seminoles and their black tributaries, to conduct guerilla operations against the Patriots. By doing so, the governor pursued a strategy that in 1738 had led to the establishment of the free black settlement of Gracia Real de Santa Teresa de Mose. Located two miles north of town, the outpost, manned by ex-slaves who had gained freedom in East Florida under the royal sanctuary policy, functioned as a key bastion against English attack. In 1812, as in 1738, local blacks and Black Seminoles clearly understood that defeat meant re-enslavement. Moreover, opportunities for government-sanctioned plunder promised to enhance blacks' material wealth, and their service to the crown in dire times would embellish their social status.[11] Thus, frontier warfare functioned as a sanctuary for East Florida's black community, because victory would buttress its liberty in a number of ways.

United States soldiers and their Patriot allies, then, had ample reasons to fear military engagements with men of color. Jane Landers and Joseph Alexander have researched how Kindelán shrewdly sought to harness black rage, alternately restraining and fanning it. On one occasion in July 1812, the governor sent his St. Augustine black militiamen on a mission to attack two rebel positions on the St. Johns River. He instructed their officers, Jorge Jacobo, Prince Witten, and Benjamin Seguí, to refrain from "excessively sanguinary" behavior. They were to conduct themselves in a "civilized" manner. That is, they were only to attack if they encountered resistance, and they were to protect the lives of prisoners of war. The expeditionaries received permission to confiscate rebel property for sustenance and hazardous-duty pay. But, at the same time, Kindelán conducted "undeclared, psychological warfare against the Patriots" by offering a bounty of ten dollars and a bottle of rum for each enemy scalp. Moreover, in Twelve Mile Swamp, when Prince Witten's force of twenty-five provincials, thirty-two Black Seminoles, and a few Indians ambushed Captain John Williams's supply wagons escorted by twenty marines and five to six dozen Patriots, the assailants wore war paint and tribal garb. Elsewhere, during their numerous forays, the Spaniards' "multiracial guerillas also engaged in scalpings and mutilations." These terror tactics significantly eroded the invaders' morale, while maintaining Spain's "overt neutrality."[12]

Black ferocity reverberated into antebellum times in the memories of East Florida's white "old inhabitants." Esteban Arnow related the governor's response to invaders who ventured "in front of the City brandishing their arms in a very insulting manner"—he "despatched a company of Black Troops (Dragoons) to lie in wait for them." Before sunrise, the dragoons left town, concealing themselves at Peter Capo's farm, two miles from the gates. As fortune would have it, "no one however appeared but a Mulatto Boy a servant of Delany one of the Patriots." This hapless slave became a scapegoat. Arnow explained that "he was on Horseback and having passed the ambuscade perceived the tracks of horses in the road before him and turned to fly." Before the bondsman could escape, "he was fired upon & killed." After mutilating his corpse, the assailants buried him next to Capo's fence. Arnow somberly noted that he "saw the ears of the Mulatto which had been cut off by the blacks—they brought them to town," along with the deceased's horse. Word of this incident spread like wildfire to the interior, where it had its intended effect upon the Patriots and their collaborators. John Jones, Isaiah D. Hart, John Uptegrove, and Lewis Hogan agreed that the slain slave had been riding Francis Richard Sr.'s valuable "stud horse," which the

Americans had confiscated. Uptegrove and Hart testified that the victim had been a messenger, "the bearer of dispatches to the American camp." The entire affair "was notoriously understood."[13] Afro-Spanish troops had made it clear that even fellow blacks would not be spared if they were in the service of the enemy.

Certainly the prospect of being killed and mutilated by men of color frayed Patriot nerves. In April 1812, twenty-five miles south of St. Augustine, at midnight on Francis Pellicer's plantation, another slave, Jim, lost his life, this time as a consequence of a rebel's jitters. Matthew Long, who was a prisoner of the twenty-five-man party, remembered the incident well: "The Patriots were walking up Pellicer's steps about 12 o'clock at night—the boy Jim came from the kitchen door, which was open, he was seen by Dill who sprang from the steps and ordered the negro to stand—but as he attempted to move, Dill shot and killed him dead. . . . Dill took Jim's gun away from him . . . negroes were allowed in those times to have guns, for the purpose of shooting game." Long pointedly accounted for the shooting by noting that the "Patriots were affraid of the negroes." Additional claims cases attest to this fear. Joseph Summerall related how his terrified daughter-in-law had fled on a raft down the St. Johns River because of "Indians and Negroes being up in the Country, and some murders having already been committed." Similarly, James R. Woodland recalled "a Spanish Company of free negroes that was scouting the country & did some mischief killed some white people." While describing wartime conditions in U.S.-occupied Fernandina, Thomas Backhouse mentioned "twenty or more free negroes" who, along with "sixty to seventy loyal [white] men," were "all anxious to avenge the country with the blood of their enemies."[14]

In addition to linking men of color with death, some antebellum witnesses associated them with the loss of property. Dr. James Hall lost a wagon that was "taken by the Black Troops from St. Augustine, at 12 mile swamp." Of course, it was the Americans who had confiscated the wagon in the first place. Since Hall never regained the vehicle, it may have been the one that Prince Witten's charges "Cut in peices" after the ambush. The "other One and the Teams," Captain Williams reported, "they took away. We Suppose to carry off their dead." The Patriots also had pressed four of John Forbes's mules and these animals witnessed the storied attack on Williams. The beasts of burden, which likely had been pulling supply wagons, were "retaken in the month of September of 1812 in the sally made by the company of Blacks." Forbes ultimately recovered the mules, but it cost him the sum of sixty dollars, which was divided among Witten's men. While testifying on behalf of his son-in-law, Philip Weedman, ninety-four-year-old Anthony Hindsman denied the invaders' responsibility for pilfering Weedman's crops, blaming "the free negroes" and white St. Augustinians instead. In subsequent testimony, however, the Minorcan Andreas Pacetty discounted

Hindsman's assertion, explaining that the old man had fallen "into childishness and dotage." Pacetty stressed that neither blacks nor anyone else from St. Augustine took anything from Weedman's plantation.[15]

In fact, many Minorcans tied the presence of black troops, both Cuban and provincial, with economic prosperity. Pacetty, while discussing St. Augustine's favorable market for vegetable farmers in Spanish times, mentioned several groups of customers, including "four companies of blacks from Havanna one Company of mulattoes from Havana and one company of blacks raised in Florida under the Command of Capt: Prince." Furthermore, the Ancient City's residents who had endured the American siege credited their very survival to local men of color serving in the provincial militia. Previous to the engagement at Twelve Mile Swamp, the black militiamen had relieved the besieged inhabitants' hunger by courageously hunting cattle in the province's hinterlands and driving them to the capital. Esteban Arnow remembered "several expeditions of free blacks to hunt up cattle." James Arnowe also testified that "some Parties of negroes and others brought into Town Some Cattle for Subsistence." Andreas (Andrés) Papy recalled how Antonio Huertas "used to get permission from the Governor to go with free negroes to bring in Cattle–giving the free negroes 1$ per head for what they brought." Francis Pellicer alluded to the danger involved in driving the cattle, explaining that at times, a herd had to be abandoned because the militiamen "were shot at by the enemy." Besides cattle, the black militia gathered additional foodstuffs for the starving city. On at least three occasions, they were sent to Pellicer's plantation by boat in order to obtain corn and other provisions.[16] Rather than disdaining local free men of color as bloodthirsty plunderers, then, numerous whites in antebellum St. Johns County portrayed them as courageous, dependable providers, thus turning paternalism upside down.

Indeed, in the memories of East Floridians, white American troops and their Patriot allies became the very antitheses of the province's stalwart free black militiamen. Francis Román Sánchez explained that once the Americans realized that parties from St. Augustine had obtained small numbers of cattle from the countryside, the invaders' policy was to corral all of the beasts that they could find or to shoot them where they were encountered. Philip Weedman hinted that "the Black soldiers," along with local butchers, had supplied the town with a "small flock," toward the beginning of the siege. Also, since a large Patriot cattle-hunting foray was sent south to the Matanzas Range at the beginning of April 1812, free blacks must have procured fresh beef prior to this time. Spanish documents reveal that from July through September alone, free blacks escorted 460 cattle to the city. The archival sources demonstrate that witnesses testifying in the Patriot War claims cases did not exaggerate the achievements of the militiamen of color. Bartolo Solana, for instance, offered no numerical estimate. He merely stated that "several gangs" were "brought in by the free negroes." José Lalderol, who had served as a "corporal in the regular Troops," surmised that blacks furnished St. Augustine with only 300 head of cattle. Lalderol, however, attested to the key role that soldiers of color had played as food providers, by swearing that the "[b]eef which the city consumed in 1812 was furnished by cattle crossed over by the free blacks to the [Anastasia] Island. . . . They were on foot and collected small gangs." Matthew Long's figure, 270 to 301, approximated Lalderol's, but he was able to cite specific quantities gathered on four separate black cattle-hunting missions. Long added that the militiamen may have rounded up additional livestock on other missions.[17]

That the halo of this black heroism continued to glow as Florida made the transition from territory to statehood can be ascertained by examining Prince Witten's Patriot War claims case, which constituted a multiethnic project to wrest compensation from the U.S. Treasury. The charismatic Witten, even after his death, appealed to persons of a variety of racial and socioeconomic backgrounds. George J. F. Clarke, the administrator of Witten's estate, filed the deceased hero's claim for damages on 26 June 1835. Clarke, who had held high positions in the local colonial administration under the Spaniards, was the son of a Protestant English father and an Irish Catholic mother and was born in East Florida in 1774, when the British ruled the colony. Nine years after Clarke died in 1836, Esteban Arnow, a Minorcan, was appointed the estate's administrator by Elias B. Gould, the judge of St. Johns County's probate court. Four of the six witnesses who testified in the lawsuit also were Minorcans: John Leonardy, Andreas Pacetty, Michael Andreu, and George Gianopoli. John M. Bowden and Juan Antonio Florencio were the other two witnesses. Bowden appears to have been born in the province circa 1791. His white parents had emigrated from English-speaking territory north of the St. Marys River. Florencio was the son of an enslaved New York native who had fled from her Savannah master and a white father. Gould, who represented Arnow in federal court before Judge Isaac H. Bronson (a Connecticut native who had spent most of his life in New York before taking up his post in 1840), was another northern immigrant.[18]

When the Patriot War erupted, Prince Witten was a family man who cultivated corn, potatoes, peas, and other "such vegetables as were usually raised," on ten or eleven acres, well enclosed with rail fences, situated fourteen miles north of St. Augustine "at Sweet Water Branch on the Pablo road," half a mile from the North River. John Leonardy, who resided on a "small plantation" a mile from Witten's place, was the landlord. Leonardy characterized his tenant's dwelling, constructed of "Sawed Lumber," as "small": twenty to twenty-five feet by fourteen to fifteen feet. Andreas Pacetty thought that it was worth five hundred dollars, or twice as much as Leonardy's home. Paling surrounded the yard, and the farm also sported a kitchen, corn house, and chicken coop. Witten's livestock consisted of four to six cows and five or six horses. He owned plain furniture, a corn mill, a canoe, a grindstone, saws, wedges, augers, chains, agricultural implements and other utensils, along with two timber carts. Furthermore, he "was in the habit of getting out Cedar & ranging timber & had considerable at the landing."[19] Witten's hard work and aspirations for upward mobility are evident from this brief description of his property. He owned his buildings and, as a carpenter, he almost certainly erected them himself.[20] His land was carefully fenced. Moreover, he and his family resided in a house built with boards rather than logs. Most tellingly, like other ambitious East Floridians, he was cashing in on the province's lumber boom. Questions regarding the quantity of timber that Witten was able to cut, in fact, turned into a point of contention pregnant with deeper meanings.

George J. F. Clarke's original petition on behalf of the Witten estate claimed that in 1812 the free black man had accumulated 10,000 superficial feet of pine ranging timber, 6,000 superficial feet of sawed lumber, 2,344 cubic feet of cedar, and one hundred cedar posts, worth a total of $1,472. Clarke's statement carried weight, since measuring and inspecting timber constituted one of his myriad duties under the Spanish regime. John Leonardy, Witten's near neighbor and landlord, testified almost a decade after Clarke had submitted his petition. He recollected Witten as having only 3,000 to 4,000 feet of ranging timber, but more than twice the cedar—5,000 to 6,000 feet, at the Twenty Mile Landing on the North River. Clarke and Leonardy generally agreed regarding the sawed lumber. Because of his close friendship with Leonardy, Andreas Pacetty, who resided in St. Augustine, visited the Witten place monthly. Pacetty judged that Witten possessed more cedar at the landing than Leonardy had sworn to—6,000 to 7,000 feet, in addition to forty other cedar logs sitting at the edge of Twelve Mile Swamp, which he believed would add a minimum of 2,000 cubic feet to the claim. He and Leonardy corroborated each other in relation to the ranging timber. Regarding the sawed lumber, Pacetty confirmed Clarke's and Leonardy's figures. Michael Andreu only "occasionally" passed by Witten's, so he knew "nothing of any ranging timber or Cedar timber." Nevertheless, about two weeks before the invaders appeared, Andreu surmised that he saw a pile at Witten's containing 9,000 to 10,000 feet of sawed lumber, an estimate that exceeded those of the other witnesses by 3,000 to 4,000 superficial feet.[21]

To summarize, conflicting information caused considerable consternation in the minds of those responsible for ascertaining the appropriate award owed to Prince Witten's estate. The ranging timber had been variously estimated as measuring from 3,000 to 10,000 superficial feet, the cedar piles as containing from

2,344 to 7,000 cubic feet, and the sawed lumber as amounting to from 5,000 to 10,000 superficial feet. Juan Antonio Florencio's testimony further muddied the waters, but it suggested that Witten had harvested and prepared for market a batch of timber that far exceeded the typical output of a small East Florida lumbering entrepreneur. Florencio emphasized that Witten was not felling, hauling, and shaping logs for anyone else. "He had plenty of people hired for getting cedar & lumber." In other words, he had worked independently of the white man, employing twelve to twenty black hands, which in turn, had permitted fellow provincials of African descent to share both his prosperity and his occupational sanctuary. The historian Lee Warner believed that free blacks who employed their fellows in such work crews were "challenging the very basis of the established Southern social order." This may have caused Witten's white witnesses to neglect to mention this key fact. Unlike the Minorcan witnesses, Florencio did not quantify Witten's arboreal treasure in terms of cubic or superficial feet. Instead, he swore that a "great pile" containing more than two hundred cedar logs, each measuring one to two feet in diameter and between ten and thirty feet long, temporarily rested at the landing, and another equally large stack of cedar lingered among the trees of the forbidding Twelve Mile Swamp. In this manner, Florencio lodged his subtle protest against American rule. From these dimensions, whites themselves could make their own calculations, so that by the very mathematics that they utilized to commodify the enslaved, they might discover the enhanced productive capacities of free blacks. All in all, then, as Florencio succinctly stated under oath, Witten owned "a good chance of cedar," in addition to "sawed boards and cypress posts."[22]

Judge Isaac H. Bronson remained particularly troubled about the cedar. Because Leonardy and Pacetty had agreed that Witten's pine amounted to 3,000 to 4,000 superficial feet, he discounted Clarke's figure and settled upon the lower number that the Minorcans proffered. Likewise, because all three men felt that Witten owned 5,000 to 6,000 feet of sawed timber, Bronson disregarded Andreu's higher estimate and again chose the smallest stated quantity. But rather than apply the same logic to the cedar, which, since both Leonardy and Pacetty had surmised Witten's logs as totaling between 5,000 and 7,000 cubic feet, would have dictated that he negate Clarke's claim of 2,344 cubic feet, he balked. The federal official hypothesized that "as in many other cases," the "lapse of time has much magnified in [witnesses'] minds the quantity & value of . . . the cedar timber." As he reasoned in another free black claim, that of Sancho Davis, "estimates and valuations are so far beyond what the losses evidently could have been, that I should entertain great suspicion of the whole testimony if I did not know the witnesses personally and from my knowledge of them believe them incapable of manufacturing testimony willfully. . . . I believe they intended to tell the truth but in these respects are greatly mistaken." Moreover, Bronson revealed his racist bias. He fumed against the "idea that such a free negro had . . . 6000 feet of cedar." Testimony of this nature simply was "not admissable." Racial prejudice also moved Bronson to discount Juan Antonio Florencio's narrative, which he "deem[ed] . . . of very little consequence."[23]

In determining the award due to Prince Witten's estate, Bronson placed great stock in George Gianopoli's testimony, as well as that offered by John Carreras in the Davis case. Gianopoli was sixteen to seventeen years of age in March 1812, and during the previous three years, he had clerked for John Forbes & Company in their St. Augustine store. His employer would purchase the cedar that "the people of the country" rafted down both the North and Matanzas Rivers. Most of the time, the town's "small shop-keepers" served as middlemen. The petty merchants either would "make advances" to rural inhabitants and "take cedar timber in payment" or purchase the prized wood directly. They in turn sold it to Forbes & Company, the only "house then at St. Augustine that shipped timber from this port." Gianopoli stated that rafts usually contained five hundred to one thousand cubic feet of cedar. The diameters of their individual logs ranged from twelve to eighteen inches. The former clerk could recall none being two feet in diameter. Lengths varied from ten to fifteen feet. Carreras estimated that a typical raft was comprised of one hundred logs. Therefore, Bronson assumed that the amount of marketable cedar in an individual log averaged between twenty and thirty cubic feet. While Gianopoli admitted that he was not "acquainted with the business of cutting," nor had he ever "been in the woods when they were getting out cedar," he believed that felling and squaring forty cubic feet per day constituted "a fair days work for a hand."[24]

These statements by Gianopoli and Carreras caused Bronson to scoff at Pacetty's estimate that one log could produce as much as four hundred cubic feet of red cedar. Consequently, the latter's "opinion" of the "quantity of a pile of timber. . . . [was] entitled to very little consideration." Since Leonardy's figure approximated Pacetty's, it, too, was ignored. In 1847, more than two years after his initial testimony, Leonardy defended his credibility. The Minorcan asserted that he (unlike Gianopoli) "was engaged in cutting Cedar timber. . . . in the 12 Mile Swamp at the time the Patriots came into the country in 1812." He then challenged Gianopoli and Carreras. Leonardy's rafts contained twenty to forty squared logs (rather than Carreras's hundred), at least one foot in diameter and never less than eighteen feet long. Therefore, if Gianopoli's judgment of a raft's cubic footage were correct, Bronson would have to upwardly revise his calculation of the average product of an individual log. Furthermore, Leonardy elaborated, because lumbering usually commenced in July, by March, he would extract five thousand to seven thousand cubic feet of cedar in a season, especially since "a good hand could cut & hew 100 feet in a day" (as opposed to Gianopoli's guess of forty). Moreover, when the Americans invaded, Leonardy maintained that he had three thousand or four thousand cubic feet of cedar piled at one landing. Finally, contrary to Gianopoli's attribution of monopoly to Forbes & Company, Leonardy swore that, unlike the "free negroes," he "never sold any [cedar] to the house," preferring instead to deal "directly" with captains of "vessels which came from the north" or to sell it "to Ysnardi" in St. Augustine when no ships were present to load cargoes.[25]

By serving as Prince Witten's advocate, therefore, John Leonardy was defending his own honor. While Leonardy's praise for Witten's lumbering enterprise was not as effusive as Florencio's, the Minorcan still insisted that the black Patriot War hero had worked as industriously and skillfully as his white neighbors. Regarding Witten's independent nature, he also agreed with Florencio, although, once again, Leonardy muffled his tribute. That is, between the lines of his testimony of 1847, he implied that like himself and unlike some other free blacks, Witten was not beholden to Forbes & Company. Unfortunately, Leonardy's plea fell upon Bronson's deaf ears. Not only did he reject the notion that Witten possessed 5,000 to 7,000 cubic feet of cedar, he also dispensed with Clarke's figure of 2,344 cubic feet, despite having noted in a previous claim that the latter had stood "high in the confidence" of the Spanish regime and had been "extremely engaged" in the lumber business. In fact, *subsequent* to his 1848 award decree for the Witten estate, Bronson lauded Clarke as "highly intelligent & well informed . . . and upon whose testimony much reliance may be placed." Nevertheless, Bronson reduced the cubic footage to 1,600, assigning a value of $400 to Witten's cedar, in place of the former provincial timber inspector's sum of $1,472.[26] In short, Bronson refused to believe that a man of color, even one of Prince Witten's ample abilities, could possibly be so economically successful.

Bronson's obstinacy regarding the capacity of free colored men to compete with whites in the marketplace offers a striking contrast between the racial attitudes of American newcomers and East Florida's white inhabitants who had lived under Spanish rule. Prince Witten was not the only claimant to suffer as a consequence of Anglo newcomers' prejudices. The timber claims of his comrades in arms also aroused Bronson's ire. Twelve miles south of St. Augustine, on the banks of Moses Creek, Isaac Bacchus and John Morell cultivated farms near those of Charles W. Clarke and his brother George J. F. Clarke, affluent and politically connected patriarchs of biracial families. Bacchus and Morell supported their dependents by erecting dwellings, outbuildings, and fencing, in addition to growing provisions on eight-acre plots. Their ambition and energy is evident by the attention they devoted to cutting cedar for export. When duty called during the Patriot War, these men of color, after escorting their loved ones to St. Augustine, served their sovereign in Witten's vaunted military unit. In his decision regarding Morell's cedar, Bronson opined that instead of accumulating a year's harvest at his landing, Morell would have rafted his cedar to market periodically. Moreover, even in an entire season, the judge sarcastically opined, if Morell had harvested 3,775 cubic feet of cedar as Clarke's petition alleged, it would have been "more, I apprehend, than any other free negro ever made by his own exertions in one year, in this or any other country."[27]

George Clarke lived some eighteen miles south of Bacchus and Morell, about two miles from Fort Matanzas, along Tony Masters Creek, a mile from the Matanzas River. This biracial man had been a fugitive from Georgia who had taken advantage of Spain's religious sanctuary policy in order to gain his freedom and a land grant. However, in 1812, Clarke and his family lived on land that they rented from Antonio Masters. There he erected a log dwelling, a kitchen, and a fence around the three-acre plot that he cultivated. Clarke's major economic activity was logging. For this enterprise, he required a "cart fixed like a dray—or a pair of timber wheels & two or three good horses." Hauling the timber to the water landing might require "cutting roads in the swamp where they got the timber." James Arnowe recalled seeing "more cedar timber at [Clarke's] landing than I saw at any other place." Joseph Manucy recollected a great deal of cedar, "quite a pile of it." Francis Triay's memory was more detailed. He estimated that Clarke had "large logs about 18 feet long hewed and squared," amounting to three thousand cubic feet of cedar, in addition to two thousand feet of pine timber, all ready to be shipped to market in St. Augustine. Slavery obviously had squelched the ambitious Clarke's potential. Although he was a "poor man" in Spanish East Florida, he was independently supporting his family and contributing to the colony's booming economy. Moreover, when the Americans invaded, he hastened to defend his adopted homeland as a soldier under Prince Witten's command.[28] Georgia's loss had been Florida's gain.

George Clarke, Isaac Bacchus, and John Morell were able to engage in the hard labor of cutting timber, which, according to Zephaniah Kingsley, was "at that time the most profitable employment or labor in which negro men slaves could be employed." What was profitable employment for slaves laboring for others would be even more so when free men of color toiling for themselves took their axes to trees. Therefore, whites' estimates of cedar that free blacks had cut in 1811–12 offered compelling evidence of the capacity of people of color to harness their energy in the independent pursuit of profits, rather than settle for dependency upon the largesse of paternalists. If free blacks in Spanish days could distinguish themselves on the battlefield and successfully cast themselves into the capitalist scramble for cedar-based wealth, then United States–era racial policies were stifling East Florida's growth by hamstringing a segment of society that historically had proven to be loyal and productive. Perhaps this explains why, in the eyes of antebellum federal judge Isaac H. Bronson, white witnesses' estimates that Morell had accumulated $1,887 worth of cedar seemed preposterous. While it is true that the cedar claims of Bacchus, Clarke, Domingo and Sancho Davis, John Howley, Abraham Rocho, and Prince Witten did not match Morell's, as they ranged from $200 to $1,440, Bronson obviously reached his compensation decisions in a racist context.[29]

This same racist mind-set, nevertheless, renders other comments by Bronson elsewhere in the claim as most remarkable, demonstrating the power that memories of Witten's Patriot War valor continued to exude thirty-six years later. The sixty-six-year-old Leonardy aimed to convince Bronson of the high esteem in which the Spaniards had held the black hero: "Prince was immediately put into the military service by Gov: Kindelan, he was made Lieut of a Black or coloured company of troops & afterward commanded the company, & served during the whole of the Patriot war." Pacetty, who was seven years younger than Leonardy, added that Witten had been promoted from lieutenant to captain and "was very active as a military man & was much depended upon by the spanish Govt." He then summoned Captain John Williams's ghost: "[Witten] had several engagements with the Patriots & I believe was well known to them, he had also an engagement with Capt Williams of the U.S. Regulars, & a party under his command at 12 mile Swamp in which the American Troops were defeated & Williams badly wounded & died soon after." Like Leonardy and Pacetty, Andreu, age fifty-one, recalled Witten's leadership of a "company of Black Troops during the Patriot war." "I saw him frequently," he reflected, "during that year in the Spanish service."[30] Clearly, Prince Witten had earned the continuing respect of his Minorcan acquaintances, who in the mid-1840s were St. Augustine's honored elders.

When Florencio, the sixty-three-year-old free man of color, added his assent, he carefully toed the fine line of folk diplomacy. In 1796, Florencio was one of eighty-one pupils enrolled in St. Augustine's integrated Catholic boys' school.[31] Presumably, unlike Leonardy and Andreu, he was literate. Significantly, Florencio did not Anglicize his name, recognizing that by clinging to his Hispanic identity, he could better navigate the perilous waters of United States rule. This Latin heritage was one of his sanctuaries. Florencio's freedom had been recorded in the city's Catholic parish registers. The Roman Catholic Church, an international entity, could therefore vouch for him. So could Spain. According to the Adams-Onís Treaty by which the United States acquired Florida, all former Spanish subjects were to enjoy the privileges of American citizenship. The treaty also required Washington to compensate the king's ex-subjects for damages caused "by the late operations of the American Army in Florida." Hence, Prince Witten's case could be heard in federal court, and Florencio, under certain conditions, could offer testimony. Moreover, the colonial government papers for East Florida remained in St. Augustine during antebellum times, and they attested to blacks' privileges. For example, in 1839, Antonio Álvarez, the Keeper of the Public Archives, swore that free persons of color under the Spaniards "possessed and enjoyed the same rights as White persons respecting the acquiring of and the alienation of property."[32]

In order to bolster his credibility, Florencio began his account by notifying his listeners of his own presence in St. Augustine during the American siege of 1812, thus linking himself to other venerable city residents by the vivid memory-bond of hunger. Next, in addition to emphasizing the *hispanidad* of the black troops, he astutely reminded the courtroom audience of the heroic role that he, Prince Witten, and other free men of color had played in staving off starvation and protecting the town from attack. At the same time, Florencio was careful to include whites in this narrative, both to quell possible guilt-inspired resentment on the part of the ruling caste and to convey the sentiment that the oppressed and the oppressors, as comrades-in-arms, had shared the dangers of battle. In modern parlance, they had been "war buddies." He also cleverly mentioned the losses of prominent Hispanic whites in order to stir further sympathy for his testimony and to gild his words with authority. That is, Florencio was reinforcing the veracity of their compensation claims:

> I was in the Spanish service during the Patriot war. Kept guard on the lines. Was under the command of *Prince Whilton*—who was a sargent.—Our white Capt—was Capt Fleming. Myself & other Spanish soldiers used to go out into the Country during the war to get cattle & bring them in for the troops, & people in the city. The parties that went out were usually commanded by Prince Whilton, & Tony Doctor, but sometimes a white seargent went with us. Sometimes we got 40, Sometimes 50 & Sometimes 60 head of cattle, just as we could find them. We used to take them wherever we could find them. We went Sometimes to Matanzas, Sometimes to Deep Creek & wherever we could find Cattle. Some that we got—belonged to Huertas. Some to Pallacier. Some to Arredondo—& some to others, don't know who. . . . they belonged to various persons—Huertas, Solana & others.

Notably absent from Florencio's reminiscences was Prince Witten's triumph at the Twelve Mile Swamp. As a man of color in 1846, he obviously felt that a recounting of this black military victory over whites would be too inflammatory coming from his mouth. Therefore, he lodged his protest against the marginalization of Afro–East Floridians more subtly.[33]

As part of his folk diplomacy, Florencio took pains to construct a bridge of victimhood between persons of color and whites. He recalled how during the siege "there was a party of 30 or 40 of us that went out into the Country up the North River." Prince Witten participated in this scouting foray. Like property owners of all ethnicities (Florencio made this point by specifically mentioning the European immigrant Dr. Philip Weedman and Weedman's free black protégé, Charles Hill, who had lived in East Florida during British rule, and who had tragically lost his wife and three children to Patriot kidnappers), when Witten reached his farm, "he found his place burned & destroyed, & all the places about in that part of the country had been burned." Leonardy also alluded to this chain of anguish that linked St. Johns County's "old inhabitants." When the governor found out about the American invasion, Leonardy explained, he sent boats up the North River to evacuate the neighborhood. The order to abandon their farms "was a sudden one," giving residents "no time to pick up anything but came off directly." "We all did quit our places accordingly," he continued, "& come into the city, & Prince Whilton came in & brought his family with the rest. . . . I came in the same day that he did." And, with a nod to Witten's bravery, he added that the black man could not have returned to his place during the war "with safety." After the invaders retreated, Leonardy "found that Princes place was all destroyed, the buildings & fences were all burned."[34]

Pacetty also attested to Prince Witten's sharing in the agony of having experienced dreams going up in smoke. He recollected seeing Prince "when he arrived in town" after having been evacuated with "his family & others" in government boats. A fortnight after the Americans abandoned East Florida, Pacetty journeyed out to Witten's place and "found that his buildings & fences had all been destroyed—burned." He noted that "[a]ll communication between that part of the country was cut off during the war & the enemy had possession of it." While not offering any specific details about the pillaging of Witten's farm, Andreu testified that the black military man, like his white neighbors, had been forced by the governor to suddenly abandon his possessions in order to serve the crown under arms. Sixty-year-old John M. Bowden not only knew Witten, but also had been one of the Patriots who had besieged St. Augustine. Bowden described the frequent trips that the invaders would make along the road between their camp outside of town to Pablo, near the mouth of the St. Johns River. During their travels, "they visited all the plantations in that part of the country. . . . I heard them say that they went to every plantation that they could find." Moreover, said Bowden, "Foraging parties were constantly sent out in all directions who brought in Cattle, Hogs, & fowls, corn, etc." Although he denied taking part in any of these expeditions, since Witten lived "on the Pablo Road," circumstantial evidence made the United States culpable for the losses.[35]

Moreover, evidence from an earlier claims case, that of the free black Philip (Felipe) Edinborough, suggests that the enemy particularly targeted the homes of militiamen of color. Charles W. Clarke and Rafael Olivares reported that Edinborough had been a noncommissioned officer in "a Company of Blacks." But, Bartolo Solana appears to have confused him with Prince Witten, crediting Edinborough with "head[ing] the black party that fought the Enemy commanded by Capt Williams U.S.A. in the 12 mile Swamp; in which engagement the Capt was killed." He was "an active Soldier during the war," Philip Weedman testified, implying that Edinborough had played a prominent role in the fighting, but not placing him at Williams's ambush. The free black Tony Proctor clarified whites' accounts, explaining that Edinborough had indeed fought in the skirmish at the Twelve Mile Swamp. News of Edinborough's martial prowess became a topic of conversation among the invaders. Gabriel Capo, who had been a prisoner of the Americans at "Fort Mosa," heard his captors speak "many times" of plundering Edinborough's farm. "Edimboro belonged to a Black company," Capo related, "and they knew it. I heard them speak of it." Witten, too, was "well known" to the Patriots. As Charles W. Clarke reminded the court, "The Patriots suffered nothing to escape them; but seized upon every article of property no matter how trifling that came in their way."[36] Given the invaders' reputation for destructiveness and their fear of black troops, it is most probable that they sought to punish the members of Witten's company by venting their outrage on their possessions.

Certainly, then, shared nightmares of sudden forced migration to town, hunger during the siege, impoverishment as a result of property loss, and dangerous military service plagued many antebellum Afro–East Floridians and whites. Furthermore, captured free people of color faced a terror not applicable to white prisoners like Capo—permanent enslavement. For some people of color, the fear was re-enslavement. One free black, Charles Hill, admitted that he had once been a slave. In the case of Abraham Rocho, Minorcans testified that the claimant had formerly served as Rocque Leonardy's bondsman. Hill and Rocho, however, had purchased their liberty. They had not gained it by applying for sanctuary. In fact, there seems to have been an aversion on the part of antebellum whites to acknowledging this Spanish policy. Numerous witnesses referred to the American occupation of Fort Mose, where decades earlier, the Spaniards had settled fugitives that had been granted religious sanctuary. Zephaniah Kingsley even mentioned that the fort had been a "post of Gen Ogelthorpe." In 1739, Georgia's founder, James Oglethorpe, invaded East Florida, aiming to stem the flow of runaway slaves seeking sanctuary in Spanish territory. On 14 June 1740, at Mose, white, black, and Indian troops defeated the British invaders, hastening their retreat from the province. Significantly, the Georgians assaulting the colony in 1812, who also hoped to strip their human chattel of the option of fleeing to Florida, conducted a flag-raising ceremony pregnant with symbolism at "old Fort Moosa under a Salute." Subsequently, Spanish parties from St. Augustine successfully attacked this position twice. Still, although Kingsley coyly hinted at the parallels, those testifying in the Patriot War claims cases did not directly connect the historical dots in court, even though evidence indicates that they remembered the sanctuary policy.[37]

In any event, the Minorcan witnesses swore that they knew nothing about Prince Witten ever having been enslaved nor having fled to East Florida seeking sanctuary for himself and his family. They simply could not imagine it, although Spanish religious records and civil documents in St. Augustine's Catholic church as well as public archives could have revealed these facts. John Leonardy merely stated that Witten "was a free Black man." Pacetty used the same words, adding that he heard that Witten had died in Cuba, after departing with the Spaniards in 1821, when the Americans took over the colony. Pacetty further asserted that he "had known Prince from childhood well. He was never a slave. I think he was born free." In 1812, Pacetty would have been about twenty-six, so he was born around the time that Witten and his family reached East Florida. Andreu, eight years Pacetty's junior, also swore that Witten "was always a free man since I remember—do not think he ever was a Slave." Florencio, whose mother, like Witten, had fled from bondage in Georgia, wisely kept silent on the subject, although he likely knew the truth.[38] The role of Spain's sanctuary policy both in Prince Witten's life and in the history of Fort Mose had become unmentionable in the public sphere.

The earnest witnesses convinced the wary Judge Bronson that Witten "was a free negro & a Spanish subject. . . . he was born, & had always lived in East Florida." Consequently, Bronson opined: "I see no reason why he is not entitled to the benefit of the provisions of the treaty & the act of Congress of 26th of June 1834, to enable him to recover from the U. States for such losses & injuries as he actually suffered." Moreover, testimony in this case and others had obviously caused the judge to recognize Witten's leadership skills, courage, and military aptitude. Indeed, Bronson's stifled feelings of astonishment and admiration evinced themselves in his brief of Witten's career: "He was immediately enrolled in a company of Black troops in the Spanish service, & had some prominent command in the company—so much so that in many of these claims, the witnesses speak of this company of coloured troops as 'Princes Black company.'" Thus, the legend of Prince Witten continued to spread. Indeed, memories of

Witten survived even during the worst days of Jim Crow segregation and lynching. Both William W. Dewhurst in 1885 and Herbert Bruce Fuller in 1906 "cite the bravery of Prince, who saved the population of St. Augustine from starvation by his action against the invaders."[39]

Prince Witten was a man of African descent who, against heavy odds, led his charges to victory on the battlefield. His charisma and talent earned him the homage of those who normally despised persons of non-European ethnicities. In St. Augustine, nostalgic whites sang the praises of Witten at informal gatherings, adopting him as one of their own and conveying their sentiments to their descendants. Although this veneration also might function as a self-serving tool for preserving the racial status quo, the life of Witten demonstrates that white associations with black heroes could ameliorate, at the individual level, broader social dysfunction. Consequently, in antebellum East Florida, white memories of Prince Witten and those who fought in his "Black Company" gave persons of color, including slaves, a certain latitude in negotiating their freedom. That is, by invoking the halcyon Spanish past in their dealings with whites, the oppressed could use their oppressors' memories against them. For this reason, it is important to examine how Witten's men were remembered. In addition, we must return to the question of the enslaved. That is, how did antebellum whites interpret the actions of their bondsmen during the Patriot War? To what extent did the experiences of the free and the enslaved overlap?

5
Prophets of the Apocalypse

We have seen how white antebellum East Floridians remembered the years immediately preceding the United States–sponsored invasion of 1812 as harbingers of a golden age. Witnesses testifying in the Patriot War claims cases blamed Washington for shattering their dreams of prosperity. Moreover, they portrayed the Americans and their allies not as missionaries of republican virtue, but instead as ruthless barbarians who shattered the very foundations of civilized life in the Spanish colony. In contrast, the region's elders elevated soldiers belonging to a local black militia unit under the charismatic leadership of Prince Witten to the status of folk heroes for their pivotal role in rescuing St. Augustine's besieged inhabitants from starvation. The historical context of whites' recollections of black valor adds poignancy to their praise, for after the Spaniards finally surrendered the Floridas to the United States in 1821, the subsequent territorial and state governments enacted a series of measures aimed at marginalizing free persons of African descent. As the color line hardened, blacks found themselves barred from their traditional role as military defenders, a role that had earned them freedom, prestige, and material gains under Catholic rule.[1]

Therefore, when antebellum testimony resurrected and recorded tales of the martial prowess of Afro-Spaniards during the Patriot War, those who proffered it, consciously or unconsciously, were lodging veiled protests against the racial policies that had arisen under the American regime. The cognitive dissonance that ensued when memories of the courage, competence, and loyalty of free men of color clashed with contemporary legal restrictions based upon their unfitness for civic responsibility furnished black folk diplomats with valuable leverage for negotiating freedom. Enslaved East Floridians also shared in the suffering that the U.S. assault of 1812 generated. More than a quarter century after the attack, whites acknowledged slaves' victimhood, which tied them to their masters in a manner that transcended the usual relationships linking bondsmen and their owners. Here, too, between the lines of their depositions, witnesses protested the regime change by depicting a peaceful Spanish slaveholding past that had "gone with the wind." In its place, American rule brought slave rebellion in the form of the Second Seminole War, as well as a spectacular escape from St. Augustine engineered by the bondsman Andrew Gué that cast East Florida into an embarrassing international spotlight. Recollections of contented and trustworthy slaves whose benign existence had been suddenly disrupted by swarming white hordes from the north further expanded the repertoire of ambassadors of color seeking to ameliorate the oppressive precepts of a government that had transformed a "society with slaves" into a "slave society."[2]

What also shines forth from the Patriot War claims cases is witnesses' tacit and sometimes direct recognition of slaves' intelligence, bravery, initiative, and overriding desire for freedom, as well as the hollowness of planters' paternalism. Combined with the inspirational valor that free blacks exhibited during the chaos of the Patriot War, this testimony indicts the U.S. slave society in Florida as wasteful and immoral. Following a "providential" interpretation of history,[3] the destruction of 1812–13 may be perceived as God's way of preventing a Spanish "society with slaves" from developing into an even more diabolical "slave society." In addition, according to this line of thought, free and enslaved blacks, by their words and deeds, acted as prophets of abolition who chastised whites for their social injustice and warned them of a coming apocalypse should they ignore the call to repentance. The Second Seminole War served as another divine chastisement. On the eve of the Civil War, a Catholic bishop issued a final warning. Then, at last, came the cataclysmic year of jubilee. Whites had not availed themselves of the opportunities for reflection and reform that a series of violent tragedies had presented to them. The result was a bloodbath that their obstinance created.

Certainly, according to white testimony in federal court during the lengthy process of the adjudication of the Patriot War claims, free men of color had posed no threat to Spanish rule. Whites portrayed them as hard-working family heads who, like other East Floridians in the boom times of 1812, were striving to increase their fortunes. Although there was much to admire concerning black property, the holdings of blacks were generally inferior to those of whites. There existed ample evidence of interracial friendships, but even these relationships seem to have been conducted within the framework of white superiority. During the throes of the American invasion, free blacks fought alongside whites as valiant comrades-in-arms who faced the enemy under special dangers due to their African heritage. Like their white neighbors, black families endured the refugee experience, in addition to the loss of their wealth at the hands of marauding rebel bands. When the change of flags took place, the vast majority of these stalwart subjects of color protested the American takeover by accompanying the Spaniards to Cuba. According to the gist of the reminiscences of East Florida's revered elders, therefore, the draconian antiblack measures that the territorial and state legislatures had passed since 1821 were without merit.

The case of Philip Edinborough illustrates many white assertions concerning Spanish-era free men of color. Jane Landers, using a variety of documentary evidence, has traced his life in some detail in her magisterial study, *Black Society in Spanish Florida.* Edinborough was an African-born slave who, through his skills, energy, and initiative, succeeded in purchasing his freedom. His understanding of colonial institutions enabled him not only to gain his liberty, but subsequently to acquire land, slaves, a position of military responsibility, and high standing as a black layman in the Catholic Church. Through fictive kinship and marriage, Edinborough enjoyed ties to prominent whites and the province's leading black families. To be sure, he was no shrinking violet. He was confident enough of his social standing to initiate lawsuits in order to settle his scores in court.[4] If, however, Edinborough had attempted to replicate his achievements under the republican U.S. regime in antebellum East Florida, he would have found it increasingly difficult merely to gain his manumission.

Whites who testified on behalf of Edinborough's Patriot War compensation suit attested to many of the facts concerning his life that Landers has unearthed in modern times. Charles W. Clarke, an important provincial official who was the brother-in-law of Edinborough's daughter's husband, described him as "an industrious man." "Edinborough labored himself," Andreas Papy recalled. "[He and his family] were industrious people." Bartolo Solana, the scion of one of the colony's eminent cattle-ranching families, called the ex-bondsman "a respectable man." The physician Philip Weedman agreed that Edinborough was "generally respected by the white people." No witness alluded to his servile origins, not even Joseph S. Sánchez, a prominent white son of the fabulously wealthy Francisco Xavier Sánchez, whom Edinborough had taken to court in a rancorous but successful freedom bid. Clarke, Weedman, and Rafael Olivares remembered that Edinborough had served as a sergeant in Prince Witten's vaunted black company. Solana, as mentioned previously, mistakenly thought that he had risen to the rank of lieutenant, and that "[h]e headed the black party that fought the Enemy commanded by Capt Williams U.S.A. in the 12 mile Swamp; in which engagement the Capt was killed."[5]

Besides voicing their agreement regarding Edinborough's good character, his loyalty to the crown, and his courage in battle, whites expressed their admiration for his property. In 1807, the governor had granted the free black man a hundred acres some three miles west of St. Augustine. By 1811, according to Dr. Philip Weedman, Edinborough had transformed his grant into "a very flourishing little place" that contained a "very good garden" of vegetables. The thirty acres on which he cultivated corn, Irish and sweet potatoes, pumpkins, peas, and melons, "indeed all kinds of provisions," were "well enclosed with a rail fence" that was "worth Considerable" since the wood for it had to be brought from a distance. His forty to fifty cattle "ran with" those of Bartolo Solana's father. He also owned a "good Chance of Hogs." The two slaves that assisted Edinborough and his diligent family in their labors "were prime." Esteban Arnow admired the farm's "very good" buildings, which Weedman estimated to be worth five hundred dollars. Edinborough, besides being a "planter," was a military man and "acted [as] a *Cattle Hunter.*" Whites also noted how Edinborough's economic interests were geographically diverse. He owned a garden and orange grove in St. Augustine, as well as additional land at Buena Vista on the St. Johns River. Indeed, prior to the Patriot War, Edinborough "was very well off in point of property." And, he was a family man.[6]

The fact that he apparently had imbibed the values of Spanish colonial society served to dispel the notion that he in any way posed a threat to the province's racial hierarchy. To be sure, white witnesses were careful to note that Edinborough's successes, while admirable, rested well within the bounds of the social order. Charles W. Clarke explained that "[h]is furniture Suited Edinborough's condition in life." Bartolo Solana, Andreas Papy, and Rafael Olivares similarly commented on the furniture, characterizing it as "coarse," "rough," and "very common,"—"[s]uch as negroes use." Clarke, Papy, and Olivares extended this depiction of innate black inferiority to their discussion of Edinborough's buildings, which they described as "small" and "made of Clapboards and covered with bark—they were common negro houses." Philip Weedman voiced the same condescending sentiment by testifying that the farm's fence "was Crooked and of real negro workmanship." As Clarke conceded, Edinborough "was in respectable circumstances for a coloured man." Olivares sighed his assent regarding the black man and his family, "[s]uppos[ing] they were as industrious as colored people usually are."[7]

Although white witnesses denied Philip Edinborough's equality to them, they readily admitted that he was their brother in suffering at the hands of the American invaders. First of all, Edinborough shared the refugee experience that continued to haunt antebellum East Florida's elders. "[T]he free people of color were ordered into Town, placed under arms, and their property fell into Enemy hands," Andreas Papy reminded the court. Rafael Olivares concurred that Edinborough "received notice and repaired suddenly to St. Augustine." So suddenly, and "under such alarm," Philip Weedman stressed, that the Edinboroughs could save no property, and "all that was *theirs,* fell into Enemy hands." The family's blackness, Weedman and Esteban Arnow pointed out, had placed it in special peril. Their "great haste" in fleeing to the Ancient City's gates was fueled by their fear of "being made captives by the Enemy," a captivity that would have resulted in their enslavement. While Arnow was a prisoner in the Patriot camp, he heard the rebels speak about pillaging Edinborough's place with a special relish, since they knew that he fought with Prince Witten's black company. In the end, the war ruined Edinborough. He "was reduced to poverty by the Rebellion," Charles W. Clarke asserted. Indeed, Bartolo Solana lamented, "[Edinborough] was living comfortably and happily" and he "was doing very well before the war." But afterward, "he was utterly broken up." Even Edinborough's most unsympathetic witness, Rafael Olivares, saw himself forced to admit that the invasion had robbed the free man of color of his "comfortable circumstances" and made him "poor."[8]

Other free men of color received similar qualified praise and sympathy from whites in the claims hearings. Isaac Bacchus, George Clarke, Domingo Davis, Sancho Davis, Scipio Fleming, Charles Hill, John Morell, Tony Primus, Abraham Rocho, Lewis Sánchez, and Benjamin Wiggins, for example, were cited as having taken up arms for the Crown during the Patriot War. They, like Edinborough, therefore, shared white veterans' esprit de corps for having risked their lives in order to defeat the American invaders. Several of these Afro-Spanish claimants also partook of the muscular entrepreneurial enterprise of logging during East Florida's pre-invasion timber boom. Regarding this lucrative activity, federal judge Isaac Bronson, during the mid-1840s, found white witnesses' glowing tributes to black drive, determination, ingenuity, skills, strength, and economic success as sincere but too incredible to swallow. Bronson, however, did not contest white testimony describing black militiamen as husbands, fathers, and caretakers. Nor did he protest when whites lauded the troops for other positive attributes. Sophia Fleming, a daughter of the legendary planter Francis P. Fatio, vouched for Scipio Fleming, claiming that "he has always borne an excellent character for truth & veracity." Likewise, James Arnowe acknowledged George Clarke's "very good" character, and Joseph S. Sánchez called Lewis Sánchez an "honest" and "very industrious man."[9]

In many instances, this white praise of black men emanated from and was intertwined with fond memories of friendships originating in the heady times of witnesses' vanished youths. Thus, the warm glow of golden days illuminated their reminiscences. Michael Andreu, for example, had known the "yellow man" Isaac Bacchus since childhood. Likewise, when they were boys living in St. Augustine, Francis Triay and Joseph Manucy first met George Clarke, a mulatto unrelated to the Spanish surveyor general, George J. F. Clarke. In 1846, the septuagenarian James Arnowe recalled that he had made the mulatto Clarke's acquaintance two decades before the Patriot War, when Arnowe was around nineteen years of age. Referring to Tony Primus, John M. Bowden deposed that he "has known claimant since he was a child and has always considered him free." Elsewhere, he swore that he had been well acquainted with another free man of color, Abraham Hannahan, since Bowden was about thirteen years old. "[F]or many years previous" to the invasion, Esteban Arnow had known the free "mulatto man" Abraham Rocho. John Leonardy, Andreas Pacetty, and Andreu had struck up friendships with Sancho Davis long before the Patriot War commenced. The sixty-seven-year-old matron Sophia Fleming, testifying in 1835, declared that her connection to Scipio Fleming stretched back some forty years.[10]

Not only did whites have nodding acquaintances with men of color, they visited blacks' homes and conversed with them about their lives. Scipio Fleming's tract on Padan Aram Creek, twenty-five miles northwest of St. Augustine, served as "a place of rest" for George Gianopoli when he would visit Sophia Fleming's father's opulent New Switzerland estate. Esteban Arnow remembered well the number of cows on Abraham Rocho's farm, some five miles north of St. Augustine, because he "drinked milk there." Michael Andreu frequently passed Rocho's place, and likely tarried there, on eighteen-mile trips to town. Arnow also recalled his frequent visits to Charles Hill's place, twelve miles north of the city, prior to the Patriot War. John Leonardy was familiar with Hill's affairs, because his father "had a plantation just along side of Hills—adjoined his." Andreas Pacetty in 1812 lived in St. Augustine, but he was frequently at Sancho Davis's, twenty miles to the north, and "stopped there many a night with him." Pacetty would visit monthly. Domingo Cercopoly made Davis's acquaintance in the course of traveling out to the Leonardy plantation from town in order to "take a hunt." Cercopoly learned more of Davis's affairs because when Davis would come to town to sell the products of his labor, he would tell Cercopoly about the property at his place. James Arnowe, Andreu, and Cercopoly spoke of fishing often at Moses Creek, twelve miles south of St. Augustine, and landing at John Morell's in order to wait for favorable tides. Leonardy stopped at George Clarke's, seven miles southward of Morell, almost every time that he visited his uncle in Matanzas, Francis Pellicer.[11]

Frequently, work, in addition to traveling and socializing, brought whites and free blacks together. Esteban Arnow knew George Clarke very well because his father used to employ the free man of color as a lumberjack and "as a kind of botch carpenter." Sancho Davis would sometimes help Michael Andreu transport tools and provisions to the Twenty Mile Swamp, near Davis's place, where Andreu would cut timber for canoes and boats. Andreu noted that he frequently stopped at Davis's. John M. Bowden recalled the time that he helped Abraham Hannahan guide a cow and calf across the St. Johns River to the free colored man's place at Laurel Grove. When Patriot marauders kidnapped Charles Hill's family in 1813, Dr. Philip Weedman assisted his distraught black neighbor by journeying to Georgia in search of them. Weedman also helped Hill to build a new vessel after the Patriots destroyed his "good" "cord Boat." Bartolo Solana asserted that he was quite familiar with Philip Edinborough, probably from working with him in his father's large-scale cattle operations.[12] In toil, as in combat, bonds with blacks originating years beforehand and nurtured by social visits solidified and indelibly became etched in white memories.

As in the case of Philip Edinborough, whites found much to admire when they remembered black property. Four miles north of St. Augustine, Lewis Sánchez, a "very industrious" and "honest hardworking man" and an "excellent farmer," was "living in a very comfortable way." The eight to ten acres that he cultivated was "in a flourishing state." His property was "under good fence." Sánchez was "well supplied with farming utensils." He also practiced carpentry, which undoubtedly enhanced his prosperity. Less than a mile north of Sánchez stood the free black settlement of Five Mile. Here, John Howley, Abraham McQueen, and Abraham Rocho, all of them family men, rented "70 or more acres" of "good hammock land" from Don Antonio Yguínez. More than thirty years after the American invasion of 1812, the land was still good enough for Daniel Hurlbert, a white man, to occupy it. The large field already had been cleared when Howley, McQueen, and Rocho took up residence. They proceeded to cut timber "in Mr. Yguinez' Hammock" and "fenced in one large field for the whole of them" and each family "used portions of it." The land was "well fenced" and the black tenant farmers made "very large crops." The tenants also constructed their own buildings, and after their lease expired, by custom, they enjoyed the right to sell them or disassemble and move them. Domingo Cercopoly and Andreas Pacetty described Howley as "honest," "industrious," and "hard-working." McQueen and Howley must have exhibited the same strengths, because a few days before the invasion, Philip Weedman "saw everything snug and strait" on the farm.[13]

Certain personal property items at Five Mile stood out in the minds of white antebellum witnesses. John Howley grew a "large quantity" of pumpkins and possessed "a good Smart pony." Abraham McQueen owned two or three "fine dogs" that were "sharp & fierce." McQueen had trained them "to pursue deer—racoon—or any kind of varment." He also could boast of a "smart bunch of Poultry." Abraham Rocho lived in a "framed house" rather than a log cabin. Eight miles north of Five Mile, on the west side of the North River, Charles Hill rented an old field from James Arnowe. Whites uttered many positive comments about Hill. John Leonardy reminded his listeners that Hill had constructed his own buildings and fences. Mrs. Mary Weedman praised the free colored man because he "always planted & made crops to support his family." Mrs. Weedman added that Hill owned horses and a cart. In fact, "[h]auling with his wagon & horses formed Hill's principal business and support—there were only three engaged in that business at the time." He also harvested fifty to sixty pounds of Sea Island cotton annually and possessed a fine four-oared boat.[14]

Prince Witten's ten-acre field was located about two miles north of Hill, on John Leonardy's land. Witten's buildings and fences especially impressed his white neighbors, who variously estimated their total value at four hundred to eight hundred dollars for the former and two hundred dollars for the latter. Some six miles north of Witten, near Cabbage Swamp, at a place called Sampson along the Pablo Road, Sancho Davis and his son Domingo cultivated government land. Whites also paid homage to their construction skills. Both father and son lived in sawed lumber dwellings. Moreover, the Davises even built their kitchens of the same material. Consequently, each man's structures were remembered as being worth four hundred to seven hundred dollars. Like Charles Hill, Sancho and Domingo Davis grew cotton along with their provisions. However, whereas Hill harvested only 50 to 60 pounds of the crop, the Davises each produced two or three 350-pound bales. Sancho Davis owned seven horses, sixty beef cattle and milk cows, sixty to seventy hogs, and a hundred poultry. Both of the Davis farms, upon which seven to ten acres were cultivated and which were located within a quarter mile of one another, were well fenced.[15]

Northwest of St. Augustine, along the St. Johns River, roughly parallel to the lands that Lewis Sánchez, John Howley, Abraham McQueen, Abraham Rocho, Charles Hill, Prince Witten, Domingo Davis, and Sancho Davis cultivated, other free black farms dotted the countryside. Five to six miles south of New Switzerland, located thirty miles from the Ancient City, Scipio Fleming owned twenty-five acres that the governor had granted to him in 1809. In 1812, corn, sweet potatoes, peas, pumpkins, melons, sugarcane, and "all other kinds of vegetables usually planted in Florida" grew there on six to seven acres surrounded by "good fences." The "great deal of poultry" that Fleming raised stood out in James R. Woodland's recollection. Approximately fifteen miles north of Fleming, Anna Madgigne (Majigeen), "a Free Woman and native of Senegal in Africa," lived in a "large and comfortable house" built of "hewn logs in fashion of a Block House with a roof of shingles." This "good new house" was a "substantial building about thirty feet square & two stories high & well finished" worth four hundred to six hundred dollars. The basement story contained a thousand bushels of corn, along with a large quantity of nails, spikes, and iron tools. Because Madgigne had "a large family with her at that time," the house contained "considerable furniture." Several slave cabins stood on her property, three or four of which were "very good log buildings," valued at one hundred dollars each. As in the case of Fleming, Madgigne's poultry dazzled white witnesses. William Bardin called it the "greatest poultry yard" that he knew of in East Florida. John M. Bowden concurred, swearing that he "did not know another poultry yard in the country equal to that." Madgigne's flock of "large English Ducks" especially impressed Bowden.[16]

Across the St. Johns River from Anna Madgigne, at Laurel Grove, "Free Abraham Hanaham," a farmer and trader, lived in a one-and-a-half- story, good and comfortable frame dwelling house worth $500 to $600. In this structure, Hannahan kept his merchandise, which included corn and salt. He also owned a considerable number of hogs, chickens, geese, and turkeys. In addition, the free man of color was in the process of erecting another structure. The frame and lumber for this large house were valued at $250. Near Madgigne, in the Mandarin settlement, Tony Primus's very modest establishment helped to support his mother and two sisters. By cultivating four acres enclosed by a "good rail fence" on Robert Gilbert Sr.'s land, and by working "as a hired Labourer," Primus managed to eke out a humble but responsible life. Since he owned a complete set of cooper's tools, he may also have followed this trade, or rented the tools to tradesmen. His military service on behalf of the Spaniards, for which he "received very trifling compensation," elicited the sympathy of white witnesses and enhanced his social standing in their eyes.[17] Along this fifteen-mile stretch of the St. Johns, as they were doing in the vicinity of the North River, free blacks were working hard to support themselves and their loved ones in ways that earned whites' respect.

Toby Herreira lived some thirty miles south of St. Augustine, "not far" from Francis Pellicer's Matanzas plantation. Curiously, witnesses made no mention of Herreira's racial status, although his first name suggests that he was a man of color. His farm was much larger than those of Bacchus and Morell—approximately twenty-five acres. Pellicer described the "hard working thrifty old man," who lived in "comfortable circumstances," as "among the early settlers in the country of Matanzas." Since Pellicer would pen his father's cattle "not more than 200 yards" from Herreira's home, he "had abundant opportunity of being in his house and on his farm." Matthew Long also knew Herreira well. Long remembered him as "an industrious man" who "generally made good crops." Herreira typically produced enough provisions to feed his family and to regularly sell corn in town. He also had been accumulating cotton for a couple of years, so he may have had as many as two bales on hand. A generation after the Patriot War, Herreira's land remained so fertile that a white man, Colonel James Williams, still managed to derive good corn yields from the soil.[18]

Despite the fact that whites had provided, in Judge Bronson's opinion, inflated estimates of blacks' cedar harvests, they still made it clear that colored men filled an inferior niche in society, thus further condemning the racial policies of the American regime. That is, according to the testimony of East Florida's respected elders, unlike the region's antebellum North American (Protestant) overlords, the (Catholic) Spaniards had astutely succeeded in harnessing blacks' talents, while at the same time keeping them in their place. White witnesses, although they praised the courage and possessions of free men of color, carefully delineated their admiration within a broader description of blacks who were hard-working, yet poor, and whose property generally was "small." For example, Isaac Bacchus owned a "small house or hut" along with a "little fowl house." Likewise, Scipio Fleming's buildings were "very common" and he grew "such crops as small planters usually plant." At the outbreak of the Patriot War, Abraham Hannahan lived on a small place of his own at Laurel Grove. After the war, in 1817, José Bergallo permitted Hannahan to occupy "a small house of mine" gratis, after U.S. troops had driven the free man of color and "his small family" from their "small one story house" in Fernandina. Toby Herreira occupied a small plantation. John Howley resided on a "small farm" in a "tolerably good small house." Howley's neighbors at Five Mile also were described as living in diminutive circumstances. Whereas in 1812, Abraham McQueen tilled "a few acres," his widow, in 1841, passed her days "on a small lot" in St. Augustine. Abraham Rocho's dwelling featured some furniture, "but not much." Tony Primus slept in "one small Log House." Domingo and Sancho Davis, according to one jaded witness, "had a kind of camp . . . or negro houses, but not any very good buildings." John Morell's abode was small and constructed of clapboards. He traveled to town in a small canoe.[19]

Charles W. Clarke's testimony in the case of Benjamin Wiggins is especially telling in this respect. Clarke lauded Wiggins's prewar peripatetic economic activities, informing the court that the free man of color would annually earn five hundred to six hundred dollars in money or cattle as a stock keeper, in addition to three dollars per diem as a regularly employed "Pilot to those who travelled through the country." When he was home, Wiggins grew provisions to support his wife and three children, who resided with his father-in-law, Philip Edinborough. Consequently, Wiggins "always had money—he always kept it private & took care not to let any body know what he had." During the siege of St. Augustine, the free man of color fought for the Crown. He received extra pay from the government, probably in connection with dangerous cattle-hunting expeditions. Additionally, Wiggins fished and gathered oysters when he was off duty. His industrious wife, "who worked herself," also made an important contribution to the family's maintenance under most trying circumstances. Like his black and white neighbors, the Patriot War "entirely reduced" Wiggins, making him "very poor directly afterwards." Nevertheless, during the 1830s, due to "his own exertions" and "what he has gotten from his fathers Estate," Wiggins was "again getting up in the world." Even if Wiggins had succeeded in rising to his pre–Patriot War standard of living, Clarke admitted that his affluence would have been relative. That is, his circumstances would have been "very good"—"for a person of color."[20]

Clarke's testimony is telling in another aspect. Although Wiggins was his brother-in-law, he makes no mention of this relationship. This is consistent with white testimony in other free black claims. Although whites did acknowledge that they had known free men of color well and dropped hints of friendships with them, they never used the words "friend," "friendship," or "intimate acquaintance." Even relatively poor whites might publicly boast of their friendships with the provincial aristocracy. William Bardin, for example, explained that he had been "intimately" acquainted with the wealthy planter Zephaniah Kingsley. John M. Bowden remembered that he had interacted with Kingsley "in the most friendly manner." Neither inequalities of gender nor social standing restricted admissions of friendship. Philip Weedman, a married man of middling status, swore that he had enjoyed a close friendship with the affluent widowed planter Mrs. Frances Kerr. Ethnicity was no barrier to friendship. The Minorcan Andreas Pacetty noted that he had been very friendly with Weedman. John Leonardy, another Minorcan, when deposing for his neighbor Juan González Montesdioca, who seems to have been a Spaniard, stated that he and González were very good friends. Bardin, Bowden, Weedman, Pacetty, and Leonardy, when serving as witnesses for free men of color, never officially characterized their relationships with blacks in these terms. In the cases of Bardin and Bowden, they did not call themselves friends of Kingsley's African wife when testifying on her behalf. On the other hand, when the free black Tony Primus referred to the four free men of color whom George J. F. Clarke had employed on his Matanzas plantation in 1812, he reported that they were "my friends and acquaintances."[21] These word choices surely reflected antebellum sensibilities, but they also informed federal authorities that under the Spaniards, it had been commonplace for people of color to productively exercise their talents without threatening the racially based social hierarchy.

White witnesses, once again, were subtly protesting the new racial regime under the United States. Similarly, when whites discussed the free black exodus to Cuba in 1821, between the lines of their testimony, they furtively mourned departed comrades-in-arms, along with the passing of the good old days of Catholic rule, when prospects were bright and youth buoyed their spirits. Prince Witten, one of Philip Edinborough's boys, the Matanzas neighbors Isaac Bacchus, George Clarke, and John Morell, former Five Mile residents John Howley and Abraham Rocho, along with the father-son combination of Sancho and Domingo Davis, were among the free blacks who rejected republicanism, opting instead to continue living as subjects of a distant monarch. Florida's loss was Cuba's gain. "[A]lmost all of the free negroes," Domingo Cercopoly wistfully and pointedly recounted in 1845, "went to Cuba." Some of the white witnesses heard news of these exiles after they had departed. Andreas Pacetty and John Leonardy found out that Witten, Howley, and Sancho Davis had died in Cuba. Around 1830, Francis Triay "heard some of the white folks . . . who had been to Havannah" say that Rocho was deceased. Triay also was informed of the deaths of Rocho's wife and son. Esteban Arnow had "heard by several persons" that Clarke had died around 1835. Arnow explained that after Clarke went to Cuba, "I used to enquire of persons coming from there about him." Domingo Cercopoly, on a visit to Cuba in 1827, acquired news of Domingo Davis's passing when he conversed with "many of the free negroes who had left [St. Augustine] previously."[22]

Like white East Floridians, the Patriot War financially ruined free persons of color. Moreover, blacks and whites both endured long waits for compensation from the United States, and when this money finally reached them or their heirs, the sums were disappointing, to say the least. Michael Andreu regretted the fact that the invaders had burned Isaac Bacchus's laboriously obtained cedar. Sophia Fleming and James R. Woodland acknowledged the bonds of suffering that united blacks and whites when they spoke of Scipio Fleming's losses occurring in the same manner as everybody else's had—through the invaders "indiscriminately" plundering everything they encountered. Matthew Long proclaimed the same interracial chains of victimhood when, in the case of Toby Herreira, he launched into a tirade, denouncing the Americans for sending "one detachment after another," which "laid waste the plantations, destroyed the growing crops, and carried away the cattle and horses of the settlers." Then Long turned specifically to Herreira, who had been driven into St. Augustine. Afterward, Long lamented, "he was in a destitute situation." Andreas Pacetty followed suit by describing a pile of goods that the Patriots had taken from the "people of the country" and ruined by burning. "A number of cart loads of these articles or the remnants of them were brought into Town," Pacetty recounted, "& they were recognized by different persons as being therr property but all so injured by fire as to be useless." John Howley's possessions, along with those of other rural free black settlers, were mixed together with whites' charred belongings. John M. Bowden specifically remembered the rebels killing Tony Primus's hogs and stealing his mare. Discovering the "irons" of Abraham Rocho's cart within the vehicle's ashes stood out in Esteban Arnow's memory more than three decades after the Patriot War. When John Leonardy served in a reconnoitering expedition two weeks after the United States evacuated East Florida, he found that Domingo Davis's place had "been laid waste and destroyed" along with whites' farms and plantations.[23]

In addition to vouching for the fact that the Patriot War had united whites and blacks in suffering at the hands of the Americans and their agents, white witnesses distinguished black victimization from that of whites. That is, people of color faced the singular danger of enslavement. This may explain why, in the sixty-six-year-old mind of Francis Triay, one of his exploits thirty-three years earlier had proven to be so indelible. Triay recollected that he and his brother accompanied five other men under the command of Pedro Trope in a government boat sent specifically to rescue George Clarke and his family. Triay stressed that no other Matanzas family was carried to town on this expedition, and that the Clarkes carried nothing away with them. He sadly added that except for himself, all of the boatmen had gone to Havana or died. Edward M. Wanton, the white patriarch of a large mixed-race family, was not as fortunate as Clarke. In 1815, during the unsettled aftermath of the U.S. evacuation, "*a Patriot band,*" part of a pack of plunderers who "continued their incursions into the country long after the withdrawal of the regular forces of the *United States,*" heaped misery upon Wanton, who had already endured "great hardship and suffering" because of his loyalty to Spain. White "*confederate borderers*" of the United States kidnapped and "carried into *Georgia*" his free daughter-in-law and grandchildren, whom Wanton described in 1834 as "a colored woman and her children belonging to his family." Fortunately, "with difficulty," he was able to recover them. Charles Hill was not. A year earlier than Wanton's family tragedy, he lost his wife, two teenaged daughters, and his ten-year-old son "by kidnapping." Hill never saw them again. Philip Weedman did not doubt that they had been taken to Georgia where they surely lost their liberty permanently.[24]

Heart-wrenching losses such as Hill's earned free people of color valuable sympathy from the white community. Moreover, the slow-paced adjudication of the Patriot War claims cases and dissatisfaction with the sums that Washington finally awarded to the victims of American-inspired violence once again made whites and free blacks comrades-in-arms. A survey of successful Patriot War claims cases of 177 whites indicates that the U.S. Treasury Department paid a mean average of 53 percent of what petitioners claimed for the losses that they had suffered in 1812–13. In the seven cases pressed in the names of white patriarchs whose heirs were people of color, the mean average was 51 percent. In fact, Washington made its highest Patriot War payments to two of these patriarchs: John Fraser ($157,146—54 percent of his claim), and Zephaniah Kingsley ($77,322—68 percent of his claim). Regarding the fourteen claims paid to free black claimants, the federal government reimbursed a mean average of only

35.5 percent of the sums that petitioners requested. Approximately 84 percent of whites received compensation at higher rates, and 70 percent garnered more money than free blacks, even though only 60 percent claimed greater sums than the fourteen successful free colored damage suits. Because the lapse of time between the claimants' losses and the commencement of the adjudication of their cases was over twenty years, and the fact that the lawsuits dragged on to at least 1855, federal judges in St. Augustine tacked on interest payments to the sums that they awarded. Unfortunately, in a travesty of justice, the Treasury Department paid no interest to any claimant—free colored or white.[25] In short, the two castes again together fell victim to Washington's meanness.

Advertisements regarding free black claims cases peppered St. Augustine newspapers throughout the antebellum period, thus giving persons of color visibility in a medium that otherwise sought to make them invisible. These printed notices placed African Americans on an equal plane with white claimants, in addition to reminding the community of black achievements during Spanish rule. At a time when Florida strove to humiliate free people of color by stripping them of their wealth, Patriot War settlement money made African Americans more financially secure and more hopeful for the future. Indeed, their vigorous pursuit of their claims demonstrates that free blacks had not acquiesced to the marginal social role that Florida had assigned to them. The federal government awarded $12,468 in the names of fourteen free people of color, and another $262,142 to blacks as heirs to the estates of eight white fathers or husbands. The individual awards ranged from $157,146 to the biracial heirs of the white patriarch John Fraser to $102 for Tony Primus. The mean average settlement given in the names of free black claimants was $983. Black heirs of whites received an average of $33,582, a figure that illustrates the economic potential of these African American elites, a class that Florida's officialdom sought to impoverish.

The fact that free people of color could indeed sue the United States for losses was due to formal diplomacy between two empires. Article IX of the Adams-Onís Treaty mandated that Washington reimburse Spanish subjects for losses caused by invading troops. It did not restrict compensation to whites only. Hence, free black subjects could and did press claims. Moreover, they also served as witnesses in claims cases. This development resulted from diplomacy at the local level that free people of color initiated. Evincing his racism, federal district judge Isaac H. Bronson apologetically explained the circumstances that enable contemporary historians to glimpse black viewpoints regarding the events of the Patriot War:

> In this case [Estate of George J. F. Clarke, Account No. 83,177] it will be observed that two free negroes were examined as witnesses on behalf of

> the claimant. . . . I am not aware of any law or regulation of the United States, in respect to the admission or exclusion of such evidence, on claims against the Government. . . . George J. F. Clarke married a negro woman by whom he had a number of children who are his heirs and devisees and directly interested in this claim. . . . And on that ground as well as for the reason that there was no law against such testimony, they claimed that it should be received. . . . I concluded to . . . let it go up "for so much as it is worth." . . . I think [it] is entitled to some consideration.[26]

Consequently, due to the astute negotiations of Clarke's biracial children, not only did white witnesses prophesy concerning the capacity of African Americans for responsible citizenship, but black voices, too, protested their marginalization under the American flag. It is likely that Clarke's biracial daughter, the widow Mrs. Felicia M. F. Garvin, with the assistance of his quadroon granddaughter, Eliza Garvin, spearheaded this diplomatic initiative.

The Patriot War claim of Mrs. Garvin's deceased white husband, William Garvin, illustrates how whites and people of color, as they had in 1812–13, worked together in an adversarial multiethnic, mixed-gender project vis-à-vis the United States. The government acknowledged her right to administer her spouse's estate. E. B. Gould, a post-1821 white American migrant to East Florida, served as her attorney. The prominent ex-Spanish officials George J. F. Clarke, her father, and Charles W. Clarke, her uncle, testified on her husband's behalf, as did a Minorcan, James Arnowe. William Garvin's acquaintance, Captain Winslow Foster, who in 1812 had commanded a U.S. gunboat that was part of the flotilla that intimidated Fernandina into surrendering to the Patriots, lent his considerable expertise to the case.[27] Working together in courtroom battles undoubtedly stoked an esprit de corps among blacks and whites that reinforced memories of their comradeship in 1812–13, thus enlarging Afro–East Floridian diplomats' room to maneuver in their antebellum negotiations to preserve their freedom.

The robust diplomacy that Felicia M. F. Garvin and her daughter Eliza exercised in furnishing black male ex-Spanish subjects with secular pulpits from which to protest and prophesy demonstrates a linkage between the national women's rights and abolitionist movements of the 1830s and 1840s, and local conditions in East Florida. To be sure, St. Augustine was not isolated from knowledge of these social developments. In the mid-1830s, perhaps 160 "strangers" per winter, most of them from the northeastern states, rented rooms in private residences, boardinghouses, and hotels. By the mid-1850s, this figure had doubled. The visitor industry offered a variety of service-related jobs for blacks and increased the town's cosmopolitan ambience. Some of the northern tourists brought attitudes toward slavery that conflicted with southern values. Through interactions with these northerners, African Americans broadened their horizons. The Ancient City also hosted weekly newspapers throughout the antebellum period that exposed its residents to the wider world.[28] Furthermore, due to memories of the region's Spanish past, during which free people of color and women enjoyed higher statuses than under United States rule, antebellum reformism meshed well with the historical experiences of these two groups. That is, history, as well as the spirit of the times certainly emboldened some free black and female witnesses in the Patriot War claims cases.

Several women, for example, recounted their assertiveness during the conflict of 1812–13, contrasting their righteous behavior with the vacillation, cowardice, and immorality of many of their male counterparts. Margaret Starrat recalled that John B. Christopher decided to join the Patriots, as did most of the other men in the vicinity, claiming that they did so to protect their property. Starrat, however, proclaimed that she had remained "a true Loyalist." Other women also trumpeted their fidelity to the Crown. In 1841, the still-seething Cynthia Sweeney assured the court that "she never belonged to any party of Robbers." When the U.S. instigator of the Patriot War, George Mathews, appeared at Susan Cashen's Amelia Island plantation in order to recruit her husband, she wrote, "I could not restrain my indignation at so gross an insult . . . rather would I see my husband stand & be shot at than he should turn traitor to the Country he got his bread in." Mrs. Frances Kerr was of the same ilk. Mrs. Ann Maria Hernández described the Tomoka planter as "fearless." Sarah B. McDonnell applied the same characterization to Lucy Fitzgerald. As previously mentioned, she remembered how Joseph Crews, Fitzgerald's overseer, had hidden himself "behind a stack of fodder" in order to elude the Patriots. His employer, even though the invaders frequently abused her, remained on the plantation "longer than it was thought prudent," while Crews fled to Georgia. McDonnell added that on one occasion, she herself had successfully prevented Gilbert Mann, "a noted Patriot & plunderer," from wresting her brother's double-barreled gun from her hands. Maria Hogans testified that Fitzgerald's encounter with Mann had not been so fortunate. Despite quarreling with him and making "a great Effort to save" her favorite horse, the Patriots pressed the animal into their service. Elsewhere, Mrs. Hernández credited herself with saving Robert McHardy's life by shaming her former overseer, who led a Patriot party that was threatening to kill him.[29]

Free black witnesses likewise asserted themselves during their testimony in the Patriot War claims cases, thus prophesying before federal officials, who duly recorded in writing their subtle cries for justice. Simon Forrester, a black East Florida native who was about sixty years of age in 1841, used his opportunity to call attention to his energy, initiative, and determination to be free. Forrester explained that he had purchased his liberty from John Forrester before the 1821 change of flags, more than a quarter of a century previously. By the time that he offered his testimony, it was increasingly difficult for the enslaved to obtain their manumission. Tony Primus, nearly fifty years old, emphasized that he had been born free in St. Augustine. Then, he spoke of black courage, reminding his audience of how the colored urban militia had saved the Ancient City from starvation. "[A] party of us," Primus intoned, "(all coloured people for no whites would go) went out to get cattle. . . . We were at the time in the service of the Spanish Government, under the command of Prince a blackman." In the 1840s, Florida would not think of sending black military units into battle. Primus further emphasized black bravery and leadership by noting that while he was cutting lumber "on wages" for George J. F. Clarke with thirteen other hands near Julington Creek, some twenty miles above antebellum Jacksonville, two white men first informed him of the American invasion. They warned him that "perhaps if [the invaders] caught me they would sell me for a slave and advised me to come in." Then, Primus attested to black wisdom. William Garvin, the white supervisor of the lumberjacks, refused to heed the admonition. When the lumbermen heard gunshots in the distance, however, Primus recollected how Garvin "could not keep us any longer."[30]

The free man of color Antonio Florencio echoed Primus's convictions. Florencio likewise alluded to the policies of a royalist regime that granted its black subjects greater freedom to develop and exercise their talents than the republican government that replaced it. In his testimony, he stressed the integrative aspects of his Patriot War experience, at the same time that he vouched for blacks' capacity for leadership. Florencio recounted how he "& other Spanish soldiers used to go out into the Country during the war to get cattle & bring them in for the troops, & people in the city." "The parties that went out," he continued, "were usually commanded by Prince Whilton, and Tony Doctor, but sometimes a white sergeant went with us." Florencio also called antebellum whites to acknowledge the bonds of suffering that they had shared with black fellow property owners by describing a bold and dangerous expedition in which he participated while the Patriots were besieging St. Augustine: "a party of 30 or 40 of us . . . went out into the Country up the North River, & went to Weedmans place & Princes place. Prince himself was one of the party, we found his place burned & destroyed, & all the places about in that part of the country had been burned. Went to Carlos Hills place & found that his house & property had been burned & destroyed also—we were after cattle at that time & got 34 I think. They belonged to various persons—Huertas, Solana & others."[31] Florencio was recollecting how whites like Weedman, Huertas, and Solana, along with men of color like Witten and Hill, still mourned their hard-earned sources of livelihood that had vanished in the chaos of the American invasion of 1812–13.

In addition to enabling free black veterans to publicly commemorate their hunger for liberty, civic responsibility, valor, suffering at the hands of the United States, and wartime/postbellum bonds with whites, some witnesses of color laid claims to pioneer status. Like numerous other elders in the region, Charles Hill had "suffered the loss of every thing by the Americans and Patriots in 1812 and 1813." Moreover, he had endured a misfortune much more poignant than the destruction of material goods. "[M]y wife and children," Hill stated in agony, "were stolen from me." A man vigorous and resourceful enough to buy his own freedom, Hill's residency in East Florida stretched back to the first Spanish period, which placed him in the company of esteemed white families such as the Solanas and Sánchezes. "I have lived in Florida near Ninety years," Hill attested in 1848. "I was born in the West Indies, and came over a man grown previous to the British occupancy." The "decrepit and blind" elderly man of color then addressed the issue of his character. "I have always endeavored to maintain an honest and good report," he proudly reflected, "and I believe have succeeded to acquire the good will and confidence of all who have ever known me." Tony Proctor, a prominent free black man, vouched for him, assuring Judge Isaac Bronson that Hill was "an old man of truth."[32] Once again, free blacks, a segment of society which American officials wished to banish into Florida's sea of enslaved laborers, had lionized and humanized themselves.

Indeed, Proctor, a skilled linguist and diplomat, who, like Hill, was a nonagenarian in 1841, had attained the status of Florida's elder statesman. He had lived in East Florida since British times. As a slave, he served as an interpreter for Panton, Leslie & Company, as well as for Forbes & Company, firms active in maintaining peace with the Seminoles through trade. Proctor added that the Spanish governor frequently had employed him as "his principal interpreter." During the Patriot War, Proctor apparently spied for the Spaniards. He recounted how the Patriots had pressed him into their service as a guide when they were hunting for cattle to feed the U.S. regulars. Proctor probably had been purposely captured and then escaped, for elsewhere he reported how careful he and Scipio Fleming had been to avoid the Patriot camp when they lost a horse while they were gathering beeves for Spain. Ever the astute diplomat, Proctor was modest and cryptic when he explained how he had obtained his freedom in 1812. His enslavement, he vaguely deposed, ended due to his "good conduct and services in behalf of the Spanish Government in East Florida." The Minorcan Esteban Arnow, who had known Proctor since he had been a bondsman of Panton, Leslie & Company, filled in the blanks: "[Proctor] was employed by the Spanish Governor to go and negociate with the Indians and act against the Patriots in 1812. He was successful in that mission and it was principally for that he was emancipated."[33]

Subsequent to his liberation, Proctor did not rest on his laurels. Arnow, accurately recording historical events while at the same time exhibiting sensitivity to East Florida's racial milieu in 1841, went on to describe Proctor's heroism: "[Proctor, along with] 25 other negroes put under his command by the Governor for [gathering cattle]—they were all armed and mounted—and the orders to them by the Governor were not to attack the whites but to defend themselves if attacked—[Proctor] went out very frequently on excursions after cattle with this Company." Unlike the favorable attitude that he exhibited toward white female witnesses, Judge Isaac Bronson intrinsically questioned the credibility of free persons of color. Arnow staked his reputation upon Proctor's veracity, but once again, he couched his confidence according to the racist tenets of his time, swearing that the black diplomat "has always been considered a very honest and worthy man—as good as any negro—and I believe him under oath as I would any negro living." Indeed, the United States considered Proctor's skills so crucial that its officials employed him as a diplomat after they took charge of Florida. Moreover, since knowledgeable white witnesses attributed the defeat of the American invaders of 1812–13 to the Hispano-Afro-Seminole alliance and Prince Witten's ambush at Twelve Mile Swamp, it is apparent that despite American Florida's draconian statutes aimed at its free black population, this community of color continued to retain the gratitude of East Florida's white old inhabitants in antebellum times.[34] As folk diplomats negotiating their freedom in a slave society, black Patriot War veterans hoped to capitalize upon these popular historical traditions.

Since the enslaved were not eligible to make damage claims against the United States, unlike free people of color, they could not offer direct testimony of their version of the Patriot War in court. We do have evidence, however, that whites sometimes consulted slaves for information pertinent to claims cases. In 1835, for example, Joseph M. Hernández sent his "servant Philip" to summon one of John Bunch's former drivers, a bondsman named Bob, to provide details about Bunch's losses in 1812–13. Another witness in the Bunch case, Philip Weedman, also admitted to making inquiries to slaves regarding the number of times that the Patriots had visited the claimant's Tomoka plantation.[35] Moreover, other white testimony in the case that describes slaves' movements, diet, and survival skills during the enemy occupation surely originated in conversations with Bunch's bond persons. Similar evidence in other cases makes it clear that a portion of the information in the Patriot War claims does indirectly reflect slave testimony. Even through the filter of whites' narratives, the strategies of enslaved folk diplomats manifest themselves.

The Bunch case illustrates several important aspects of this folk diplomacy. One of the damages for which the Bunch estate sued the United States was "the injury done to the habits of his slaves by being obliged to withdraw them from their usual or regular labor and discipline." Prior to the Patriot War, on his plantation situated forty-six miles south of St. Augustine on Tomoka Creek, Bunch's "negroes," who labored "under good management and discipline," produced as much as sixty to sixty-five bales of cotton annually. Francis Pellicer characterized them as "intelligent negroes" who were "orderly and well behaved . . . obedient and good to work." They were, Pellicer continued, "contented on the Plantation and happy there doing all that was required of them." Mrs. Mary Weedman remembered that all of the slaves on the Tomoka plantations were "quiet orderly well behaved negroes—never heard any complaint of any of them—and those of Mr. Bunch's were as good as the best of them." Likewise, Mrs. Mary Douglass Dummet recalled that Bunch's workers, who had been brought to East Florida from the Bahamas, were "tractable industrious & maneageable," in addition to being "very intelligent negroes rather more so than usual and not timid or easily alarm[ed]." They "worked well," Mrs. Ann Maria Hernández opined. Bunch's neighbors considered them to be "an excellent gang."[36]

Modern scholarship, interestingly enough, adds a certain credence to this testimony. In Spanish East Florida, planters utilized the task system, and permitted their bondsmen to raise or gather their own provisions. Coupled with Spanish law and Roman Catholicism, the province's enslaved benefited from an environment that, as Jane Landers explained, "tolerated slave mobility, free market and feast days, an internal slave economy, and permitted the slaves relatively free cultural expression." Moreover, bond persons "lived in fairly durable families and developed extensive and long-term networks of kin, shipmates, and friends across plantations and in the city." Unfortunately, this idyllic scenario suddenly unraveled. The American invasion, Bunch's witnesses contended, corrupted the slaves. Matthew Long estimated that "Negro property was reduced one half in value by the Revolution of 1812 and 1813." Francis Pellicer echoed this assessment. Because the fighting left "nobody to make the negroes work," Philip Weedman (an experienced overseer) expounded, they were "not under the control of anybody—they did as they pleased." Weedman stressed that "[y]ou can't manage a gang of negroes without an overseer—they will do what they please." Pellicer, another overseer, who had "been accustomed to negroes all the days of his life," hammered home Weedman's point. "[I]t is the nature of the negro, when an opportunity offers," Pellicer intoned, "to avoid work they are naturally lazy, and unless overseers are with them all the time they will not work."[37]

Thus, Pellicer concluded, because the invasion resulted in a dearth of overseers due to the fact that they all were bearing arms, John Bunch, a sexagenarian plagued by rheumatism that often confined him to bed, saw his slaves choose "rather to be idle." Paradoxically, however, as witnesses toiled to convince the court of the veracity of Bunch's claim for compensation due to the Patriot War's corrosive effect on his slaves, their commentary on blacks' innate slothfulness rang hollow. Instead, what emerges is a portrait of enslaved East Floridians who were prudent, resourceful, and freedom loving. Moreover, this white testimony affords us a glimpse of slaves' folk diplomacy. In the same breath by which Pellicer tarred Bunch's slaves as idlers, he added that they were also afraid of the Patriots, "which interfered with their labours." "Certainly the Negroes had a great horror of the Patriots," Weedman admitted, "and [they] were afraid of being carried into Georgia." Pellicer added that "all the overseers in the province" could not have kept the slaves tilling the soil, because if they had "attended regularly" to fieldwork, they would have been captured. Indeed, Pellicer continued, the slaves had a reason to be alarmed. Their uneasiness was not "fictitious." The U.S. regulars and the Patriots "did 'hunt' negroes for the purpose of taking them off to sell," and Bunch's bond persons did not know at "what moment they might be pounced upon." To make matters worse, because there was no work for slaves in besieged St. Augustine, and it was very expensive to support them there, Bunch decided to leave his blacks "in the Country to shift for themselves."[38] White witnesses had exposed the fiction of paternalism.

These same witnesses also eroded the notion that blacks would not work unless whites coerced them. Bunch's slaves surely understood the difference between enslavement in Georgia and East Florida. Hence, when Bunch issued a "general instruction" to the slaves "to keep out of the way of the Patriots," the interests of the master and his bond persons meshed. Accordingly, the "negroes sought refuge from their fears in the swamps and hammocks." Because they found themselves "unprotected by any one" and with no whites to "superintend" them, the vaunted intelligence of Bunch's laborers entered the historical record. "Bunch's as well as the other negroes of the [Tomoka] settlement well knew" that the Patriots sought "young and active" slaves to sell in Georgia, not "old and infirm ones." Therefore, the latter remained on Bunch's and neighboring plantations. Those left behind formed a communication network that would keep the vulnerable youths apprised of conditions in the settlement. The taskable hands then took Bunch's maneuverable small boats across Tomoka Creek to Gabriel W. Perpall's Mount Oswald plantation, a half mile away. From there, they journeyed two miles south by crossing the "three quarters of a mile wide" Halifax River, and took refuge on "a beach or slip of Sand covered with Hammock . . . where they remained & Subsisted upon fish & Counti [root] wildfowl & Deer." Most of the time, the black refugees stayed "upon the Beach," but occasionally, they "came over and worked a little in the fields." At this point of his testimony,

Matthew Long revealed his insightful understanding of black "laziness": "The negroes were not compelled to work in 1812—they will not work unless compelled; if left to themselves—they will do a little work but very trifling. Bunch's negroes would not work the cotton field unless forced to do so—they might have come over and worked the corn field a little with a view to their own advantage." Philip Weedman also realized that the slaves would not work voluntarily if "there was no prospect of reaping a benefit from their labors."[39] Once again, whether they realized it or not, whites were indicting slavery.

The survival saga of John Bunch's slaves surely struck a sensitive chord with Matthew Long and Francis Pellicer. In 1812, Long resided at Matanzas, twenty miles north of Bunch. Pellicer, aged twenty-four, and his brother James, seventeen, who lived three or four miles away, were Long's closest neighbors. George Long, Matthew's father, was a rancher, planter, and innkeeper who enjoyed "prosperous circumstances," the blessings of a "large family," contentment, and moderate independence. Then, in 1812, "the Invader came, drove him from his home, pillaged his property—devastated his farm, burnt his houses—imprisoned his *sons.*" The Patriots impelled the elder Long to cross the Matanzas River to Little Bar Island, where he "built a temporary cabin." "*[L]iterally heart broken,*" the patriarch died in the late summer or autumn of 1812, due to "the exposure of his situation and grief for the Loss and total destruction of all his property." As of 1834, his family still lived "in *Poverty.*" His embittered son Matthew railed that the United States "*have it not in their Treasury*" just compensation "for a father's death, or for a life of poverty and blasted prosperity." James Pellicer, his younger siblings, mother, and two slaves also knew something about fleeing to an island to escape the Patriots. For two months they "suffered much" on an Anastasia Island beach near the protective guns of Fort Matanzas, living in tents, with no possessions except for some bedding and "a pot to cook in."[40] Furthermore, numerous other white witnesses had been forced to run from the Patriots and avoid them by hiding in swamps and hammocks. In fact, the claims cases are replete with such examples.

Whites also spent a great deal of time explaining the choices that they made during the Patriot War. Some steadfastly maintained their loyalty to the crown. These "Royalists" frequently suffered close confinement or restricted movement, property destruction, banishment, unpaid labor as royal troops, death threats, crippling wounds, and death itself, as a consequence of their fidelity. A few East Floridians willingly joined the Patriots. More required little persuasion when faced with exile, imprisonment, and the confiscation of their hard-earned assets, on the one hand, or five-hundred-acre land bounties and the promise of a quick and inevitable toppling of the Spanish regime due to the Patriots being backed by the powerful United States military fighting under orders of the president in Washington, on the other. Numerous men, after being marched to enemy camps "in strings" or in files at the points of bayonets, saw themselves with no recourse but to join the "rebellion." Once they joined, a certain portion of the conscripts "made a frolick of it." Many of the "forced" Patriots, however, "escaped" as soon as they perceived a "fair chance" to do so. Often, these white fugitives ended up as desperately poor refugees, or they opted to "skulk about" swamps, forests, and hammocks to avoid recapture. The invaders particularly targeted the Tories or their descendants who had fled to East Florida at the time of the American Revolution. Fear of undergoing the same calamities as they had under the U.S. Patriots of an earlier generation induced a segment of this populace to jump aboard the latter-day Patriot bandwagon. In short, the loyalty or disloyalty of a substantial number of settlers, including a few who had risen high in the Patriot ranks, was hazy, prompting Dr. James Hall to remark, "How far persons can be rebels & subjects at the same time [I leave] to the casuists to determine." Tomoka's slaves, including those belonging to Bunch, also faced choices, particularly in the unsettled aftermath of the American retreat, when Patriot bands and other invaders continued to plunder East Florida.[41]

Following the lead of previous slaves who had taken advantage of frontier geopolitics in order to negotiate their freedom, some Tomoka bondsmen bore arms for their sovereign. Philip Weedman remembered how, in 1812, the Patriots who foraged in the region always feared that the Spaniards "would send out their Black Troops to intercept and cut them off from the Camp before St. Augustine." Indeed, fear of Afro-Spanish troops radiated to Georgia and Washington. American officials recoiled at the real possibility that the presence of soldiers of color might turn East Florida into "the refuge of fugitive slaves [from the United States] and from thence emissaries . . . will be detached to bring about the revolt of the black population of the United States." In expeditions against small Patriot detachments along the St. Johns River, Governor Sebastián Kindelán not only sent out black soldiers, but he authorized them to arm Patriots' slaves. In July 1817, six of Joseph M. Hernández's bondsmen carried guns, along with those of the Tomoka area planters, who "had gathered and armed many of their slaves," in order to fight, along with white and free black units, a force that the anti-Spanish rebel Gregor MacGregor had dispatched from Amelia Island after seizing Fernandina. Most of MacGregor's soldiers were whites from Georgia and South Carolina. The Spaniards' multiracial troops engaged the enemy at Thomas Addison's plantation along Tomoka Creek, some five miles south of John Bunch's estate. They killed ten of MacGregor's men in an ambush and wounded others. The only royalist casualty suffered a minor wound. The slave-soldiers, under the command of a black officer, were to escort the white prisoners to St. Augustine by land. Thus, "a handful of Spanish troops aided by local planters inflicted a serious defeat on the insurgents."[42]

White memories of armed slaves loyally defending their plantations in the rocky aftermath of the U.S. evacuation of East Florida were alive and well in antebellum times. Joseph M. Hernández, who served as a general during the Second Seminole War, recounted how in 1814 and 1815, he had "applied to the Governor for arms and ammunition, and placed his slaves under arms, for the purpose of repelling aggression which was continually expected." Matthew Long testified that on the Samuel Williams estate, about fifteen miles south of Bunch, "Such was the confidence of their owners in them that they several times during the troubles armed [slaves] for their own defence." While Long stressed the bondsmen's loyalty, the phrase "for their own defence" indicates the slaves' true motivation. Elsewhere, Francis Pellicer recalled how Hernández, with government assistance, "had armed his Negroes—they had arms and ammunition at command, to enable them to protect themselves against marauders."[43] As in 1812, they did not wish to be separated from their families by being carried off to Georgia. Furthermore, the opportunity to kill white oppressors, as well as to reap psychological and material benefits associated with military service, also would have impelled them to risk their lives.

In 1814, these same slaves who Long had described as "faithful & obedient" could be coaxed to produce only five bales of cotton. A year later, "with hard fighting," the recalcitrant laborers packed fifteen bales, a quantity far below the fifty-eight that they had cultivated before the Patriot War. Indeed, they drove their exasperated mistress, Samuel Williams's widow, to "finally abandon" her plantation, citing the "permanent injury & depreciation in the value" of her labor force. She would later marry Joseph M. Hernández, who had also armed his slaves. On the Bunch plantation, a similar situation prevailed. As Bunch's overseer, Francis Pellicer "found it difficult with constant attention to [the slaves], and some severity—to make them make any thing of a crop." Pellicer complained that "whoever undertook the management of Slaves after the Revolution, took in hand a severe job; the habits of the slaves were greatly changed for the worse."[44] By fending for themselves and defending themselves, the Tomoka slaves had tasted freedom. They had seen terrified masters behave in cowardly fashions.[45] They had gained self-confidence. Therefore, these enslaved men and women were no longer so tractable. Moreover, the chaos of unsettled times provided an atmosphere for successful resistance. So, too, did a diplomatic revolution.

In the first half of the eighteenth century, the slaves of Anglo-Americans, acting as folk diplomats, had played off Spain against England in order to gain freedom in East Florida, a freedom intimately linked to Catholicism and security concerns. When the United States gained its independence, it took England's place as the enemy of black liberty, and Spanish East Florida continued to serve as a sanctuary for fugitive slaves from the north. During the War of 1812, however, the British emerged as the liberator of American, as well as Spanish, bond persons, to whom they offered, in a secularized cooption of the region's historical traditions, freedom in return for military service. Matthew Long remembered how Captain George Woodbine "had sent messages through the Indians to the negroes who were anxious to accept the invitation so conveyed to them." That is, "[t]he negroes were promised freedom and protection by the English Government if the[y] would go to Woodbine." Because Woodbine "was endeavoring to seduce the negroes from their fidelity to their owners," according to Dr. Philip Weedman, planters "humoured their slaves and suffered them to do very much as they pleased least on the slightest provocation they should . . . fly to the Indians and to Woodbine." Once more, slaves were playing off the British against the Spaniards. Despite masters' indulgences, Weedman estimated that in 1815, a hundred slaves deserted the plantations south of St. Augustine. Francis Pellicer placed the number of those "induced" to flee by the "promises of liberty" made by the "Indian negroes" whom Woodbine sent to infiltrate the southern plantations at 114.[46]

In the future, as Britain moved toward abolition, and ultimately ended slavery in its empire, its colony in the Bahamas would become the preferred destination of runaways from Florida. Slaves who perceived that bondage under the Spaniards was better than enslavement in Georgia still had made their dissatisfaction with any kind of bondage known to their owners. When the Spanish flag was lowered over East Florida for the last time in 1821, life with the Seminoles or on the British islands off the peninsula's coast would become even more attractive to the region's slaves. During the hearings connected to the Patriot War claims cases, whites and blacks had attested to the talents of people of color, as well as to their deep desire for liberty. Consciously and inadvertently, they had acted as prophets who protested the injustice of American Florida's racial policies, called on the regime to reform, and predicted the outcome if their jeremiads went unheeded. Their prophecies materialized in the late 1830s and the early 1840s in the person of the enslaved Andrew Gué, who, driven by "one of the great dynamics of human history," the "human quest for freedom,"[47] emerged as a resurrected Prince Witten. Gué's message would reverberate in Washington and London—the very seats of Anglophone empires. Following the diplomatic folk traditions of his eighteenth-century forebears, he would take advantage of a new sanctuary policy, and he would use the sea as his pathway to freedom.

6
The Notorious Andrew Gué

On 25 July 1843, Andrew Gué, William Hernández, Joe Williams, Robert Williams, James Ashe, Gasper Mickler, and Harvey (alias Henry) Fontané threw St. Augustine "into a state of unusual excitement." Four of these slaves had served aboard the U.S. schooner *Walter M,* then anchored in port. The conspirators boarded the vessel and seized a compass, a spyglass, "seven stand of muskets," and victuals. Then, on one of the schooner's small boats, they rowed to nearby Fish's Island. The bondsmen had planned their mission well. Requiring a vessel capable of an ocean voyage, they transferred their navigation instruments, weapons, and provisions to the harbor pilots' "large whale boat," which just had been repaired. Since one of the fugitives hailed from the Bahamas, that was their presumed sanctuary.[1] Gué and his comrades acted as folk diplomats steeped in history. They would strain relations between the United States and Great Britain, ultimately prodding white elites to promote their agenda and to disseminate their history.

It would take a mixture of skill, daring, persistence, and luck to attain freedom in the Bahamas. Fergus Bordewich's description of a contemporary whale boat illustrates the conditions under which the runaways labored. These vessels were small, perhaps twenty-five feet in length, quite seaworthy, and equipped with "fore and main spritsails." When the wind was not blowing, they could be rowed. But, they provided no protection from the sun, saltwater, and rain. Sleeping was difficult. Wet clothing, thirst, and "claustrophobic" conditions caused "extreme" discomfort. Moreover, the mariners had to keep a constant watch for captors eager to administer "sure and swift punishment." At times, they had to land in order to dry their clothes, cook, and gather water.[2]

Between 25 July and 7 August 1843, the fugitives from St. Augustine reached Key Biscayne, near modern Miami. Under favorable weather conditions, they could have made Nassau after a full day and night of sailing. For some reason, they failed in their attempt to cross the Gulf Stream. Consequently, they decided to return to familiar territory in order to gather supplies for another attempt. "Having suffered much for want of water," they came ashore at North Beach, ten miles from St. Augustine, where at John Seguí's place, they filled a "three gallon jug" with water and gathered a "quantity of Water Melons." Then, they set sail again. Because Seguí was a "simple man" and alone when the fugitives approached him, he dared not challenge them. The Minorcan farmer did send word to town of the appearance of Gué and his comrades. Immediately, two search parties were dispatched, one by land and the other by sea. Four days later, the land party spotted the runaways in the Tomoka region, on the beach opposite Bulow Plantation, in the vicinity of modern-day Daytona Beach. When they discerned their pursuers' approach, the bondsmen, trapped by high surf, saw themselves forced to carry their pilot boat for a distance of 150 yards to Bulow Creek. From here they hurried down the Halifax River, eluding their pursuers.[3]

By 1 September 1843, the fugitives were back on Key Biscayne, after a series of unsuccessful supply raids on settlers along the Miami River. In 1804, the Spaniard Pedro Fornills had settled Key Biscayne with several St. Augustine slaves, but he abandoned his 175-acre land grant the next year, leaving behind some blacks who had vanished into a neighboring swamp. For the next twenty years, according to Marvin Dunn, "escaped slaves from Georgia and other southern states" used the island, which "stands nearer to . . . the Gulf Stream, than any other piece of land," as a way station to Andros Island. More than a hundred slaves and Indians searched for food on Key Biscayne in 1821, while they waited for boats to take them to the Bahamas. Moreover, Cape Florida, on the island's southern tip, was a well-known source of fresh water.[4] Thus, it was no accident that Andrew Gué and company found themselves seeking sustenance along the shores of Biscayne Bay.

Between 18 and 22 September, desperately in need of provisions, they entered the dwelling of John Henry Geireen, a German immigrant who had left his wife behind in New York. Here they gathered pork, biscuit, flour, clothing, and a rifle. Only Geireen's daughter, Anna, about six years of age, was at home. During the intrusion, one of the slaves placed his hands over the girl's mouth to prevent her from screaming. When they departed, Anna rushed to her father, who was fishing nearby with her brother. Geireen grabbed his rifle and chased the fugitives. Moments later, at about 5:30 P.M., Geireen's children heard two shots, followed by a series of agonizing cries from their father. In thirty minutes, he died. After a terrifying night in hiding, the children found Geireen's body, which bore two six-inch wounds on the left side of the chest and neck. No other people lived on the island, but a wrecker happened upon the traumatized youngsters late in the day.[5] Now, the St. Augustine fugitives' dash for freedom would become even more desperate.

Gué and his companions continued to be daring and elusive foes of the United States. Their boat was spotted leaving Key Biscayne after Geireen's death, but several days later, they returned to the island's thick mangrove swamps. On 3 October 1843, news of their whereabouts reached Key West. The *Walter M* left the next day for Key Biscayne with a force of twenty soldiers and orders to capture the blacks dead or alive. The revenue cutter *Nautilus* and the U.S. schooner *Flirt* joined the chase. General William Worth conducted the operations. He also made arrangements with the Seminoles to turn the fugitives over to him should they encounter them. After a fruitless search of the island on 6 October, the soldiers, with reinforcements, spent the next week in boats scouring the banks of the Miami River and sixty to seventy miles of some old Indian hunting grounds, again to no avail. Returning to the Miami settlements, they discovered that Gué and his men already had sailed up and down the river. During their travels, the Gué gang had added another St. Augustine slave to their number—Anson Murphy, as well as an additional black man. These two, however, do not seem to have sailed on to Nassau. The fearful settlers excused their refusal to confront Gué, pleading that they were "not strong enough" to do so.[6]

Because of five or six days of good weather, Worth surmised that Gué had outfoxed him. Indeed, Nassau's *Royal Gazette* reported that on 10 October 1843, the *Springbird,* a schooner returning from a "wrecking or droghing voyage," carried "seven persons" from a "whale boat" that had "fallen in with" the Bahamian vessel. Upon reaching their long-cherished sanctuary, Gué and his companions, in a statement pregnant with meaning, represented "themselves to be the slaves of a Mr. William Williams, of St. Augustine, E. F."[7] This simple assertion unlocks the door to their history.

As the scholar Mark M. Smith pointed out, however, unlocking the history of "ostensibly silent and inarticulate" men necessitates "hard logic, historical reasoning, and a good deal of speculation." A list of slaves belonging to the Samuel Williams estate at Tomoka, dated 1814, contains a family composed of the biracial John, his wife Hester, and their son Andrew, aged two months. According to a St. Augustine newspaper, this matches Andrew Gué's approximate age. The same list includes William, a son of the slaves Friday and Lucy. Also enumerated are Bob, the son of Boatswain and Nancy, along with Harry, the son of Long John and Betty. Perhaps they were the William Hernández, Robert Williams, and Henry Fontané who were Gué's comrades in 1843. Joe Williams obviously belonged to the Williams family. The connection of James Ashe and Gasper Mickler to this family is unclear, but Ashe's wife was a Mickler bondswoman. Under the Spaniards, East Florida's black militiamen typically were tied to one another by blood, marriage, and baptism.[8] By raiding a federal vessel, Gué's men operated as a military unit exhibiting elements of Spanish-era kinship patterns.

Therefore, by claiming to be Williams's slaves, Gué and his comrades acknowledged their community ties both to one another and to blacks in the Bahamas. During the American Revolution's aftermath, Loyalists who mainly had evacuated the mainland via St. Augustine transported some four thousand slaves to uninhabited islands, thereby establishing outposts of African American culture throughout the British possession. The Williams family had held bond persons in the archipelago—slaves who in 1843 were free and who thus would sympathize with other Williams slaves more personally. Kinship ties had forged the fugitives to one another, steeling them for a perilous saltwater quest for liberty. Now they invoked these ties, which Florida slaveholders had severed, in order to secure their still-precarious freedom in a new land. They understood (using Alan Cobley's general analysis), the fundamental importance of kinship in "small, 'people-sized' communities in the Caribbean, where everyday life is negotiated through a series of deeply imbedded local networks."[9]

Moreover, the fugitives' timing proved crucial. On 9 August 1842, Washington, after much difficulty and through President John Tyler's dogged informal negotiations, signed the Webster-Ashburton Treaty, which settled a simmering border controversy with Canada that had threatened to erupt into war. Moreover, the agreement had endowed Anglo-American relations with a much more positive tenor, holding out the happy prospect of future cooperation between the two nations. Since British animosity constituted the top threat to U.S. security, this promising state of affairs was no mean accomplishment. In 1843, London lawmakers passed the enabling act that put into effect Article 10 of the treaty. This bill troubled abolitionists on opposite Atlantic shores since it did not specifically exclude slaves from extradition to the United States on criminal charges. Because Andrew Gué's escape took place on the heels of this enabling act, it garnered anxious international scrutiny. Abolitionists viewed it as a "test case." The Reverend J. H. Hinton of the British and Foreign Anti-Slavery Society wrote to the Earl of Aberdeen, Her Majesty's foreign secretary, that "the eyes of nations . . . the eyes of the world . . . will be fixed on the proceedings which are taken in respect to [the case of the seven Florida fugitives]."[10]

The Gué party had followed a long-standing tradition of East Florida folk diplomacy, a strategy that persons of African descent in many locales likewise had utilized and in the future would employ in negotiating their freedom. Emulating the seventeenth- and eighteenth-century black fugitives from Carolina who had forced Spain's sovereign to make a decision regarding religious sanctuary, these seven St. Augustinians of color harnessed geopolitical rivalries to impel white elites to speak out on their behalf. Gué's men, in Steven Hahn's words, had "constituted themselves as political actors in a society that tried to refuse them that part."[11]

On 13 November, the Grand Jury of the Counties of Monroe and Dade indicted the seven fugitives, as well as Anson Murphy, for robbery and murder. A week later, the United States requested that the British government order a warrant to be issued for their arrest, and "upon the exhibition to the proper British Colonial authorities . . . of such evidence as may be deemed sufficient under the provisions of the 10 article of the Treaty of Washington," to deliver the prisoners to Joseph B. Browne, the U.S. marshal from Key West. The British minister in Washington, Henry S. Fox, acceded to this request. Fox sent instructions to the governor of the Bahamas, Sir Francis Cockburn, in duplicate packets, one of which Marshal Browne received at Key West on 17 December. The local federal judge and the district attorney advised Browne that in addition to Fox's instructions, certified copies of the grand jury's indictments, along with a person who could identify Gué and his comrades, would constitute sufficient evidence for the extradition. Browne sailed for Nassau the following day, arriving there on Christmas Eve. The lawman had a private axe to grind, which made the fulfillment of his official duties more urgent in his mind. Seven months previously, in May 1843, Coleman Royal, one of his own slaves, with a party of four men and a woman, stole the pilot boat *Mary Neavis* from Key West and sailed to Andros Island with a "considerable amount of property in money and goods" of Browne's. They subsequently were declared free in Nassau.[12]

Governor Cockburn received a copy of Fox's instructions on 10 December. Cockburn was "particularly careful" that "its contents should not transpire, as had its purport been known it might have induced to such of the Fugitives as were at the time in Nassau quitting the place." He well understood the power of local black opinion regarding the liberation of U.S. runaways. Despite his precaution, he could not stifle the black maritime communication network. A vessel arriving at nearby Harbour Island from Key West already had reported that the U.S. schooner *Nautilus* was waiting at the latter port to transport Browne to Nassau. Consequently, Cockburn suspected that "as soon as the 'Nautilus' was seen off the few of [the fugitives] who might previously have been here, were on their way to quit the Island." The plight of Andrew Gué and company had generated sizable support in Nassau. The black community pressured British authorities to hold firm in their policy of liberation. Additionally, the colonial capital's Friendly Society, "composed of emancipated Negroes," hired an attorney on Gué's behalf. Browne responded by employing his own barrister.[13]

Meanwhile, Andrew Gué's white supporters also mobilized. Annie Abel and Frank Klingberg noted that the British and Foreign Anti-Slavery Society (BFASS) "ferret[ed] out information . . . in the most remote places." American abolitionists "aimed and managed to keep their British friends thoroughly well informed of all conditions at home likely to affect the cause they mutually had at heart." Ironically, the anxious, detailed reports furnished by St. Augustine's newspapers inadvertently built the fugitives a transnational stage. A mid-November 1843 letter from Boston, undoubtably based on these accounts, informed Thomas Clarkson, the BFASS president, of the presence of the Florida fugitives in the Bahamas. By 6 December, it had been forwarded to the Earl of Aberdeen, Britain's foreign affairs secretary. An enclosure reminded Lord Aberdeen of the "intense anxiety" of the "British public" regarding such matters. Eight days later, a British abolitionist asked Henry Capern in Nassau to lobby the local colonial authorities on Gué's behalf. In early 1844, the *British and Foreign Anti-Slavery Reporter,* using words that critics had employed to describe the Second Seminole War, chided the United States for conducting a "national negro hunt." Although federal officials maintained that Gué and company were "fugitives from justice," the *Reporter* lionized them as refugees "from oppression."[14]

Evidentiary matters were of utmost importance. The United States indictments were not based upon eyewitness accounts of the shooting on Key Biscayne. The dead man's two children, who were between six and nine years of age, merely heard shots. For this reason, although Marshal Browne brought people to Nassau who could identify the seven fugitives as those who had fled St. Augustine, they could not place them on Key Biscayne nor determine whether or not Geireen's homicide, because of self-defense, was justifiable. This point was crucial, because in order for extradition to take place under Article 10, the defendants' actions had to meet the definition of murder in the Bahamas as well as in the United States. Moreover, indictments coming from slave owners, who had a vested societal interest in ensuring that human property was recovered, were suspect in British circles. Thus, the Florida grand jury was perceived as being prone to fraud and capable of corrupting local colonials. Also, when runaways were extradited, even if they were tried and found to be innocent, they still were reenslaved. In 1842, before the signing of the Webster-Ashburton Treaty, Canada had extradited the escaped Arkansas slave Nelson Hacket. Since the Gué case was the first to fall under the new extradition agreement, the nervous abolitionist J. H. Hinton asked Reverend Capern if the black men could be moved to "any spot where they would be safer than at Nassau?"[15]

The *New York Evangelist* opined that the Bahamian authorities' decision in the Gué case would "have an important bearing, and disclose[s] more fully than any other decision which has yet occurred, the determination of Great Britain with regard to our fugitive slaves." Marshal Browne and Governor Cockburn treated the affair with urgency. Although it was Christmas Day and Cockburn was scheduled to attend "Divine Service at St. Matthews Church" at 10 o'clock, he agreed to meet Browne and the U.S. consular agent at Government House at 9:30 A.M. The following day, Cockburn caused a warrant to be issued to Chief Justice J. C. Lees for the arrest of the fugitives. On 28 December, Lees and his two associated justices received Browne's evidence. After the "most mature consideration," they "reluctantly" decided the next day that it was "quite impossible" to issue a warrant based upon "mere Indictments without any evidence upon which they were framed." That is, they refused to accept indictments from a "jury in Florida" without "*viva voce evidence*" or copies of the depositions upon which the original warrant was granted. The justices pointedly reasoned that what constituted murder in Florida might be "very far" from the definition of the crime in Great Britain or the "Northern States of America." Browne departed on 30 December, thanking Cockburn "for the Courtesy and good feeling evinced toward him personally, and in his official character." Despite vigorous U.S. protests, London stood its ground. Andrew Gué and his comrades were free. By 1 January 1844, Cockburn believed that they had "left this Colony." The still-wary *Boston Daily Advertiser* advised them to "take care of themselves." Indeed, during the 1830s and 1840s, several black mariners from the Bahamas had been kidnapped and sold in Florida.[16]

During the Gué affair, sectional controversy over slavery's expansion, especially in regard to Texas, raged within the Union. In fact, on 8 May 1843, Secretary of State Daniel Webster resigned because of his disagreement with the Tyler administration over this issue. Webster's replacement, Abel P. Upshur, made Texas his top priority. After Gué had reached Nassau and Upshur had succeeded Webster, Edward Everett, the U.S. ambassador to the Court of St. James, informed his new superior that it was "impossible for Her Majesty's Government to make the slightest compromise . . . when slaves were found within the British jurisdiction, by whatever means or from whatever quarter, they were *ipso facto* free." Indeed, abolitionists noted in early 1844 that Congress had been "remarkably quiet" about the Gué affair. When John C. Calhoun, whom historian Edward Rugemer characterized as "slavery's most prominent apologist," replaced Upshur, he pressured Everett to pin down the slippery Aberdeen regarding the extradition of fugitive slaves. Aberdeen remained prudently evasive. But, Calhoun had bigger fish to fry. Believing that the annexation of Texas was critical to U.S. security, he, like Upshur, focused his attention on this issue.[17] Washington's preoccupation with Texas, along with a healthy respect for British military power, paved the way for Andrew Gué's freedom. He had injected himself onto the international scene at a most propitious moment.

The British refusal to deliver Gué and company to a federal marshal set a comforting albeit shaky precedent. For the remainder of the antebellum period, London handed no runaway slaves over to the Americans. Wherever the Union Jack flew, those fleeing bondage found sanctuary. On 18 October 1860, Boston's African American community hailed this "shelter [where] so many thousands of their race, fugitives from American slavery, find safety and rest," praying that God would continue to "bless England while her law is Justice and her sceptre secures Liberty!"[18] It was in the national interest both of Britain and the United States to maintain the positive direction of their relations that the hard-won Webster-Ashburton Treaty had inaugurated. The English-speaking powers also shared a mutual concern regarding the extradition of criminals. Nevertheless, the question of the criminality of a bond person's acts en route to self-emancipation represented a diplomatic sticking point, especially in instances of homicide. Ironically, the same issue, in seventeenth-century East Florida, had soured Spain's relations with England.

To be sure, history informed Andrew Gué's diplomacy. Local traditions, personal experiences, and contemporary conditions impacted the timing and tactics of his freedom flight. During British, Spanish, and antebellum American rule, the Tomoka region was an angry place. Under Britain, from 1763–84, slaves along the Tomoka River, as the historian Daniel L. Schafer wrote, "overcame enormous environmental obstacles through arduous land and swamp clearance" to establish profitable plantations for their owners. At the same time, family separations occasioned by agricultural entrepreneurs like Richard Oswald, who ripped fifty children from their loved ones in Africa, forced the grueling Middle Passage upon them, and deposited them into the midst of a Florida hell hole, generated a miasma of suffering. "These involuntary immigrants to British North America," Schafer pointed out, "created families and histories in addition to wealth for their owners." He added that "[t]heir life histories await a biographer." In 1803, twenty planters left the Bahamas to settle in Spanish territory on the Halifax and Hillsborough Rivers. Samuel Williams was one of them. Williams, a Loyalist who had evacuated his land in the Carolinas during the American Revolution, owned a plantation on Watling Island, in addition to Nassau property.[19] These planters repeated the cycle of misery that earlier slaveholders had inflicted upon their black labor force. The Gué escape reflects Tomoka's somber history.

It will be recalled from the previous chapter that during the Patriot War large numbers of slaves in the Tomoka region fended for themselves while the American invaders plundered their owners' plantations. After U.S. troops withdrew from East Florida, as discussed earlier, bondsmen bore arms for allies of the Spaniards, resisted the reimposition of work regimens, and fled to British forces on the peninsula's western shores. Antebellum white witnesses, in addition to recollecting these black experiences, preserved vivid memories of East Florida slaves who made it to the Bahamas. For example, Robin, a thirty-two-year-old carpenter and expert "Boat Builder," was Prudence Plummer's "best hand." The widow utilized him as "a Mechanic as well as a very ingenious and useful field hand." When rented, he brought Mrs. Plummer twenty to thirty dollars per month, and he was her only slave who could be profitably employed in the lucrative lumbering business. During the Patriot War, she evacuated her plantation on the east side of the St. Johns River, thirty-two miles from St. Augustine, taking "all her family Black and White," which included fifteen slaves, to Amelia Island. Robin thereafter ran to the Indians via St. Augustine. Oral tradition maintained that he met his death on the Apalachicola River at the Negro Fort. A slave who survived the fort's explosion recounted this story to Francis R. Sánchez. This informant, however, may have been protecting Robin's liberty, since subsequent to the war, the Spaniards had "insisted upon the restoration of negro property by the Indians" in return for a reward of fifty dollars per captive. The Seminoles accordingly delivered some runaways, "but many of the fugitives did not remain with the Indians—they went down to the Capes and many passed over to the Bahamas."[20]

Whites also remembered three more fugitive slaves from plantations along the St. Johns River whose ultimate destination was the Bahamas. Stephen, a slave of John Crichton, Mrs. Plummer's neighbor, ran, like Robin, to St. Augustine, and thence to the Seminoles. Eventually, according to "common report," he made his way to the British, who "took him off to the Keys." Roger, aged thirty-eight, a "good carpenter" whom his master, Farquhar Bethune, normally hired out to "work at his trade," absconded in the summer of 1812, along with his wife, Phoebe, a field hand. Sánchez heard that the couple "went in the direction of Cape Florida," a staging area for transportation to the British island colony. Furthermore, it is likely that a number of the 114 Tomoka slaves who fled to the British in the immediate post–Patriot War period also ended up there.[21]

If whites passed down oral traditions of black flights to the Bahamas, so did blacks. Furthermore, memories of black military heroes formed part of what historian Lizabeth Cohen has described as "resistance passed from generation to generation." On 15 January 1812, near Puerto Príncipe, Cuba, a charismatic free black sporting a sharp historical consciousness, José Antonio Aponte, masterminded a widespread Cuban slave insurrection that lasted until mid-March. Aponte, a sculptor and militia captain, drew his inspiration from George Washington, Ethiopian monarchs, and Haitian revolutionary leaders. The scholar Matt Childs described how "stories about the insurrection circulated immediately following the movement's suppression," causing it to become a "common and well-known event in Cuban history." In June 1812, 270 soldiers of color arrived in

St. Augustine from Cuba. They would have brought news of the Aponte Rebellion. Through the black grapevine, this information surely reached the ears of Tomoka bond persons fending for themselves in seaside mangrove swamps and near abandoned plantations during the Patriot War. Aponte, then, would have become known to Andrew Gué's parents. Even after the Civil War, in fact, the ex-slave Jack Smith still fondly recalled the discipline, intelligence, skills, and military bearing of these Cuban soldiers of color. Smith also remembered some seven hundred slaves (which included fugitives from East Florida) who took up arms for Britain's Corps of Colonial Marines during the War of 1812 at Cumberland Island, Georgia.[22]

Gué's parents certainly heard of Jorge Biassou, an ex-bondsman who had commanded troops on Spain's behalf during the revolutionary turmoil that shook the island of Hispaniola in the 1790s. After the Spaniards made peace with France, they exiled Biassou to St. Augustine, where he demanded dinner with the governor, as well as other perquisites normally preserved for white elites. Before his death in 1801, he battled, along with the future black Patriot War hero Prince Witten, the forces of William Augustus Bowles threatening the provincial government. In this conflict, the colonial authorities also armed slaves. Jane Landers called Biassou a "significant role model for blacks—decorated, militant, independent and propertied." He was buried after an "impressive military funeral."[23]

Andrew Gué and his comrades would have been raised on legends of local black military heroes such as Biassou, Witten, Philip Edinborough, and Antonio Proctor, men whose skills, dignity, and courage played significant roles in fending off Spain's enemies. Cassandra Pybus found that during the American Revolution "[t]ales of black heroes . . . made thrilling listening." As the Patriot War claims cases demonstrate, they did so in antebellum East Florida as well. Even prior to their adjudication of the claims, we have evidence that whites, and therefore people of color, talked about "black heroes." In 1823, for instance, the wealthy white planter Zephaniah Kingsley lauded "about 50 coloured militia inhabitants of this then Province saved by their Bravery and fidelity the City of St. Augustine from being taken & Plundered." Steven Hahn, alluding to the Civil War, noted the "élan . . . of black troops" and "their growing sense of themselves as . . . saviors of the Union and the liberators of their people." Hahn also emphasized "their view of military service as a personally and collectively transfiguring experience, and the very powerful effect that this political process had on white colleagues and observers."[24]

Hahn's conclusions are relevant to the Patriot War. In the conflict's wake, whites noted the surly attitudes of their unfree laborers. Furthermore, Spanish officers had difficulty commanding the colored troops who manned garrisons on the St. Johns River. These soldiers were pledging both to assist Georgia runaways by "accepting [them] into their ranks" and to "slap any white man's jaws who would dare to say anything not pleasing to them." To be sure, Childs's analysis of events leading up to the Aponte Rebellion applies to East Florida: "militia service . . . instilled confidence in free people of color in their daily interactions with colonial officials that the government regarded as arrogant and even threatening."[25] In this charged atmosphere, seething with resistance to involuntary servitude and whites' notions of racial superiority, Andrew Gué drew his first breaths.

Andrew Gué, then, heard about Prince's Black Company, soldiers of color from Havana, ex-slaves serving in the Corps of Colonial Marines, and Tomoka slaves bearing arms for the East Florida's Spanish and British regimes. His community told him tales of hiding out along the Halifax River, flight to the Seminoles, and voyages to the Bahamas via Key Biscayne. Spain's sanctuary policy, along with memories of Fort Mose, also would have been passed along to him. In all likelihood, Gué entered his teenage years steeped in black oral historical traditions. Also, through the workings of the wonderfully efficient slave grapevine, he was exposed to waves of revolt emanating from national and overseas flashpoints. History, then, easily could have inspired him in his boyhood to immortalize himself through his own wartime exploits.[26]

When Joseph M. Hernández wed the widowed Mrs. Samuel Williams, slaves who had fended for themselves in Tomoka during the Patriot War and who had been armed in its aftermath were united under a common ownership. Actions that Hernández-Williams slaves took during the Second Seminole War demonstrate a rebellious spirit that links them to the servile unrest in the Tomoka region a generation earlier. Stephen Hernández fought with the Seminoles, while Alick Hernández was "a most active leader in every measure of hostility and depredations." A slave named Alick is inscribed in the previously mentioned enumeration of Williams's slaves. Since he is listed as the son of Friday and Lucy, he may have been the sibling of Andrew Gué's comrade, William Hernández. On 22 November 1839, the *St. Augustine News* reported that a "negro belonging to J. HERNANDEZ, Esq., of this city, secreted himself on board the Southerner, just before she left the wharf for Charleston on her last trip." The stowaway was discovered en route and returned to his master. Perhaps he was William Hernández, for this name appears alongside Gué's atop the reward notice for the 1843 runaways, who were characterized, with "one or two exceptions," as "most faithful negroes" who "stood high in the estimation of their owners." In November 1842, Amos, Sandy, and Brass, fugitives belonging to William H. Williams, a son of Samuel Williams, stole James Keogh's yawl boat during their escape. Gué, too, grabbed headlines during the Seminole War, a circumstance that links him to Tomoka and to the Hernández and Williams bondsmen.[27]

If one is mindful of East Florida's black history, it is not difficult to understand why, when the Second Seminole War exploded, large numbers of enslaved workers, as they had done during Patriot War times, fled from "Tomoka & Smyrna" to the Indians. According to the historian Larry Rivers, "more than one thousand" slaves "may have fled in East Florida alone during the opening stages of the Second Seminole War," making the conflict "probably . . . the largest slave rebellion in United States history." Hands from the Depeyster plantation, for instance, donned war paint in solidarity with their master's Seminole foes. On 22 September 1836, Castillo, a Depeyster bondsman, was convicted of arson in St. Augustine. Prominent among the black emissaries recruiting warriors in Tomoka were John Caesar and Abraham. They apparently enlisted Andrew Gué, who, in the summer of 1836, absconded to the Seminoles. Gué subsequently recruited in the Ancient City, where hundreds of plantation slaves had been taken by their panic-stricken masters. Many of these forced refugees of color "had wives among the Indian negroes, and the Indian negroes had wives among them." Cognizant of these ties, General Duncan L. Clinch predicted the danger of a black-Seminole alliance prior to the outbreak of hostilities.[28] His admonition proved well founded.

"These coloured persons are giving us much trouble," a Florida militia officer complained in July 1836, "and there is scarcely a doubt that some of them have . . . given information to the Indians." In fact, Andrew Gué and two other slaves were "in the habit of coming into town at night and being harboured aided and fed." On these visits, Gué boasted of his position of confidence with the Seminoles and "only wanted a white man's scalp to make him a great man." Like Prince Witten and other black Spanish-era East Florida military heroes, Gué was an ambitious man. Jeffrey Bolster maintained that among the enslaved "social distinctions and terms of respect were highly regarded." In Seminole culture, according to John Mahon and Brent Weisman, "personal bravery and stealth" demonstrated in raids on the enemy won "increased prestige among the warrior's peers, the privilege of wearing a tattoo, and the opportunity for a young man to earn an adult or warrior's name." Thus, during the summer of 1836, while the troops were in the field and only an "inefficient patrol" of eight or ten civilians kept watch, two Seminoles forded the St. Sebastian River on the Ancient City's western fringe and "rode through the town and went out at the gates." "The icon of elite frontier masculinity," Edward Baptist found, "was the 'hot-blooded fellow' who not only submitted to no one but also attempted to compel obeisance from all others in his world." From the research of these scholars, therefore, at least four cultural influences upon Gué's bold behavior can be discerned. In early 1837, along with Joe Merritt and John Bicenty, he convinced the free biracial Randall Erwin at his home on Anastasia Island, far to the city's south, to furnish cloth, needles, thread, and tobacco, and to obtain other provisions in St. Augustine.[29]

The following night, on 16 January, Gué, Merritt, and Bicenty helped attack J. M. Hanson's plantation, some two miles west of St. Augustine's defense lines. Sentinels posted at the city gates heard the raiders' shots. On the eighteenth, mounted militiamen happened upon "the negro camp at Williams Plantation," some sixteen miles south of town, and fired upon it, killing Merritt, along with two "remarkably large and well proportioned" Black Seminoles. Gué, although wounded three times, managed to escape. Whites also discovered "[a]bout a pound of good rifle powder" that had been "recently purchased in town." In a manner not revealed in the sources, authorities soon learned of Gué's contacts with Randall Erwin. Consequently, Erwin, in addition to Merritt's father and sister, faced charges of treason. The Hanson raid had "revived something of the panic of the early days of the war." Dread of an impending slave uprising, which, according to a local newspaper, carried the potential for a "consequence" that "we well may shutter at," drew troops back to town, thus making it easy for warriors to operate outside of the city. Merritt's death shocked whites because he had disguised his defection by feigning his own drowning, which had "called forth sympathies of the people much in his favor." It also must have troubled them that his grandfather was an Englishman and that Erwin's father was a white South Carolinian.[30]

Meanwhile, Gué eluded whites for a time, relying upon black sympathizers to support him. Eventually, in March 1837, he was taken into custody. The *Florida Herald,* under a screaming headline, announced the capture of the "notorious" runaway slave. Newspapers in faraway places like South Carolina and New Hampshire reprinted the story. There is no record of his punishment, although Kenneth Porter has surmised that it consisted of "rather light" jail time.[31]

Afterward, Gué seemed, in fact, to have "reformed" over time, perhaps due to a parting of ways between the Seminoles and their black warriors in 1838. The city of St. Augustine, in 1839, even paid Gué for work in connection with a burial. We know that he was accumulating cash, because in 1842 he owed $9.42 to the merchant Isaac Avery. The former firebrand had self-purchase on his mind. His own master's family had been amenable to such arrangements. Francis Gué conveyed one of his slaves, Juana, to Andrew Pow, who previously had bought his own freedom from Pablo Sabate.[32]

Andrew Gué's aspirations for freedom also are evinced in Catholic records. Like hundreds of other black East Floridians, by participating in Catholic sacraments, he resisted slavery. Slightly over a year before his sea escape, Henrietta Boyé, on 10 July 1842, bore him a daughter, who was baptized on 23 July as

Fanny Rufina Gué. Spiritually, in an age of high infant mortality, the baptismal waters saved her from limbo, ensuring that if she died before she could reason, heaven was her certain reward. Also, by gathering parents, sponsors, and the infant, the baptismal ceremony, in the historian Stephanie Smallwood's words, "ignite[d] the eternal flame of kinship." Through the sacrament, the scholar Cyprian Davis concluded, East Florida slaves acquired "a status and a name . . . as well as a family and spiritual relations, and even a history."[33]

Blacks in the region had been able to do this for centuries. By comparison, William Lee, George Washington's bondsman, who appeared in the background of several of his master's portraits, and who, according to Douglas Egerton, was the "single most recognized slave in Revolutionary America," did not have "an identifiable birth date and recognized parentage." Eugene Genovese surmised that "most slaves in the South probably did not know their exact age." In Gué's daughter's case, however, a white representative of a prestigious international organization had written her essential genealogical data into an official document. Furthermore, the sacrament linked her to St. Augustine's Spanish past, a time when blacks had enjoyed rights that the Americans no longer honored, but which, in the eyes of her fellow parishioners, constituted a distinguishing feature of a regime whose passing they still lamented. Additionally, baptism made the infant the spiritual equal of whites, "dangerous and heady stuff," in the historian Robert Hall's analysis.[34]

Fanny Rufina Gué's baptism, therefore, exemplifies what W. Fitzhugh Brundage has termed "rituals as a forum for black protest." It also fits Sharon Ann Holt's definition of "symbolic rebellions." The baby's godparents, Antonio Fontané and "Elisa," by sponsoring her, engaged in a "service act" that "undermined" the slave society by buttressing a black family that, because its members were unfree, had no civil standing. Moreover, Holt would argue that the sacrament itself, because it "testif[ied] to the family ties which the laws of slavery refused to honor," was a liturgy of "symbolic affiliation." On his part, Robert N. Bellah would classify the anointing as a "practice of commitment," an "ethically good" deed that "keep[s] the community alive." Since Bellah maintained that typical communities are historical in nature, Gué's christening helped preserve memories of Afro–East Floridians' heroic role in defending Catholicism under the Spaniards. Besides providing her with a social safety net, the infant's godparents represented, like the Church itself, potential curbs on her owner's power over her.[35] Gué's paternal grandmother likely had suffered sexual abuse at the hands of a white man, and she perhaps had expressed her rage and shame to her mixed-race son. Gué may have absorbed this anger. In any event, he was determined to assert his paternity in writing. According to slaveholders' common practice, Fanny would have been the property of her mother's master, Christian

Boyé. Yet, in parentheses, the priest recorded her surname as "Gue." Andrew Gué may have persuaded the priest to do this because he was in a state of quasi-freedom, having made a Spanish-style arrangement to buy his freedom in installments. Expecting to be a free man in the near future, and intending to purchase his daughter's, freedom, he was able to, as the scholar David Brion Davis wrote, subvert slavery by a "subtle triumph that uncloak[ed] a master's pretensions to god hood."[36]

In 1843, however, it was becoming clear that the old Spanish institution of *coartación,* a government- and Church-sanctioned system by which slaves could have an arbitrator set their freedom prices and buy themselves incrementally, was on its deathbed. This sad circumstance may well have been the major motivating factor for Gué's desperate escape attempt. The case of Jimmy Gibbs illustrates this phenomenon. In 1839, George Gibbs was planning to leave St. Augustine. When one of his slaves, Jimmy, protested that this move would separate him from his wife, "Old Mr. Gibbs" made a bargain with his distraught bondsman. He would part with the black man if the latter could find someone who would pay seven hundred dollars for him and who would agree to free him once he repaid this sum. This agreement reflects a trace survival of *coartación.* Jimmy Gibbs, in effect, had his price declared (although not officially as in Spanish times), and was permitted to seek a master who would emancipate him on the installment plan. The problem was that he could not count on American law should a dispute arise regarding his manumission. Under Spain's rule, a slave could take his master to court. No such right existed under the Stars and Stripes.[37]

Cognizant of the obstacles that the new regime had placed in his path, Jimmy Gibbs found a free black purchaser. Gibbs's new master, Andrew Pow, would have been very familiar to Andrew Gué. To be sure, he easily could have served as Gué's role model. Pow had bought his own freedom in 1829 for four hundred dollars. He fathered at least two children by Juana, the aforementioned slave of Gué's owner. In 1833, after emancipating Juana in exchange for $350, Pow paid $173.50 for a St. Augustine lot next to the Presbyterian church. Gibbs and Pow worshiped together in a Baptist congregation. Seeking to the greatest extent possible to replicate the sanctions of Spanish-style *coartación,* albeit within a Protestant setting, Gibbs conducted his negotiations with Pow by means of a lengthy discussion in the presence of other black congregants. But, when he asked Pow to put the terms of their freedom pact in writing, the latter refused. "You know brother Jimmy," Pow replied, "you and I are [Christian] brethern and . . . not of this world . . . our [oral] agreement is more binding than any in writing." As a free man of color, however, Pow had to secure the approval of his white guardian. With the explicit understanding that Gibbs would be manumitted upon delivering seven hundred dollars to Pow, the guardian consented. Only George

Gibbs is known to have criticized this informal *coartación.* He complained that on the open market, his slave would have fetched nine hundred dollars.[38]

Inspired by the prospect of freedom, Jimmy Gibbs worked hard for Pow. He accumulated his market value of nine hundred dollars, which he handed over to his brother in Christ. Pow, however, steadfastly refused to execute the legal paperwork necessary to certify Gibbs's liberty. Meanwhile, he was taking measures to bolster his own precarious freedom. Utilizing another Protestant imitation of a pattern that East Florida's black community had established in Spanish times, Pow sanctified his relationship with the former Juana Gué in the Presbyterian church in April 1841. Thereafter, Pow purchased his son from Francis Gué for seven hundred dollars, mortgaging his town lot to do so. At the same time, Pow's relationship with Gibbs deteriorated. Seeing Pow's expenditure on his son, Gibbs pressed Pow for his freedom papers, only to hear Pow angrily remind him that he was his slave, threaten him with the whip, and have him jailed.[39] Ties of blood were stronger than the waters of baptism.

A day after Gibbs's arrest, his lawyer had him released on a writ of habeas corpus. Joshua Joyner, Pow's former guardian (who had witnessed and approved the free black man's promise to eventually manumit Gibbs), it turns out, had entered a deposition supporting the bondsman's case. Gibbs testified on his own behalf, thereby hoping "to be liberated by process of law," as he would have been under the Spaniards. The magistrate deciding the case ordered another hearing. He therefore remanded Gibbs to the custody of James Gould, Pow's current white guardian. Ultimately, Gibbs lost his appeal. He had no standing in court. Even if he had executed a written agreement with Pow, it would have carried no legal weight, for it now was impossible for an unfree person to make a binding contract. Thus, the arrangement between Gibbs and Pow was a private affair, unenforceable in the judicial system.[40] Clearly, by 1842, the official Spanish Catholic practice of *coartación* had fallen victim to Florida's slave society.

Andrew Gué would have viewed these proceedings with trepidation. After all, if he worked during his free time to manumit himself from Francis Gué, what was to prevent the white man from simply pocketing the money and reneging on his pledge? Florida's legislature, in 1829 and 1842, launched vigorous attacks on those seeking to emancipate their slaves. Indeed, Gué's master had been pressuring him in the early 1840s. A newspaper advertisement on 8 July 1841 warned the public not to hire the bondsman nor transact any business with him, without Francis Gué's express written permission. This restriction of his anonymity certainly did not sit well with the former Seminole warrior and diplomat, for in June of 1843, he ran away for a time. Due to the social changes that American rule had inaugurated, it would be very difficult for Andrew Gué to emulate Andrew Pow. The Jimmy Gibbs case, as well as Francis Gué's proscriptions, meant that his opportunities to buy his own freedom, let alone the liberty of Henrietta Boyé and his daughter, were shrinking. Moreover, there is a hint that Boyé either died or was separated from him before his electrifying sea escape. She never again appeared in St. Augustine's Catholic parish registers, and census records indicate that the family who owned her left St. Augustine between 1842 and 1850.[41]

Historically, in efforts to counteract the expansionist Americans, the Seminoles and their black allies had conducted diplomacy in Nassau. In 1819, for example, Chief Kenadgie and his party paddled to the island of New Providence for this purpose. Bond persons in Spanish East Florida had grown accustomed to appealing successfully to the judiciary for their liberty. Jimmy Gibbs's case demonstrates that this practice still formed part of the freedom strategy of the region's enslaved. It also showed blacks, however, that the U.S. legal system, unlike the Spaniards', was hostile to manumission. Traveling north as a stowaway via what Fergus Bordewich termed the "saltwater underground," as the aforementioned slave of Joseph M. Hernández discovered, was increasingly risky in the 1840s.[42] Therefore, Gué and his comrades, combining Black Seminole and Afro-Hispanic diplomatic traditions, opted to bring their "freedom suit" before British judges.

Between 1821 and 1827, Black Seminoles, after gathering at Cape Florida, sailed 150 miles to Andros Island, at times assisted by Bahamian wreckers. One scholar, Rosalyn Howard, characterized this movement as an "exodus . . . born of desperation." Already living on Andros were black Loyalists from the American Revolution, as well as Africans whom the British navy had liberated in the wake of London's ban on the slave trade in 1807. Among the Black Seminole refugees were veterans who had served in the British military in 1812. The governor of the Bahamas, J. Carmichael Smyth, a man fervently dedicated to abolishing slavery, permitted these African Americans to remain.[43]

In 1825, Britain's Colonial Office decided that "any slave brought to the Bahamas from outside the British West Indies would be manumitted." More than 350 American bond persons who were fugitives to or shipwrecked in the archipelago would be liberated under this ruling. Almost half of this number came from the *Comet,* a United States ship that wrecked off Abaco in 1831. When the 165 slaves on board were brought into Nassau, they "caused an excitement" among local bond persons, "who came in crowds to view the [Bahamian] vessels [which delivered them from Abaco] as they approached the town." Three years later, when the British freed 42 U.S. slaves traveling aboard the *Encomium,* which also foundered near Abaco, their owners charged that the colonial authorities had threatened to hang them if they attempted to remove their human "property" and that Nassau's free blacks had "abused" them.[44]

One way that news of the *Comet* and *Encomium* affairs would have reached St. Augustine's slaves was through mariners of color, who were "for black people in the Atlantic world what newspapers and the royal mail service were for white elites: a mode of communication integrating local communities into the larger community of color." The Ancient City's whites also suspected visiting Englishmen of spreading provocative propaganda. In 1839, for example, they accused William Henry Shadgett of being an "Abolition Emissary." Furthermore, many free people of color in town were literate and some, "too many perhaps," of its bond persons also could read. Thus, many black St. Augustinians might learn about sea escapes and the Bahamas as a sanctuary, directly from the writings of whites. The local newspapers, for instance, devoted extensive coverage to the U.S. Supreme Court's decision to free the slaves who had participated in the famous shipboard revolt on the *Amistad.* In January 1842, Florida's governor, Richard Keith Call, warned the legislature that because of the Territory's "sparse white population," the "extent of [its] seaboard," and its "proximity to the British islands," it was "slumbering on a volcano." The St. Augustine press duly reported Call's admonition.[45]

Only months after the *Amistad* decision, and several weeks subsequent to Governor Call's dire warning, news of the *Creole* mutiny reached St. Augustine's newspapers. While voyaging to New Orleans from Hampton Roads, Virginia, 135 slaves seized the vessel. Cognizant both of Britain's abolition of slavery in its colonies during the 1830s, as well as London's policy of emancipating foreign bond persons reaching its far-flung possessions, the black mutineers brought the *Creole* to Nassau, where they were declared free by the colonial authorities. Before the latter had acted, fifty local boats from Nassau's overwhelmingly black populace surrounded the *Creole,* threatening to free the American slaves "by something approaching mob action."[46]

Indeed, the winds of self-liberation were swirling about the Gulf Stream, and the fragrance of freedom sweetened the nostrils of East Florida's slaves like orange blossoms on a spring day. On 2 July 1841, Ned or Edward Dixon, a twenty-three-year-old carpenter, fled from his master in a small boat. Dixon, a "bright Mulatto or Quadroon" with straight hair and the "letters E D on his arm in Indian ink," could pass for a white man. In November 1842, the aforementioned fugitives belonging to William H. Williams—Amos, Sandy, and Brass—absconded with a yawl. Five to six months later, six slaves in Key West stole a boat from the harbor and, though "closely pursued," succeeded in reaching the Bahamas, where, the *St. Augustine News* lamented, "they have ever since been sheltered and have no doubt been made free."[47]

The U.S. secretary of state, Daniel Webster, of course, did not view Bahamian sanctuary in a positive light. Rather, in August 1842, he saw the islands' official policy regarding slavery as a threat to U.S. national security:

> The Bahama Islands approach the coast of Florida within a few leagues . . . and the navigation [is]difficult and dangerous. . . . necessity often compels vessels of The United States . . . to seek shelter in the ports of these islands. Along this passage the Atlantic States hold intercourse with the States on the gulf and the Mississippi, and . . . find a main outlet to the sea in their destination to the markets of the world.
>
> No particular ground of complaint exists as to the treatment which American vessels usually receive in these ports, unless they happen to have slaves on board; but in cases of that kind, complaints have been made . . . of officious interference of the colonial authorities with the vessel, for the purpose of changing the condition in which these persons are by the laws of their own country, and of setting them free.

By acquiring Florida, John Lewis Gaddis explained, Washington had sought to quash security concerns emanating from what twenty-first-century commentators would call a "failed state." But, the republic now had another problem: "how to keep that expansion itself from generating new sources of insecurity." As Florida's territorial period came to a close, its lawmakers perceived the British colony as a menace to the system of bondage that was the foundation of the peninsula's wealth.[48]

St. Augustine's bond persons delighted in the possibilities that Webster's complaint brought to mind. Indeed, a few days before Andrew Gué's burglary of the *Walter M* in July of 1843, one of the black conspirators had told another Ancient City slave that a "British vessel would soon be off the port, and that there would then be a good opportunity for those who wished it, to obtain their freedom." On the day of Gué's escape, whites observed a suspicious ship, purportedly carrying salt from Rum Key, in the Bahamas, lingering outside of St. Augustine's harbor. When the harbor pilots boarded this ship, they found "rather a numerous crew," though the ship itself "appeared to be . . . only in ballast." At the same time, Joseph Simeon Sánchez wrote to his son that his slave Ben had been "making abolition speeches." Sánchez felt that Ben knew perhaps "too much" about either abolition or the Gué conspiracy (or both). Soon, the city council requested naval patrols between St. Augustine and Key West so as to "form a check on our slaves" and on those who, "probably in the Bahama Islands," maintained "a regularly organized system" for the "aiding and abetting" of fugitives from East Florida.[49]

The trepidation that St. Augustine's city councilmen expressed had been brewing for years. Almost from the beginning of United States rule, territorial officialdom voiced its fear that the archipelago would replace Spanish Florida as a sanctuary for black fugitives. In 1823, for example, Governor William P. Duval complained to Secretary of War John C. Calhoun: "I have been informed by Gentlemen upon whom I can rely, that there are about ninety negros, fugitives from this Province and the neighboring States, on St. Andrews Island one of the Bahamas, & about thirty more on the Great Bahama & the neighboring Islands, those Negros went from Tampa Bay & Charlotte Harbour, in boats to the Florida Keys from whence they were taken to the Bahamas by the Providence Wreckers." Undoubtably, Tomoka bond persons were numbered among these runaways. Sixteen years later, one Ancient City newspaper editor described the threat of "Black Regiments" that abolitionist Britain maintained in the Bahamas. Some 3,500 Africans whom the British navy had liberated in the wake of London's ban on the slave trade in 1807 arrived in the islands from 1811 to 1841. Many of them enlisted in Nassau's Second West India Regiment. Florida's governor, Robert R. Reid, warned in 1841 that blacks from the "British West India Islands are, as I am credibly informed, holding intercourse with the Main, and Abolitionism is preparing itself for a vigorous onset."[50] Thus, high-ranking policy makers in Washington, Florida's governors, and St. Augustine's councilmen, as well as East Florida slaves, nervously eyed the British colonial archipelago, albeit for different reasons.

Spain's seventeenth-century sanctuary policy and Britain's similar nineteenth-century stance bear striking resemblances. In East Florida, the Spaniards needed settlers and defenders in order to check English pretensions. Therefore, they welcomed runaway slaves from their Protestant imperial rival's estates. Fugitives who converted to Catholicism received liberty and, in exchange for bearing arms, land. This policy remained in place after the Americans won their independence. Georgia planters deeply resented it. As Larry Rivers indicated, when the United States took over in 1821, the former Spanish possession "had been renowned for generations as a haven for fugitive slaves . . . and as a nightmare for slaveholders to the north." Consequently, while the nearby British Caribbean colonies were expanding blacks' rights, the young republic celebrated Andrew Jackson's democratic reforms by targeting Florida's free people of color for elimination or marginalization. London lacked laborers in places like Jamaica, Guiana, and Trinidad. A number of American slaves who joined royalist invaders during the War of 1812, for example, received freedom and land on the latter island. In the Bahamas, between 1811 and 1860, some six thousand Africans whom the British had seized from international slave traders were incorporated into the military or settled on sparsely populated Out Islands as a bulwark against the United States. These Africans also were to be Christianized and taught marketable skills. Howard Johnson has compared these requirements to the *encomienda* laws that Spain had applied to its *conquistadores.* At one time, more than a thousand soldiers of color protected the Bahamas, causing antebellum southerners to rail against the threat of a black invasion.[51]

Such relatively favorable conditions for blacks, as they previously had done in Spanish East Florida, attracted American slaves to the British archipelago in what Steven Hahn (referring to the post–Civil War African American exodus from the South) described as "chains of migration." In Jeffrey Bolster's analysis, seagoing vessels thus became "conduits for political dissent." The sea, as Kären Wigen reminded us, is "both barrier and connector—an elusive target for legal regimes and police powers alike." With Andrew Gué's escape fresh in their minds, the white inhabitants of St. Johns County soon saw further evidence of the black "grape vine," as well as the lengths to which African Americans would go in order to free themselves from bondage. Sometime during the summer of 1844, eight blacks employed as oarsmen by "an association of Pilots" at the mouth of the Mississippi River, near Balize, Louisiana, seized the pilot boat *Lafayette* and headed toward the Bahamas. En route, the Louisiana fugitives became stranded upon a reef, where a Key West wrecking schooner encountered the desperate men. They told the wrecker's captain that they had been without water for over three days and that they were bound to Jamaica from Boston. After carrying the black castaways to Tortugas Key, the suspicious skipper, noticing the pilot boat's freshly lettered name, rubbed off the paint, thus revealing the vessel's true identity. The runaways then confessed. Since the U.S. judge at Key West was absent, the wreckers brought the *Lafayette* to Judge Isaac H. Bronson in St. Augustine, seeking salvage rights.[52]

Two of the captured fugitives claimed to be free mariners. Judge Bronson therefore allowed them the opportunity to prove their claims. The other six prisoners he ordered sold at auction, along with the *Lafayette.* Forty percent of the net proceeds were earmarked for the wreckers. About two weeks later, however, on 10 August 1844, the *Vigilant,* a U.S. revenue schooner, arrived in St. Augustine with a "demand from the Governor of Louisiana" for the return of all eight runaways, six of whom had been sold four days previously. Apparently, the *Vigilant* left St. Augustine with only the two men whom Bronson had delayed auctioning. The revenue schooner later perished in a "[t]remendous" October hurricane that slammed Key West. Among the passengers presumed dead were Robert Cooper, one of the Louisiana pilots who had employed the apprehended runaways, and "two of the negroes who deserted with the Pilot boat from the

Balize." The entire affair had caused quite a stir in St. Augustine, especially since it had followed on the heels of Andrew Gué's escape and his subsequent freedom in the Bahamas.[53]

The summer of 1844 brought St. Johns countians additional news of a spectacular attempted flight to the Bahamas. On the night of 22 June, Jonathan Walker, a Massachusetts "ship-wright," departed from Pensacola, the former Spanish capital of the province of West Florida, with seven slaves. They sought, with Walker's assistance, freedom under the Union Jack. On 8 July, two Key West wreckers descried the fugitives some forty or fifty miles from Cape Florida, on the peninsula's southeastern tip, from whence Walker, like Andrew Gué, would have headed across the Gulf Stream. As in the case of the *Lafayette,* wary wreckers decided to tow the vessel to Key West, where the runaways were arrested. Back in Pensacola, one slave committed suicide. Walker was pilloried, pelted with rotten eggs, and branded by the federal government, a punishment that served to stoke the flames of abolitionism in the North.[54] The failures of the Louisiana and Pensacola fugitives illustrate how skilled and fortunate Gué and his comrades had been.

In 1847, seven slaves failed to reach the British archipelago after a cleverly conceived escape from their toil at Fort Jefferson, seventy miles west of Key West. Seven years later, in 1854, twelve slaves successfully fled from Key West to Andros Island, in the Bahamas, where their arrival generated great popular support. These fugitives had stolen a seaworthy vessel from a lighthouse. With the guidance of a free black pilot, they safely disembarked as free persons. Two more groups of bond persons, each containing at least one person bearing the surname "Browne," attempted to sail to freedom under the Union Jack in February and March of 1858. The earlier group, which included men and their families, succeeded. Perhaps tales of Andrew Gué's escape inspired them. By the 1850s, significant numbers of St. Augustine's free people of color had migrated to Key West.[55]

These migrants, along with slaves from the Ancient City who were laboring on the island, would have carried reminiscences of Gué there with their oral traditions. Furthermore, those blacks who were living in Key West at the time of Gué's flight would have remembered the successful freedom voyage of Marshal Joseph B. Browne's bond persons, as well as the black maritime communication network that had warned Gué that Browne was preparing to come to Nassau to seize him. Thus, East Florida's African American diplomatic folk tradition of exploiting geopolitics was alive and well in the 1850s, and it would continue to thrive during the Civil War, when Union gunboats patrolling the St. Johns River became for slaves the new archipelago of freedom. Indeed, shortly before the outbreak of that fratricidal conflict, in a striking parallel to their seventeenth-century forebears, eight black runaways made their way to U.S. troops stationed at Florida's Fort Pickens and asked for liberty.[56]

Florida's racial policies had made Andrew Gué's prospects for manumission by self-purchase increasingly slim. Even if he were able to liberate himself and his family, as Andrew Pow had, they, like Pow, would have found themselves under harrowing legal pressure. Of course, bondage was much worse, for as long as he and his loved ones were enslaved, their domestic lives remained in serious jeopardy. The black community that Gué had left behind faced serious threats to their marriages and families as Florida took its place in the Union in 1845. According to Eugene Genovese, "[o]ppressed peoples cannot avoid admiring their own nihilists, who are the ones most dramatically saying 'No.' . . . [b]ut for the whole people the aim remains to live, not to die heroically."[57] Like Andrew Gué, East Florida's larger enslaved population recognized that their geopolitical circumstances had shifted due to forced Seminole migrations. Unlike Gué and his fellow fugitives, however, the vast majority neither were positioned nor willing to risk death on freedom voyages with minuscule prospects for success. Instead, they devised a way to voyage slowly to liberty while still remaining in East Florida. Using religious rituals, they would perform the past, thereby utilizing time travel in order to reach a sanctuary.

7
The Cana Sanctuary

Andrew Gué's dramatic escape manifested the depth of the desperation and dread that wracked St. Augustine's enslaved community in the wake of the Second Seminole War. Over the centuries, Afro–East Floridians had become adept at exploiting geopolitical conflict in order to expand the boundaries of their liberty. Ominously, however, as the 1840s unfolded, the Seminole defeat had virtually eliminated a traditional sanctuary, as well as a pillar of black folk diplomacy. The promise of political stability that followed the war meant that the region's enslaved population, in an era of rapidly shrinking opportunities for self-emancipation or legal manumission, would have to adjust long-standing strategies aimed at ameliorating the abuses that accompanied bondage. In doing so, diplomats of color contested versions of the past that masters constructed to buttress Florida's slave society. They also kept alive their time-honored practice of orchestrating the white dissemination of the black political agenda. Through astute negotiations grounded in the art of history, they strove to protect their women and families.

Catholic records provide ample evidence of the vulnerability of enslaved women under Spain's regime. For the Second Spanish Period (1784–1821), Jane Landers found that a quarter of the approximately 1,600 blacks baptized were biracial. Among the eighty-eight white fathers who acknowledged these children were planters, military officers, and government officials, as well as soldiers, sailors, merchants, urban craftsmen, small farmers, and physicians. In fact, some of the colony's brightest luminaries sired "large mulatto families (sometimes in addition to their white families)," Landers reported. These patriarchs "recognized their mulatto children, educated them, and provided for them in their wills."

Provincial shakers and movers such as Francisco Xavier Sánchez, Francis P. Fatio, Jesse Fish, George J. F. Clarke, Mateo Solana, Zephaniah Kingsley, John Fraser, and Francis Richard Jr. fit Landers's description, as do Francisco Gué, Francis Marín, Andreas Papy, and Pablo Sabate, less prominent men who nevertheless hailed from important families long associated with St. Augustine.[1]

Notwithstanding some white fathers' laudable actions, many scholars would contend that these relationships were inherently exploitative. Statistics from the final decades of Spanish rule reflect the prejudice and power discrepancies that characterized them. Of the eighty women of color whose white partners acknowledged their paternity in Catholic records, a third were themselves biracial and 35 percent were free. By contrast, only one-eighth of the 116 whom whites had impregnated without admitting it were free, and less than one-seventh were biracial. In short, whites were more likely to own up to their responsibilities if the women of color in their lives were light skinned and free. David Weber viewed these pregnancies on North America's Spanish frontier as consequences of a dearth of white women in a culture that defined masculinity according to "sexual conquest." Robert Paquette, speaking of colonial Cuban society, to which East Florida enjoyed close ties, highlighted the "vulnerability of mulatto girls." In his comparative study of nineteenth-century New Orleans and Havana, Daniel Walker asserted that because whites controlled black "life, death, manumission, enslavement, and social mobility," and could furnish "rewards [to] . . . their biracial progeny," miscegenation was fundamentally a "weapon of domination."[2]

As the Civil War approached, miscegenation continued to loom large in East Florida society, but it became more secretive and subjected whites to less pressure to honor their parental responsibilities. Due to anti-miscegenation statutes, gaps in parish registries, and the legalization of Protestantism, however, statistical evidence is sketchy. After 1832, no father of "colored" offspring was identified as white in St. Augustine's Catholic records. Nevertheless, the baptismal books, along with secular sources, hint that prominent lawyers, politicians, planters, civil officials, and physicians such as Edgar Macon, George Center, Morris Sánchez, Rafael B. Canova, David Levy, John Peck, and Joseph B. Lancaster may have sired biracial babies. Anecdotal evidence strongly supports these possibilities. In 1841, while discussing miscegenation, newspaper editor D. W. Whitehurst attested that "there are many walking evidences [of the practice] to be seen daily in our streets." Visitors to the Ancient City as well noticed numerous mixed-race persons. William Cullen Bryant was impressed in 1843 by the "agreeable, open, and gentle physiognomy" of the African Americans he observed at Mass. The "Spanish race," Bryant noted, "blends more kindly with the African, than does the English, and produces handsomer men and women." Four years later, a private letter reported that a white man, Francis Forward, recently had been caught spending the night with a young mulatto female.[3]

Thus, in East Florida, with its historical tradition of widespread interracial sex, Americanization threatened to exacerbate a problem that Hispanic cultural and religious practices had to a certain degree ameliorated. As in the rest of the antebellum South, there was no legal recognition of slave marriages in Florida. The Spaniards had acknowledged the matrimonial rights of the enslaved. So had the British in the nearby Bahamas. But the Americans adamantly refused to do so, contending that they did not wish to undermine slaveholders' property rights. Owners faced no statutory obstacles when, in order to promote their own agendas, they wished to separate husbands from wives or children from parents. Even the most elaborate wedding festivities that "benevolent" paternalists sponsored for their slaves were nothing more than shams that could be annulled according to shifting circumstances. Indeed, southern legislatures repeatedly balked at sanctioning bond persons' connubial rights. In short, as John Blassingame stated, "the slave family was an extraordinarily precarious institution."[4]

Enslaved East Floridians clearly understood that they needed legal marriages to protect their families, and they passed this belief down to their children. During the 1930s, Edward Lycurgus related how, as a boy, he reveled in his father's tale of the first time that he saw Lycurgus's mother, Julia Gray, the daughter of David and Barbara Gray, pampered slaves of the wealthy Fleming family. When Mr. Fleming died, some of his heirs who harbored abolitionist sensibilities decided to exchange their share of the estate's human chattel for cash. Thus, when Cupid's arrow struck George Lycurgus, a free-born black mariner from England, Julia was standing on the auction block at St. Augustine's slave market, where whites were "barter[ing] off po niggers lake dey was hogs." "Whole families sold together and some was split," the elder Lycurgus would tell his children. "An dey shore did git rid uf some pretty gals." He recounted how "Dey always looked so shame and pitiful upon dat stand wid all dem men standin dere lookin at em wid what dey had on dey minds shinin' in they eyes." Julia's beauty, sadness, and shock due to having belonged to a "family where nobody ever was sold" moved the visiting seaman to buy her for $950.[5]

Antebellum documents do not support George Lycurgus's rescue saga, which he claimed took place around the time of the Civil War. They instead indicate that David Gray (alias Fleming) paid his wife's freedom price of five hundred dollars in installments from 1824 to 1829. Her name was Barbara, or Bobet, a black woman belonging to the estate of Bartolomé de Castro. Sometime before 1837, the couple had solemnized their vows before a Catholic priest. In 1850, Julia Gray was ten years old, so she would have been born free. By 1860, she was Julia "Keigus," the free black mother of two young children.[6] Therefore, the written evidence suggests that Lycurgus was telling his children about how their grandfather had rescued their grandmother (and hence their mother). He was contesting white history by declaring that under the best of conditions, slavery blatantly dehumanized African Americans. In addition to explaining the security that freedom afforded to domestic happiness, Lycurgus also was extolling legal marriage's power to secure kinship bonds among African Americans.

At the same time, by a clever twist of history, George Lycurgus was comparing himself to antebellum white patriarchs such as Zephaniah Kingsley and George J. F. Clarke, both of whom had "rescued" their respective enslaved consorts, Anna Madgigne Ndiaye and Flora Leslie. Lycurgus proclaimed his moral superiority to these men by contrasting his pure motives with those of slaveholders, whose intentions he characterized as lascivious. Indeed, Ndiaye was a thirteen-year-old girl fresh from Africa when Kingsley spied her in Havana, and, according to our twenty-first-century standards, raped her, before hustling her to East Florida. Leslie already had borne Clarke's child when she was sold to him. Although Kingsley and Clarke formed lifetime relationships with these former slaves and formally recognized their biracial offspring, they never legally married them. In fact, Kingsley sired children by other enslaved "wives." Beginning in 1825–26, Clarke, at the age of fifty, commenced a sexual relationship with the slave Hannah Benet, a young woman who had not yet turned twenty. Meanwhile, Leslie suffered as a blind invalid from 1824 until her death around 1832. Her palsy attacks were so severe that she had to be fed as if she were an infant.[7]

To be sure, most enslaved women in Florida did not share the relative good fortune of Anna Madgigne Ndiaye and Flora Leslie. From 1790 to 1860, more than a million African Americans were banished from Atlantic coastal regions and the Upper South to fresh agricultural lands nearer to the Gulf of Mexico. The historian Edward Baptist asserted that in some way, these hellish long-distance journeys impacted all slaves in the nineteenth-century South. During economic downturns, when the internal slave trade languished, plunging commodity prices drove planters to bankruptcy. Estates would be liquidated. Laborers would be mortgaged. In times good and bad, probate proceedings split kinfolk. Marriages might inspire the giving of gifts in the form of "servants." Renting slaves or selling them locally constituted yet other means to shatter black family life. If an owner held multiple plantations, or engaged in enterprises at scattered locations, unfree workers might be shuttled back and forth. House servants could be required to live separately from other bond persons. Even the "kindest master," Thomas Webber explained, "was occasionally forced to sell his slaves or to divide them in his will." As a consequence of this astounding variety of separation threats, "a large number of blacks" passed their days "in fear."[8]

After the United States acquired Florida in 1821, masters forced blacks into the territory by the thousands, lacing the peninsula's psychological environment with poisonous memories of splintered kinships. Middle Florida, the land between the Apalachicola and Suwannee Rivers, received most of these traumatized African American immigrants. This north-central region became the cotton belt, home to politically powerful planters. After statehood, between 1845 and 1860, Florida's population doubled. Forty percent of its inhabitants were enslaved. Although East Florida contained some sizable plantations, Larry Rivers has characterized its economic "norm" as "[s]mall and diversified farming." Only around 15 percent of Florida's slaves resided there, and 87 percent of the region's masters, who enjoyed a reputation for commanding the state's most stable slave families, held less than twenty bond persons. Moreover, these masters characteristically employed the task system rather than the gang system on their agricultural enterprises, which gave slaves more time to attend to their own needs. Also, the long Hispanic presence had softened local customs relating to race and manumission.[9]

Despite these relatively benign conditions, enslaved East Floridians faced serious threats to their domestic lives. Rivers noted that the "large majority" lived in locales that were isolated from dense concentrations of African Americans. This meant that many were obliged to seek spouses held by masters other than their own, and that two-parent households would be difficult to maintain. They remained subject to their owners' fates and whims, particularly the ubiquitous regional practice of renting out bond persons, which strained kinship ties for extended periods. Wilma Dunaway, in her study of small plantations in Appalachia, contended that on "micromanaged" holdings, slaves suffered more frequent sexual abuse, as well as family breakups, than on large estates.[10] Her findings suggest that East Florida's bond persons may have faced more serious threats to their family unity than scholars have thought.

The internal slave trade certainly touched this former Spanish colony. Wrenched from her South Carolina husband in 1846, the cook Mary Abbott ended up in East Florida. Her son, Samuel, born close to the time of her journey south, hints of why Abbott was separated from her loved ones; he was so light in complexion that Union army officers later described him as "white." The case of Douglas Dorsey illustrates this point. During the Great Depression, the elderly ex-bondsman swore that color had doomed his brother. Dorsey recounted how the "exceedingly mean" wife of his master ("Colonel" Louis Mattair, whose family had branched out from East Florida) forced the fair-skinned baby "from its mother's breast at the age of eight months and auctioned [it] off on the first day of July to the highest bidder," a "Captain Ross," who removed the infant to another county. Mattair, a man who was "very kind to his slaves," vigorously had denied his paternity, but ultimately, to secure his own domestic tranquility, he destroyed that of the Dorseys.[11]

To help secure her spouse's fidelity to his marital vows, the biracial Mary K. Sammis, like Mrs. Mattair, forced a slave separation by striking a bargain with her white husband. Mrs. Sammis, the daughter of the wealthy planter-polygamist Zephaniah Kingsley and Anna Madgigne Ndiaye, strove to avoid her mother's fate. After one of her slaves bore the Bostonian John S. Sammis a boy, she consented to the bondswoman's manumission in return for her philandering Yankee spouse's pledge to end his relationship with his black paramour. The son in question, Albert Sammis, detailed the arrangement decades later. "I was to remain with Sammis," he explained, "till I was 21." As he matured, he served as a "house boy" on the huge agribusiness near Jacksonville supported by 250 slaves. Subsequently, his father apprenticed him to a blacksmith, so he was absent on weekdays. One of Albert Sammis's friends, Henry Adams, married a slave of "Colonel" Sammis. Although he toiled in involuntary servitude a mile away from the colonel's place, he slept on the grand estate with his enslaved wife almost nightly. In 1890, as he testified on his friend's behalf before a federal pension officer, Adams seethed. When he no longer could contain his rage, he hijacked the interview. "I had three children sold away from me," Adams angrily interjected, thereby striking a blow against white southern mythology and impelling a government official to record this crime for posterity.[12]

Unlike Mrs. Mary K. Sammis, Diana Hatcher could not salvage her marriage, which suffered the same tragic demise as Mary Abbott's. Hatcher belonged to David Palmer of Duval County, while her husband, Samuel Sams, was the property of one Mr. Haines. In the late 1840s, after Hatcher celebrated Christmas with Sams, she never saw him again. Only in April did she learn that her beloved spouse had been "sold off to a negro trader" who carried him to Louisiana or Mississippi. Fifty years later, Hatcher, like Adams, remained embittered; Sams "had been sold and I did not know it." The man whom she married after the Civil War, St. Augustine native Benjamin Hatcher, it seems, also had been torn from his own wife and two sons during his enslavement.[13]

The tattered nuptials of Richard Simmons and Elsie Dupont demonstrate that in the reputedly benign slaveholding region of East Florida, the most solicitous of patriarchs could and did behave with mercurial thoughtlessness. In his 1852 will, the wealthy St. Johns County planter Abraham Dupont piously intoned that "families shall not be separated." Dupont had been conscientious in his efforts to promote Christianity among his dependents of color. In 1855, for instance, Bishop Francis H. Rutledge, an Episcopalian, confirmed twenty-two slaves on Dupont's plantation and distributed communion as well. Yet, Dupont's stated principles and his religious scruples failed to deter him from giving Elsie Dupont to his daughter, who subsequently relocated to Charleston, thereby dissolving her slave's marriage to Tony Baya's bondsman, Richard Simmons. The latter eventually would wed Susan Baya, whose matrimonial bonds also had been torn asunder by white desires.[14]

During an estate sale circa 1852, when she was twelve years old, Susan Loring had been sold to Simmons's master at St. Augustine's marketplace. Afterward, her new owner sent her out of town, away from her friends and family, to his plantation on the St. Johns River, near Palatka. There, she met Archie Morris, Clark Simpkins's slave, who resided six miles away. With their respective owners' permission, an itinerant preacher who specialized in slave weddings married the woman now called Susan Baya to Morris, who would go "home every Wednesday night and every Saturday, whenever I wanted to." His wife bore him four children, two of whom she "lost." Morris stressed the seriousness of his marriage bonds. "[I]t wasn't like we marry now," he reflected, "but they called it lawfully at that time. . . . I was married to her, but we did not have a license the same as we do these days." His master, unfortunately, did not share this sense of "legality." When the Civil War erupted, he hurried Morris to the more secure Confederate stronghold of Middle Florida, where he eventually wed Mary Ann, another Simpkins slave. Susan, on her part, then took Simmons, a fellow slave of Tony Baya's, as her husband. Archie Morris and Susan Baya expressed outrage over whites' sordid acts decades after they had transpired.[15]

Even highly regarded house servants belonging to prestigious families with deep historical roots in East Florida were not shielded from the agony of profit-motivated family separations. Jane Sánchez entered the world in St. Augustine circa 1800. Her master, Don Francisco Xavier Sánchez, was a man of wealth and influence whose ancestors had lived in the region since the First Spanish Period (1565–1763). In 1883, a federal pension investigator described her as "one of the best old colored women I have ever known." Don Francisco's granddaughter, Frances E. Dewees, singing the praises of white paternalism, declared that the elderly woman's former owners had been supporting their ex-slave for two decades, because "we esteem her highly as She was a good faithful Servant & regret that we cant do more for her." When Dewees's mother, a Sánchez, married Philip Dewees, Jane became a wedding gift. Fortunately, her new mistress remained in the city. Prior to the Civil War, a justice of the peace had "legally married" her to Charles Fatio, another Sánchez family slave. She bore Fatio seventeen children before he died in 1858.[16]

One of these children, Adam Fatio, was born in 1822 in St. Augustine. His mistress, Doña María del Carmen Sánchez y Dewees, assisted at his birth. Fatio lived with Mrs. Dewees in town, and when she and her husband moved to Jacksonville, his enslaved parents accompanied him there. He never was rented "for any length of time." Perhaps there was little demand for him, for he had grown into a poor-sighted, "large & very fleshy" man who was "very clumsy & not active." Nevertheless, when opportunity knocked in 1849, the Dewees family sold Fatio to a Key West physician. On the island, he sometimes shoveled coal, but since he was not very "robust," he mostly did lighter work. From his exile, Fatio wrote frequently to the Deweeses, expressing a strong attachment to them. His letters always ended with the sentence, "I am glad to say I am well & I hope you all are the same." He would express special solicitude for his mother, who fondly remembered him as a "very kind son."[17]

Fatio obviously felt the pain of separation from his loved ones. The fact that he was absent from his father's deathbed must have grieved him deeply. When he heard the bad news, he forwarded nine dollars and three dresses to his mother. Frances E. Dewees swore that Fatio continued to send money to the widow in amounts ranging from five to fifteen dollars, even after his enlistment into the Union army. Relaying such sums involved no small sacrifice, especially when he was enslaved and had to turn the great portion of his wages over to his master. Fatio's close Key West friend, George Johnson, cited his "good Moral habbits" as the source of his ability to accumulate funds. "We often tried to get him to go with us in some frolic," Johnson reflected, "but he would say that he could not afford to spend his money in that way—as he had an old mother that depended on him." Jane Sánchez did not doubt that her son had mailed her money on numerous occasions. She swore, however, that it only reached her once—shortly after her husband's passing.[18]

Her excellent reputation, along with the depositions of her well-regarded black witnesses and Dewees's self-serving testimony, painted a shameful picture of white avarice overpowering paternalism. The Dewees family not only had profited from Adam Fatio's sale, they also had pocketed a portion of his earnings, even though he was no longer their slave. Fatio's aged and beloved mother, cognizant that she had been robbed, bit the white hands that were feeding her by contesting the Jim Crow era's benign orthodox interpretation of slavery. She used white elites to disseminate an African American counternarrative. In doing so, Jane Sánchez was following a strategy that black diplomats long had employed in East Florida in order to negotiate their community's liberties.

Slavery's assault on the black family and women of color, to be sure, haunted its victims for the rest of their days. After growing up on the St. Johns River near Jacksonville, Julia Holder married William A. Hart, a Key West native who had been free in antebellum times and a sergeant in the Union army during the Civil War. According to one acquaintance, he was "almost a white man—you would not suspect that he was not a white man." Subsequent to her wedding to this groom twenty years her senior in 1874, Holder accompanied him to Savannah, where the couple baptized five children in St. Stephen's Episcopal Church. Mr. Hart worked in an iron factory and his family resided in an adjoining company house. Whites thought highly of the Harts, regarding them as "very respectable colored people."[19]

Two years after her husband's death by heart attack in 1898, Mrs. Hart's life further unraveled. Ironically, in the process, her self-interested effort to embrace the white version of history unintentionally contested it. She always had claimed to be the legitimate daughter of free parents, Joe and Nellie Holder. Also, she swore that her marriage to Hart had taken place "in the country," just outside of Beaufort, South Carolina, at the home of the Reverend Isaac Johnson. Although a special examiner for the U.S. Bureau of Pensions admitted that Mrs. Hart enjoyed a "good reputation for truth and her witnesses [were] among the most respectable people" in Savannah, her "rather flimsy" explanation for her lack of a marriage license aroused his suspicions. An investigation revealed that Reverend Johnson had first married her to one Edward Raines and that she and Raines never had divorced after they broke up a couple of years later. Furthermore, her biracial mother had been a slave. Mrs. Hart's father was her master, Joe Holder. Thus, she was her father's slave. Mr. Holder, a witness stressed, took "mighty good care" of Julia, never treating her as such.[20]

Regardless, young Julia Holder was, by law, chattel, and thus, like thousands of enslaved East Floridians, she was vulnerable to the fickle winds of commerce. When his wife died, Joe Holder gave Julia and his other biracial progeny to his white daughter, Susan, who had married Thomas Tillis. The Tillises subsequently "sold the yellow children of old man Joe Holder to Wade Sparkman," the proprietor of a nearby plantation. Sadly, the future Mrs. Hart's own sister could not resist the temptation to profit by the sale of blood relatives. Because of Hart's perjury, the government instituted criminal proceedings against her in 1901. Luckily, the federal prosecutor had second thoughts, so the statute of limitations killed the case.[21] Nevertheless, the scandal was punishment enough.

Undoubtedly, competing historical narratives circulated in antebellum East Florida. The historian David R. Colburn has described St. Augustine as a "historic community" where people are "heavily influenced by the traditions of the past." The city's white inhabitants, he pointed out, generally have prided themselves on their "excellent" relationships with African Americans.[22] What Colburn found in twentieth-century St. Augustine rang true in pre–Civil War times. Yet, nineteenth-century blacks countered benign characterizations of antebellum race relations. Enslaved residents faced a relentless, daunting mission merely to protect the fundamental human right to a secure family life. Each day, they grappled with the prospect of whites separating them from their loved ones or sexually abusing them. As a result, they saw themselves compelled, like Andrew Gué, to rebel, but to do so subtly, symbolically, and diplomatically. As Steven Hahn suggested, their "struggle to form relations among themselves and to give these relations customary standing in the eyes of masters and slaves alike was both the most basic and the most profound of political acts in which they engaged."[23]

To protect their women and families, blacks in the vicinity of St. Augustine concluded that they could wield history as a weapon. Accordingly, many opted to flaunt their Catholic Hispanic identity, thus distinguishing themselves from blacks who had more recently entered Florida from Protestant regions. The Spaniards had fostered what the historian James Bennett called a "triracial order," in contrast to the "binary" hierarchy that the United States aimed to impose. Colonial Spanish officials had bestowed special privileges upon an intermediate class—East Florida's free people of color. The treaty of cession between the United States and Spain recognized these privileges, and the ongoing Patriot War claims cases that some blacks were pressing served as reminders of them. By stressing their connections to the old regime, antebellum blacks also could harness the resentments of "old inhabitants" and their influential families, who, as the Patriot War claims likewise demonstrated, still had not forgiven the Americans for seizing East Florida. Moreover, the blood of many of these esteemed white elders flowed through blacks' veins. In Louisiana, by pursuing a similar strategy, some people of color had carved out a protective niche for themselves. To summarize, a large number of the Ancient City's residents of African descent established an "ethnicity" that might permit them to better defend their domestic relationships. Utilizing the Catholic sacrament of Holy Matrimony constituted an important part of this strategy. Historically, both seventeenth-century Afro-Mexicans and eighteenth-century inhabitants of Fort Mose had used it to cement ethnic bonds.[24]

In East Florida, an exposed frontier colony, the major source of black prestige under the Spaniards had been military service. The foundation of their freedom and human rights had been Catholicism. By 1843, whites had stripped Afro–East Floridians of their historical role of protecting the region's security. Blacks, then, would have to find another source of prestige. But the Catholic Church, in a muted though still relevant form, remained open to them. Enslaved diplomats recognized that under the Americans they could utilize this institution, with its deep local roots and its far-flung branches, to spiritually and materially succor their imperiled families. Nationally, during the initial years of the 1840s, Protestant church schisms over the slavery issue, along with abolitionist critiques from the North and abroad, touched off a fervent competition among denominations to bring slaves into their respective folds. In St. Augustine, this translated into sectarian challenges to Catholicism. Blacks' lives in bondage had demanded that they learn to sensitize themselves to whites' prevailing moods and to adeptly take advantage of them. Thus, the enslaved became masters at exploiting conflicts that wracked white society. Late-antebellum East Florida, to be sure, presented black diplomats with ample opportunities to work their magic.[25]

Slaves also could skillfully harness paternalism to work in their favor. Transnational debates in the 1840s, besides touching off a drive to evangelize slaves impelled by an ideology that the historian Blake Touchstone called "Christian paternalism," led to a professed concern, out of psychological, religious, reformist, and economic needs, for the protection of blacks' morals. Whites understood that bond persons highly valued "legal" marriages for the protection that they might afford their families. By embracing the practice of conducting slave nuptials as formal church liturgies, the various denominations could attract black converts and inculcate Christian sexual morality among them. Masters therefore might salve their consciences while demonstrating "noblesse oblige" both to their neighbors and to slavery's vociferous critics. Additionally, the resulting boost to the morale and self-discipline of their labor force would permit planters to reap burgeoning financial rewards without entailing any real risk to their ability to dispose of their human property as they pleased, since the states still gave no civil standing to slave marriages.[26]

John Blassingame has gathered statistics illuminating the workings of this Christian paternalism. He concluded that "many denominations required all slave members to take their marriage vows in the church." Antebellum documents, he added, support the notion that ministers attempted to put this ideal into practice. "[T]housands" of bond persons exchanged vows in churches throughout the South from 1800 to 1860. Of the 1,228 Episcopal church weddings in South Carolina, Alabama, North Carolina, Georgia, Louisiana, Mississippi, and Virginia in 1860, nearly 40 percent joined enslaved couples. Between 1830 and 1860, "[a]t many times . . . more slaves were married in the Episcopal churches in some states than were whites." In South Carolina, for example, during the two decades before the Civil War, a majority of Episcopal nuptials were marriages between slaves. During these same decades, in almost every state with extant records, bond persons "accounted for a larger percentage of the marriages than they did of the members of the Episcopal church." Thus, in Alabama, although slaves never reached 8 percent of Episcopalians, they constituted from 15 to 33 percent of that denomination's church marriages. Furthermore, after the ceremonies, "[w]hite churches continued to exercise moral oversight" by "frequently" investigating "charges of adultery and fornication" among the slaves.[27]

The southern social setting, therefore, proved propitious for slaves desiring to make their marital commitments as "legal" as possible. This was true in St. Augustine, especially for Catholic bond persons. After years of instability under

U.S. rule, the Catholic Church, as 1840 approached, once more established a firm foundation in the Ancient City. In 1836, Bishop Michael Portier, from his see in Mobile, Alabama, assigned Father Claude M. Rampon there as a "permanent pastor." The Frenchman remained at his post until 1843, the longest continuous presence of a Catholic priest since 1821. Under Rampon, according to Michael Gannon, Catholicism "waxed strong once more" and "parishioners [became] . . . assiduous in the practice of their faith." Two local boys, Dominic Manucy and Anthony Pellicer, attest to this. They found their priestly vocations under Rampon's tutelage, eventually becoming bishops after the Civil War. In 1844, Bishop Portier sent two more French priests in Rampon's stead, Benedict Madeore and Edmond Aubril. Madeore and Aubril built mission churches in Fernandina, Jacksonville, Mandarin, and Black Creek. The following year, Portier also designated a priest for Key West. As the 1850s unfolded, St. Augustine became part of a new diocese centered at Savannah, a city situated within relatively easy traveling distance. Seven years later, Rome decided to establish in Florida a bishopric based in St. Augustine. Because of this vicariate's missionary status, its prelate would report directly to Europe.[28]

Catholicism's reinvigorated presence in St. Augustine formed part of what Randall Miller has described as an "ambitious extension of dioceses in the South." At the same time, the American hierarchy pressed the clergy to "subject all parishioners to church discipline and to impose regular, uniform devotional practices." This ecclesiastical policy applied to enslaved parishioners as well, which melded with bond persons' desires to utilize church weddings to better secure their families. Moreover, in areas of the antebellum South where priests maintained a strong presence, Catholic masters exercised a greater respect for the church's precepts regarding the sanctity of slave marriages.[29]

Statistical evidence suggests that black East Floridians seized upon this milieu in order to place their relationships upon a firmer legal footing—at least according to Catholic canon law, which, practically speaking, represented the best juridical option available. From 1821 to 1862, eight hundred black Catholic baptisms appear in St. Augustine's parish registries, about half the total denoted in the Second Spanish Period (1784–1821). Despite the large number of black baptisms under the Spaniards, however, the historian Jane Landers discovered only fifty-one solemnized marriages involving persons of color. During the antebellum U.S. regime, Catholic clergymen recorded forty-eight black nuptials, which, unlike baptisms, almost equaled the number that they presided over in the days when Spain permitted legally recognized slave matrimony. Furthermore, a closer examination of the records reveals thirty-six additional ecclesiastically recognized black unions, after taking into account baptized children of color who priests classified as legitimate rather than natural offspring. When twelve Protestant weddings and five civil ceremonies are added to the mix, there exists written evidence for ninety-nine formalized nuptials, nearly double the number celebrated under the Spaniards.[30]

Furthermore, Civil War pension applications suggest that the above figures understate the incidence of Catholic black marriages in antebellum East Florida, though by how much will never be known. In 1898, for example, Sally Growles testified that while enslaved in 1850, and a few days after delivering her son, James Filomena Rogero, she married the bondsman Handy Canova "in the Big Catholic church" before "the Priest," Father Edmond Aubril. Growles admitted that she previously had delivered a son to a white man, the aforementioned Frank Forward. Canova, on his part, had sired a son by Mary, a slave of Mauricio Sánchez, but "didnt really have Mary for a wife." He "just caught her on the fly." After the affair ended, Mary commenced a relationship with another slave, none other than the previously discussed Richard Simmons. Joshua Hagaman (whose status in the church can be measured by the large number of black children that he sponsored for baptism), along with William Nateel, swore that they had witnessed the wedding in the historic Spanish edifice. Ecclesiastical records, however, do not record it. It is known, nevertheless, that the Rogero, Canova, and Solana families, to whom the couple had belonged, on other occasions had permitted their slaves to partake in sacramental ceremonies. And, the fact that Handy Canova had served as an official witness to a Catholic wedding in 1858 is evidence of his good standing within the church. He and Sally Growles also stood as godparents during antebellum times, another indication of their Catholic leadership status.[31]

Similarly, during the 1890s, the ex-slave Peter Johnson claimed that Father Aubril had officiated at his marriage to Amanda (Hermana) Canova, which appears to have taken place in the late 1830s and which was blessed with ten children. A free man of color, Abraham Lancaster, supported Johnson's claim, as did John Williams, who recalled of the Johnsons that he "used to go to their house quite often" and knew that "they lived together and were known as husband and wife." In addition, the couple's son, John Mills, deposed that his parents had been "lawfully married in slave time by Rev Father Obree." Yet, the four children of the Johnsons who appear in Catholic baptismal records, like those of Sally Growles, are not described as legitimate, nor is the father named, circumstances that challenge claims of a sanctified union. Nevertheless, the Johnsons, like the Growles, were active and respected parishioners, sponsoring seven godchildren. Also, Peter Johnson's owner, Susan Murphy, was a Catholic who left a legacy of one hundred dollars to Father Aubril.[32]

Surprisingly, St. Johns County actually issued a civil marriage license to the free-born Abraham Lancaster and Jane Canova, a house slave, on 5 December

1857, despite Florida's refusal to recognize bond persons' unions. Although county records confirm that Father Aubril "legally" united the pair on 6 January 1858, the marriage is not recorded in parish registries. After the Civil War, however, Martin Dixon and Domingo Papy recalled the wedding taking place when they were boys. Thomas Williams, a former slave and Lancaster's childhood playmate, also recollected the marriage. Lancaster's niece, a girl about ten years old in 1858, still could visualize the bridal wreath that Canova had worn on her head. The niece remembered that the ceremony had taken place in the "Cathedral," but she differentiated between this ceremony and the "wedding" that was held at her grandmother Tyra Lancaster's house on Charlotte Street. Thomas Richardson, another former slave, testified that the nuptials took place on a Saturday night. Finally, the baptismal records of 1860 list the couple's enslaved son, John Vulter Canova, as legitimate.[33]

The fact that the Lancaster-Canova nuptials found their way into government record books demonstrates the corrosive effect on the laws of bondage that regularly conducted Catholic slave marriages could have in a city that sported a majority Catholic population. It also illustrates, as the historian John Boles reminds us, that in the South, "strict uniformity in anything was the exception." St. Johns County granted marriage licenses to two other enslaved Catholic couples in 1839 and to a mixed-status Catholic couple seventeen years later. In an ambience that featured intense competition for black converts, it followed that Protestant slaves also were issued county marriage licenses. Two enslaved Episcopalians, and two other bond persons belonging to that denomination who wed free partners, appear in civil documents from 1843 to 1846. County officials may have extended civil recognition to at least three additional Protestant slave unions.[34] In antebellum St. Johns County, slave nuptials that the state regarded as mere water had been transformed by white officials into the wine of government-sanctioned marriages. This Cana Sanctuary, if expanded, might erode one of the legal foundations of the U.S. slavery.

Further evidence of black Catholic nuptials may have been lost in fires or natural disasters. Other sacramental vows may have gone unrecorded because of irregular visits by the clergy during the 1820s to the late 1830s. Moreover, priests in some southern locales were empowered to conduct clandestine marriages in cases where masters refused permission for their slaves to wed. Additionally, in certain instances, when priests registered the names of both of an enslaved natural child's parents, they were recognizing a marriage by inference. Thus, enslaved diplomats, by manipulating local history, international controversies enveloping the United States slave society, and the internal dynamics of the Catholic Church, had placed their families on a firmer foundation.[35]

Nonetheless, sacramental nuptials, although they bolstered slaves' families, were no substitute for legal recognition. Peter Johnson sadly discovered this fact. Johnson's life deteriorated as his Catholic owner of at least twenty years, Susan Murphy, lingered on her deathbed in 1855–56. While his fellow slave Belinda managed to obtain a promise of liberty by Murphy's will, Johnson saw himself conveyed in trust to the prominent Episcopalian George R. Fairbanks. Next, at the age of forty-one, he suffered ten lashes for cursing an out-of-town physician attending to the elderly widow. For a time, it looked like Venancio Sánchez, a wealthy Catholic merchant-planter, would buy Johnson. When this deal fell through, U.S. senator David L. Yulee (born David Levy), a Protestant friend of Mrs. Murphy's and one of her heirs, sent him north to Fernandina, away from his family. In 1893, a still-anguished Johnson reminded federal pension officials, "I was compelled to come [to Fernandina]. I was separated from my wife by my owner." Abraham Lancaster confirmed that "they were separated by the white people." When the Civil War ignited, Yulee made matters worse by shuffling Johnson to Florida's interior, away from both Yankee troops and the black man's beloved family.[36]

Certainly, then, black diplomats had their work cut out for them, despite the spike in church marriages that Christian paternalism had made possible. But history was working in their favor. Under the impact of romanticism as well as a number of economic and political stresses, Middle Florida's planter elite had begun to view themselves as beneficent medieval lords who chivalrously protected their dependent black "serfs." Accompanying this fascination with the Middle Ages was an idealization of Florida's Hispanic roots. The beginnings of this historical sensibility, the early 1840s, coincided with the Patriot War claims cases being argued in St. Augustine's federal court. As we have seen, venerable witnesses in these lawsuits had painted the American invaders as heartless, destructive barbarians who had shattered East Florida's golden age. Stingy U.S. treasury officials and federal judges, as well as the heavy weight of the hard times that U.S. rule had brought to the region, led St. Augustine's citizens, like Middle Florida's cotton barons, to contemplate the Spanish past more intensely. In examining this past, they liked what they saw. When economic prosperity returned in the 1850s, as winter tourists packed its hotels, the inhabitants of the Ancient City likely realized that history might profit them. A newspaper article, for example, described Spanish-era coins that one resident had discovered among his possessions. The paper also printed the words of the Minorcan *formatjada* hymn of the Easter season in English and Catalan. George R. Fairbanks, a St. Augustinian, perceived enough interest in the past to found the Florida Historical Association in 1856. Father Madeore, whose church-related forays into local history can be traced to at least 1848, enlisted as a charter member.[37]

Black East Floridians could, therefore, manipulate this romantic historical interest of Tallahassee-area cotton planters and white St. Augustinians in the Spanish past. The Patriot War claims hearings had enabled some blacks to officially boast of their role as valiant protectors of Hispanic civilization. Indeed, by whites' own admission, they had rescued the province from the greedy Americans, just as George Lycurgus had saved the young and beautiful Julia Gray from the auction block. Indeed, their forebears had attained their freedom, rights, and social recognition under Catholic Spain. They had fought as black knights in the defense of Catholicism. They had helped construct the very cathedral that dominated the town plaza. "Heritage counted for much in East and West Florida during the four decades prior to the Civil War," the historian Larry Rivers concluded in his study of slavery in Florida, and "the traditions behind it in good part were Spanish."[38] Therefore, each time that they attended Mass or participated in the sacraments, black St. Augustinians kept alive in their minds and those of the white congregation their unique historical role.

Thus, they contested the white version of history that held them to be incapable of responsible citizenship. The church was a sanctuary from the self-serving history that the U.S. slave society had formulated. When blacks married each other under Catholic auspices, they sought to erect a sacramental sanctuary for their families. In the words of the historian Sharon Ann Holt, they "undermined their masters' fictions" and engaged in "symbolic rebellions." They publicly challenged, as did black performers in New Orleans's Congo Square and Afro-Cuban celebrants in Havana's *El Día de Reyes* festivities, the notion that their women were libidinous creatures incapable of chastity and marital fidelity and thus undeserving of white respect. When St. Augustine's Catholic couples of color clad in their best clothing marched up the aisle of the city's venerable Spanish-era church or baptized their children within its walls, they evoked memories of black heroes, thereby reminding whites that they had denied them their historical prominence, while reminding themselves what future freedom held in store.[39]

Another way that they resurrected memories was through the exercise of what foreign policy experts call "moral suasion." By publicly exhibiting their ethical high ground vis-à-vis their masters through their participation in the sacraments, Catholic East Floridians of color used piety in order to recover a measure of the prestige that they had lost when the Americans barred them from military service. During antebellum American rule, approximately 482 Catholic godparents of persons of color can be identified with a reasonable degree of certainty. Forty percent were godfathers. Of these men, two-thirds had only one godchild. This is true for 70 percent of the godmothers. Another 19 percent of the men and 16 percent of the women sponsored two godchildren, while a mere 7 percent and 5 percent respectively counted three persons of color as their ritual progeny. All in all, 93 percent of the godfathers, and 91 percent of the godmothers sponsored only one to three godchildren. Only six black men and ten black women served as godparents for six or more persons. The leaders were the slaves Joshua Hagaman, also known as Joshua Dummett, and Betsy Benet, who each sponsored twenty-three baptismal candidates.[40]

The second most popular black godfather was Sprig Mosby, who sponsored twelve people of color. His life demonstrates how, through Catholic leadership, a man might garner social respect at a time when whites gave blacks little if any opportunity to do so. In 1825, Mosby stood as godfather for George D. Clarke, one of the biracial heirs of the former Spanish colonial official George J. F. Clarke. At this time, Mosby was a married, property-owning free black businessman. In time, however, he fell into a spiral of drunkenness and poverty. From 1842 to 1849 he vanished from the historical record, only to resurface in 1850, apparently having undergone a spiritual rebirth. Over the next eight years, after an absence of a quarter century from the baptismal registries, Mosby served as godfather for ten persons and witnessed two marriages. When his material circumstances bottomed out in 1859, an alderman brought to the St. Augustine city council's attention the "miserable and unfortunate condition of Mosby." White support for the elderly black man was unflagging. Prominent Anglos and Minorcans, Protestants and Catholics, rushed to his aid, recalling how he had "extended daily the hand of charity to many of our poor population particularly widows," as well as to a deranged white man whom he had sheltered "on his premises." From 1859 to 1862, the city supported him. In the latter year, the financial exigencies caused by the onset of the Civil War halted payments to all paupers "Excepting Spirigg Moseby."[41]

In this setting, Jean-Pierre Augustin Marcellin Verot, St. Augustine's newly appointed Catholic bishop, commenced his role as shepherd of the recently established vicariate of East Florida. On 22 May 1858, when Verot left Doughoregan Manor, the Maryland community in which he enthusiastically had ministered to the enslaved, blacks dressed in their Sunday best touchingly bid the Frenchman farewell in song, and each of the serenaders presented him with a small gift. The scholar Michael Gannon noted that as the "bishop walked among them, the slaves knelt reverently to receive his blessing." The scene must have impacted Verot to the core of his earliest memories of Catholicism. At his birthplace, LePuy, France, on each fifteenth of August, "tens of thousands of pilgrims wound through her ancient streets in processions honoring the Black Virgin." On 6 June 1858, shortly after his arrival in St. Augustine, Bishop Verot's parishioners of color, in a gesture that hints that they had formed some type of religious society, offered their new prelate a pectoral cross.[42]

Through this gift-giving, black diplomacy was very much in evidence. The Maryland slaves were hoping to curry the favor of Verot's replacement in their own quest for shelter from slavery's storm. Moreover, their gifts would remind the southern-bound churchman of his duty to promote blacks' welfare. Surmising that the prelate would display these gifts before East Florida's African American congregants, Verot's former charges were, in effect, furnishing their Ancient City counterparts with veritable "letters of recommendation." Black St. Augustinians completed this diplomatic maneuver. Their pectoral cross reinforced the Marylanders' symbolic admonitions. Additionally, each time that the bishop wore this traditional symbol of his ecclesiastical authority, white Catholics would be reminded of blacks' piety, as well as their ties to the Spanish golden age that the Americans had shattered more than four decades earlier.

The historian Robert Kapitzke has argued that from St. Augustine's earliest days "foreignness . . . was measured by religious adherence rather than by nativity or race." Therefore, by their very Catholicism, black St. Augustinians were informing their new spiritual leader that they were linked inextricably to the history of their sixteenth-century city. And, as it turned out, the history of the place impressed Verot. He was, according to Michael Gannon, "attracted by" its "Spanish atmosphere." After conducting his own historical investigation, Verot issued a pastoral letter in which he referred longingly to the region's Catholic past, expressing a desire to resurrect those days as a solution to the contemporary problems that his flock faced. Subsequent to the Civil War, after learning about local traditions regarding the spot where the Spaniards had celebrated St. Augustine's first Mass in 1565, he purchased the land and restored the old church that once stood there. The prelate also added a painting of this storied Mass to the cathedral. At Fernandina, he built a church at the place where he believed a Spanish missionary had been martyred during colonial times. A year after the war, the bishop pressed Rome to make St. Augustine a full-fledged diocese, citing its "antiquities & precious reminiscences" among his arguments. Verot once more demonstrated his love of history when, in 1871, he traveled to Havana in search of St. Augustine's parish records. He found them there, with their baptismal registers dating to 1594.[43] History, then, constituted a means by which black parishioners could relate to Verot.

On an 1860 voyage to Key West, however, the bishop observed firsthand an ugly side of East Florida's heritage: the suffering that the international slave trade inflicted on African captives. He deemed this trade immoral, as Pope Gregory VI had proclaimed in 1839. As far as the domestic institution was concerned, Verot believed that the South's Christian paternalism generally had furnished the enslaved with adequate food, shelter, and clothing. What seriously concerned him was the sexual immorality that the slave system imposed on bond persons, who, due to the ease with which whites split African American families, improvised by constructing a variety of conjugal arrangements that, as did the assaults of their masters on black kinship ties, fell outside of the bounds of Catholic morality. The freedman Washington McDuffie, speaking after the Civil War of the aforementioned bondsman Richard Simmons, for example, did not know whether Elsie Dupont had been the latter's slave wife, because Simmons "lived with so many." On the same subject, Minda Hammond commented that Simmons would "dip about all around." Verot certainly knew about such activities. "Marriage," he wrote in reference to the slaves of his vicariate, "is scarcely known among them." Verot undoubtably heard stories of St. Augustine's worsening legacy of miscegenation from his priests. Free and enslaved blacks also must have related their woes concerning their family lives to their confessors. Therefore, he was determined to correct this historical injustice. Like elite planters and numerous St. Augustinians, an idealized Hispanic past enthralled the prelate. Accordingly, he strove to resurrect the golden glory days of Spanish rule, when the church had ensured that the civil authorities recognized slave marriages. Thus, Verot informed the French office of the Propagation of the Faith that he would "seize every possible opportunity and means to extend a helping hand to extricate [the slaves] from ignorance and corruption."[44]

Verot's sense of history, then, drew him to defend black families. Moreover, there was a historical precedent in St. Augustine for what an "activist" prelate could do for the enslaved. In 1788, for example, Bishop Cyril de Barcelona, on a visit from New Orleans, held the sword of excommunication over the heads of those who, in ministering to or owning slaves, failed to catechize, baptize, promote church marriages, and preserve families. Along these lines, evidence exists that in 1859, St. Augustine nuns who recently had established a school for whites, obviously with Bishop Verot's approval, were also instructing children of color. His Sulpician religious order had championed the education of African Americans in Maryland. Also, during the mid-1840s, in Baltimore, African American Catholics conducted prayer services in the cathedral basement, so the new bishop was predisposed to initiate or continue similar gatherings at his new post. But history can be a double-edged sword. Using the false historical analogy of medieval Europe, Verot believed that if American slavery could be ameliorated, the Catholic Church, as it had done centuries before, would slowly strangle the institution. The key, in his mind, was a sincere return to Spanish-era precepts. The Roman curia, realizing that such an approach was not applicable to nineteenth-century exigencies, had abandoned this philosophy. Verot, however, in company with the overwhelming majority of his fellow U.S. Catholic bishops, adhered to the same backward-looking thinking as the Spaniards had, when, in trying to head off slave revolts in Cuba during the 1840s, they promulgated a slave code reminiscent of the island's pre-sugar-boom years.[45]

Regardless, St. Augustine's black folk diplomats patiently sought small victories one step at a time. Their goal was to exploit Christian paternalism in search of privileges that they could transform into rights. The diplomats' top priority was the protection of enslaved families. They could not do this with any certainty, however, unless slave marriages were legalized. Therefore, they needed elite whites to speak on their behalf. They found a spokesman in Bishop Verot, who well understood that as a leader of a faith whose adherents comprised only 10 percent of slaveholders, he would somehow have to enhance Catholic prestige in the South so that he could achieve his goal of bolstering the black family.

On 4 January 1861, the fair-skinned, blue-eyed, five-foot-two "bantam" prelate who almost a decade earlier, at the age of forty-seven, had thought that his most influential days had passed, preached, in his characteristic "slow, clear," and intellectual style, a sermon that subsequently would be published throughout the Confederacy, earning him the dubious title of "Rebel Bishop." The occasion was President James Buchanan's national day of prayer and fasting on the Civil War's eve.[46]

When Verot sat down to compose his famous sermon, he likely contemplated gifts from Maryland slaves and touched the pectoral cross that his black congregants had given him. But, a dilemma taunted the prelate. Two-thirds of St. Augustinians belonged to his flock, nearly a third of which was black. The preponderant segment of the white Catholics were Minorcans, an ethnic group still smarting from an inferiority complex due in part to Anglo-Americans associating them with eighteenth-century indentured servitude. On the one hand, then, Verot did not wish to alienate these parishioners, a minority people practicing a minority faith. Therefore, if he defended African American rights too directly, he risked, as the Minorcans' spiritual leader, making this already-suspect Hispanic population less "Southern" and less "white." Moreover, such inflammatory words were sure to be hotly contested by Dixie's Protestants, rendering Catholicism worse than irrelevant and subjecting its adherents to possible nativist attacks. On the other hand, at least half (and probably many more) of the Ancient City's slaves were Catholics. Ministers ardently competed with priests for these enslaved souls. Too militant of a championing of masters' practices would cause Verot to violate his own conscience and to lose credibility among people of color. In the end, the Frenchman opted to sugarcoat his scathing critique of slaveholders and his defense of the black family by invoking Christian paternalism, the traditional teachings of the U.S. Catholic Church regarding slavery, and the reigning ideology of white supremacy. He also utilized a long-standing Protestant practice of wrapping his condemnation of planters within the mantle of God's impending wrath. His evocation of Judgment Day also would have caught the attention of the enslaved, who continually perused the natural world for signs of their impending deliverance by their heavenly Father.[47]

After justifying involuntary servitude by scripture and history, Verot proclaimed black inferiority and the duties associated with it. This is the portion of the sermon that southern whites celebrated. Their reading of the bishop's pro-slavery argument caused them to become unwitting heralds of the black version of the institution's history, as their printing presses and postal system spread Verot's analysis throughout the rebel states. But African Americans attending biracial churches were accustomed to ignoring such admonitions. They had learned to focus instead upon the more uplifting elements of Christian preaching.[48] Thus, it was the second part of the bishop's homily that delighted them.

Here, in unprecedentedly strong language, Verot linked the impending national bloodshed to God's anger at the sexual exploitation of black women. He demanded a sanctuary for them. He emphasized the need for "holiness of life in masters." Unless white men desisted from sexually abusing their African American charges, and encouraged as well as respected slave marriages and black families, they could not expect to triumph in their cause, for "the Almighty" might be using the "present disturbances" to destroy the "frequent occasions of immorality, which the subservient and degraded position of the slave offers to the lewd." According to Verot, Christian paternalism thus far had failed miserably. Whites ignored this aspect of the prelate's jeremiad at first, but as defeats on the battlefield accumulated, Verot's words began to unnerve them. Their encounters with black Union troops soon demonstrated to planters that, as the Frenchman had prophesied, the apocalypse had arrived. For the northeast Floridian Hattie Reed, it came in the form of a black infantryman fighting under the Stars and Stripes, who told the trembling planter's daughter that he had come to avenge the commercial conveyance of his enslaved wife to Georgia. The exbondsman demanded to "meet Pa face to face to teach him what it is to part man and wife."[49]

We would now celebrate Augustin Verot as a great man (rather than as merely a complicated though basically good one), if prior to the Civil War (as he vociferously did after the bloody conflict ended), he unequivocally had condemned involuntary servitude. But, Verot's antebellum reluctance to do so should not mask the stellar black diplomatic achievement of pressuring him to publicly defend enslaved families. According to Gannon, Verot was the first United States Catholic bishop to "enter national politics on an issue not directly affecting Catholicism as such." And, as the historian Albert Raboteau pointed out, although southern antebellum churches were "sincerely troubled by the issue of slave marriage," they never "even considered . . . petition[ing]" for its legalization. The scholar Barbara Mattick concluded that "[s]uch concern for female slaves and the open admission that the sexual abuse they often suffered was criminal was startling, especially coming from a Southern bishop." The fact that the Confederacy lapped up Verot's words attests to how superbly he packaged his outrage against white attacks on the black family. Scholars have acknowledged that the slave code that the St. Augustine prelate proposed soon was adopted by southern Episcopalians before spreading more widely throughout the seceded states.[50]

Verot's sermon, when viewed through the prism of African American folk diplomacy, takes on a new meaning. It reflects a "hidden" diplomatic history whose intellectual foundation originated with sixteenth-century black "cultural brokers" who interposed themselves between whites and Florida's native peoples. At the end of the next century, slaves fleeing to St. Augustine from South Carolina exploited geopolitics in order to pressure the Spanish Crown to decree a Catholic sanctuary for them in East Florida. During the subsequent decades of Spain's rule, black troops won glory and honors defending this sanctuary. Later, as the Second Seminole War raged, blacks had functioned as ambassadors or "sensebearers" for indigenous chieftains so that they might protect a maroon sanctuary from the machinations of Florida's American masters.[51]

At the same time, in St. Augustine, as the Patriot War claims cases continued to drag on, people of color, playing upon whites' financial interests, paternalism, and legalism, masterfully induced their oppressors to violate a long-standing ban on recording black historical accomplishments, for slaveholders well understood that "[p]astness," as the scholar Immanuel Wallerstein wrote, "is a tool persons use against each other."[52] White East Floridians, however, were using the past to wrest monetary concessions from the federal government. In the process, they inadvertently attested to blacks' bravery and dignity, as well as their oppression. African Americans in St. Augustine brandished this "usable past"[53] as a weapon in order to evoke and then attach themselves to whites' mental images of a Spanish golden age that wonderfully blended with the romanticism sweeping late-antebellum Florida. By exploiting their Hispanic Catholic heritage, they rode the wave of this romanticism in order to press their political agenda, which prioritized the protection of their families.

The Afro–East Floridian usable past (significantly grounded in Patriot War heroics that lived on in oral histories and were recorded in federal hearings) was performed liturgically in the Catholic Church and thereby constituted a rebellion against the U.S. slave society. Thus, they "wrote" their history for all to see in a sacred environment that temporarily suspended time.[54] One consequence of this strategy was that the sacrament of matrimony became a bulwark for black family lives. Elsewhere, by their astute reading of his personal history, black diplomats gauged Bishop Augustin Verot's interior sympathies. Seeing his potential as an ally, they succeeded, through their piety and the dissemination of their history, in enlisting Verot both as their ambassador and their historian. Incredibly, as a result, the Confederacy and its supporters became their sensebearers and their *griots.* During the eighteenth-century Stono Revolt, slaves fleeing South Carolina for religious sanctuary in St. Augustine had demonstrated the "revolutionary potential of Afro-Catholicism."[55] Within the hallowed confines of the Ancient City's historic Spanish-era house of worship, this Catholic militancy produced the antebellum Cana Sanctuary.

Notes

I have standardized the spellings of surnames in the text, but in the notes I have left them as they appear in the sources cited.

INTRODUCTION

1. Jane Landers, *Black Society in Spanish Florida* (Urbana: University of Illinois Press, 1999), 24, 291n93.

2. Ibid., 14–15, 23–25.

3. Ibid., 28–30, 34–39, 45–49, 56–62; Jane G. Landers, "Francisco Xavier Sanchez, *Floridano* Planter and Merchant," in *Colonial Plantations and Economy in Florida*, ed. Jane G. Landers (Gainesville: University Press of Florida, 2000), 85–86.

4. Landers, *Black Society*, 76–79; James G. Cusick, *The Other War of 1812: The Patriot War and the American Invasion of Spanish East Florida* (Gainesville: University Press of Florida, 2003), 149, 179–80, 210; Patricia C. Griffin, "The Spanish Return: The People-Mix Period 1784–1821," in *The Oldest City: St. Augustine, Saga of Survival*, ed. Jean Parker Waterbury (St. Augustine: St. Augustine Historical Society, 1983), 131–33, 148.

5. Landers, *Black Society*, 32, 107.

6. Colored Baptisms, Colored Marriages, Cathedral Parish Records, St. Augustine, Florida, St. Augustine Historical Society Research Library.

7. Thomas E. Will, "Weddings on Contested Grounds: Slave Marriage in the Antebellum South," *The Historian* 62 (Fall 1999): 99–117.

8. Michael V. Gannon, *The Cross in the Sand: The Early Catholic Church in Florida, 1513–1870* (Gainesville: University of Florida Press, 1965), 152.

9. Will, "Weddings on Contested Grounds," 102–3.

10. Herman L. Bennett, "Genealogies to a Past: Africa, Ethnicity, and Marriage in Seventeenth-Century Mexico," in *New Studies in the History of American Slavery*, ed. Edward E. Baptist and Stephanie M. H. Camp (Athens: University of Georgia Press, 2006), 129.

11. Mark M. Smith, "Remembering Mary, Shaping Revolt: Reconsidering the Stono Rebellion," *Journal of Southern History* 67 (August 2001): 513–34.

12. Bennett, "Genealogies to a Past," 130, 138–43; Virginia Gould, "In Full Enjoyment of Their Liberty: The Free Women of Color of the Gulf Ports of New Orleans, Mobile, and Pensacola, 1769–1860" (PhD diss., Emory University, 1989), 268–72.

13. Clive Parry, ed., *The Consolidated Treaty Series* (Dobbs Ferry, NY: Oceana, 1969), 70: 11; Herbert Bruce Fuller, *The Purchase of Florida: Its History and Diplomacy* (Cleveland: Burrows Brothers, 1906), 373–74; Landers, *Black Society,* 183; Daniel L. Schafer, "'A Class of People Neither Freemen Nor Slaves': From Spanish to American Race Relations in Florida, 1821–1861," *Journal of Social History* 26 (Spring 1993): 152; Canter Brown Jr., "Race Relations in Territorial Florida, 1821–1845," *Florida Historical Quarterly* 73 (January 1995): 304.

14. Cusick, *The Other War of 1812,* 4–11, 104–7, 169, 183, 185–86, 195, 209, 214–15, 265–66, 298; John Lewis Gaddis, *Surprise, Security, and the American Experience* (Cambridge, MA: Harvard University Press, 2004), 17–18; Michael Gannon, *Florida: A Short History* (Gainesville: University Press of Florida, 1993), 27–28; Jane G. Landers, introduction to *Colonial Plantations and Economy in Florida,* 1–10.

15. Cusick, *The Other War of 1812,* 4, 7–9, 15, 216–23, 231–35, 265–69, 292.

16. Parry, *The Consolidated Treaty Series,* 70: 11; Richard Peters, ed., *The Public Statutes at Large of the United States of America . . .* (Boston: Charles C. Little and James Brown, 1846), 3: 768, 6: 569; Rembert W. Patrick, *Florida Fiasco: Rampant Rebels on the Georgia-Florida Border, 1810–1815* (Athens: University of Georgia Press, 1954), 302.

17. Settled Miscellaneous Treasury Accounts, September 6, 1790–September 29, 1894, Office of the First Auditor, Records of the Accounting Officers of the Department of the Treasury, Record Group 217, National Archives, College Park, Maryland.

18. Sherry Johnson, "The St. Augustine Hurricane of 1811: Disaster and the Question of Political Unrest on the Florida Frontier," *Florida Historical Quarterly* 84 (Summer 2005): 28–56.

19. Gregg D. Kimball, "African, American, and Virginian: The Shaping of Black Memory in Antebellum Virginia, 1790–1860," in *Where These Memories Grow: History, Memory, and Southern Identity,* ed. W. Fitzhugh Brundage (Chapel Hill: University of North Carolina Press, 2000), 57–77.

20. Larry Eugene Rivers, *Slavery in Florida: Territorial Days to Emancipation* (Gainesville: University Press of Florida, 2000), 13.

21. John Hope Franklin and Loren Schweninger, *Runaway Slaves: Rebels on the Plantation* (New York: Oxford University Press, 1999), 291–92; Rivers, *Slavery in Florida,* 201–3.

22. Rivers, *Slavery in Florida,* 192, 224; Landers, *Black Society,* 229–35; Rosalyn Howard, *Black Seminoles in the Bahamas* (Gainesville: University Press of Florida, 2002), 31–32, 44–48.

23. Frank Marotti Jr., "Negotiating Freedom in St. Johns County, Florida, 1812–1862" (PhD diss., University of Hawai'i, 2003), 86–90.

24. Ibid., 196–99.

25. Gannon, *The Cross in the Sand,* 163–65, 169–70.

26. John B. Boles, *Black Southerners, 1619–1869* (Lexington: University Press of Kentucky, 1983), 213; W. Fitzhugh Brundage, "No Deed but Memory," in Brundage, *Where These Memories Grow,* 23; Eugene Genovese, *Roll, Jordan, Roll: The World the Slaves Made* (New York: Random House, 1974), xvii; Lawrence W. Levine, *Black Culture and Black Consciousness: Afro-American Folk Thought from Slavery to Freedom* (New York: Oxford University Press, 1977), xiv.

27. Kenneth S. Greenberg, "Name, Face, Body," in *Nat Turner: A Slave Rebellion in History and Memory,* ed. Kenneth S. Greenberg (New York: Oxford University Press, 2003), 3.

CHAPTER 1

1. Whitwell to Peck, Brooklyn, New York, 30 May 1868, "1840–1886 Part 1, legal battle over Alachua land grant (Garvin tract)," Peck Papers, St. Augustine Historical Society Research Library, St. Augustine, Florida (hereafter cited as SAHSL); J. P. Whitwell to J. R. Poinsett, Secretary of War, Boston, 12 January 1840, Letters received by the Adjutant General's Office, 1822–1860, Microfilm Publication M567, microfilm roll 220, 1840, V221-W193, #0287, #0228, Records of the Adjutant General's Office, Record Group 94, National Archives, Washington, D.C. (hereafter cited as RG 94); Registers of Enlistment in the U.S. Army, 1798–1914, Microfilm Publication M233, microfilm roll 20, Volume 41, 1835–1837, p. 231, RG 94; *St. Augustine Tatler,* 27 January 1894, SAHSL.

2. Louise Biles Hill, "George J. F. Clarke, 1774–1836," *Florida Historical Quarterly* 21 (January 1943): 197, 205–8, 216–21, 225, 228–29, 234; "Clarke, George F., Last Will and Testament," 28 August 1834, Clarke Papers, SAHSL; award of Judge Isaac H. Bronson, Account No. 94415, Charles Witter Clarke, Settled Miscellaneous Treasury Accounts, September 6, 1790–September 29, 1894, Office of the First Auditor, Records of the Accounting Officers of the Department of the Treasury, Record Group 217, National Archives, College Park, Maryland (hereafter cited as RG 217).

3. *St. Augustine Tatler,* 27 January 1894.

4. Whitwell to Peck; Undated clipping from the *St. Augustine Record,* [Spring 1890s?], William Whitwell Dewhurst Papers, SAHSL.

5. Daniel S. Papp, Loch K. Johnson, and John E. Endicott, *American Foreign Policy: History, Politics, and Policy* (New York: Pearson Longman, 2005), 49, 76–77.

6. Testimony of F. R. Sanches, Account No. 73008, Farquhar Bethune, RG 217; testimony of F. R. Sanchez, Account No. 73340, Manuel Solana, RG 217; testimony of Mrs. Mary Smith, Account No. 85848, William Fitzpatrick, RG 217; testimony of Zephaniah Kingsley, Account No. 86225, Henry Yonge, RG 217; testimony of Dr. James Hall, Account No. 84671, Prudance Plummer, RG 217; testimony of Matthew Long, Account No. 74759, Toby Herreira, RG 217; testimony of Charles W. Clarke, Account No. 83763, Clarke & Garvin, RG 217; testimony of George J. F. Clarke, Account No. 73347, Francisco D. and Peter Pons, RG 217; testimony of Mrs. Sarah Acosta, Account No. 95167, Joseph Summerall, RG 217.

7. Jane Landers, *Black Society in Spanish Florida* (Urbana: University of Illinois Press, 1999), 237–38, 242, 365n34; David J. Weber, *The Spanish Frontier in North America* (New Haven, CT: Yale University Press, 1992), 298; testimony of John Moses Bowden, Account No. 83177, George J. F. Clarke, RG 217; testimony of John Chevalier, Account No. 88415, Zephaniah Kingsley, RG 217; testimony of George J. F. Clarke, Account No. 73801, William Garvin, RG 217; testimony of George J. F. Clarke, Account No. 73347, Francisco D. & Peter Pons, RG 217; testimony of Joseph M. Hernandez, Account No. 85766, John Fraser, RG 217; testimony of Thomas Backhouse, Account No. 87923, Hibberson & Yonge, RG 217.

8. Weber, *The Spanish Frontier,* 274, 280–81; Landers, *Black Society,* 74–75; testimony of George J. F. Clarke, Account No. 73801, William Garvin, RG 217; testimonies of John Uptegrove, Charles Sibbald, Account No. 87923, Hibberson & Yonge, RG 217; testimony of William Brodnax, Account No. 85371, John H. McIntosh, RG 217; testimony of Zephaniah Kingsley, Account No. 76455, Francisco P. Fatio, Sr., RG 217.

9. Petition of George J. F. Clarke, testimonies of John Moses Bowden, Seymore Picket, Joseph Lourcey, Charles W. Clarke, Mathew Long, Simon Forrester, Tony Primus, Account No. 83177, George J. F. Clarke, RG 217; testimony of Seymore Pickitt, Account No. 94415, Charles Witter Clarke, RG 217; testimony of Charles W. Clarke, Account No. 83763, Clarke & Garvin, RG 217.

10. Petition of George J. F. Clarke, testimonies of Seymore Picket, Joseph Lourcey, Charles W. Clarke, John Moses Bowden, John Leonardy, Matthew Long, Peter Pons, John J. Abernathy, Tony Primus, award of Judge Isaac H. Bronson, Account No. 83177, George J. F. Clarke, RG 217.

11. Testimonies of John Moses Bowden, John Leonardy, Joseph Lourcey, Lorenzo Gracesqui, Peter Pons, Pedro Rodriguez, Account No. 83177, George J. F. Clarke, RG 217.

12. James G. Cusick, *The Other War of 1812: The Patriot War and the American Invasion of Spanish East Florida* (Gainesville: University Press of Florida, 2003), 67–68; Petition of John Houston McIntosh, testimonies of Gabriel Priest, Samuel Swearingen, William Brodnax, Samuel Russell, Account No. 85371, John H. McIntosh, RG 217.

13. Judge Isaac H. Bronson to Secretary of the Treasury W. M. Meredith, St. Augustine, 9 June 1849, Account No. 102005, Manuel Romero, RG 217; petition of John Houston McIntosh, testimonies of Gabriel Priest, John G. Rushing, Samuel Russell, Zephaniah Kingsley, John M. Bowden, William Brodnax, Account No. 85371, John H. McIntosh, RG 217; testimony of Joseph M. Hernandez, Account No. 85766, John Fraser, RG 217.

14. Testimony of Zephaniah Kingsley, Account No. 85371, John H. McIntosh, RG 217; petition of Zephaniah Kingsley; testimonies of John M. Bowden, Francis Richard, Seymour Picket, Account No. 88415, Zephaniah Kingsley, RG 217.

15. Amended petition of the Executor of the Estate of John Fraser; testimonies of Farquhar Bethune, Francis Richard, George Gianopoli, Joseph M. Hernandez, Philip Weadman; award of Judge Isaac H. Bronson, Account No. 85766, John Fraser, RG 217; Joseph M. Hernandez to John C. Spencer, Secretary of the Treasury, Washington, D.C., 12 January 1844, Account No. 88415, Zephaniah Kingsley, RG 217.

16. Petition of Cornelius Taylor; testimonies of Mrs. Jane Redding, Philip Dewees; petition of Winslow Foster, Account No. 75008, Catherine Baker, RG 217; See maps in Cusick, *The Other War of 1812*, 94, and Landers, *Black Society*, 103; George M. Bibb, Secretary of the Treasury, to the Accounting Officers of the Treasury Department, 26 April 1844, J. J. Papy, attorney for the claimants, to G. M. Bibb, Secretary of the Treasury, St. Augustine, 5 October 1844, Account No. 91018, James Black & Dorcas Black, RG 217; testimonies of James G. Mattair, James Bardin, Mrs. Sarah Acosta, Charles B. Penrose, Solicitor of the Treasury, to Thomas Ewing, Secretary of the Treasury, 27 April 1841, Account No. 81650, Sarah Petty, RG 217; testimony of Jane Reddin[g], Account No. 87900, Mary Dewees, RG 217; award of Isaac H. Bronson, Account No. 82466, Mary O'Neill, RG 217.

17. Testimonies of Jane Redding, Philip Dewees, John Floyd, Joseph Mattair, Account No. 75008, Catherine Baker, RG 217; testimonies of Thomas Suarez, Seymour Pickett, Maria Hogans, Sarah B. McDonnell, Account No. 92003, Lucy Fitzgerald, RG 217; amended petition of Benjamin A. Putnam, testimony of Margaret Starrett, Account No. 86134, Mary E. Saunders, RG 217; amended petition of Margaret Starrat, petition of Joseph L. Smith, testimonies of Robert Harrison, Samuel Swearingen, Ferdinand D. McDonald, Thomas Suarez, Samuel Russell, Thomas J. Andrew, Account No. 78509, Margaret Starrat, RG 217.

18. Testimonies of Philip Weedman, Ann Maria Hernandez, Account No. 84638, John Bunch, RG 217; petition of Joseph M. Hernandez and Anna Maria Hernandez, testimonies of Philip Weedman, Sr., Francis Pellicer, will of Samuel Williams, Account No. 76042, Samuel

Williams, RG 217; petition of Mrs. Sarah P. Anderson, testimonies of Mrs. Ann Maria Hernandez, General Joseph M. Hernandez, Account No. 73358, Mrs. Frances Kerr, RG 217; petition of Charles Lawton, testimonies of Mrs. Ann Maria Hernandez, General Joseph M. Hernandez, Account No. 108178, James & Emanuel Ormond, RG 217.

19. Daniel L. Schafer, "'A Swamp of an Investment'?: Richard Oswald's British East Florida Plantation Experiment," in *Colonial Plantations and Economy in Florida,* ed. Jane G. Landers (Gainesville: University Press of Florida, 2000), 33n18; petition of George J. F. Clarke, testimonies of Joseph Lourcey, Charles W. Clarke, John Moses Bowden, John Leonardy, Pedro Rodriguez, Zephaniah Kingsley, Mathew Long, Lorenzo Gracesqui, James Arnowe, Account No. 83177, George J. F. Clarke, RG 217.

20. Petition of George J. F. Clarke, testimonies of James Arnowe, Lorenzo Gracesqui, Peter Pons, Bartolo Pons, award of Judge Isaac H. Bronson, Account No. 83177, George J. F. Clarke, RG 217; petition of George J. F. Clarke, testimonies of Charles W. Clarke, Pedro Rodriguez, Mathew Long, John Leonardi, Account No. 83763, Clarke & Garvin, RG 217; testimony of George J. F. Clarke, award of Judge Isaac H. Bronson, Account No. 73801, William Garvin, RG 217.

21. Petition of George J. F. Clarke, testimonies of Mathew Long, Charles W. Clarke, John Leonardy, Pedro Rodriguez, Bartolo Ponce, Bartolo Leonardy, Tony Primus, Account No. 83177, George J. F. Clarke, RG 217; Petition of Charles W. Clarke, award of Judge Isaac H. Bronson, testimonies of Seymore Pickitt, Tony Primus, Francis Pellicer, Martin Canovas, Lawrence Graceski, Joseph S. Sanchez, Matthew Long, Account No. 94415, Charles W. Clarke, RG 217; testimony of Charles W. Clarke, Account No. 90173, Justo Lopez, RG 217; testimony of Mathew Long, Account No. 75214, Francis Pellicer, RG 217; "Sitiki, 'The Story of Uncle Jack' Draft 2," Buckingham Smith Papers, Manuscript Division, New York Historical Society, New York, New York.

22. Testimony of Estevan Arnow, Account No. 73629, Jose E. Pomar & Juana Rogero & others, RG 217; testimonies of Joseph Baya, Andreas Pacetty, Sr., Mateo Lorenzo, Account No. 87746, Margarita Acosta, RG 217.

23. Petition of Pablo Sabate, testimonies of Pedro Fouchar, John Moses Bowden, James Arnowe, Paul Masters, award of Judge Isaac H. Bronson, Account No. 85093, Pablo Sabate, RG 217.

24. Petition of Margarita Acosta, testimonies of Jose Baya, Andreas Pacetty, Sr., Mateo Lorenzo, Account No. 87746, Margarita Acosta, RG 217.

25. Testimony of Esteven Arnow, Andreas Pacetti, Sr., Account No. 82538, Christopher Lopez, RG 217; testimony of Estevan Arnow, Account No. 73629, Jose E. Pomar & Juana Rogero & others, RG 217; testimonies of Joseph Baya, Francis Triay, Benet Segui, Account No. 89739, Andreas Pacetti, RG 217; testimonies of Joseph Baya, Estevan Arnow, Account No. 82542, John Lawrence, RG 217.

26. Patricia C. Griffin, "Blue Gold: Andrew Turnbull's New Smyrna Plantation," in Landers, *Colonial Plantations,* 39–68; Griffin, "Mullet on the Beach: The Minorcans of Florida, 1768–1788," special issue, *El Escribano: The St. Augustine Journal of History* 27 (1990): 1, 3–4; Weber, *The Spanish Frontier,* 278.

27. Testimonies of Andres Pacetti, Bennet Segui, Account No. 72686, Joseph Baya, RG 217; testimony of Andreas Pacetty, Account No. 102832, John Capo, RG 217.

28. Testimonies of Bartolo Pons, Mateo Lorenzo, Andreas Pacetti, Sr., Esteven Arnow, Account No. 82538, Christopher Lopez, RG 217.

29. "Sitiki, The Story of Uncle Jack"; testimony of John M. Bowden, Account No. 88415, Zephaniah Kingsley, RG 217; testimony of Sophia Fleming, Account No. 94405, Francis P.

Fatio, Jr., RG 217; testimonies of Zephaniah Kingsley, Louis Fleming, Farquhar Bethune, Account No. 89602, Francis P. Fatio, Sr., RG 217; testimonies of Philip Weedman, Sr., John Leonardi, George Petty, Zephaniah Kingsley, Account No. 76455, Francis P. Fatio, Sr., RG 217.

30. Claim of Andrew Atkinson, Patriot War Papers & Patriot War Claims, 1812–1846, SAHSL; testimonies of John M. Bowden, Francis Richard, William Barden, Seymour Picket, award of Judge Isaac H. Bronson, Account No. 88415, Zephaniah Kingsley, RG 217; testimonies of Michael Andrew, Philip Weedman, Bartolome Leonardi, Account No. 75878, Jose Peso de Burgos, RG 217; testimonies of William Bardin, Philip Weedman, Account No. 80361, Edward M. Wanton, RG 217; Landers, *Black Society,* 219.

31. Daniel L. Schafer, "Zephaniah Kingsley's Laurel Grove Plantation, 1803–1813," in Landers, *Colonial Plantations,* 115n13; claim of Delores English, Patriot War Papers & Patriot War Claims, 1812–1846, SAHSL; John Fontane v. Felicia M. Garvin (1846), 117-14, St. Johns County Court Cases, SAHSL.

32. Testimonies of Charles W. Clarke, John Leonardy, Bartolo Leonardy, Tony Primus, Account No. 83177, George J. F. Clarke, RG 217; testimony of Joseph Summerall, Account No. 81650, Sarah Petty, RG 217; Michael Williams, *Americans and Their Forests: A Historical Geography* (Cambridge: Cambridge University Press, 1989), 72, 74.

33. Petition of Geronima Tatin, testimony of Michael Andrew, Account No. 75878, Jose Peso de Burgos, RG 217; Daniel L. Schafer, *Anna Kingsley* (St. Augustine: St. Augustine Historical Society, 1994), 21; "Sitiki, The Story of Uncle Jack"; testimonies of George Cla, John Masters, Sr., Paul Masters, Account No. 81371, Pedro Cocifacio, RG 217; Griffin, "Mullet on the Beach," 16, 32, 64, 66, 144, 151, 154, 156–57, 169, 179–80.

34. Petition of Susan Follis, testimonies of Joseph Summerlin, George Petty, Henry Hartly, John M. Bowden, James Plummer, Philip Weedman, Joseph Lourcey, Michael Sloane, Account No. 81613, Follis & Gunby, RG 217.

35. Testimonies of Francis R. Sanchez, Joseph Lourcey, Account No. 81613, Follis & Gunby, RG 217; testimonies of Andrew Pacetti, Estevan Arnow, Joseph Baya, Account No. 76104, Bennet Segui, RG 217.

36. Certified translation of the loyalty oath of Robert Hutchinson, testimonies of Elijah Higginbotham, Francis R. Sanches, Thomas Higginbotham, James R. Woodland, Elizabeth Jones, Samuel Swearingen, Joseph Higginbotham, Account No. 94416, Robert Hutchinson, RG 217.

37. Testimony of John Broward, Account No. 89730, Peter B. Maxey, RG 217.

38. Testimonies of John Houston, James Woodland, William Houston, Account No. 84647, Spicer Christopher, RG 217; Testimonies of John Houston, James Mattair, Account No. 86381, Lewis Christopher, RG 217.

39. Testimony of General Joseph M. Hernandez, Account No. 86282, Fernando de la Maza Arredondo, Jr., RG 217; testimonies of Robert Harrison, James Woodland, Samuel Russell, Jeremiah Wingate, Account No. 84647, Spicer Christopher, RG 217; testimony of Francis Pellicer, Account No. 74759, Toby Herreira, RG 217; testimony of George J. F. Clarke, Account No. 73347, Francisco D. and Peter Pons, RG 217; testimony of Charles Seton, Account No. 73008, Farquhar Bethune, RG 217; testimony of James Green, Account No. 98529, Samuel Sauls, RG 217; testimony of Zephaniah Kingsley, Account No. 86225, Henry Yonge; testimonies of General Joseph M. Hernandez, Bartolo Solana, Account No. 86282, Fernando de la Maza Arredondo, Jr., RG 217; testimony of Francis R. Sanchez, Account No. 73340, Manuel Solana, RG 217.

40. Petition of James Pellicer, testimonies of Francis Pellicer, John Pellicer, award of Judge Robert R. Reid, Account No. 75877, Joseph Hughes, RG 217; testimony of General Joseph

M. Hernandez, Account No. 86282, Fernando de la Maza Arredondo, Jr., RG 217; award of Judge Isaac H. Bronson, testimonies of Philip Weedman, Sr., John Moses Bowden, Account No. 85040, Arredondo & Huertas, RG 217; petition of Felipe Solana, testimony of Francis R. Sanchez, award of Judge Robert R. Reid, Account No. 73340, Manuel Solana, RG 217.

41. Testimony of Samuel Swearingen, Account No. 98529, Samuel Sauls, RG 217; testimonies of William Black, Mrs. Cynthia Sweeny, Account No. 87748, John Black, RG 217.

42. Jane G. Landers, "Francisco Xavier Sanchez, *Floridano* Planter and Merchant," in Landers, *Colonial Plantations,* 83–90; Landers, *Black Society,* 85.

43. Landers, "Francisco Xavier Sanchez," 90–92; Kim Hazouri, "From Jose Mariano Hernandez to Joseph Martin Hernandez: 1788–1856," 12, unpublished manuscript, SAHSL; testimonies of John Masters, Estevan Arnowe, Ann Maria Hernandez, Francis Roman Sanchez, Account No. 74969, Estate of Francis X. Sanchez, RG 217.

44. Testimony of Charles W. Clarke, Account No. 83177, George J. F. Clarke, RG 217; testimony of Mathew Long, Francis Pellicer, Account No. 94415, Charles Witter Clarke, RG 217; testimonies of James Pellicer, Francis Pellicer, Account No. 86282, Fernando de la Maza Arredondo, Jr., RG 217; testimony of John Pellicer, Account No. 75877, Joseph Hughes, RG 217; testimony of Francis Pellicer, Account No. 89469, John B. Ferreira, RG 217; testimonies of George J. F. Clarke, Charles W. Clarke, James Arnowe, Account No. 73801, William Garvin, RG 217.

45. Testimony of Captain Winslow Foster, Account No. 73801, William Garvin, RG 217; award of Judge Robert R. Reid, Account No. 82538, Christopher Lopez, RG 217; Judge Robert R. Reid to the Secretary of the Treasury, St. Augustine, 31 August 1836, Records of Letters Sent, Florida Claims 1834–1842, Correspondence, General Records of the Department of the Treasury, Record Group 56, National Archives, College Park, Maryland; award of Judge Isaac H. Bronson, Account No. 94421, John Morell, RG 217.

46. Award of Judge Isaac H. Bronson, Account No. 102005, Manuel Romero, RG 217; testimonies of Francis Richard, Sr., William Munroe, award of Judge Isaac H. Bronson, Account No. 83831, Rebecca E. Read, RG 217; testimonies of Rebecca E. Read, Dr. James Hall, Account No. 83129, Francis Richard, Sr., RG 217; Weber, *The Spanish Frontier,* 353–60; Jane G. Landers, introduction to *Colonial Plantations,* 1.

47. Weber, *The Spanish Frontier,* 347–53.

48. *St. Augustine Tatler,* 27 January 1894; Landers, *Black Society,* 150–53, 171; Daniel L. Schafer, "'A Class of People Neither Freemen Nor Slaves': From Spanish to American Race Relations in Florida, 1821–1861," *Journal of Social History* 26 (Spring 1993): 587–610.

49. *St. Augustine Tatler,* 27 January 1894; "Sitiki, The Story of Uncle Jack"; Daniel Schafer, "Zephaniah Kingsley's Laurel Grove Plantation, 1803–1813," in Landers, *Colonial Plantations,* 120n35; John Lewis Gaddis, *The Cold War: A New History* (New York: Penguin Press, 2005), 192.

CHAPTER 2

1. Testimony of Thomas Suarez, Account No. 78699, Thomas Andrew, Settled Miscellaneous Treasury Accounts, September 6, 1790–September 29, 1894, Office of the First Auditor, Records of the Accounting Officers of the Department of the Treasury, Record Group 217, National Archives, College Park, Maryland (hereafter cited as RG 217).

2. Larry E. Rivers, *Slavery in Florida: Territorial Days to Emancipation* (Gainesville: University Press of Florida, 2000), 203.

3. Testimony of Mrs. Sarah Acosta, Account No. 95167, Joseph Summerall, RG 217; tes-

timony of Estevan Arnow, Account No. 73629, Juan Pomar, RG 217; testimony of John Egan, Account No. 83129, Francis Richard, Sr., RG 217; testimony of William Monroe, Account No. 85848, William Fitzpatrick, RG 217; testimony of Samuel Swearingen, Account No. 85371, John H. McIntosh, RG 217; testimony of Zephaniah Kingsley, Account No. 86225, Henry Yonge, RG 217.

4. Testimony of John Bowden, Account No. 83761, Henry Hartley, RG 217; testimony of Abraham Daniels, Account No. 82248, James Dell, RG 217; testimony of Mrs. Mary Smith, Account No. 85848, William Fitzpatrick, RG 217; testimony of Estevan Arnow, Account No. 73639, Juan Pomar, RG 217; petition of Mathew Long, Account No. 74862, George Long, RG 217.

5. Testimony of Mateo Lorenzo, Account No. 75214, Francis Pellicer, RG 217; testimony of Rebecca Read, and petition of Francis Richard, Jr., Account No. 83129, Francis Richard, Sr., RG 217; testimony of Rebecca E. Read, Account No. 81651, Francis Richard, Jr., RG 217; testimony of Gabriel Priest, Account No. 84719, Nathaniel Wilds, RG 217.

6. Testimonies of John Bowden, James Plummer, Account No. 83761, Henry Hartley, RG 217; testimony of Gabriel Priest, Account No. 84719, Nathaniel Wilds, RG 217; testimony of Thomas J. Andrew, Account No. 79230, William Braddock, RG 217; testimony of Joseph Lourcey, Account No. 85848, William Fitzpatrick, RG 217; testimony of James Pellicer, Account No. 74862, George Long, RG 217.

7. Testimony of William Black, Account No. 81651, Francis Richard, Jr., RG 217; testimony of Paul Masters, Account No. 81371, Pedro Cocifacio, RG 217; testimony of Enoch Daniels, Account No. 92279, John Dixon, RG 217.

8. Testimony of James Mattair, Account No. 88510, Horatio Low, RG 217; testimonies of John Masters Senior, Anthony Masters, Paul Masters, Account No. 81371, Pedro Cocifacio, RG 217.

9. Testimony of Thomas Suarez, Account No. 86134, Mary E. Saunders, RG 217; testimony of James R. Woodland, Account No. 104775, Lodovic Ashley, RG 217; testimony of Philip Weadman, Account No. 100476, Antonio Andrew (the younger), RG 217; testimony of Rebecca E. Read, Account No. 83129, Francis Richard, Sr., RG 217.

10. Testimony of John Wingate, Account No. 78259, Michael & Garrit Ledwith, RG 217; testimony of Mathew Long, Account No. 75214, Francis Pellicer, RG 217; testimony of Zephaniah Kingsley, Account No. 86225, Henry Yonge, RG 217; testimony of Joseph A. Mattair, Account No. 79403, Samuel Harrison, RG 217; testimony of John D. Braddock, Account No. 84719, Nathaniel Wilds, RG 217; testimony of Samuel Harrison, Account No. 86134, Mary E. Saunders, RG 217; testimony of James Green, Account No. 98529, Samuel Sauls, RG 217; testimony of William McCullough, Account No. 83057, Stephen Vanzandt, RG 217.

11. Testimonies of James Woodland, William McCullough, Jesse Long, William Munro, Account No. 83057, Stephen Vanzandt, RG 217.

12. Testimonies of Samuel Swearingen, James Green, Account No. 98529, Samuel Sauls, RG 217.

13. Testimonies of Francis R. Sanchez, James R. Woodland, Elizabeth Jones, Samuel Swearingen, Joseph Higginbotham, oath of allegiance of Robert Hutchinson, Account No. 94416, Robert Hutchinson, RG 217.

14. Testimony of George J. F. Clarke, Account No. 73350, Francisco D. & Peter Pons, RG 217; testimony of Seymour Pickett, Stephen Williamson, Account No. 82301, Gabriel Priest, RG 217; testimony of Zephaniah Kingsley, Account No. 86225, Henry Yonge, RG 217; testimonies of Seymore Pickitt, Lawrence Graceski, Account No. 94415, Charles Witter Clarke,

RG 217; testimony of Joseph Lourcey, Account No. 90774, George Atkinson, RG 217; testimonies of Henry Sweeney, Charles Sibbald, Account No. 87923, Hibberson & Yonge, RG 217; testimony of James A. Rogers, Account No. 104775, Lodovic Ashley, RG 217; testimony of Stephen Williamson, Account No. 85371, John H. McIntosh, RG 217; testimony of Joseph Lourcey, Account No. 81613, Follis & Gunby, RG 217; testimony of John Leonardi, Account No. 76455, Francis P. Fatio, Sr., RG 217; testimonies of Farquhar Bethune, Samuel Sauls, Account No. 89063, William Mills, RG 217; testimony of Ramon Sanchez, Account No. 80681, Bernardino & Joseph Sanchez, RG 217.

15. Testimonies of Britton Knight, Henry Sweeney, and letter from Justo Lopez to Don Sebastian Kindelan, 18 June 1812, Account No. 87923, Hibberson & Yonge, RG 217; testimony of George J. F. Clarke, Account No. 73801, William Garvin, RG 217; testimony of James Woodland, Account No. 108413, John D. Braddock, RG 217; petition of Sophia Fleming and Lewis Fleming, Account No. 89454, George Fleming, RG 217; testimony of Lewis Fleming, Account No. 94405, Francis P. Fatio, Jr., RG 217.

16. Testimony of Jeremiah Wingate, Account No. 77524, Eleazer Waterman, RG 217; testimony of John Jones, Account No. 81651, Francis Richard, Jr., RG 217; testimony of James Plummer, Account No. 89416, Robert Gilbert, Sr., RG 217; testimony of Jeremiah Wingate, Account No. 82467, Eber O'Neill, RG 217.

17. Testimony of Joseph Lourcey, Account No. 85848, William Fitzpatrick, RG 217; testimonies of John M. Bowden, Francis Richard, Account No. 88415, Zephaniah Kingsley, RG 217; testimony of John D. Braddock, Account No. 79367, William Berrie, RG 217; testimony of James Hall, Account No. 73800, John Crichton, RG 217; testimony of James Pellicer, Account No. 74862, George Long, RG 217; testimonies of Francis Richard, Jr., Joseph M. Hernandez, Account No. 85766, John Fraser, RG 217; testimony of James Plummer, Account No. 83761, Henry Hartley, RG 217; testimony of Joseph Manucy, Account No. 87751, Francis Triay, RG 217; testimony of James Mattair, Account No. 89730, Peter B. Maxey, RG 217; testimony of Henry Hartley, Account No. 82782, David S. H. Miller, RG 217; testimony of William Braddock, Account No. 83762, William O'Neil, RG 217.

18. Testimony of Rebecca E. Read, Account No. 83129, Francis Richard, Sr., RG 217; testimony of Francis Pellicer, Account No. 89050, Robert McHardy, RG 217.

19. Susan R. Parker, "The Cattle Trade in East Florida, 1784–1821," in *Colonial Plantations and Economy in Florida,* ed. Jane G. Landers (Gainesville: University Press of Florida, 2000), 161; testimony of George J. F. Clarke, Account No. 77834, Philip R. Yonge, RG 217; testimony of Zephaniah Kingsley, Account No. 86225, Henry Yonge, RG 217; testimony of Joseph M. Hernandez, Account No. 85766, John Fraser, RG 217; testimonies of James A. Rogers, Joseph Haddock, Account No. 104775, Lodovic Ashley, RG 217.

20. Testimony of Robert Harrison, Account No. 73313, Fernando D. McDonnell, RG 217; testimony of Joseph A. Mattair, Account No. 77822, Antonio Suarez, RG 217; testimony of Mathew Long, Account No. 75214, Francis Pellicer, RG 217; testimonies of Mathew Long, Philip Weadman, Account No. 84638, John Bunch, RG 217; testimonies of Samuel Swearingen, Mrs. Susan Murphy, Account No. 89535, James Cashen, RG 217; testimonies of John Houston, James Mattair, Account No. 86381, Lewis Christopher, RG 217; testimony of Seymour Picket, Account No. 88415, Zephaniah Kingsley, RG 217.

21. Testimony of James A. Mattair, Account No. 77822, Antonio Suarez, RG 217; testimony of Samuel Swearingen, Account No. 83229, Robert Andrew, RG 217; testimony of Samuel Swearingen, Account No. 97178, Daniel Hogans, RG 217; testimonies of Harry Hartley, William Bardin, Account No. 83229, John Crichton, RG 217.

22. Testimony of Mrs. Ann Marie Hernandez, Account No. 108178, James Ormond, RG 217; testimonies of Jesse Long, John M. Bowden, Account No. 89454, George Fleming, RG 217; testimony of John Uptegrove, Account No. 83129, Francis Richard, Jr., RG 217; testimony of Pedro Rodriguez, Account No. 102005, Manuel Romero, RG 217; testimonies of John G. Rushing, John M. Bowden, Account No. 85731, John H. McIntosh, RG 217.

23. Testimonies of Kingsley B. Gibbs, Joseph M. Hernandez, Account No. 88415, Zephaniah Kingsley, RG 217; testimony of Paul Masters, Account No. 81371, Pedro Cocifacio, RG 217; testimonies of Dr. James Hall, John Leonardi, Account No. 76455, Francis P. Fatio, Sr., RG 217; testimony of Juan Leonardi, Account No. 76003, Joseph Floyd, RG 217; testimony of John M. Bowden, Account No. 89454, George Fleming, RG 217; testimony of Philip Weadman, Account No. 84638, John Bunch, RG 217; testimony of John G. Rushing, Account No. 85371, John H. McIntosh, RG 217; testimony of James Mattair, Account No. 86146, John B. Christopher, RG 217; testimony of Zephaniah Kingsley, Account No. 86225, Henry Yonge, RG 217; testimony of George Gianopoli, Account No. 85766, John Fraser, RG 217; petition of Joseph M. Hernandez & wife Anna Maria, Account No. 76042, Samuel Williams, RG 217.

24. Testimony of Charles W. Clarke, Account No. 83177, George J. F. Clarke, RG 217; testimony of Philip Weadman, Account No. 73915, John Forbes, RG 217; testimony of Sophia Fleming, Account No. 94405, Francis P. Fatio, Jr., RG 217; testimony of John Leonardi, Account No. 76455, Francis P. Fatio, Sr., RG 217; testimony of George Petty, Account No. 88415, Zephaniah Kingsley, RG 217; testimonies of John Houston, Robert Harrison, William Houston, Account No. 84647, Spicer Christopher, RG 217; testimonies of Seymour Pickitt, Robert Harrison, Sarah B. McDonell, Thomas Suarez, Account No. 92003, Lucy Fitzgerald, RG 217; petition of Susan Murphy, Account No. 82290, James Cashen, RG 217.

25. Testimony of Charles W. Clarke, Account No. 83763, Clarke & Garvin, RG 217; testimonies of Charles W. Clarke, Lorenzo Gracesqui, Bartolo Ponce, Pedro Rodriguez, James Arnowe, John Moses Bowden, Peter Pons, Account No. 83177, George J. F. Clarke, RG 217; testimonies of George J. F. Clarke, Charles W. Clarke, Account No. 73801, William Garvin, RG 217.

26. Testimonies of Peter Pons, John J. Abernathy, Bartolo Ponce, Joseph Lourcey, Lorenzo Gracesqui, Account No. 83177, George J. F. Clarke, RG 217; testimony of Charles W. Clarke, Account No. 83763, Clarke & Garvin, RG 217.

27. Testimony of Phillip Weadman, Account No. 89050, Robert McHardy, RG 217; testimony of Phillip Weadman, Account No. 73358, Frances Kerr, RG 217; testimony of George Gianopoly, Account No. 78184, James Smith, RG 217; testimony of John Chevalier, Account No. 88415, Zephaniah Kingsley, RG 217; testimonies of Charles W. Clarke, Lawrence Graceski, Account No. 90713, Justo Lopez, RG 217; testimony of Peter A. Masters, Account No. 81371, Pedro Cocifacio, RG 217; testimony of Catherine Taylor, Account No. 80150, Philip Dewees, RG 217.

28. Testimony of Phillip Weadman, Account No. 89050, Robert McHardy, RG 217; testimonies of John G. Rushing, John M. Bowden, George Petty, Account No. 85371, John H. McIntosh, RG 217.

29. Testimony of Paul Masters, Account No. 81371, Pedro Cocifacio, RG 217; testimony of Philip Dewees, Account No. 86138, William Dewees, RG 217; testimony of Joseph A. Mattair, Account No. 77822, Antonio Suarez, RG 217.

30. Testimonies of Robert Harrison, Thomas Suarez, John D. Vaughn, Seymour Pickitt, Account No. 92003, Lucy Fitzgerald, RG 217.

31. Testimonies of Margaret Starratt, Maria Hogans, Sarah B. McDonell, Thomas Suarez, Robert Harrison, Account No. 92003, Lucy Fitzgerald, RG 217.

32. Testimony of William Gardner, Account No. 97406, William Bardin, RG 217; testi-

mony of Seymour Pickett, Account No. 73358, John J. Lowe, RG 217; testimonies of Samuel Russell, Samuel Swearingen, Account No. 82989, Joseph Higginbotham, RG 217; testimony of Stephen Williamson, Account No. 87381, William Nelson, RG 217; testimony of John Jones, Account No. 81651, Francis Richard, Jr., RG 217; testimony of Samuel Swearingen, Account No. 83762, William O'Neil, RG 217; testimony of Henry Sweeney, Account No. 82248, James Dell, RG 217; testimony of George Petty, Account No. 102005, Manuel Romero, RG 217; testimonies of James E. Mattair, Thomas Suarez, Account No. 86134, Mary E. Saunders, RG 217; testimony of John Bowden, Account No. 83761, Henry Hartley, RG 217.

33. Testimony of Samuel Russell, Account No. 85371, John H. McIntosh, RG 217; testimony of Charles W. Clarke, Account No. 90713, Justo Lopez, RG 217; testimony of Catherine Taylor, Account No. 80150, Philip Dewees, RG 217; testimony of Rafael Olivares, Account No. 99518, Fernando Fulany, RG 217; testimony of Samuel Swearingen, Account No. 82989, Joseph Higginbotham.

34. Testimony of Anthony Masters, Account No. 81371, Pedro Cocifacio, RG 217; testimonies of Mrs. C. Taylor, Philip Dewees, Account No. 76003, Joseph Floyd, RG 217; testimony of Seymour Pickett, Account No. 78259, Michael & Garrit Ledwith, RG 217; testimony of Antonio Andrea, Account No. 74385, Peter Meastre, Sr., RG 217; testimony of Rebecca E. Read, Account No. 77890, William Hart, RG 217; testimony of James Pellicer, Account No. 77132, Gabriel W. Perpall, RG 217; testimonies of William Lofton, Harry Hartley, Account No. 89416, Robert Gilbert, Sr., RG 217; testimony of John M. Bowden, Account No. 89454, George Fleming, RG 217; testimony of James Plummer, Account No. 73800, John Crichton, RG 217; testimony of William Broadnax, Account No. 101109, George Morrison, RG 217; testimony of Mateo Lorenzo, Account No. 75214, Francis Pellicer, RG 217; testimony of Matthew Long, Account No. 84638, John Bunch, RG 217.

35. Testimony of William Braddock, Account No. 83762, William O'Neil, RG 217; testimonies of George Petty, William Gardner, Harry Hartley, James Plummer, Account No. 89416, Robert Gilbert, Sr., RG 217; testimonies of Louisa Fatio, Sophia Fatio, John M. Bowden, Account No. 89454, George Fleming, RG 217; testimony of Lewis Fleming, Account No. 76455, Francis P. Fatio, RG 217; testimony of Mrs. Sarah Acosta, Account No. 95167, Joseph Summerall, RG 217; testimonies of Philip Weadman, William Bardin, petition of Edward M. Wanton, Account No. 80361, Edward M. Wanton, RG 217.

36. James Cusick, *The Other War of 1812: The Patriot War and the American Invasion of Spanish East Florida* (Gainesville: University Press of Florida, 2003), 195; Parker, "The Cattle Trade in East Florida," 150.

37. Testimony of Dr. James Hall, Account No. 73340, Manuel Solana (the Elder), RG 217; statement of Isaac H. Bronson, Account No. 85040, Fernando de la Maza Arredondo, Sr. & Antonio Huertas, RG 217; testimony of General Joseph M. Hernandez, Account No. 74969, Estate of Francis X. Sanchez, RG 217; testimony of George J. F. Clarke, Account No. 73350, Francisco D. & Peter Pons, RG 217; testimony of George Petty, Account No. 73800, John Crichton, RG 217; testimony of Ramon Sanchez, Account No. 75214, Francis Pellicer, RG 217; testimony of Thomas J. Andrews, Account No. 77094, John D. Vaughan, RG 217; testimony of Francis Pellicer, Account No. 94415, Charles Witter Clarke, RG 217.

38. Charles W. Arnade, "Raids, Sieges, and International Wars," in *The New History of Florida,* ed. Michael Gannon (Gainesville: University Press of Florida, 1996), 102; Michael Gannon, *Florida: A Short History* (Gainesville: University Press of Florida, 1993), 8–10.

39. Testimony of General Joseph M. Hernandez, Account No. 86282, Fernando de la Maza Arredondo, Jr., RG 217; testimony of John Pellicer, Account No. 75877, Joseph Hughes, RG 217; testimonies of Philip Weadman, Sr., Ramon Sanchez, Lewis Fleming, Bartolo So-

lana, George Petty, John Moses Bowden, Andres Papy, Isaac H. Bronson, Account No. 85040, Fernando de la Maza Arredondo, Sr. & Antonio Huertas, RG 217; testimonies of Dr. James Hall, John Bowden, Francis R. Sanchez, Account No. 73340, Manuel Solana (the Elder), RG 217; testimony of Francis R. Sanchez, petition of Ramon Sanchez & Jose E. Sanchez, Account No. 75015, Ramon and Nicholas Sanchez, RG 217; testimonies of Francis R. Sanchez, John Masters, Estevan Arnowe, Account No. 74969, Estate of Francis X. Sanchez, RG 217; testimony of Charles W. Clarke, Account No. 73063, Felipe Solana, RG 217.

40. Testimonies of James Woodland, Samuel Russell, Jeremiah Wingate, Account No. 76531, John D. Braddock, RG 217; testimony of John M. Bowden, Account No. 85371, John H. McIntosh, RG 217; testimony of James Woodland, Account No. 83057, Stephen Vanzandt, RG 217; testimony of Gabriel Priest, Account No. 84719, Nathaniel Wilds, RG 217; testimony of Bennet Maxey Dell, Account No. 83832, William Dell, RG 217; testimony of William Gardner, Account No. 97406, William Bardin, RG 217; testimonies of John M. Bowden, Charles W. Clarke, Account No. 73063, Felipe Solana, RG 217.

41. Testimonies of Gabriel Priest, Samuel Russell, John M. Bowden, Account No. 85371, John H. McIntosh, RG 217; testimony of George Petty, Account No. 77889, John M. Bowden, RG 217; testimony of Joseph Summerlin, Account No. 81613, Follis & Gunby, RG 217; testimony of Samuel Swearingen, Account No. 98529, Samuel Sauls, RG 217.

42. Testimony of William Daniels, Account No. 108207, Hardin Lanier, RG 217; testimony of R. Sanchez, Account No. 82248, James Dell, RG 217; testimonies of Henry Sweeny, Joseph S. Sanchez, Account No. 87060, Francis R. Sanchez, RG 217; testimony of Francis R. Sanchez, Account No. 74969, Estate of Francis X. Sanchez, RG 217; testimony of Emanuel Mott, Account No. 76339, John Ashton, RG 217; testimonies of Jeremiah Wingate, Isaac Wingate, Account No. 75783, John Wingate, RG 217; testimonies of Estevan Arnou, Francis Triay, Account No. 87753, Peter Trope, RG 217; testimony of Andres Pacetti, Account No. 72686, Joseph Baya, RG 217.

43. Testimony of William Williamson, Account No. 87381, William Nelson, RG 217; testimonies of William Black, Mrs. Cynthia Sweeney, petition of John Black, Account No. 87748, John Black, RG 217; testimonies of John Worley, David Turner, James R. Woodland, Account No. 99331, Jane Lane, RG 217; testimony of Mathew Long, Account No. 75214, Francis Pellicer, RG 217; testimony of Francis Pellicer, Account No. 89469, John B. Ferreira, RG 217; testimony of James Pellicer, Account No. 86282, Fernando de la Maza Arredondo, Jr., RG 217.

44. Testimony of Francis R. Sanchez, Account No. 73340, Manuel Solana (the Elder), RG 217; testimony of Seymour Pickett, Account No. 86282, Fernando de la Maza Arredondo, Jr., RG 217; testimony of John M. Bowden, Account No. 85371, John H. McIntosh, RG 217; testimony of John Leonardy, Account No. 75182, Gaspar Pappy, RG 217.

45. Testimony of Francis R. Sanchez, Account No. 73340, Manuel Solana (the Elder), RG 217; testimony of Felipe Solana, Account No. 87747, Mattias Pons, RG 217; testimonies of Francis Pellicer, James Pellicer, Account No. 86282, Fernando de la Maza Arredondo, Jr., RG 217; testimonies of Ramon Sanchez, Mathew Long, James Dell, Account No. 75214, Francis Pellicer, RG 217; testimony of Francis Pellicer, Account No. 89469, John B. Ferreira, RG 217; testimony of James Pellicer, Account No. 80681, Bernardino & Joseph Sanchez, RG 217; testimony of Robert Hodges, Account No. 108206, Willoughby Hodges, RG 217; testimony of Thomas Suarez, Account No. 79022, Lewis Mattair, RG 217; testimony of John M. Bowden, Account No. 85371, John H. McIntosh, RG 217; testimony of Mrs. Sarah Acosta, Account No. 95167, Joseph Summerall, RG 217.

46. Testimony of Charles W. Clarke, Account No. 73063, Felipe Solana, RG 217; testi-

mony of Philip Weadman, Sr., Account No. 85040, Fernando de la Maza Arredondo, Sr. & Antonio Huertas, RG 217; testimony of Stephen Williamson, Account No. 85371, John H. McIntosh, RG 217; testimony of John Uptegrove, Account No. 83129, Francis Richard, Sr., RG 217; testimony of Pablo Masters, Account No. 75015, Ramon & Nicholas Sanchez, RG 217; testimony of Isaac Wingate, Account No. 75783, John Wingate, RG 217; testimony of William Black, Account No. 87748, John Black, RG 217; testimony of Paul Masters, Account No. 82775, John Segui, RG 217; testimony of Dr. James Hall, Account No. 74969, Estate of Francis X. Sanchez, RG 217; testimony of Francis R. Sanchez, Account No. 84671, Prudance Plummer, RG 217; testimony of Mrs. Eliza Crews, Account No. 94405, Francis P. Fatio, Jr., RG 217.

47. Daniel L. Schafer, *Anna Kingsley* (St. Augustine, FL: St. Augustine Historical Society, 1994), 29; testimonies of Estevan Arnowe, General Joseph M. Hernandez, Account No. 74969, Estate of Francis X. Sanchez, RG 217; testimony of Thomas Suarez, Account No. 90713, Justo Lopez, RG 217; testimony of John Uptegrove, Account No. 83128, Francis Richard, Sr., RG 217; testimonies of James Woodland, Samuel Russell, Jeremiah Wingate, Account No. 108413, John D. Braddock, RG 217; testimonies of Charles W. Clarke, Miguel Papy, Account No. 73063, Felipe Solana, RG 217; testimony of John Houston, Account No. 84647, Spicer Christopher, RG 217; testimony of Philip Dewees, Account No. 83318, William Dewees, RG 217; testimony of Seymour Pickett, Account No. 78259, Michael & Garrit Ledwith, RG 217; testimony of Samuel Russell, Account No. 79022, Lewis Mattair, RG 217; testimony of Robert Harrison, Account No. 73313, Fernando D. McDonnell, RG 217; testimony of William Odam, Account No. 73924, Seymour Pickett, RG 217.

48. Testimonies of Jeremiah Wingate, John Wingate, Samuel Russell, Account No. 85341, Samuel S. Christopher, RG 217; testimonies of George Hartley, George Petty, Account No. 90228, Frederick Hartley, RG 217; testimonies of James A. Rogers, John Haddock, Account No. 104775, Lodovic Ashley, RG 217; testimonies of Thomas Suarez, Ephraim Harrison, Account No. 77094, John D. Vaughan, RG 217; testimonies of William Braddock, Samuel Russell, Account No. 83762, William O'Neil, RG 217; testimonies of Abraham Daniels, William Daniels, Account No. 82248, James Dell, RG 217; testimony of James Dell, Account No. 92279, John Dixon, RG 217; Francis Marine, in James Falany, "Papers Relating to Claims by the Inhabitants of Florida Under the Treaty of Spain of 1819," Box No. 2, Florida, Land Suits, 1829–1880, Records of the Solicitor of the Treasury, Record Group 206, National Archives, College Park, Maryland.

49. Testimony of Philip Weadman, Sr., Account No. 77118, Lorenzo Solana, RG 217; testimony of James R. Woodland, Account No. 92475, David Turner, RG 217; testimony of Francis Pellicer, Account No. 76042, Samuel Williams, RG 217; testimony of Lewis Fleming, Account No. 94405, Francis P. Fatio, Jr., RG 217.

CHAPTER 3

1. James M. Denham and Keith L. Huneycutt, eds., *Echoes from a Distant Frontier: The Brown Sisters' Correspondence from Antebellum Florida* (Columbia: University of South Carolina Press, 2004), 57n7; Robert Raymond Reid to the Secretary of the Treasury, St. Augustine, 31 August 1836, Records of Letters Sent, Florida Claims 1834–1842, Correspondence, General Records of the Department of the Treasury, Record Group 56, National Archives, College Park, Maryland (hereafter cited as RG 56); Testimony of Mrs. Jane Redding, Account No. 75008, Catherine Baker, Settled Miscellaneous Treasury Accounts, September 6, 1790–

September 29, 1894, Office of the First Auditor, Records of the Accounting Officers of the Department of the Treasury, Record Group 217, National Archives, College Park, Maryland (hereafter cited as RG 217); testimony of James Plummer, Account No. 81613, Arbino Follis & Levin Gunby, RG 217; J. Clark, Solicitor, to Thomas Corwin, Secretary of the Treasury, Washington, D.C., 12 March 1852, Account No. 79230, William Braddock, RG 217.

2. Susan R. Parker, "Success through Diversification: Francis Philip Fatio's New Switzerland Plantation," in *Colonial Plantations and Economy in Florida,* ed. Jane G. Landers (Gainesville: University Press of Florida, 2000), 69–71, 76, 79; testimony of Sophia Fleming, Account No. 94405, Francis P. Fatio, Jr., RG 217.

3. Parker, "Success through Diversification," 73, 79.

4. Testimony of James Arnowe, Account No. 79073, Juan Leonardy, RG 217; testimony of Samuel Swearingen, Account No. 85371, John H. McIntosh, RG 217.

5. Testimony of Lewis Fleming, Account No. 89602, Francis P. Fatio, Sr., RG 217; testimony of Lewis Fleming, Account No. 76455, Francis P. Fatio, Sr., RG 217; testimony of Lewis Fleming, Account No. 94405, Francis P. Fatio, Jr., RG 217; Robert Raymond Reid to the Secretary of the Treasury, St. Augustine, 31 August 1836, RG 56; award of Isaac H. Bronson, Account No. 94405, Francis P. Fatio, Jr., RG 217.

6. Petition of John L'Engle and David R. Dunham, testimonies of Sophia Fleming, Mrs. Eliza Crews, award of Isaac H. Bronson, Account No. 94405, Francis P. Fatio, Jr., RG 217; testimonies of W.E. Broadnax, Farquhar Bethune, Zephaniah Kingsley, John M. Bowden, Account No. 89602, Francis P. Fatio, Sr., RG 217; testimonies of Farquhar Bethune, William Broadnax, George Petty, Philip Weedman, Sr., Francis Roman Sanchez, Account No. 76455, Francis P. Fatio, Sr., RG 217; petition of John L'Engle and David R. Dunham, Account No. 76455, Francis P. Fatio, Sr., RG 217.

7. Testimonies of Mrs. Eliza Crew, Sophia Fleming, Account No. 94405, Francis P. Fatio, Jr., RG 217.

8. Testimonies of Sophia Fleming, Mrs. Eliza Crews, Account No. 94405, Francis P. Fatio, Jr., RG 217; petition of John L'Engle and David Dunham, Account No. 76455, Francis P. Fatio, Sr., RG 217; testimonies of John Leonardi, William Brodnax, James Hall, Lewis Fleming, Account No. 89602, Francis P. Fatio, Sr., RG 217; testimony of Zephaniah Kingsley, Account No. 76455, Francis P. Fatio, Sr., RG 217.

9. Testimonies of Mrs. Eliza Crews, Sophia Fleming, Account No. 94405, Francis P. Fatio, Jr., RG 217; testimony of Mrs. Sophia Fleming, Account No. 89602, Francis P. Fatio, Sr., RG 217; testimony of William Brodnax, Account No. 76455, Francis P. Fatio, Sr., RG 217.

10. Testimonies of Mrs. Eliza Crews, Sophia Fleming, Account No. 94405, Francis P. Fatio, Jr., RG 217; testimony of Farquhar Bethune, Account No. 89602, Francis P. Fatio, Sr., RG 217; John K. Mahon, "Daniel Newnan: A Neglected Figure in Florida History," *Florida Historical Quarterly* 74 (Fall 1995): 148–49; Denham and Huneycutt, *Echoes from a Distant Frontier,* 5n5; testimonies of Farquhar Bethune, Francis R. Sanchez, Account No. 94405, Francis P. Fatio, Jr., RG 217; testimony of William Brodnax, Dr. James Hall, Account No. 76455, Francis P. Fatio, Sr., RG 217.

11. Testimonies of Sophia Fleming, Lewis Fleming, William Brodnax, Francis R. Sanchez, Henry Hartley, George Petty, Farquhar Bethune, Account No. 76455, Francis P. Fatio, Sr., RG 217; testimonies of John M. Bowden, Farquhar Bethune, W. E. Broadnax, George Petty, Zephaniah Kingsley, Account No. 89602, Francis P. Fatio, Sr., RG 217; testimony of Mrs. Eliza Crews, 94405, Francis P. Fatio, Jr., RG 217; testimony of W.E. Broadnax, Account No. 88415, Zephaniah Kingsley, RG 217.

12. James G. Cusick, *The Other War of 1812: The Patriot War and the American Invasion of Spanish East Florida* (Gainesville: University Press of Florida, 2003), 240–43; testimony of William Gardner, Account No. 97406, William Bardin, RG 217; testimonies of John M. Bowden, Mrs. Mary Ann Bowden, Account No. 116929, John Beardon, RG 217; testimony of William Black, Account No. 87748, John Black, RG 217; testimony of Zephaniah Kingsley, Account No. 82290, James Cashen, RG 217; testimonies of J. M. Bowden, John Houston, W.E. Broadnax, Account No. 88415, Zephaniah Kingsley, RG 217; testimonies of John M. Bowden, William E. Broadnax, Account No. 101109, George Morrison, RG 217; testimony of John G. Rushing, Account No. 85371, John H. McIntosh, RG 217; testimonies of Francis R. Sanchez, Doctor James Hall, William Monroe, Account No. 84671, Prudence Plummer, RG 217; testimony of Mrs. Sarah Acosta, Account No. 95167, Joseph Summerall, RG 217; testimony of Michael Sloan, Account No. 88590, George Petty, RG 217; testimony of Elijah Higginbotham, Claim of James Erwin, Patriot War Papers & Patriot War Claims (hereafter cited as Patriot War Claims), St. Augustine Historical Society Research Library, St. Augustine, Florida (hereafter cited as SAHSL).

13. Testimony of Mrs. Eliza Crews, Account No. 94405, Francis P. Fatio, Jr., RG 217; testimonies of John M. Bowden, George Petty, William Bardin, Francis Richard, John Houston, Samuel Swearingen, Account No. 88415, Zephaniah Kingsley, RG 217; testimony of Sophia Fleming, Account No. 89454, George Fleming, RG 217.

14. Cusick, *The Other War of 1812,* 141, 240, 246, 276–77, 280, 287–91, 308; Chris Monaco, "Fort Mitchell and the Settlement of the Alachua Country," *Florida Historical Quarterly* 79 (Summer 2000): 9–11, 22, 25.

15. Award of Isaac H. Bronson, Account No. 94405, Francis P. Fatio, Jr., RG 217; testimony of Catherine Taylor, Account No. 80150, Philip Dewees, RG 217; testimony of William Daniels, Account No. 108206, Willoughby Hodges, RG 217; testimony of Sarah B. McDonell, Account No. 92003, Lucy Fitzgerald, RG 217; testimony of Andrew Fullwood, Account No. 98530, Ezekial Hudnall, RG 217; Cusick, *The Other War of 1812,* 268–69; testimony of James R. Woodland, Claim of James Erwin, Patriot War Claims, SAHSL.

16. D. Levy to Secretary of the Treasury[?], n.d., testimonies of Ferdinand McDonald, Philip Weedman, A. A. Massias, Account No. 82290, James Cashen, RG 217; testimonies of James Mattair, Thomas Suarez, Account No. 89536, James Cashen, RG 217; testimonies of Mrs. Susan Murphy, Seymore Pickett, Account No. 89535, James Cashen, RG 217.

17. Testimonies of Mrs. Susan Murphy, Samuel Swearingen, John Ennis, Account No. 89535, James Cashen, RG 217; testimonies of Zephaniah Kingsley, A. A. Massias, Jeremiah Wingate, Account No. 82290, James Cashen, RG 217.

18. Testimonies of Joseph Lourcey, Thomas Suarez, Account No. 89536, James Cashen, RG 217; testimonies of Samuel Swearingen, Mrs. Susan Murphy, Account No. 89535, James Cashen, RG 217.

19. David Bushnell, "The Republic of Florida: An Overview," in *La Republica de las Floridas: Texts and Documents,* comp. David Bushnell (Mexico City: Pan American Institute of Geography and History, 1986), 7, 9–10, 14–16; L. David Norris, "Failure Unfolds: The Loss of Amelia Island," in Bushnell, *La Republica de las Floridas,* 19; Gerald E. Poyo, "La Republica de las Floridas: The Mexican Connection, 1814–1817," in Bushnell, *La Republica de las Floridas,* 35, 38–41; Charles H. Bowman Jr., "Amelia Island and Vicente Pazos of Upper Peru," in Bushnell, *La Republica de las Floridas,* 45, 48, 53–54.

20. Bushnell, "The Republic of Florida," 10, 16; Norris, "Failure Unfolds," 19, 26; Bowman Jr., "Amelia Island," 48; testimony of Domingo Acosta, Account No. 89486, Jose Ber-

gall, RG 217; testimony of Joseph Lourcey, Account No. 108169, Mathew Long, RG 217; testimony of Joseph Lourcey, Account No. 106617, Henry Groves, RG 217; testimony of Seymour Picket, Account No. 94420, Arbina Follis, RG 217; testimony of Joseph Lourcey, Account No. 89536, James Cashen, RG 217.

21. Testimonies of Seymour Picket, Thomas Suarez, Joseph Lourcey, John Middleton, Account No. 106617, Henry Groves, RG 217; testimonies of Antonio Dias, Ynocencio Cardonar, John Middleton, Andrew Lopez, Account No. 97445, Antonio Diaz, RG 217.

22. Testimonies of James Mattair, Joseph Lourcey, Account No. 89536, James Cashen, RG 217; testimony of Mrs. Susan Murphy, Account No. 89535, James Cashen, RG 217.

23. Award of Isaac H. Bronson, Account No. 119599, Joseph Arnow, RG 217; award of Isaac H. Bronson, Account No. 83177, George J. F. Clarke, RG 217; Robert Raymond Reid to the Secretary of the Treasury, 31 August 1836, RG 56; award of Joseph L. Smith, Account No. 89486, Jose Bergall, RG 217; testimonies of Farquhar Bethune, Witter Clarke, George J. F. Clarke, award of Joseph L. Smith, Account No. 86402, Charles F. Sibbald, RG 217.

24. Testimony of Sarah Acosta, Account No. 73915, John Forbes, RG 217.

25. Testimony of George J. F. Clarke, Account No. 73350, Francisco D. & Peter Pons, RG 217; Cusick, *The Other War of 1812,* 203; Gil Jose Pacot to Don Sebastian Kindelan, 2 May 1813, Account No. 90774, George Atkinson, RG 217.

26. Testimonies of Jose Lalderol, Matthew Long, George Gianoply, Account No. 75214, Francis Pellicer, RG 217; testimonies of Domingo Circoply, Francis Pellicer, Account No. 89469, John B. Ferreira, RG 217; testimony of James Pellicer, Account No. 86282, Fernando de la Maza Arredondo, Jr., RG 217.

27. Testimonies of John M. Bowden, Jacob Summerlin, Account No. 75214, Francis Pellicer, RG 217; testimony of Francis Pellicer, Account No. 89469, John B. Ferreira, RG 217.

28. Testimony of Joseph Baya, Account No. 87746, Margarita Acosta, RG 217; testimony of Benet Segui, Account No. 89739, Andreas Pacetti, RG 217; testimonies of Stephen Arnow, Francis Marine, Account No. 72384, John Gianoply, RG 217; testimony of Antonio Canovas, Account No. 83784, Bartolo Canovas, RG 217; testimony of Estevan Arnow, Account No. 76104, Bennet Segui, RG 217; award of Robert R. Reid, Account No. 72686, Joseph Baya, RG 217.

29. Award of Robert R. Reid, testimony of John Masters, Account No. 75187, John Andrew, RG 217; petition of Peter Capella, testimonies of Esteban Arnau, John Leonardy, John Carreras, Antonio Pons, Joseph Pacetty, Account No. 103431, Andrew Capella, RG 217; testimonies of Diego Hernandez, Ramon Rogero, in James Falany, "Papers Relating to Claims by the Inhabitants of Florida Under the Treaty of Spain of 1819," Box No. 2, Florida, Land Suits, 1829–1880, Records of the Solicitor of the Treasury, Record Group 206, National Archives, College Park, Maryland (hereafter cited as RG 206); testimony of James Arnowe, Account No. 81194, Roque Leonardi, RG 217; testimony of Antonio Capo, Account No. 75881, Philip Weadman, RG 217; testimony of Antonio Capo, Account No. 76339, John Ashton, RG 217; testimonies of George Gianople, Philip Weadman Senior, John M. Bowden, Account No. 76528, Lewis Scofield, RG 217; testimony of Mrs. Mary Weedman, Account No. 79073, Juan Leonardy, RG 217; testimony of Antony Hinsman, Account No. 75881, Philip Weadman, RG 217; testimonies of Andrew Paceti, Joseph Lourcey, Domingo Circople, John Leonardy, Account No. 82629, Anthony Hindsman, RG 217.

30. Testimony of J. M. Bowden, Account No. 88415, Zephaniah Kingsley, RG 217; testimony of Ramon Sanchez, Account No. 76340, Lazaro Ortega, RG 217; petition of Ramon Sanchez and Jose E. Sanchez, testimony of Peter Masters, Account No. 75015, Ramon Sanchez

and Nicholas Sanchez, RG 217; petition of Joseph M. Hernandez and wife Anna Maria, testimony of Philip Weedman, Sr., Account No. 76042, Samuel Williams, RG 217; testimonies of Ann Maria Hernandez, Philip Weedman, Mrs. Mary Weadman, Francisco Pellicer, Account No. 84638, John Bunch, RG 217; testimony of Francis Pellicer, Account No. 74862, George Long, RG 217; testimonies of Seymour Pickett, James Pellicer, Account No. 86282, Fernando de la Maza Arredondo, Jr., RG 217; testimonies of Mathew Long, Jose Lalderol, Account No. 75214, Francis Pellicer, RG 217.

31. Testimonies of Charles W. Clarke, Miguel Papy, Account No. 73063, Felipe Solana, RG 217; testimony of George Petty, Account No. 88415, Zephaniah Kingsley, RG 217; testimony of Estevan Arnowe, Jr., Account No. 102005, Manuel Romero, RG 217; testimonies of James Arnowe, John Moses Bowden, Account No. 85093, Pablo Sabate, RG 217; testimonies of Domingo Sarcopoli, Bennet Segui, Account No. 76105, James Arnow, RG 217.

32. Testimony of Charles W. Clarke, Account No. 73063, Felipe Solana, RG 217; testimony of James Arnow, Account No. 75880, Domingo Segui, RG 217; testimony of James Arnowe, Account No. 85093, Pablo Sabate, RG 217.

33. Testimonies of Estevan Arnow, Francis Triay, Andres Pacetti, Paul Masters, Antonio Masters, Account No. 82775, John Segui, RG 217; testimony of Antonio Maestre, Account No. 100475, Antonio Andrew, RG 217.

34. Testimonies of Paul Masters, Antonio Masters, Estevan Arnow, Francis Triay, Andres Pacetti, Account No. 82775, John Segui, RG 217; testimony of Antonio Maestre, Account No. 100475, Antonio Andrew, RG 217.

35. Testimonies of Andres Pacetti, Francis Triay, Account No. 72686, Joseph Baya, RG 217; testimonies of Estevan Arnow, Mateo Lorenzo, Account No. 73629, Jose E. Pomar & Juana Rogero & others, RG 217; testimonies of Diego Hernandez, John Carreras, in James Falany, RG 206; testimony of Sophia Fatio, Account No. 89454, George Fleming, RG 217; testimony of Andres Papy, Account No. 75214, Francis Pellicer, RG 217; testimonies of Estevan Arnow, Bartolo Pons, Account No. 82538, Christopher Lopez, RG 217; testimony of Joseph Baya, Account No. 89739, Andreas Pacetty, RG 217; testimony of Andreas Pacetti, Account No. 79073, Juan Leonardy, RG 217; testimony of Antonio Masters, Account No. 75015, Ramon Sanchez and Nicholas Sanchez, RG 217; testimony of Estevan Arnow, Account No. 76104, Bennet Segui, RG 217; testimony of Estevan Arnow, Account No. 82542, John Lawrence, RG 217.

36. Testimony of Esteven Arnau, Account No. 81942, Albert Rogero, RG 217; testimony of Bennet Segui, Account No. 87750, John Triay, RG 217; testimonies of Andrew Pacetti, Joseph Baya, Account No. 76104, Bennet Segui, RG 217; testimonies of Andres Pacetti, Bennet Segui, Francis Triay, Account No. 72686, Joseph Baya, RG 217; testimonies of Estevan Arnow, Andreas Pacetti, Sr., Bartolo Pons, Account No. 82538, Christopher Lopez, RG 217.

37. Testimonies of Andreas Pacetti, Sr., Estevan Arnow, Account No. 82538, Christopher Lopez, RG 217; testimonies of Joseph Baya, Francis Triay, Benet Segui, Account No. 89739, Andreas Pacetti, RG 217; testimony of Joseph E. Pomar, Account No. 73629, Jose Hernandez, RG 217; testimony of Francis Triay, Account No. 72686, Joseph Baya, RG 217; testimonies of Joseph Baya, Joseph Manucy, Account No. 87751, Francis Triay, RG 217; testimonies of Stephen Arnou, John Carreras, Account No. 102832, John Capo, RG 217; testimony of Estevan Arnow, Account No. 76104, Bennet Segui, RG 217; testimonies of Joseph G. Manucy, Peter Trope, John Carreras, Account No. 82859, Francis Triay, RG 217; testimony of Joseph Baya, Account No. 82543, Margarita Bevis Santana, RG 217; testimony of Mrs. Mary Weadman, Account No. 79073, John Leonardy, RG 217.

38. Testimony of Bennet Segui, Account No. 72686, Joseph Baya, RG 217; testimony of Estevan Arnow, Account No. 82538, Christopher Lopez, RG 217; testimony of George J. F. Clarke, Account No. 73350, Francisco D. and Peter Pons, RG 217; testimony of John Carreras, Account No. 82859, Francis Triay, RG 217; testimony of Estevan Arnow, Account No. 76104, Bennet Segui, RG 217; testimony of Antonio Canovas, Account No. 83784, Bartolo Canovas, RG 217; testimony of Joseph Manucy, Account No. 72384, John Gianoply, RG 217; testimony of Joseph E. Pomar, Account No. 73629, Jose Hernandez, RG 217; testimony of Mrs. Mary Weedman, Account No. 79073, Juan Leonardy, RG 217; testimony of Bartolo Ponce, Account No. 73629, Juan Pomar, RG 217.

39. Testimony of Jose Baya, Account No. 87746, Margarita Acosta, RG 217; testimonies of Gabriel W. Perpall, John Masters Senior, Account No. 81371, Pedro Cocifacio, RG 217; testimony of Joseph E. Pomar, Account No. 73629, Francisco Yanobar, RG 217; testimony of Joseph E. Pomar, Account No. 73629, Jose Hernandez, RG 217; testimony of Estevan Arnow, Account No. 76104, Bennet Segui, RG 217; testimonies of James Arnow, Matteo Lorenzo, Account No. 75880, Domingo Segui, RG 217; testimony of Joseph G. Manucy, Account No. 82859, Francis Triay, RG 217; testimony of Joseph Manucy, Account No. 87751, Francis Triay, RG 217; testimony of Antonio Canovas, Account No. 83784, Bartolo Canovas, RG 217; testimonies of Sophia Fleming, Bartolo Leonardy, Account No. 94405, Francis P. Fatio, Jr., RG 217; testimony of Joseph Manucy, Account No. 72384, John Gianoply, RG 217; testimony of Estevan Arnow, Account No. 82538, Christopher Lopez, RG 217; testimonies of Rafael Olivares, Francis Marine, John Pellicer, Account No. 99518, Fernando Fulany, RG 217; testimony of Peter A. Masters, Account No. 100475, Antonio Andrew, RG 217; testimony of Francis Triay, Account No. 87747, Mattias Pons, RG 217; testimony of Mathew Long, Account No. 89469, John B. Ferreira, RG 217.

40. Testimony of Estevan Arnow, Account No. 82538, Christopher Lopez, RG 217; testimony of Zephaniah Kingsley, Account No. 86225, Henry Yonge, RG 217.

41. Testimony of Charles W. Clarke, Patriot War Claims, Benjamin Wiggins, SAHSL; testimony of George Petty, Account No. 88415, Zephaniah Kingsley, RG 217; testimony of Francis Pellicer, Account No. 76042, Samuel Williams, RG 217; testimony of Francis Pellicer, Account No. 89469, John B. Ferreira, RG 217; testimony of James Pellicer, Account No. 75215, Isaac Weeks, RG 217; testimony of Francis Marine, Account No. 72384, John Gianoply, RG 217; testimony of Bartolo Ponce, Account No. 73629, Juan Pomar, RG 217; testimony of Andres Pacetti, Account No. 72686, Joseph Baya, RG 217; testimony of Martin Canovas, Account No. 94415, Charles Witter Clarke, RG 217; testimony of Philip Weadman, Account No. 100476, Antonio Andrew (the younger), RG 217; testimony of Ramon Rogero, in James Falany, RG 206; testimony of Francis Triay, Account No. 72686, Joseph Baya, RG 217; testimony of Joseph Baya, Account No. 82543, Margarita Bevis Santana, RG 217; testimony of Bennet Segui, Account No. 87751, Francis Triay, RG 217; testimony of Andreas Papy, Account No. 75214, Francis Pellicer, RG 217; testimony of Ann Maria Hernandez, Account No. 84638, John Bunch, RG 217.

42. Testimony of Francis Roman Sanchez, Account No. 73063, Felipe Solana, RG 217; testimony of Andreas Papy, Account No. 75214, Francis Pellicer, RG 217; testimony of General Joseph M. Hernandez, Account No. 108178, James Ormond, RG 217; testimony of Matteo Lorenzo, Account No. 74768, Bartolome Leonardi, RG 217; testimony of Sophia Fatio, Account No. 89454, George Fleming, RG 217; testimony of Andrew Pacetti, Account No. 76104, Bennet Segui, RG 217; testimony of Matteo Lawrence, Account No. 81963, John Ponce, RG 217; testimony of Joseph Summerlin, Account No. 81613, Arbina Follis and Levin

Gunby, RG 217; testimony of Bartolo Pons, Account No. 82538, Christopher Lopez, RG 217; testimonies of Andres Pacetti, Francis Triay, Account No. 72686, Joseph Baya, RG 217; testimony of Joseph Baya, Account No. 89739, Andreas Pacetti, RG 217; testimony of Estevan Arnow, Account No. 82538, Christopher Lopez, RG 217; testimony of Lawrence Graceski, Account No. 90713, Justo Lopez, RG 217; testimony of George J. F. Clarke, Account No. 73350, Francisco D. and Peter Pons, RG 217; testimony of Lawrence Gracesqui, Account No. 108172, Daniel Hurlbert, RG 217; testimony of James Arnowe, Account No. 81194, Roque Leonardi, RG 217; testimony of Zephaniah Kingsley, Account No. 86225, Henry Yonge, RG 217.

CHAPTER 4

1. Ryan Buncher, "Perfect Name for Great New Ken QB," *Tarentum (PA) Valley News Dispatch* (hereafter cited as VND), 29 October 1995, special section, "Greatest 11: Area's Greatest High School Football Players as Chosen by the Readers," 4, 9; George Guido, "Thrower's Legacy Didn't Dim with Age," VND, 21 February 2002, sec. B, 4; John Vivirito Jr., "Ken High Retains Title with Shutout," VND, 31 October 1993, special section, "Greatest Area High School Football Games of All Time," 9.

2. Buncher, "Perfect Name for Great New Ken QB," 9; John Vivirito Jr., "A Little Nudge Is All Big Mo Needed," VND, 29 October 1995, "Greatest 11," 6; Rob Amen, "Ken High Football Great Dies," VND, 21 February 2002, sec. A, 1; Guido, "Thrower's Legacy Didn't Dim with Age," 1, 4; Stephanie A. Rex, "Willie Thrower Statue Takes Its Place," VND, 25 July 2006, http://www.pittsburghlive.com/x/pittsburghtrib/news/mostread/s463282.html (accessed 5 September 2009).

3. Buncher, "Perfect Name for Great New Ken QB," 9; Rob Amen, "Gentle Giant: NFL Pioneer Willie Thrower Dies at 71," VND, 21 February 2002, sec. B, 1; Guido, "Thrower's Legacy Didn't Dim with Age," 1.

4. Amen, "Gentle Giant"; Chuck Finder, "Trail Blazer: Willie 'The Pro' Thrower Opened Door for Black Quarterbacks," *Pittsburgh Post-Gazette,* 24 February 2002, http://www.post-gazette.com/sports/columnists/20020224finder0224p1.asp, 1–3 (accessed 19 February 2004).

5. Testimony of Francis Roman Sanchez, Account No. 73063, Felipe Solana, Settled Miscellaneous Treasury Accounts, September 6, 1790–September 29, 1894, Office of the First Auditor, Records of the Accounting Officers of the Department of the Treasury, Record Group 217, National Archives, College Park, Maryland (hereafter cited as RG 217); Jane Landers, *Black Society in Spanish Florida* (Urbana: University of Illinois Press, 1999), 77, 88, 97, 101–2, 122.

6. Landers, *Black Society,* 77, 119, 128.

7. J. H. Alexander, "The Ambush of Captain John Williams, U.S.M.C.: Failure of the East Florida Invasion 1812–1813," *Florida Historical Quarterly* 56 (January 1978): 280, 293–95; *St. Augustine Florida Herald,* 31 August 1836; Captain John Williams to Lieutenant Colonel Franklin Wharton, Commandant of the Marine Corps, Davis Creek Block House, East Florida, 15 September 1812, Volume 16. Letters Received, 1798–1817, Office of the Commandant, Headquarters, U.S. Marine Corps, Record Group 127, National Archives, Washington, D.C. (hereafter cited as RG 127); Joseph H. Alexander, "Swamp Ambush in Florida," *Military History* 14 (March 1998): 40, 44.

8. Testimony of George J. F. Clarke, Account No. 73350, Francisco D. & Peter Pons, RG 217; testimonies of Robert Harrison, Margaret Sterret, Thomas Suarez, Account No. 73313,

Fernando D. McDonnell, RG 217; testimony of Charles W. Clarke, Account No. 73063, Felipe Solana, RG 217.

9. Williams to Wharton, 15 September 1812, RG 127; Alexander, "The Ambush of Captain John Williams," 293; testimony of George J. F. Clarke, Account No. 73350, Francisco D. & Peter Pons, RG 217; Zephaniah Kingsley, "Address to the Legislative Council of Florida on the Subject of Its Coloured Population by Z. Kingsley a Planter of That Territory," 1823, Manuscript Collection 11, Florida Collection, State Library of Florida, Tallahassee; testimonies of Zephaniah Kingsley, Account No. 86225, Henry Yonge, RG 217; testimony of Zephaniah Kingsley, Account No. 82290, James Cashen, RG 217.

10. Louise Biles Hill, "George J. F. Clarke, 1774–1836," *Florida Historical Quarterly* 21 (January 1943): 198–253. For details on Kingsley's family, see Daniel L. Schafer, *Anna Madgigine Jai Kingsley: African Princess, Florida Slave, Plantation Slaveowner* (Gainesville: University Press of Florida, 2003); testimony of Dr. James Hall, Account No. 74969, Estate of Francis X. Sanchez, RG 217; award of Isaac H. Bronson, Account No. 98273, Prince Whilton, RG 217; *St. Augustine Florida Herald,* 31 August 1836.

11. Landers, *Black Society,* 28, 30, 221–26.

12. Ibid., 223–26; Alexander, "The Ambush of Captain John Williams," 289, 291.

13. Testimony of Esteven Arnow, Account No. 82988, Peter Capo, RG 217; petition of Francis Richard, Jr., testimonies of John Jones, Isaiah D. Hart, John Uptegrove, Lewis Hogan, Account No. 83129, Francis Richard, Jr., RG 217.

14. Testimony of Mathew Long, Account No. 75214, Francis Pellicer, RG 217; testimony of Joseph Summerall, Account No. 81650, Sarah Petty, RG 217; testimony of James R. Woodland, Account No. 89050, Robert McHardy, RG 217; testimony of Thomas Backhouse, Account No. 87923, Hibberson & Yonge, RG 217.

15. Testimony of John M. Bowden, Account No. 72942, James Hall, RG 217; Williams to Wharton, RG 127; petition of William Travers, Account No. 73915, John Forbes, RG 217; testimonies of Antony Hinsman, Andreas Pacetti, Account No. 75881, Philip Weadman, RG 217.

16. Testimony of Andreas Pacetty, Sr., Account No. 87746, Margarita Acosta, RG 217; testimony of Estevan Arnow, Account No. 82538, Christopher Lopez, RG 217; testimony of James Arnowe, Account No. 79073, Juan Leonardy, RG 217; testimony of Andreas Papy, Account No. 75214, Francis Pellicer, RG 217; testimony of Francis Pellicer, Account No. 75215, Isaac Weeks, RG 217.

17. Testimony of Francis R. Sanchez, Account No. 73340, Manuel Solana (the Elder), RG 217; testimony of Philip Weedman, Account No. 75215, Isaac Weeks, RG 217; testimony of James Pellicer, Account No. 86282, Fernando de la Maza Arredondo, Jr., RG 217; Landers, *Black Society,* 362n100; testimony of Bartolo Solana, Account No. 73063, Felipe Solana, RG 217; testimony of Jose Lalderol, Mathew Long, Account No. 75214, Francis Pellicer, RG 217.

18. Petition of George J. F. Clarke, appointment of the administrator of the estate of Prince Whilton by Elias B. Gould, testimonies of John Leonardy, Andreas Pacetty, Michael Andreu, George Gianopoli, John M. Bowden, Juan Antonio Florencio, "In the matter of the Claim of the Administrator of Prince Whilton decd. For losses in East Florida in 1812 and 1813," 28 June 1847, by I. H. Bronson, Account No. 98273, Prince Whilton, RG 217; Hill, "George J. F. Clarke, 1774–1836," 203–6; baptismal certificate of John Moses Bowden, Account No. 77889, John M. Bowden, RG 217; Cathedral Parish Records, St. Augustine, Florida, Colored Baptisms, vol. I, entries 125, 126, St. Augustine Historical Society Research Library, St. Augustine, Florida (hereafter cited as SAHSL); James M. Denham and Keith L.

Huneycutt, eds., *Echoes from a Distant Frontier: The Brown Sisters' Correspondence from Antebellum Florida* (Columbia: University of South Carolina Press, 2004), 157n17; Elias B. Gould, Biography File, SAHSL.

19. Testimonies of John Leonardy, Andreas Pacetty, Account No. 98273, Prince Whilton, RG 217.

20. Testimony of Andreas Pacetti, Account No. 79073, Juan Leonardy, RG 217; testimony of Andreas Pacetti, Account No. 89455, Prince Whilton, RG 217.

21. Petition of George J. F. Clarke, testimonies of John Leonardy (1845 and 1847), Andreas Pacetty, Michael Andreu, Account No. 98273, testominy of RG 217; testimony of George J. F. Clarke, Account No. 73801, William Garvin, RG 217.

22. Testimony of Juan Antonio Florencio, Account No. 98273, Prince Whilton, RG 217; Lee H. Warner, *Free Men in an Age of Servitude: Three Generations of a Black Family* (Lexington: University Press of Kentucky, 1992), 43–44.

23. Award of Isaac H. Bronson, Account No. 98273, Prince Whilton, RG 217; award of Isaac Bronson, Account No. 98272, Sancho Davis, RG 217.

24. Testimony of George Gianopoli, award of Isaac H. Bronson, Account No. 98273, Prince Whilton, RG 217; testimony of John Carreras, Account No. 98272, Sancho Davis, RG 217.

25. Award of Isaac H. Bronson, testimonies of Andreas Pacetty, John Leonardy, George Gianopoly, Account No. 98273, Prince Whilton, RG 217.

26. Award of Isaac H. Bronson, petition of George J. F. Clarke, testimonies of John Leonardy, Andreas Pacetty, Account No. 98273, Prince Whilton, RG 217; award of Isaac H. Bronson, Account No. 83177, George J. F. Clarke, RG 217; Isaac H. Bronson to the Secretary of the Treasury, 1849, Account No. 102005, Manuel Romero, RG 217.

27. Testimony of Mathew Long, Account No. 94415, Charles W. Clarke, RG 217; testimonies of J. Arnau, Michael Andreu, Domingo Circopley, Tony Primus, Account No. 94419, Isaac Bacchus, RG 217; testimonies of James Arnau, Michael Andreu, Domingo Cercopoly, award of Isaac H. Bronson, petition of George J. F. Clarke, Account No. 94421, John Morell, RG 217.

28. Testimonies of John Leonardy, Francis Triay, James Arnow, Joseph Manucy, Stephen Arnou, certified copy of Spanish land grant, Account No. 98270, George Clarke, RG 217.

29. Testimony of Michael Andreu, petition of George J. F. Clarke, Account No. 94419, Isaac Bacchus, RG 217; testimony of Michael Andreu, award of Isaac H. Bronson, Account No. 94421, John Morell, RG 217; testimony of Francis Pellicer, Account No. 74759, Toby Herreira, RG 217; testimony of Zephaniah Kingsley, Account No. 86225, Henry Yonge, RG 217; petition of Charles W. Clarke, Account No. 98370, George Clarke, RG 217; testimony of George J. F. Clarke, Account No. 98271, Domingo Davis, RG 217; testimony of Charles W. Clarke, Account No. 98272, Sancho Davis, RG 217; memorial of George Gianopoli, Account No. 89455, John Howley, RG 217; memorial of George J. F. Clarke, Account No. 99162, Abraham Rocho, RG 217; memorial of George J. F. Clarke, Account No. 98273, Prince Whilton, RG 217.

30. Testimonies of John Leonardy, Andreas Pacetty, Michael Andreu, Account No. 98273, Prince Whilton, RG 217.

31. Landers, *Black Society*, 116–17.

32. Clive Parry, ed., *The Consolidated Treaty Series* (Dobbs Ferry, NY: Oceana, 1969), 70: 11; Herbert Bruce Fuller, *The Purchase of Florida: Its History and Diplomacy* (Cleveland: Burrows Brothers, 1906), 373–74; testimonies of John Leonardy, Michael Andreu, John M.

Bowden, Juan Antonio Florencio, memorandum of Isaac H. Bronson, Account No. 98273, Prince Whilton, RG 217; testimony of Antonio Alvarez, 27 August 1839, "On the Case of Philip Edimboro," 16 May 1843, "Papers Relating to Claims by Inhabitants of Florida Under the Treaty of Spain of 1819," Box No. 2, Florida, Land Suits, 1829–1880, Records of the Solicitor of the Treasury, Record Group 206, National Archives, College Park, Maryland (hereafter cited as RG 206).

33. Testimony of Juan Antonio Florencio, Account No. 98273, Prince Whilton, RG 217.

34. Testimonies of Juan Antonio Florencio, John Leonardy, Account No. 98273, Prince Whilton, RG 217; testimony of Antony Hinsman, Account No. 75881, Philip Weadman, RG 217; petition of Charles Hill, testimony of Philip Weadman, Senior, Account No. 97990, Charles Hill, RG 217; declaration of Charles Hill, n.d., RG 206; testimony of Charles Hill, Account No. 85048, Abraham McQueen, RG 217.

35. Testimonies of Andreas Pacetty, Michael Andreu, John M. Bowden, Account No. 98273, Prince Whilton, RG 217.

36. Testimonies of Charles W. Clarke, Rafael Olivares, Bartolo Solana, Philip Weadman, Tony Proctor, Gabriel Capo, Account No. 86844, Philip Edinborough, RG 217; testimony of Andreas Pacetty, Account No. 98273, Prince Whilton, RG 217.

37. Testimonies of Philip Weadman, Gabriel Capo, Account No. 86844, Philip Edinborough, RG 217; testimony of Tony Proctor, Account No. 99008, Scipio Fleming, RG 217; testimonies of Philip Weadman, Andrew Pacetti, Account No. 97990, Charles Hill, RG 217; testimony of Andreas Pacetti, Account No. 89455, John Howley, RG 217; testimony of Philip Weadman, Account No. 85048, Abraham McQueen, RG 217; testimony of James Plummer, Account No. 84941, Tony Primus, RG 217; testimony of Charles Hill, Account No. 85048, Abraham McQueen, RG 217; testimonies of Estaban Arnow, John Leonardy, Account No. 99162, Abraham Rocho, RG 217; testimony of Zephaniah Kingsley, Account No. 82290, James Cashen, RG 217; testimonies of John M. Bowden, William Barden, Account No. 88415, Zephaniah Kingsley, RG 217; testimony of Estevan Arnau, Account No. 82538, Christopher Lopez, RG 217; Exposition of Facts by Gabriel W. Perpall, Account No. 77132, Gabriel W. Perpall, RG 217; testimony of Stephen Arnau, Account No. 82859, Francis Triay, RG 217; testimony of Zephaniah Kingsley, Account No. 86225, Henry Yonge, RG 217; Landers, *Black Society,* 35–37; testimonies of Henry Hartly, James Plummer, Account No. 84941, Tony Primus, RG 217; Frank Marotti Jr., "Negotiating Freedom in St. Johns County, Florida, 1812–1862" (PhD diss., University of Hawai'i, 2003), 133–35.

38. Testimonies of John Leonardy, Andreas Pacetty, Michael Andreu, Juan Antonio Florencio, Account No. 98273, Prince Whilton, RG 217.

39. Award of Isaac H. Bronson, Account No. 98273, Prince Whilton, RG 217; Alexander, "The Ambush of Captain John Williams," 296.

CHAPTER 5

1. Daniel L. Schafer, "'A Class of People Neither Freemen Nor Slaves': From Spanish to American Race Relations in Florida, 1821–1861," *Journal of Social History* 26 (Spring 1993): 587–610; Frederick P. Bowser, "Colonial Spanish America," in *Neither Slave Nor Free: The Freedman of African Descent in the Slave Societies of the New World,* ed. with an intro. by David W. Cohen and Jack P. Greene (Baltimore: Johns Hopkins University Press, 1972), 46, 58; Jane G. Landers, "Free Black Plantations and Economy in East Florida, 1784–1821," in *Co-*

lonial Plantations and Economy in Florida, ed. Jane G. Landers (Gainesville: University Press of Florida, 2000), 126.

2. Ira Berlin, *Many Thousands Gone: The First Two Centuries of Slavery in North America* (Cambridge, MA: Harvard University Press, 1998), 8, 12, 17, 306.

3. Daniel Lord Smail, *On Deep History and the Brain* (Berkeley and Los Angeles: University of California Press, 2008), 110.

4. Jane Landers, *Black Society in Spanish Florida* (Urbana: University of Illinois Press, 1999), 95–96, 121, 127, 147, 197, 216–18.

5. Ibid., 104, 147; testimonies of Charles W. Clarke, Andreas Papy, Bartolo Solana, Philip Weadman, Joseph S. Sanchez, Rafael Olivares, Account No. 86844, Philip Edinborough, Settled Miscellaneous Treasury Accounts, September 6, 1790–September 29, 1894, Office of the First Auditor, Records of the Accounting Officers of the Department of the Treasury, Record Group 217, National Archives, College Park, Maryland (hereafter cited as RG 217).

6. Certified translation of John M. Fontane, testimonies of Philip Weadman, Bartolo Solana, Charles W. Clarke, Andreas Papy, Stephen Arnow, Account No. 86844, Philip Edinborough, RG 217.

7. Testimonies of Charles W. Clarke, Bartolo Solana, Andreas Papy, Rafael Olivares, Philip Weadman, Account No. 86844, Philip Edinborough, RG 217.

8. Testimonies of Andreas Papy, Rafael Olivares, Philip Weadman, Stephen Arnow, Charles W. Clarke, Bartolo Solana, Account No. 86844, Philip Edinborough, RG 217.

9. Testimonies of James Arnau, Domingo Circopley, award of Isaac H. Bronson, Account No. 94419, Isaac Bacchus, RG 217; testimonies of Sophia Fleming, George Gianopoli, Capt. Don Jorge Fleming, Account No. 99008, Scipio Fleming, RG 217; testimonies of Philip Weadman Sen[r], Andrew Pacetti, Stephen Arnow, Account No. 97990, Charles Hill, RG 217; testimonies of James Arnau, Michael Andreu, Domingo Cercopoly, award of Isaac H. Bronson, Account No. 94421, John Morell, RG 217; testimonies of James Plummer, Henry Hartley, Moses Bowden, Account No. 84941, Tony Primas, RG 217; testimonies of Esteban Arnow, John Leonardy, Francis Triay, award of Isaac H. Bronson, Account No. 99162, Abraham Rocho, RG 217; testimonies of John Leonardy, Stephen Arnou, Francis Triay, James Arnow, award of Isaac H. Bronson, Account No. 98270, George Clarke, RG 217; testimonies of John Leonardy, Andreas Pacetty, Domingo Cercopoly, Michael Andreu, award of Isaac H. Bronson, Account No. 98271, Domingo Davis, RG 217; testimonies of John Leonardy, Andreas Pacetty, Domingo Cercoply, Michael Andreu, award of Isaac H. Bronson, Account No. 98272, Sancho Davis, RG 217; testimony of Col. Jos. S. Sanchez, claim of Lewis & Diana Sanchez, Patriot War Papers and Patriot War Claims (hereafter cited as Patriot War Papers), St. Augustine Historical Society Research Library, St. Augustine, Florida (hereafter cited as SAHSL); testimony of Charles W. Clarke, claim of Benjamin Wiggins, Patriot War Papers, SAHSL; award of Isaac H. Bronson, Account No. 98273, Prince Whilton, RG 217.

10. Testimony of Michael Andreu, Account No. 94419, Isaac Bacchus, RG 217; testimony of James Arnau, Account No. 94421, John Morell, RG 217; testimonies of Francis Triay, Joseph Manucy, John Leonardy, James Arnow, Account No. 98270, George Clarke, RG 217; testimony of John M. Bowden, Account No. 84941, Tony Primas, RG 217; testimony of John M. Bowden, claim of Abraham Hanahan, Patriot War Papers, SAHSL; testimony of Esteban Arnow, Account No. 99162, Abraham Rocho, RG 217; testimonies of John Leonardy, Andreas Pacetty, Michael Andreu, Account No. 98272, Sancho Davis, RG 217; testimony of Sophia Fleming, Account No. 99008, Scipio Fleming, RG 217.

11. Testimony of Sophia Fleming, George Gianopoli, Account No. 99008, Scipio Fleming, RG 217; testimony of Sophia Fleming, Account No. 94405, Francis P. Fatio, Jr., RG 217; testimonies of Esteban Arnow, Michael Andreu, Account No. 99162, Abraham Rocho, RG 217; testimonies of Stephen Arnow, John Leonardy, Account No. 97990, Charles Hill, RG 217; testimonies of Andreas Pacetty, Domingo Cercopoly, Account No. 98272, Sancho Davis, RG 217; testimonies of James Arnau, Michael Andreu, Domingo Cercopoly, Account No. 94421, John Morell, RG 217; testimony of John Leonardy, Account No. 98270, George Clarke, RG 217.

12. Testimony of Steven Arnou, Account No. 98270, George Clarke, RG 217; testimony of Michael Andreu, Account No. 98272, Sancho Davis, RG 217; testimony of John M. Bowden, claim of Abraham Hanahan, Patriot War Papers, SAHSL; testimony of Philip Weadman Sen[r], Account No. 97990, Charles Hill, RG 217; testimony of Bartolo Solana, Account No. 86844, Philip Edinborough, RG 217.

13. Testimony of Col. Jos. S. Sanchez, claim of Lewis & Diana Sanchez, Patriot War Papers, SAHSL; testimonies of Michael Andreu, Esteban Arnow, Francis Triay, John Leonardy, Account No. 99162, Abraham Rocho, RG 217; testimonies of Andres Pacetti, Philip Weadman Sen[r], Account No. 85048, Abraham McQueen, RG 217; testimonies of John Leonardy, Andreas Pacetti, Domingo Cercopoly, Account No. 89455, John Howley, RG 217.

14. Testimony of Andreas Pacetti, Account No. 89455, John Howley, RG 217; testimony of Andres Pacetti, Account No. 85048, Abraham McQueen, RG 217; testimonies of Esteban Arnow, Francis Triay, Account No. 99162, Abraham Rocho, RG 217; testimonies of Stephen Arnow, John Leonardy, Mrs. Mary Weadman, Philip Weadman, Sen[r], Account No. 97990, Charles Hill, RG 217.

15. Testimonies of John Leonardy, Andreas Pacetty, Michael Andreu, Account No. 98273, Prince Whilton, RG 217; testimonies of John Leonardy, Andreas Pacetty, Domingo Cercopoly, Michael Andreu, Account No. 98272, Sancho Davis, RG 217; testimonies of John Leonardy, Domingo Cercopoly, Michael Andreu, Account No. 98271, Domingo Davis, RG 217; Philip Weadman Sen[r], Account No. 97990, Charles Hill, RG 217.

16. See James G. Cusick, *The Other War of 1812: The Patriot War and the American Invasion of Spanish East Florida* (Gainesville: University Press of Florida, 2003), 94; certified translation of Spanish land grant, testimonies of Sophia Fleming, Lewis Fleming, George Gianopoli, James R. Woodland, Account No. 99008, Scipio Fleming, RG 217; testimonies of Sophia Fleming, Mrs. Eliza Crews, Account No. 94405, Francis P. Fatio, Jr., RG 217; petition of Anna Madgigne, testimonies of John Moses Bowden, William Bardin, claim of Anna Madgigne, Patriot War Papers, SAHSL.

17. Testimony of John Moses Bowden, claim of Anna Madgigne, Patriot War Papers, SAHSL; testimonies of William Bardin, John M. Bowden, claim of Abraham Hanahan, Patriot War Papers, SAHSL; testimonies of George Petty, William Lofton, James Plummer, Account No. 89416, Robert Gilbert, Sr., RG 217; testimonies of Henry Hartley, John M. Bowden, James Plummer, Moses Bowden, Account No. 84941, Tony Primas, RG 217; Cusick, *The Other War of 1812,* 94.

18. Testimonies of Francis Pellicer, Mathew Long, Account No. 74759, Toby Herreira, RG 217.

19. Testimony of J. Arnau, Account No. 94419, Isaac Bacchus, RG 217; testimonies of James R. Woodland, Lewis Fleming, Account No. 99008, Scipio Fleming, RG 217; testimony of John M. Bowden, claim of Abraham Hanahan, Patriot War Papers, SAHSL; testimonies of Jose Bergallo, William McGower, Account No. 68379, Abraham Hannaham, RG 217; tes-

timonies of John Leonardy, John M. Bowden, Account No. 89455, John Howley, RG 217; testimony of Andreas Papy, Account No. 85048, Abraham McQueen, RG 217; testimony of Esteban Arnow, Account No. 99162, Abraham Rocho, RG 217; testimony of James Plummer, Account No. 84941, Tony Primas, RG 217; testimony of John Carreras, Account No. 98272, Sancho Davis, RG 217; testimony of Domingo Cercopoly, Account No. 94421, John Morell, RG 217.

20. Testimony of Charles W. Clarke, claim of Benjamin Wiggins, Patriot War Papers, SAHSL.

21. Landers, *Black Society,* 104; testimonies of William Bardin, J. M. Bowden, Account No. 88415, Zephaniah Kingsley, RG 217; testimony of Andreas Pacetti, Account No. 75881, Philip Weadman, RG 217; testimony of Philip Weedman, Account No. 73358, Frances Kerr, RG 217; testimonies of John Leonardy, John M. Fontane, Account No. 82632, Juan E. Gonzalez alias Juan Gonzalez Montesdioca, RG 217; testimonies of John M. Bowden, William Bardin, claim of Anna Madgigne, Patriot War Papers, SAHSL; testimony of Tony Primus, Account No. 83177, George J. F. Clarke, RG 217.

22. Testimony of Andreas Pacetty, Account No. 98273, Prince Whilton, RG 217; testimony of Joseph S. Sanches, Account No. 86844, Philip Edinborough, RG 217; testimony of Domingo Circopley, Account No. 94419, Isaac Bacchus, RG 217; testimony of Stephen Arnau, Account No. 98270, George Clarke, RG 217; testimony of John Leonardy, Account No. 89455, John Howley, RG 217; testimonies of John Leonardy, Francis Triay, Account No. 99162, Abraham Rocho, RG 217; testimonies of John Leonardy, Domingo Cercopoly, Account No. 98271, Domingo Davis, RG 217; testimonies of Domingo Cercopoly, Andreas Pacetty, Account No. 98272, Sancho Davis, RG 217.

23. Testimony of Michael Andreu, Account No. 94419, Isaac Bacchus, RG 217; testimonies of Sophia Fleming, James R. Woodland, Account No. 99008, Scipio Fleming, RG 217; testimony of Mathew Long, Account No. 74759, Toby Herreira, RG 217; testimony of Andreas Pacetty, Account No. 89455, John Howley, RG 217; testimony of John M. Bowden, Account No. 84941, Tony Primus, RG 217; testimony of Esteban Arnow, Account No. 99162, Abraham Rocho, RG 217; testimony of John Leonardy, Account No. 98271, Domingo Davis, RG 217.

24. Testimony of Francis Triay, Account No. 98370, George Clarke, RG 217. See Frank Marotti Jr., "Edward M. Wanton and the Settling of Micanopy," *Florida Historical Quarterly* 73 (April 1995): 456–77; petition of Edward M. Wanton, award of Robert R. Reid, Account No. 80361, Edward M. Wanton, RG 217; memorial of Charles Hill, testimonies of Philip Weadman Sen[r], Andrew Pacetti, Stephen Arnow, Account No. 97990, Charles Hill, RG 217.

25. Last will and testament of John Fraser, Account No. 85766, John Fraser, RG 217; last will and testament of Zephaniah Kingsley, Account No. 88415, Zephaniah Kingsley, RG 217; explanatory note of Isaac H. Bronson, Account No. 83177, George J. F. Clarke, RG 217; explanatory note of Isaac H. Bronson, Account No. 94415, Charles W. Clarke, RG 217; Marotti, "Edward M. Wanton and the Settling of Micanopy," 456–77; John Fontane v. Felicia M. Garvin (1846), 117-14, St. Johns County Court Cases (hereafter cited as CCC), SAHSL; Richard Peters, ed., *The Public Statutes at Large of the United States of America . . .* (Boston: Charles C. Little and James Brown, 1846), 6: 569; award of Isaac H. Bronson, testimony of James Arnau, Account No. 119599, Joseph Arnow, RG 217.

26. Clive Parry, ed., *The Consolidated Treaty Series* (Dobbs Ferry, NY: Oceana, 1969), 70: 11; explanatory note of Isaac H. Bronson, Account No. 83177, George J. F. Clarke, RG 217.

27. Frank Marotti Jr., "Negotiating Freedom in St. Johns County, Florida, 1812–1862"

(PhD diss., University of Hawai'i, 2003), 51–53, 227–31; Fontane v. Garvin, 117-14, CCC, SAHSL; "The Claim of Felicia M Garvin Admix of W[m] Garvin," testimonies of George J. F. Clarke, Charles W. Clarke, James Arnowe, Captain Winslow Foster, Account No. 73801, William Garvin, RG 217.

28. Marotti Jr., "Negotiating Freedom," 21, 28, 86.

29. Testimony of Margaret Starratt, Account No. 86146, John B. Christopher, RG 217; testimony of Cynthia Swiney, Account No. 87382, Reuben Hogans, RG 217; "Reminiscences of S. Murphy," International Claims, Spain, 1819 East and West Florida Claims—Papers, Documents, Etc., In Case of the Estate of Susan Murphy, Records of the Boundary and Claims Commissions and Arbitrations, Record Group 76, National Archives, College Park, Maryland; testimonies of Sarah B. McDonell, Maria Hogans, Account No. 92003, Lucy Fitzgerald, RG 217; testimony of Mrs. A. M. Hernandez, Account No. 89050, Robert McHardy, RG 217; testimony of Ann Maria Hernandez, Account No. 84638, John Bunch, RG 217.

30. Testimonies of Simon Forrester, Tony Primus, Account No. 83177, George J. F. Clarke, RG 217.

31. Testimony of Juan Antonio Florencio, Account No. 98273, Prince Whilton, RG 217.

32. Deposition of Charles Hill, 1848[?], "Papers Relating to Claims by Inhabitants of Florida Under the Treaty of Spain of 1819," Box 2, Florida, Land Suits, 1829–1880, Records of the Solicitor of the Treasury, Record Group 206, National Archives, College Park, Maryland (hereafter cited as RG 206); testimony of Charles Hill, Account No. 85048, Abraham McQueen, RG 217; testimony of Tony Proctor, Account No. 99008, Scipio Fleming, RG 217.

33. Testimonies of Tony Proctor, Stephen Arnow, Account No. 86884, Philip Edinborough, RG 217; Landers, *Black Society,* 171; testimony of Tony Proctor, Don Jorge Fleming to Govr Enrique White, St. Augustine, East Florida, 2 October 1809, Account No. 99008, Scipio Fleming, RG 217.

34. Landers, *Black Society,* 223; testimony of Stephen Arnow, Account No. 86844, Philip Edinborough, RG 217; award of Isaac H. Bronson, Account No. 90774, George Atkinson, RG 217; award of Isaac H. Bronson, Account No. 94405, Francis P. Fatio, Jr., RG 217; testimonies of Michael Sloan, Account No. 88590, George Petty, RG 217; testimony of Dr. James Hall, Account No. 74969, Estate of Francis X. Sanchez, RG 217; testimony of Zephaniah Kingsley, Account No. 82290, James Cashen, RG 217; testimony of George J. F. Clarke, Account No. 75350, Francisco D. & Peter Pons, RG 217.

35. Testimonies of John T. Williams, Philip Weadman, Account No. 84638, John Bunch, RG 217.

36. Petition of Joseph M. Hernandez, testimonies of Matthew Long, Philip Weadman Sr., Francis Pellicer, Mrs. Mary Weadman, Mrs. Mary Douglass Dummit, Mrs. Ann Maria Hernandez, Account No. 84638, John Bunch, RG 217.

37. Landers, *Black Society,* 246; testimonies of Matthew Long, Philip Weadman, Sr., Francis Pellicer, Account No. 84638, John Bunch, RG 217.

38. Testimonies of Francis Pellicer, Philip Weedman, Mathew Long, Gabriel W. Perpall, Account No. 84638, John Bunch, RG 217.

39. Testimonies of Philip Weedman, Francis Pellicer, Mathew Long, Account No. 84638, John Bunch, RG 217.

40. Testimony of Mathew Long, Account No. 84638, John Bunch, RG 217; petition of Mathew Long, testimonies of Francis Pellicer, James Pellicer, Account No. 74862, George Long, RG 217; testimony of James Pellicer, Account No. 86282, Fernando de la Maza Arre-

dondo, Jr., RG 217; testimonies of F.R. Sanchez, Jose Lalderol, Mathew Long, Account No. 75214, Francis Pellicer, RG 217.

41. See, for examples, testimonies of Zephaniah Kingsley, Gabriel Priest, Account No. 85371, John H. McIntosh, RG 217; testimony of Philip Weedman, Account No. 80361, Edward Wanton, RG 217; testimony of Mrs. Ann Hurlbert, Account No. 108172, Daniel Hurlbert, RG 217; testimony of Ramon Rogero, case of James Falany, RG 206; testimony of James Pellicer, Account No. 77132, Gabriel W. Perpall, RG 217; testimony of James R. Woodland, Account No. 89050, Robert McHardy, RG 217; testimony of Bennet Segui, Account No. 87751, Francis Triay, RG 217; testimony of Lorenzo Gracesqui, Account No. 83177, George J. F. Clarke, RG 217; testimony of George J. F. Clarke, Account No. 73350, Francisco D. & Peter Pons, RG 217; testimony of Felipe Solana, Account No. 87747, Mattias Pons, RG 217; testimony of Thomas Suarez, Account No. 92003, Lucy Fitzgerald, RG 217; testimony of I. D. Hart, Account No. 90774, George Atkinson, RG 217; testimony of Zephaniah Kingsley, Account No. 80150, Philip Dewees, RG 217; testimonies of Michael Sloan, Henry Hartley, Account No. 88590, George Petty, RG 217; testimonies of R. Sanchez, Abraham Daniels, Henry Sweeny, Account No. 82248, James Dell, RG 217; testimony of James A. Rogers, Account No. 104775, Lodovic Ashley, RG 217; testimony of Dr. James Hall, Account No. 73008, Farquhar Bethune, RG 217; testimonies of James Plummer, George Petty, Account No. 77889, John M. Bowden, RG 217; testimony of Samuel Swearingen, Account No. 98530, Ezekial Hudnall, RG 217; testimony of James Woodland, Account No. 108413, John D. Braddock, RG 217; testimony of Jeremiah Wingate, Account No. 85341, Samuel S. Christopher, RG 217; testimony of Dr. James Hall, Account No. 74969, Estate of Francis X. Sanchez, RG 217; testimony of Farquhar Bethune, Account No. 87060, Francis R. Sanchez, RG 217.

42. Testimonies of Philip Weedman, Ann Maria Hernandez, Account No. 84638, John Bunch, RG 217; Landers, *Black Society,* 222–23; testimony of Philip Weadman, Account No. 89050, Robert McHardy, RG 217; "A Diagram of the Country . . . ," Account No. 76042, Samuel Williams, RG 217; David Bushnell, "The Florida Republic: An Overview," in *La Republica de las Floridas: Texts and Documents,* comp. David Bushnell (Mexico, D.F.: Pan American Institute of Geography and History, 1986), 7–10; L. David Norris, "Failure Unfolds: The Loss of Amelia Island," in Bushnell, *La Republica de las Floridas,* 24–25.

43. Testimony of General Joseph M. Hernandez, Account No. 108178, James Ormond, RG 217; testimonies of Mathew Long, Ann Maria Hernandez, Account No. 84638, John Bunch, RG 217; testimony of Philip Weadman, Account No. 89050, Robert McHardy, RG 217; "A Diagram of the Country . . . ," petition of Joseph M. Hernandez & wife Anna Maria, testimony of Francis Pellicer, Account No. 76042, Samuel Williams, RG 217.

44. Testimony of Francis Pellicer, petition of Joseph M. Hernandez & wife Anna Maria, Account No. 76042, Samuel Williams, RG 217; testimony of Francis Pellicer, Account No. 84638, John Bunch, RG 217.

45. See Jonathan Fifi'i, "World War II and the Origins of Maasina Rule," in *The Big Death: Solomon Islanders Remember World War II,* ed. Geoffrey White et al. (Suva, Fiji: Institute of Pacific Studies, 1988), 222.

46. Landers, *Black Society,* 229–31; Cusick, *The Other War of 1812,* 302; testimonies of Mathew Long, Doctor Philip Weadman, Francisco Pellicer, Account No. 84638, John Bunch, RG 217.

47. George Weigel, *Witness to Hope: The Biography of Pope John Paul II* (New York: Harper Perennial, 2005), 850.

CHAPTER 6

1. *St. Augustine Florida Herald & Southern Democrat* (hereafter cited as FHSD), 31 July 1843.

2. Fergus M. Bordewich, *Bound for Canaan: The Epic Story of the Underground Railroad, America's First Civil Rights Movement* (New York: HarperCollins, 2005), 271–74, 283–87.

3. Ibid., 288; FHSD, 7 August 1843.

4. Marvin Dunn, *Black Miami in the Twentieth Century* (Gainesville: University Press of Florida, 2002), 7–14, 164; George Klos, "Blacks and the Seminole Removal Debate, 1821–1835," in *The African American Heritage of Florida*, ed. David R. Colburn and Jane L. Landers (Gainesville: University Press of Florida, 1995), 133; FHSD, 10 October, 31 October 1843; *St. Augustine News* (hereafter cited as SAN), 7 October 1843; SAN, 4 November 1843; indictments of Andrew Gue and companions, SEN 28A-E3, Records of the U.S. Senate, Record Group 46, National Archives, Washington, D.C. (hereafter cited as SEN 28A-E3); Bordewich, *Bound for Canaan*, 287.

5. FHSD, 10 October 1843; SAN, 7 October 1843; SEN 28A-E3.

6. FHSD, 31 October 1843; SAN, 4 November 1843; SEN 28A-E3.

7. SAN, 4 November, 2 December 1843; *British and Foreign Anti-Slavery Reporter*, 10 January 1844, 2.

8. Mark M. Smith, "Remembering Mary, Shaping Revolt: Reconsidering the Stono Rebellion," *Journal of Southern History* 67 (August 2001): 517, 534; petition of Joseph M. Hernandez & wife Anna Maria, formerly Ann Maria Williams, Account No. 76042, Samuel Williams, Settled Miscellaneous Treasury Accounts, September 6, 1790–September 29, 1894, Office of the First Auditor, Records of the Accounting Officers of the Department of the Treasury, Record Group 217, National Archives, College Park, Maryland (hereafter cited as RG 217); *St. Augustine Florida Herald* (hereafter cited as FH), 21 March 1837; Cathedral Parish Records, St. Augustine, Florida, Colored Baptisms (hereafter cited as CB), vol. 3, p. 323, St. Augustine Historical Society Research Library, St. Augustine, Florida (hereafter cited as SAHSL); Jane Landers, *Black Society in Spanish Florida* (Urbana: University of Illinois Press, 1999), 219.

9. Spanish Land Grants (hereafter cited as SLG), Confirmed, microfilm reel 51-I, entry W-29, P. K. Yonge Library of Florida History, University of Florida, Gainesville, Florida (hereafter cited as PKY); last will and testament of Samuel Williams, Account No. 76042, Samuel Williams, RG 217; Ianthe Bond Hebel, "The Samuel Williams Family," *Journal of the Halifax Historical Society* 2, no. 1 [1952?]: 25; Michael Craton, "Loyalists Mainly to Themselves: The 'Black Loyalist' Diaspora to the Bahamas, 1783–c. 1820," in *Working Slavery, Pricing Freedom: Perspectives from the Caribbean, Africa and the African Diaspora*, ed. Verene A. Shepherd (Kingston, Jamaica: Ian Randle, 2002), 44–45, 50–52, 54, 61, 65; Alan Gregor Cobley, "That Turbulent Soil: Seafarers, the 'Black Atlantic,' and Afro-Caribbean Identity," in *Seascapes: Maritime Histories, Littoral Cultures, and Transoceanic Exchanges*, ed. Jerry H. Bentley, Renate Bridenthal, and Kären Wigen (Honolulu: University of Hawai'i Press, 2007), 164.

10. Robert J. Morgan, *A Whig Embattled: The Presidency under John Tyler* (Lincoln: University of Nebraska Press, 1954), 129–31; Kenneth E. Shewmaker, "Webster-Ashburton Treaty," in *Encyclopedia of U.S. Foreign Relations*, ed. Bruce W. Jentleson and Thomas G. Paterson (New York: Oxford University Press, 1997), 4: 314–15; Howard Temperly, *British Antislavery, 1833–1870* (London: Longman, 1972), 203–5; David M. Turley, "'Free Air' and Fugitive Slaves: British Abolitionists Versus Government Over American Fugitives, 1834–1861," in *Anti-slavery, Religion and Reform: Essays in Memory of Roger Anstey*, ed. Christine Bolt and

Seymour Drescher (Folkestone, England: Wm. Dawson & Son, 1980), 163, 173–76; Hinton to Aberdeen, London, 6 December 1843 in *A Side-Light on Anglo-American Relations, 1839–1858: Furnished by the Correspondence of Lewis Tappan and Others with the British and Foreign Anti-Slavery Society,* ed. Annie Heloise Abel and Frank J. Klingberg (Lancaster, PA: Association for the Study of Negro Life, 1927), 153n119.

11. Landers, *Black Society,* 23–29; Douglas R. Egerton, *Death or Liberty: African Americans and Revolutionary America* (New York: Oxford University Press, 2009), 72–74, 151, 203, 210; John B. Boles, *Black Southerners, 1619–1869* (Lexington: University Press of Kentucky, 1983), 54–56, 187–90. For similar black strategies, see for example, Azza Salama Layton, *International Politics and Civil Rights Policies in the United States, 1941–1960* (New York: Cambridge University Press, 2000); Steven Hahn, *A Nation Under Our Feet: Black Political Struggles in the Rural South, From Slavery to the Great Migration* (Cambridge, MA: Harvard University Press, 2003), 1.

12. SEN 28A-E3; Upshur to Fox, Washington, D.C., 20 November 1843, Fox to Upshur, Washington, D.C., 21 November 1843, 28th Cong., 1st sess., 1844, H.R. Exec. 160, 2–3; Browne to Upshur, Key West, 17 December 1843, Records of the U.S. Senate, Record Group 46, National Archives, Washington, D.C. (hereafter cited as RG 46); Cockburn to Stanley, Nassau, 1 January 1844, Governor 2/25, Duplicate Governor's Despatches, 18 January 1843–30 December 1846, Department of Archives, Nassau, Bahamas (hereafter cited as Gov 2/25); Turtle to Webster, Nassau, 17 May 1843, Despatches from U.S. Consuls in Nassau, West Indies, 1821–1906, Records of the Department of State, Record Group 59, National Archives, College Park, Maryland (hereafter cited as RG 59).

13. Cockburn to Stanley, Nassau, 11 December 1843, Cockburn to Fox, Nassau, 30 December 1843, Gov 2/25; Michael Craton and Gail Saunders, *From the Ending of Slavery to Twenty-First Century,* vol. 2 of *Islanders in the Stream: A History of the Bahamian People* (Athens: University of Georgia Press, 1998), 11.

14. Abel and Klingberg, *A Side-Light on Anglo-American Relations,* 3, 24. Leavitt to John Beaumont, Boston, 15 November 1843; Hinton to Aberdeen, London, 6 December 1843; Hinton to Capern, London, 14 December 1843; all in Abel and Klingberg, *A Side-Light on Anglo-American Relations,* 122n94, 149, 153–156n119. *British and Foreign Anti-Slavery Reporter,* 10 January 1844, 2, 21 February 1844, 25; Junius P. Rodríguez, "Caesar, John (c. 1770–1837)," in *Encyclopedia of Slave Resistance and Rebellion,* ed. Junius P. Rodríguez (Westport, CT: Greenwood Press, 2007), 1: 93–94.

15. *British and Foreign Anti-Slavery Reporter,* 10 January 1844, 2; *British and Foreign Anti-Slavery Reporter,* 21 February 1844, 25; Turley, "'Free Air' and Fugitive Slaves," 171, 173. Thomas Clarkson, President, British and Foreign Anti-Slavery Society, to the Earl of Aberdeen, Her Majesty's Principal Secretary of State for Foreign Affairs, London, 13 February 1843; Joshua Leavitt to John Beaumont, Boston, 15 November 1843; Clarkson to Aberdeen, London, 11 October 1843; J. H. Hinton to Aberdeen, London, 6 December 1843; Hinton to Capern, 14 December 1843; all in Abel and Klingberg, *A Side-Light on Anglo-American Relations,* 122–124n94, 149–157n119; Donald V. Macdougall, "Habeas Corpus, Extradition and a Fugitive Slave in Canada," *Slavery & Abolition,* 7 (September 1986): 120.

16. *British and Foreign Anti-Slavery Reporter,* 17 April 1844, 63; Cockburn to Darling, Nassau, 25 December 1843, Gov 2/25; Lees to Cockburn, Nassau, 30 December 1843, Gov 2/25; Browne to Cockburn, Nassau, 30 December 1843, Gov 2/25; House, 28th Cong., 2nd sess., 1845, H.R. Exec. 114; Cockburn to Stanley, Nassau, 1 January 1844, Gov 2/25; *British and Foreign Anti-Slavery Reporter,* 21 February 1844, 25; Sandra Riley, *Homeward Bound: A History*

of the Bahama Islands to 1850 with a Definitive Study of Abaco in the American Loyalist Plantation Period (Miami: Island Research, 1983), 226.

17. Claude H. Hall, *Abel Parker Upshur: Conservative Virginian, 1790–1844* (Madison: State Historical Society of Wisconsin, 1964), 194, 198, 201–2, 211–12; Everett to Upshur, London, 27 February 1844, in Clyde N. Wilson, ed., *The Papers of John C. Calhoun* (Columbia: University of South Carolina Press, 1988), 18: 55; *British and Foreign Anti-Slavery Reporter,* 21 February 1844, 25; Calhoun to Everett, Washington, D.C., 7 August 1844, 28 January 1845, in 28th Cong., 2d sess., 1845, H.R. Exec. 114, 1–12; Edward B. Rugemer, "Robert Monroe Harrison, British Abolition, Southern Anglophobia and Texas Annexation," *Slavery and Abolition* 28 (August 2007): 180; Robert L. Paquette, *Sugar Is Made of Blood: The Conspiracy of La Escalera and the Conflict between Empires over Slavery in Cuba* (Middleton, CT: Wesleyan University Press, 1988), 188–91, 202–4, 265.

18. Turley, "'Free Air' and Fugitive Slaves," 170–75; Temperly, *British Antislavery,* 203–5; "Address of Colored Citizens of Boston to the Prince of Wales," in Abel and Klingberg, *A Side-Light on Anglo-American Relations,* 111; Abel and Klingberg, *A Side-Light on Anglo-American Relations,* 92n58.

19. Daniel L. Schafer, "'A Swamp of an Investment'?: Richard Oswald's British East Florida Plantation Experiment," in *Colonial Plantations and Economy in Florida,* ed. Jane G. Landers (Gainesville: University Press of Florida, 2000), 15, 19–20, 28–29.

20. Testimonies of William Lofton, Dr. James Hall, Francis R. Sanchez, Henry Hartley, James Plummer, John M. Bowden, George Petty, Zephaniah Kingsley, William Broadnax, award of Robert R. Reid, Account No. 84671, Prudence Plummer, RG 217.

21. Testimonies of James Hall, Harry Hartley, George Petty, James Plummer, award of Robert R. Reid, Account No. 73800, John Crichton, RG 217; petition of Farquhar Bethune, testimonies of Dr. James Hall, F. R. Sanchez, Mrs. Matilda Seton, award of Robert R. Reid, Account No. 73008, Farquhar Bethune, RG 217; Landers, *Black Society,* 237; testimony of Francis Pellicer, Account No. 84638, John Bunch, RG 217.

22. Lizabeth Cohen, *A Consumers' Republic: The Politics of Mass Consumption in Postwar America* (New York: Random House, 2003), 42; Matt D. Childs, *The 1812 Aponte Rebellion in Cuba and the Struggle against Atlantic Slavery* (Chapel Hill: University of North Carolina Press, 2006), 1–3, 9; James G. Cusick, *The Other War of 1812: The Patriot War and the American Invasion of Spanish East Florida* (Gainesville: University Press of Florida, 2003), 182–83; testimony of Philip Weedman, Account No. 84638, John Bunch, RG 217; "Sitiki, 'The Story of Uncle Jack' Draft 2," Buckingham Smith Papers, Manuscript Division, New York Historical Society, New York, New York; John McNish Weiss, *The Merikens: Free Black American Settlers in Trinidad, 1815–16,* rev. ed. (London: McNish & Weiss, 2002), 36, 40–48, 59–61, 64–67.

23. Jane Landers, "Free and Slave," in *The New History of Florida,* ed. Michael Gannon (Gainesville: University Press of Florida, 1996), 179–80; Jane Landers, "Black Society in Spanish St. Augustine, 1784–1821" (PhD diss., University of Florida, 1988), 184–95, 211nn51–52.

24. Cassandra Pybus, *Epic Journeys of Freedom: Runaway Slaves of the American Revolution and Their Global Quest for Liberty* (Boston: Beacon Press, 2006), 32–33; Zephaniah Kingsley, "Address to the Legislative Council of Florida on the Subject of Its Coloured Population," 1823, Manuscript Collection 11, Florida Collection, State Library of Florida, Tallahassee; Hahn, *A Nation Under Our Feet,* 99.

25. Daniel L. Schafer, "Zephaniah Kingsley's Laurel Grove Plantation, 1803–1813," in Landers, *Black Society,* 98–100; Cusick, *The Other War of 1812,* 273; Childs, *The 1812 Aponte Rebellion,* 86.

26. John McNish Weiss, "The Corps of Colonial Marines 1814–16: A Summary," *Immigrants & Minorities,* 15 (March 1996): 80–81. For discussions of slaves' historical memories of resistance and the role of the black grapevine in disseminating them, see John W. Blassingame, *The Slave Community: Plantation Life in the Antebellum South* (New York: Oxford University Press, 1972), 126; Gregg D. Kimball, "African, American, and Virginian: The Shaping of Black Memory in Antebellum Virginia, 1790–1860," in *Where These Memories Grow: History, Memory, and Southern Identity,* ed. W. Fitzhugh Brundage (Chapel Hill: University of North Carolina Press, 2000), 61–65; Wilma A. Dunaway, *Slavery in the American Mountain South* (Cambridge: Cambridge University Press, 2003), 206; slave interview with Neil Coker, [n.d.], Grandin, Florida, in George P. Rawick, ed., *Florida Narratives,* vol. 17 of *The American Slave: A Composite Autobiography* (Westport, CT: Greenwood Press, 1972), 83–84; Kenneth S. Greenberg, "Name, Face, Body," in *Nat Turner: A Slave Rebellion in History and Memory,* ed. Kenneth S. Greenberg (New York: Oxford University Press, 2003), 84; Hahn, *A Nation Under Our Feet,* 52; Jeffrey Bolster, *Black Jacks: African American Seamen in the Age of Sail* (Cambridge, MA: Harvard University Press, 1997), 36, 153; Phillip Troutman, "Grapevine in the Slave Market: African American Geopolitical Literacy and the 1841 *Creole* Revolt," in *The Chattel Principle: Internal Slave Trades in the Americas,* ed. Walter Johnson (New Haven, CT: Yale University Press, 2004), 203–4; Douglas R. Egerton, "The Tricolor in Black and White: The French Revolution in Gabriel's Virginia," in *Slavery in the Caribbean Francophone World: Distant Voices, Forgotten Acts, Forged Identities,* ed. Doris Y. Kadesh (Athens: University of Georgia Press, 2000), 96; Thomas L. Webber, *Deep Like the Rivers: Education in the Slave Quarter Community, 1831–1865* (New York: W. W. Norton, 1978), 241–42. For the role of black troops in East Florida, see Daniel L. Schafer, "'Yellow Silk Ferret Tied Round Their Wrists': African Americans in British East Florida, 1763–1784," in Colburn and Landers, *The African American Heritage of Florida,* 94–95; Weiss, *The Merikens,* 2–4, 9; David Bushnell, "The Florida Republic: An Overview," in *La Republica de las Floridas: Texts and Documents,* comp. David Bushnell (Mexico City: Pan American Institute of Geography and History, 1986), 7–10; L. David Norris, "Failure Unfolds: The Loss of Amelia Island," in Bushnell, *La Republica de las Floridas,* 24–25; testimonies of General Joseph M. Hernandez, Account No. 108178, James Ormond, RG 217; testimonies of Mathew Long, Ann Maria Hernandez, Account No. 84638, John Bunch, RG 217; testimony of Philip Weadman, Account No. 89050, Robert McHardy, RG 217; testimony of Francis Pellicer, Account No. 76042, Samuel Williams, RG 217.

27. Kenneth W. Porter, "John Caesar: Seminole Negro Partisan," *Journal of Negro History* 31 (April 1946): 198; General Thomas Jesup to Brigadier General Joseph M. Hernandez, Tampa Bay, 18 June 1837, Letters Sent, 9 May–11 July 1837, General Jesup's Papers, Records of the Office of the Adjutant General, Record Group 94, National Archives, Washington, D.C. (hereafter cited as RG 94); petition of Joseph M. Hernandez & wife Anna Maria, formerly Ann Maria Williams, Account No. 76042, Samuel Williams, RG 217; SAN, 22 November 1839; FHSD, 31 July 1843; SAN, 19 November 1842; FH, 21 March 1837.

28. Kenneth W. Porter, "Florida Slaves and Free Negroes in the Seminole War, 1835–1842," *Journal of Negro History* 28 (October 1943): 393–95; Larry Eugene Rivers, *Slavery in Florida: Territorial Days to Emancipation* (Gainesville: University Press of Florida, 2000), 13, 149; "Petition to Congress by Inhabitants of St. Augustine," March 1836, in Clarence Edwin Carter, ed., *The Territory of Florida, 1834–1839,* vol. 25 of *The Territorial Papers of the United States* (Washington, D.C.: Government Printing Office, 1960), 265; Kenneth Wiggins Porter, *The Negro on the American Frontier* (New York: Arno Press, 1971), 34, 266–69, 273–75, 341, 347,

400–401; George E. Buker, "The Americanization of St. Augustine," in *The Oldest City: St. Augustine, Saga of Survival,* ed. Jean Parker Waterbury (St. Augustine: St. Augustine Historical Society, 1983), 164–65; Duncan L. Clinch to Brevet Brigadier General A. Jones, Adjutant, Fort King, Florida, 22 January 1835, and Clinch to Jones, St. Augustine, 9 October 1835, Duncan Clinch Letterbook, 1834–1836, and Slave List 1859, Camden County, Georgia, Records of the Ante-Bellum Southern Plantations from the Revolution to the Civil War, Series C, Selections from Holdings of the Library of Congress, Part 2, Alabama, Georgia, and South Carolina, microfilm reel 1, Library of Congress, Washington, D.C.

29. B.A. Putnam to R.K. Call, Governor of Florida, St. Augustine, 26 July 1836, and Putnam to Lewis Cass, Secretary of War, St. Augustine, 31 July 1836, "Letterbook & Accounts for B.A. Putnam, 1836–1844," Calhoun Putnam Papers, SAHSL; FH, 22 September 1836, 26 January, 21 March 1837; Landers, "Free and Slave," 175, 177; Bolster, *Black Jacks,* 137; John K. Mahon and Brent R. Weisman, "Florida's Seminole and Miccosukee Peoples," in Gannon, 184; Edward A. Baptist, *Creating an Old South: Middle Florida's Plantation Frontier before the Civil War* (Chapel Hill: University of North Carolina Press, 2002), 103.

30. Porter, *The Negro on the American Frontier,* 34, 265–66, 273–75, 349, 400–401; FH, 19 January, 26 January, 21 March 1837; testimony of Captain J. M. Hanson, 30 January 1837, "Letters Received Petitions from Citizens," RG 94; FHSD, 7 August 1843; SAN, 16 March, 23 March, 30 March 1839; petition of the inhabitants of the City of St. Augustine, 14 September 1838, "Blacks: 1824–1855," City of St. Augustine Papers, SAHSL; Deed Book D, 11–14, St. Johns County Courthouse, St. Augustine, Florida (hereafter cited as SJCCH); SLG, Confirmed, microfilm reel 50-G, E10, PKY; claim of James Erwin, Patriot War Papers & Patriot War Claims (hereafter cited as Patriot War Papers), SAHSL; John Fontane v. Felicia M. Garvin (1846), 117-14, St. Johns County Court Cases,(hereafter cited as CCC), SAHSL; manuscript returns of the Seventh United States Census, 1850, Florida, St. Johns County, National Archives, Washington, D.C.; CB, vol. 4, p. 1; Deed Book M, 304–5, SJCCH; SAN, 17 November 1838; FHSD, 11 July 1839; FH, 19 January, 1 March, 21 March, 29 March 1837; CB, vol. 1, entries 258, 259; Landers, *Black Society,* 260; SLG, Confirmed, microfilm reel 50-C, B58, and Unconfirmed, microfilm reel 52-C, W28, PKY; Asbury Dickins and John W. Forney, eds., *American State Papers: Documents of the Congress of the United States in Relation to Public Lands . . .* (Washington, D.C.: Gales and Seaton, 1860), 6: 113; Cathedral Parish Records, St. Augustine, Florida, Colored Marriages (hereafter cited as CM), entries 17, 51, SAHSL; CB, vol. 2, entries 139, 496, 616; CB, vol. 3, entries 298, 362, 421; Account No. 74759, Toby Herreira, RG 217; SAN, 30 March 1839.

31. Porter, *The Negro on the American Frontier,* 347; Porter, "John Caesar," 198–99; FH, 21 March 1837; *New-Hampshire Sentinel,* 6 April 1837, *America's Historical Newspapers,* retrieved 6 January 2007 from http://infoweb.newsbank.com/iw-search/we/HistArchive/?p_products= . . . ; CB, vol. 3; Gil Wilson, "An African American Fight for Freedom," *The Ancient City Geneaologist* 3, no. 1 (1992): 16.

32. Rivers, *Slavery in Florida,* 206; Receipts, 1838–1839, City of St. Augustine Papers, SAHSL; List of Persons Indebted to the Estate of Isaac W. Avery, January 8, 1842, Inventories, "Old Book 3:1840–1861," St. Johns County Probate Records, 1784–1933, 64–65, Division of Archives, History, and Records Management, State Library, Tallahassee, Florida; Deed Book H, 314, SJCCH; Deed Book I & J, 14, SJCCH; Deed Book K, 104–6, SJCCH; CB, vol. 1, entries 285, 461, 527.

33. CB, vol. 3, entry for 23 July 1842; Luís González, *San José de Gracia: Mexican Village in*

Transition, trans. John Upton (Austin: University of Texas Press, 1974), 51, 323, 325; Stephanie E. Smallwood, *Saltwater Slavery: A Middle Passage from Africa to American Diaspora* (Cambridge, MA: Harvard University Press, 2007), 58, 198; Cyprian Davis, *The History of Black Catholics in the United States* (New York: Crossroads, 1990), 71–72.

34. Egerton, *Death or Liberty,* 3–4; Eugene Genovese, *Roll, Jordan, Roll: The World the Slaves Made* (New York: Random House, 1974), 293; Randall M. Miller, "Slaves and Southern Catholicism," in *Masters and Slaves in the House of the Lord: Race and Religion in the American South, 1740–1870,* ed. John B. Boles (Lexington: University Press of Kentucky, 1988), 230n10; Landers, *Black Society,* 107; Robert L. Hall, "Black and White Christians in Florida, 1822–1861," in Boles, *Masters and Slaves in the House of the Lord,* 97.

35. W. Fitzhugh Brundage, "No Deed but Memory," in Brundage, *Where These Memories Grow,* 12; Sharon Ann Holt, "Symbol, Memory, and Service: Resistance and Family Formation in Nineteenth-Century African America," in *Working Toward Freedom: Slave Society and Domestic Economy in the American South,* ed. Larry E. Hudson Jr. (Rochester, NY: University of Rochester Press, 1994), 194–200, 203–6, 207n3; Robert N. Bellah et al., *Habits of the Heart: Individualism and Commitment in American Life* (New York: Harper & Row, 1986), 153–54, 333, 335; Diana Paton, "Family," in *The Historical Encyclopedia of World Slavery,* ed. Junius P. Rodríguez (Santa Barbara, CA: ABC-CLIO, 1997), 1: 265–66.

36. CB, vol. 3, entry 243; David Brion Davis, *Challenging the Boundaries of Slavery* (Cambridge, MA: Harvard University Press, 2003), 7.

37. Paquette, *Sugar Is Made of Blood,* 63–64; Jimmy Gibbs v. Andrew Pow, alias Andrew Sabate (1842), 91-2, CCC, SAHSL; Deed Book N, 386, SJCCH; Landers, *Black Society,* 149–57, 171n15.

38. Deed Book H, 314, SJCCH; Deed Book I & J, 14, SJCCH; Deed Book K, 104–6, SJCCH; CB, vol. 1, entries 285, 461, 527; Gibbs v. Pow, 91-2, CCC, SAHSL.

39. Gibbs v. Pow, 91-2, CCC, SAHSL; Marriage Licenses, Volume A, 6, Judgment Record A, 7–8, Deed Book O, 518, SJCCH.

40. Gibbs v. Pow, 91-2, CCC, SAHSL; Judgment Record A, 7, Deed Book O, 518, SJCCH; Order Book A, 3, SJCCH; Emanuel Aguiar's Statement, "Blacks: 1824–1855," City of St. Augustine Papers, SAHSL; Entry D49, 7 December 1858, entry D45, & December 1858, Negro Passes and Permits, SAHSL.

41. Daniel L. Schafer, "'A Class of People Neither Freemen Nor Slaves': From Spanish to American Race Relations in Florida, 1821–1861," *Journal of Social History* 26 (Spring 1993): 591–93; FHSD, 9 July 1841, 31 July 1843; CB, vol. 3, p. 319; Ancestry.com, *1840 United States Federal Census* [database on-line], Provo, UT, USA: The Generations Network, Inc., 2004 (hereafter cited as AC-[year]). Original data: United States of America, Bureau of the Census, *Sixth Census of the United States, 1840,* Washington, D.C.: National Archives and Records Administration, 1840, M704, Roll 36, p. 109; AC-1850, *Seventh Census of the United States, 1850,* M432, Roll 59; AC-1860, *Eighth Census of the United States, 1860,* M653, Roll 108, p. 390.

42. Rosalyn Howard, *Black Seminoles in the Bahamas* (Gainesville: University Press of Florida, 2002), 30–32; Jane Landers, "Traditions of African American Freedom and Community in Spanish Colonial Florida," in Colburn and Landers, *The African American Heritage of Florida,* 30, 33; Jane Landers, "Africans and Native Americans on the Spanish Florida Frontier," in *Beyond Black and Red: African-Native Relations in Colonial Latin America,* ed. Matthew Restall (Albuquerque: University of New Mexico Press, 2005), 69; Bordewich, *Bound for Canaan,* 273–74.

43. Howard, *Black Seminoles,* 31–32, 44–48; Howard Johnson, *The Bahamas in Slavery and Freedom* (Kingston, Jamaica: Ian Randle, 1991), 32, 35.

44. Whittington B. Johnson, *Race Relations in the Bahamas, 1784–1834: The Nonviolent Transformation from a Slave to a Free Society* (Fayetteville: University of Arkansas Press, 2000), 162–65; Storr to Van Buren, Nassau, 17 January, 24 January, 17 February 1831, *Nassau Royal Gazette and Bahama Advertiser,* 15 January 1831 [enclosure], RG 59; Huyler to McLane, Nassau, 12 February, 24 February 1834 [with enclosures], RG 59; Balfour to Ogilby, Nassau, 14 May 1834, RG 59.

45. Bolster, *Black Jacks,* 17, 21, 26, 39, 147–51; FHSD, 5 July, 26 September 1839, 9 July 1841; SAN, 11 October 1839, 31 January, 15 May, 1840, 5 March 1841, 29 January 1842.

46. Howard Jones, "The Peculiar Institution and National Honor: The Case of the *Creole* Slave Revolt," *Civil War History* 21 (March 1975): 31–35.

47. SAN, 19 November 1842, 30 September 1843; FHSD, 9 July 1841; Turtle to Webster, Nassau, 17 May 1843, RG 59.

48. Daniel Webster to Lord Ashburton, Washington, D.C., 1 August 1842, *British and Foreign State Papers* (London: James Ridgway and Sons, 1858), 30: 182–83; John Lewis Gaddis, *Surprise, Security, and the American Experience* (Cambridge, MA: Harvard University Press, 2004), 16–18, 21; Richard Kluger, *Seizing Destiny: How America Grew from Sea to Shining Sea* (New York: Alfred A. Knopf, 2007), 305, 333–34, 336; Bordewich, *Bound for Canaan,* 291.

49. FHSD, 31 July 1843; Sanchez to son, St. Augustine, 14 August 1843, Sanchez Papers, SAHSL; SAN, 30 September 1843.

50. SAN, 22 November 1839, 29 January 1841; FHSD, 27 June 1839; Howard, *Black Seminoles,* 31–32; Johnson, *The Bahamas in Slavery and Freedom,* 32, 35; "Governor Duval to the Secretary of War," St. Augustine, 23 September 1823, in *The Territory of Florida, 1821–1824,* vol. 22 of *The Territorial Papers of the United States,* ed. Clarence Edwin Carter (Washington, D.C.: Government Printing Office, 1956), 744–45.

51. Kathleen Deagan and Darcie MacMahon, *Fort Mose: Colonial America's Black Fortress of Freedom* (Gainesville: University Press of Florida, 1995), 19–20; Landers, *Black Society,* 79, 248; Rivers, *Slavery in Florida,* 189; Johnson, *Race Relations in the Bahamas,* 157, 162, 164; Klos, "Blacks and the Seminole Removal Debate," 128; Johnson, *The Bahamas in Slavery and Freedom,* 31–32, 38, 40, 43–44, 50; Craton and Saunders, *From the Ending of Slavery,* 9; Weiss, *The Merikens,* 10–11; Rugemer, "Robert Monroe Harrison," 174; David Weber, *The Spanish Frontier in North America* (New Haven, CT: Yale University Press, 1992), 278.

52. Hahn, *A Nation Under Our Feet,* 456, 467–68; Bolster, *Black Jacks,* 40; Kären Wigen, introduction to Bentley, Bridenthal, and Wigen, 12, 14; FHSD, 6 August 1844.

53. FHSD, 30 July, 6 August, 13 August, 22 October 1844.

54. Jonathan Walker, *Trial and Imprisonment of Jonathan Walker at Pensacola, Florida for Aiding Slaves to Escape from Bondage, with an Appendix, Containing a Statement of His Life* (Boston: Antislavery Office, 1846), 9, 12–15, 39–40, 105–6; Herbert Aptheker, *Abolitionism: A Revolutionary Movement* (Boston: Twayne, 1989), 111–12.

55. Mark A. Smith, "Engineering Slavery: The U.S. Army Corps of Engineers and Slavery at Key West," *Florida Historical Quarterly* 86 (Spring 2008): 498, 505, 508–9; Julia Floyd Smith, *Slavery and Plantation Growth in Antebellum Florida, 1821–1860* (Gainesville: University of Florida Press, 1973), 106; Frank Marotti Jr., "Negotiating Freedom in St. Johns County, Florida, 1812–1862" (PhD diss., University of Hawai'i, 2003), 204–5, 212–14.

56. Daniel L. Schafer, "Freedom Was as Close as the River: African Americans and the Civil War in Northeast Florida," in Colburn and Landers, *The African American Heritage of*

Florida, 157; Ira Berlin, *Generations of Captivity: A History of African-American Slaves* (Cambridge, MA: Harvard University Press, 2003), 249–50.

57. Genovese, *Roll, Jordan, Roll*, 398, 594, 598, 629, 657.

CHAPTER 7

1. Jane Landers, *Black Society in Spanish Florida* (Urbana: University of Illinois Press, 1999), 118–19; Cathedral Parish Records, St. Augustine, Florida, Colored Baptisms (hereafter cited as CB), vols. 1–3, St. Augustine Historical Society Research Library, St. Augustine, Florida (hereafter cited as SAHSL); Account No. 88415, Zephaniah Kingsley, Settled Miscellaneous Treasury Accounts, September 6, 1790–September 29, 1894, Office of the First Auditor, Records of the Accounting Officers of the Department of the Treasury, Record Group 217, National Archives, College Park, Maryland (hereafter cited as RG 217); Account No. 85766, John Fraser, RG 217.

2. CB, vols. 1–3; David J. Weber, *The Spanish Frontier in North America* (New Haven, CT: Yale University Press, 1992), 331; Robert L. Paquette, *Sugar Is Made of Blood: The Conspiracy of La Escalera and the Conflict between Empires over Slavery in Cuba* (Middleton, CT: Wesleyan University Press, 1988), 113; Daniel E. Walker, *No More, No More: Slavery and Cultural Resistance in Havana and New Orleans* (Minneapolis: University of Minnesota Press, 2004), 73, 78.

3. *St. Augustine Florida Herald* (hereafter cited as FH), 15 March, 12 July 1832; CB, vol. 3, entry 573, and pp. 320–21, 326, 337; CB, vol. 4, pp. 1, 33–34; manuscript returns of the Seventh and Eighth Censuses, 1850, 1860, Florida, St. Johns County, National Archives, Washington, D.C.; Wills and Letters of Administration, vol. 1, 422, 436–38, St. Johns County Courthouse, St. Augustine, Florida (hereafter cited as SJCCH); *St. Augustine News* (hereafter cited as SAN), 25 December 1841; William Cullen Bryant, *Letters of a Traveller or Notes of Things Seen in Europe and America* (New York: George P. Putnam, 1850), 111; Robert Reid to George Burt, 23 September 1847, Burt Papers, SAHSL.

4. John W. Blassingame, *The Slave Community: Plantation Life in the Antebellum South*, rev. ed. (New York: Oxford University Press, 1979), 90, 151, 153, 165–67, 170–71; Peter Kolchin, *American Slavery, 1619–1877* (New York: Hill and Wang, 1993), 122–23; Albert J. Raboteau, *Slave Religion: The "Invisible Institution" in the Antebellum South* (New York: Oxford University Press, 1978), 228; Madeleine Hooke Rice, *American Catholic Opinion in the Slavery Controversy* (Glouster, MA: Peter Smith, 1964), 37; Randy J. Sparks, "Religion in Amite County, Mississippi, 1800–1861," in *Masters and Slaves in the House of the Lord: Race and Religion in the American South, 1740–1870*, ed. John B. Boles (Lexington: University Press of Kentucky, 1988), 73–74; Gary B. Mills, "Piety and Prejudice: A Colored Catholic Community in the Antebellum South," in *Catholics in the Old South: Essays on Church and Culture*, ed. Randall M. Miller and Jon L. Wakelyn (Macon, GA: Mercer University Press, 1983), 175; Whittington B. Johnson, *Race Relations in the Bahamas, 1784–1834: The Nonviolent Transformation from a Slave to a Free Society* (Fayetteville: University of Arkansas Press, 2000), 166–70; Eugene Genovese, *Roll, Jordan, Roll: The World the Slaves Made* (New York: Random House, 1974), 27–33, 52–53; Brenda E. Stevenson, *Life in Black and White: Family and Community in the Slave South* (New York: Oxford University Press, 1996), 244–45, 249–50; Thomas E. Will, "Weddings on Contested Grounds: Slave Marriage in the Antebellum South," *The Historian* 62 (Fall 1992): 103; John W. Blassingame. *The Slave Community: Plantation Life in the Antebellum South* (New York: Oxford University Press, 1972), 91.

5. Slave interview of Edward Lycurgus, Jacksonville, Florida, 15 December 1936, in *Florida Narratives,* vol. 17 of *The American Slave: A Composite Autobiography,* ed. George P. Rawick (Westport, CT: Greenwood Press, 1972), 204–8.

6. Deed Book H, 311–12, SJCCH; Cathedral Parish Records, St. Augustine, Florida, White Baptisms, vol. 4, entry for 2 August 1837, p. 438, SAHSL; Deed Book P, 45, SJCCH; Eighth Census of the United States, 1860, Florida, St. Johns County.

7. Daniel L. Schafer, *Anna Kingsley* (St. Augustine, FL: St. Augustine Historical Society, 1994), 5–8, 12–13; Louise Biles Hill, "George J. F. Clarke, 1774–1836," *Florida Historical Quarterly* 21 (January 1943): 200, 211–12; John Fontane v. Felicia M. Garvin (1846), 117-14, St. Johns County Court Cases (hereafter cited as CCC), SAHSL; Seventh Census of the United States, 1850, Florida, St. Johns County; Order Book A, 2, SJCCH; CB, vol. 3, entry 561.

8. Phillip Troutman, "Grapevine in the Slave Market: African American Geopolitical Literacy and the 1841 *Creole* Revolt," in *The Chattel Principle: Internal Slave Trades in the Americas,* ed. Walter Johnson (New Haven, CT: Yale University Press, 2004), 204–5; Ann Patton Malone, *Sweet Chariot: Slave Family and Household Structure in Nineteenth-Century Louisiana* (Chapel Hill: University of North Carolina Press, 1992), 207, 212–13, 216; Edward A. Baptist, *Creating an Old South: Middle Florida's Plantation Frontier before the Civil War* (Chapel Hill: University of North Carolina Press, 2002), 62, 197; Herbert Aptheker, *Negro Slave Revolts in the United States: 1526–1860* (New York: International Publishers, 1939), 11; Kolchin, *American Slavery,* 125; Thomas L. Webber, *Deep Like the Rivers: Education in the Slave Quarter Community, 1831–1865* (New York: W. W. Norton, 1978), 103.

9. Larry Eugene Rivers, *Slavery in Florida: Territorial Days to Emancipation* (Gainesville: University Press of Florida, 2000), xii, 16–17, 68–70, 73, 89–90; Michael Gannon, *Florida: A Short History* (Gainesville: University Press of Florida, 1993), 40.

10. Rivers, *Slavery in Florida,* 70, 80–83, 87, 92, 94–97; Wilma A. Dunaway, *Slavery in the American Mountain South* (Cambridge: Cambridge University Press, 2003), 5, 241–43, 245–48.

11. Samuel Abbott, Soldier's Certificate No. 350564, Civil War and Later Pension Files, Records of the Veterans' Administration, Record Group 15, National Archives, Washington, D.C. (hereafter cited as RG 15); Samuel Abbott, Company D, Regimental Descriptive Book, 33d United States Colored Infantry, Bound Records, (descriptive books), Book Records of Volunteer Union Organizations, Records of the Adjutant General's Office, Record Group 94, National Archives, Washington, D.C. (hereafter cited as RG 94); slave interview of Douglas Dorsey, South Jacksonville, Florida, 11 January 1937, in Rawick, *From Sundown to Sunup,* 93–95; Account No. 79022, Lewis Mattair, RG 217; Baptist, *Creating an Old South,* 192.

12. Albert Sammis, Soldier's Certificate No. 503989, RG 15; Schafer, *Anna Kingsley,* 13, 21, 32.

13. Benjamin Hatcher, Soldier's Certificate No. 439056, RG 15; Benjamin Hatcher, Company A, Regimental Descriptive Book, 21st United States Colored Infantry, RG 94.

14. Last Will and Testament of Abraham Dupont, 173–229, CCC, SAHSL; Richard Simmons, Soldier's Certificate No. 535664, RG 15; Robert L. Hall, "Black and White Christians in Florida, 1822–1861," in Boles, 88.

15. Richard Simmons, Soldier's Certificate No. 535664, RG 15.

16. Landers, *Black Society,* 73; Jane G. Landers, "Francisco Xavier Sánchez, *Floridano* Planter and Merchant," and "Free Black Plantations and Economy in East Florida, 1784–1821," in *Colonial Plantations and Economy in Florida,* ed. Jane G. Landers (Gainesville: University Press of Florida, 2000), 89, 121; Adam Fashion, Soldier's Certificate No. 217272, RG 15.

17. Adam Fashion, Soldier's Certificate No. 217272, RG 15.

18. Ibid.

19. William A. Hart, Soldier's Certificate No. 782658, RG 15.

20. Ibid.

21. Ibid.

22. David R. Colburn, *Racial Change and Community Crisis: St. Augustine, Florida, 1877–1980* (New York: Columbia University Press, 1985), 21–24, 207, 217–21; Thomas Graham, *The Awakening of St. Augustine: The Anderson Family and the Oldest City, 1821–1924* (St. Augustine: St. Augustine Historical Society, 1978), 19.

23. Sharon Ann Holt, "Symbol, Memory, and Service: Resistance and Family Formation in Nineteenth-Century African America," in *Working Toward Freedom: Slave Society and Domestic Economy in the American South,* ed. Larry E. Hudson Jr. (Rochester, NY: University of Rochester Press, 1994), 206; Steven Hahn, *A Nation Under Our Feet: Black Political Struggles in the Rural South, From Slavery to the Great Migration* (Cambridge, MA: Harvard University Press, 2003), 17.

24. James B. Bennett, *Religion and the Rise of Jim Crow in New Orleans* (Princeton, NJ: Princeton University Press, 2005), 142, 144–45; Schafer, *Anna Kingsley,* 30; Bennett, "'A Class of People Neither Freemen Nor Slaves': From Spanish to American Race Relations in Florida, 1821–1861," *Journal of Social History* 26 (Spring 1993): 587–609; Raboteau, *Slave Religion,* 272; Mills, "Piety and Prejudice," 174–79; Immanuel Wallerstein, "The Construction of Peoplehood: Racism, Nationalism, Ethnicity," in *Race, Nation, Class: Ambiguous Identities,* ed. Etienne Balibar and Immanuel Wallerstein (London: Verso, 1991), 78–79; Herman L. Bennett, "Genealogies to a Past: Africa, Ethnicity, and Marriage in Seventeenth-Century Mexico," in *New Studies in the History of American Slavery,* ed. Edward E. Baptist and Stephanie M. H. Camp (Athens: University of Georgia Press, 2006), 131–33; Jane Landers, "The Central African Presence in Spanish Maroon Communities," in *Central Africans and Cultural Transformations in the American Diaspora,* ed. Linda M. Heywood (Cambridge: Cambridge University Press, 2002), 229; Robert L. Hall, "African Religious Retentions in Florida," in *The African American Heritage of Florida,* ed. David R. Colburn and Jane L. Landers (Gainesville: University Press of Florida, 1995), 57.

25. Landers, *Black Society,* 107, 202; Jane G. Landers, "Acquisition and Loss on a Spanish Frontier: The Free Black Homesteaders of Florida, 1784–1821," in *Against the Odds: Free Blacks in the Slave Societies of the Americas,* ed. Jane G. Landers (London: Frank Cass, 1996), 93; Jane Landers, "Traditions of African American Freedom and Community in Spanish Colonial Florida," in Colburn and Landers, *The African American Heritage of Florida,* 26; CB, vol. 3, entry for 23 July 1842; Kenneth S. Greenberg, "Name, Face, Body," in *Nat Turner: A Slave Rebellion in History and Memory,* ed. Kenneth S. Greenberg (New York: Oxford University Press, 2003), 4–6, 10; Robert L. Kapitzke, *Religion, Power, and Politics in Colonial St. Augustine* (Gainesville: University Press of Florida, 2001), 1, 4, 6, 28; Alan Gregor Cobley, "That Turbulent Soil: Seafarers, the 'Black Atlantic,' and Afro-Caribbean Identity," in *Seascapes: Maritime Histories, Littoral Cultures, and Transoceanic Exchanges,* ed. Jerry H. Bentley, Renate Bridenthal, and Kären Wigen (Honolulu: University of Hawai'i Press, 2007), 164; Cassandra Pybus, *Epic Journeys of Freedom: Runaway Slaves of the American Revolution and Their Global Quest for Liberty* (Boston: Beacon Press, 2006), 26; Genovese, *Roll, Jordan, Roll,* 293.

26. Webber, *Deep Like the Rivers,* 109; Baptist, *Creating an Old South,* 161, 168–70, 190; Daniel L. Schafer, "U.S. Territory and State," in *The New History of Florida,* ed. Michael Gannon (Gainesville: University Press of Florida, 1996), 211; SAN, 25 December 1841; *St. Au-*

gustine Florida Herald & Southern Democrat (hereafter cited as FHSD), 3 December 1841, 23 January 1843; testimonies of Emanuel Garrido, Betsey, Jim, 2 May 1837, "Blacks: 1824–1855," City of St. Augustine Papers (hereafter cited as City Papers), SAHSL; Blake Touchstone, "Planters and Slave Religion in the Deep South," in Boles, *Masters and Slaves in the House of the Lord,* 99–102, 105, 108–9, 124; Hall, "Black and White Christians," 88, 95; Genovese, *Roll, Jordan, Roll,* 4–5, 7, 189–90; Hahn, *A Nation Under Our Feet,* 64, 166, 367; Douglas R. Egerton, "Nat Turner in a Hemispheric Context," in Greenberg, "Name, Face, Body," 139; Kolchin, *American Slavery,* 127, 129, 145; Allan Gallay, "Planters and Slaves in the Great Awakening," in Boles, 35; Blassingame, *The Slave Community,* 168–70; Clarence L. Mohr, "Slaves and White Churches in Confederate Georgia," in Boles, 155, 157; Donald G. Mathews, "Religion and Slavery—The Case of the American South," in *Anti-slavery, Religion and Reform: Essays in Memory of Roger Anstey,* ed. Christine Bolt and Seymour Drescher (Folkestone, England: Wm. Dawson & Son, 1980), 226; Stevenson, *Life in Black and White,* 228–29, 232.

27. Blassingame, *The Slave Community,* 167–70.

28. Michael Gannon, *The Cross in the Sand: The Catholic Church in Florida, 1513–1870* (Gainesville: University of Florida Press, 1965), 132, 150–52, 157–58, 162.

29. Randall M. Miller, "A Church in Cultural Captivity: Some Speculations on Catholic Identity in the Old South," in Miller and Wakelyn, *Catholics in the Old South,* 26; Randall M. Miller, "Slaves and Southern Catholicism," in Boles, *Masters and Slaves in the House of the Lord,* 138–39, 141–42.

30. CB, vols. 3–4; Landers, *Black Society,* 124–26; Cathedral Parish Records, St. Augustine, Florida, Colored Marriages, 1784–1882, SAHSL (hereafter cited as CM); Marriage Licenses, 1830–1840, SAHSL; Marriage Bonds, 1823–1833, SAHSL; Marriage Licenses, Volume A, SJCCH; Minutes and register of the Trinity Episcopal Church, St. Augustine, Florida, vol. 1, SAHSL.

31. Handy Growles, alias Goud, Soldier's Certificate No. 469919, RG 15; CB, vol. 4, pp. 17, 48, 57; CM, p. 62.

32. John Mills, Soldier's Certificate No. 490204, RG 15; CB, vol. 3, pp. 317, 327; CB, vol. 4, pp. 32, 40, 42, 50, 53, 61, 63, 71, 75; *In Supreme Court, Florida, February Term, 1860, D. L. Yulee Appellee, caveator. Ads Francis Bridier, Executor, Brief of G.R. Fairbanks Counsel of Appellee* (Jacksonville: Columbus Drew, 1860), 26; East and West Florida Claims, Treaty of 1819, Florida Claims, Claims of Spanish Citizens, c. 1812–1866, Spain, International Claims, Records of Boundary and Claims Commissions and Arbitrations, Record Group 76, National Archives, College Park, Maryland.

33. Abraham Lancaster, Soldier's Certificate No. 671600, RG 15; CB, vol. 4, p. 75; St. Johns County Marriage Licenses, Volume A, pp. 4, 215, SJCCH.

34. John B. Boles, introduction to *Masters and Slaves in the House of the Lord,* 12; James M. Denham, *"A Rogue's Paradise": Crime and Punishment in Antebellum Florida, 1821–1861* (Tuscaloosa: The University of Alabama Press, 1997), 121, 130; Canter Brown Jr., "Race Relations in Territorial Florida, 1821–1845," *Florida Historical Quarterly* 73 (January 1995): 307; Gannon, *Cross in the Sand,* 152; Rivers, *Slavery in Florida,* 86; St. Johns County Marriage Licenses, 15 April 1839, 15 June 1839, 20 February 1843, 16 July 1845, 26 February 1846, 9 May 1856, 16 June 1841, 29 January 1842, 10 February 1847, SJCCH; Kapitzke, *Religion, Power, and Politics,* 16–18; Lawrence W. Levine, *Black Culture and Black Consciousness: Afro-American Folk Thought from Slavery to Freedom* (New York: Oxford University Press, 1977), 92, 137.

35. Handy Growles, alias Goud, Soldier's Certificate No. 469919, RG 15; Miller, "Slaves and Southern Catholicism," 128, 138, 230n10; Boles, introduction to *Masters and Slaves in the*

House of the Lord, 12; Abel Poitrineau, "Demography and the Political Destiny of Florida during the Second Spanish Period," *Florida Historical Quarterly* 66 (April 1988): 427; Mills, "Piety and Prejudice," 180, 182; Cyprian Davis, *The History of Black Catholics in the United States* (New York: Crossroads, 1990), 42; Cyprian Davis and Jamie Phelps, eds., "*Stamped with the Image of God": African Americans as God's Image in Black* (New York: Orbis, 2003), 20–22, 274n54.

36. Annie Heloise Abel and Frank J. Klingberg, eds., *A Side-Light on Anglo-American Relations, 1839–1858: Furnished by the Correspondence of Lewis Tappan and Others with the British and Foreign Anti-Slavery Society* (Lancaster, PA: The Association for the Study of Negro Life, 1927), 30n27; "The Susan Murphy Will Case, Testimony at Trial," Eastern Circuit of Florida In the Circuit for St. Johns County, Spring Term, 1858, In the matter of the Contested Will of Susan Murphy decd. Francis Bridier Exct. Propounder ats David L. Yulee Caveator, RG 76; Fairbanks Brief, RG 76; John Mills, Soldier's Certificate No. 490204, RG 15.

37. W. Fitzhugh Brundage, "Le Reveil de la Louisiane: Memory and Acadian Identity, 1920–1960," in *Where These Memories Grow: History, Memory, and Southern Identity,* ed. W. Fitzhugh Brundage (Chapel Hill: University of North Carolina Press, 2000), 274, 292; Baptist, *Creating an Old South,* 156, 247, 249–50, 256, 260–61, 275; Nathalie Dessens, *Myths of the Plantation Society: Slavery in the American South and the West Indies* (Gainesville: University Press of Florida, 2003), 157–59; Gannon, *Cross in the Sand,* 27, 121, 128, 150, 152–56, 159–60, 165; Michael Gannon, *Rebel Bishop: Augustin Verot, Florida's Civil War Prelate* (Milwaukee: Bruce, 1964; reprint, Gainesville: University Press of Florida, 1997), 25–26; Weber, *The Spanish Frontier,* 347–48; FHSD, 13 March 1854; *St. Augustine Ancient City,* 5 January 1850; *St. Augustine Examiner,* 29 October 1859, 7 April 1860, 21 April 1860, 18 August 1860, 25 August 1860.

38. Jane Landers, "Black Society in Spanish St. Augustine, 1784–1821" (PhD diss., University of Florida, 1988), 141n13; Rivers, *Slavery in Florida,* 66; Levine, *Black Culture,* 262, 268, 368–69, 389; Mark M. Smith, "Remembering Mary, Shaping Revolt: Reconsidering the Stono Rebellion," *Journal of Southern History* 67 (August 2001): 513, 533; Raboteau, 6, 111; Hall, "African Religious Retentions," 42–43, 47, 49, 53.

39. Walker, *No More, No More,* 89–90, 93, 100, 103–4; David W. Blight, *Race and Reunion: The Civil War in American Memory* (Cambridge, MA: Harvard University Press, 2001), 89–93; Deborah Gray White, *Ar'n't I a Woman? Female Slaves in the Plantation South,* rev. ed. (New York: W. W. Norton, 1999), 143; Holt, "Symbol, Memory, and Service," 194–97, 199–200, 203–6, 207n3; Shulamith Lev-Aladgem, "Remembering Forbidden Memories: Community Theatre and the Politics of Memory," *Social Identities* 12 (May 2006): 269–72; Robert N. Bellah et al., *Habits of the Heart: Individualism and Commitment in American Life* (New York: Harper & Row, 1986), 153–54; David Thelen, "Memory and American History," *Journal of American History* 75 (March 1989): 1125–26; W. Fitzhugh Brundage, "No Deed but Memory," in Brundage, *Where These Memories Grow,* 12; Pybus, *Epic Journeys to Freedom,* 26; Schafer, "U.S. Territory and State," 225; Levine, *Black Culture,* 134; Baptist, *Creating an Old South,* 10.

40. Daniel S. Papp, Loch K. Johnson, and John E. Endicott, *American Foreign Policy: History, Politics, and Policy* (New York: Pearson Longman, 2005), 329–330; CB, vols. 3–4.

41. Raboteau, *Slave Religion,* 301–02; Seventh and Eighth Censuses of the United States, 1850 and 1860, Florida, St. Johns County; CB, vol. 3, entries 540–42; CB, vol. 2, pp. 68–69, 198; Deed Book F, 160–62, SJCCH; Deed Book P, 317–18, SJCCH; Judgment Record A, 20, SJCCH; Deed Book E, 202–3, SJCCH; Deed Book G, 31–36, SJCCH; Dirk Fleischman v. Mosby and Fish (1826–1827), 116–19, CCC, SAHSL; S. Mosby v. W. M. Simmons (1840),

98–45, CCC, SAHSL; *St. Augustine East Florida Herald,* 8 August 1826; Department of the South, November 1864, Report of the Census for Jacksonville, Fernandina, and St. Augustine, Florida, Report of the Census of SAHSL; CB, vol. 4, pp. 14, 16–17, 22–24, 32, 63–64, 71; CB, vol. 3, p. 14; Order Book A, 7–8, SJCCH; CM, p. 56; Minute Book B, pp. 16, 20, 27, 74, 76, 78, 195, 205–6, City Papers; petition of R. B. Canovas and others asking weekly allowance and shelter for Moseby, 6 January 1860, "Blacks: 1824–1855," City Papers.

42. Kapitzke, *Religion, Power, and Politics,* 19; Paquette, *Sugar Is Made of Blood,* 125; Walker, *No More, No More,* 103; Mills, "Piety and Prejudice," 174–79; Weber, *The Spanish Frontier,* 337; Gannon, *Cross in the Sand,* 152, 163; Gannon, *Rebel Bishop,* 5, 17, 22, 26, 248n59.

43. Kapitzke, *Religion, Power, and Politics,* 1, 9; Gannon, *Rebel Bishop,* 26, 160, 235–38, 243.

44. Kenneth J. Zanca, comp. and ed., *American Catholics and Slavery: 1789–1866, An Anthology of Primary Documents* (Lanham, MD: University Press of America, 1994), 175, 239–42; Davis, *The History of Black Catholics,* 39; Stevenson, *Life in Black and White,* 226–28, 233, 241–43, 257; George Rawick, *From Sundown to Sunup: The Making of the Black Community* (Westport, CT: Greenwood Press, 1972), 79; Richard Simmons, Soldier's Certificate No. 535664, RG 15.

45. Gannon, *Cross in the Sand,* 96–97, 111, 163; Gary Wray McDonogh, *Black and Catholic in Savannah, Georgia* (Knoxville: University of Tennessee Press, 1993), 38; Zanca, *American Catholics and Slavery,* 1321; Gannon, *Rebel Bishop,* 130; Rice, *American Catholic Opinion,* 12, 21, 153; Joseph Kelly, "Charleston's Bishop John England and American Slavery," *New Hibernia Review* 5 (Winter 2001): 52–53; Davis, *The History of Black Catholics,* 50, 52, 56–57, 64, 86–87, 107–9; Paquette, *Sugar Is Made of Blood,* 61–62, 77–78, 267, 270; Genovese, *Roll, Jordan, Roll,* 182; Hall, "Black and White Christians," 108; Gwendolyn Midlo Hall, *Social Control in Slave Plantation Societies: A Comparison of St. Domingue and Cuba* (Baltimore: Johns Hopkins University Press, 1971), 43–44.

46. Gannon, *Rebel Bishop,* 7, 15, 18; Gannon, "Verot, Augustin (1805–76)," in *The Encyclopedia of American Catholic History,* ed. Michael Glazier and Thomas J. Shelley (Collegeville, MN: Liturgical Press, 1997), 1432.

47. Gannon, *Cross in the Sand,* 152–53, 165; Gannon, *Rebel Bishop,* 143; Davis, *The History of Black Catholics,* 33; Hall, "Black and White Christians," 95; slave interview of Christine Mitchell, St. Augustine, Florida, 10 November 1936, in *Florida Narratives,* 226; Randall M. Miller, "The Failed Mission: The Catholic Church and Black Catholics in the Old South," in *The Southern Common People: Studies in Nineteenth-Century Social History,* ed. Edward Magdol and Jon L. Wakelyn (Westport, CT: Greenwood, 1980), 41, 48; Boles, *Black Southerners,* 16; Graham, *The Awakening of St. Augustine,* 14–16; Patricia C. Griffin, "Mullet on the Beach: The Minorcans of Florida, 1768–1788," special issue, *El Escribano: The St. Augustine Journal of History* 27 (1990): 16, 32, 64, 66, 151, 154; E. P. Panagopoulos, *New Smyrna: An Eighteenth-Century Greek Odyssey* (Gainesville: University of Florida Press, 1966), 90; Weber, *The Spanish Frontier,* 337; Miller, "A Church in Cultural Captivity," 52; Rice, *American Catholic Opinion,* 21, 148n49; Genovese, *Roll, Jordan, Roll,* 189; Baptist, *Creating an Old South,* 186–87, 189, 191, 236; Mohr, "Slaves and White Churches," 160, 162.

48. Augustin Verot, *A Tract for the Times. Slavery & Abolition Being the Substance of a Sermon, Preached in the Church of St. Augustine, Florida, on the 4th Day of January 1861, Day of Public Humiliation, Fasting and Prayer,* new edition (New Orleans: Catholic Propagator, 1861), 5–6, 15–16, 19.

49. Verot, *A Tract for the Times,* 17–19; Boles, introduction to *Masters and Slaves in the House of the Lord,* 11; Genovese, *Roll, Jordan, Roll,* 70; Mohr, "Slaves and White Churches,"

168–69; Hahn, *A Nation Under Our Feet,* 99; Katherine L. Dvorak, "After Apocalypse, Moses," in Boles, *Masters and Slaves in the House of the Lord,* 176; Daniel L. Schafer, "Freedom Was as Close as the River: African Americans and the Civil War in Northeast Florida," in Colburn and Landers, *The African American Heritage of Florida,* 172.

50. Kelly, "Charleston's Bishop John England," 56; Mathews, "Religion and Slavery," 220; Mohr, "Slaves and White Churches," 168–71; Gannon, *Rebel Bishop,* 52, 118, 144, 250; Gannon, *Cross in the Sand,* 171, 183; Raboteau, *Slave Religion,* 187, 208; Genovese, *Roll, Jordan, Roll,* 69–71, 186–87; Miller, "A Church in Cultural Captivity," 16; Davis, *The History of Black Catholics,* 53, 55–56, 64–65, 276n79; Zanca, *American Catholics and Slavery,* 201; Hahn, *A Nation Under Our Feet,* 77, 83; Miller, "Slaves and Southern Catholicism," 130, 233; Michael J. McNally, *Catholicism in South Florida, 1868–1898* (Gainesville: University Presses of Florida, 1982), 3; John B. Boles, *Black Southerners, 1619–1869* (Lexington: University Press of Kentucky, 1983), 194, 197; Barbara E. Mattick, "Ministries in Black and White: The Catholic Sisters of St. Augustine, Florida, 1859–1920" (PhD diss., Florida State University, 2008), 29.

51. Peter Linebaugh and Marcus Rediker, *The Many-Sided Hydra: Sailors, Slaves, Commoners, and the Hidden History of the Revolutionary Atlantic* (Boston: Beacon Press, 2000); Landers, *Black Society,* 23–25, 167; George Klos, "Blacks and the Seminole Removal Debate, 1821–1835," in Colburn and Landers, *The African American Heritage of Florida,* 138, 141; Rivers, *Slavery in Florida,* 201, 205.

52. Gregg D. Kimball, "African, American, and Virginian: The Shaping of Black Memory in Antebellum Virginia, 1790–1860," in Brundage, *Where These Memories Grow,* 66; Baptist, *Creating an Old South,* 82; Dunaway, *Slavery in the American Mountain South,* 206; Wallerstein, "The Construction of Peoplehood," 78.

53. Kimball, "African, American, and Virginian," 66.

54. Kapitzke, *Religion, Power, and Politics,* 16–17; Lev-Aladgem, "Remembering Forbidden Memories," 269–72; Brundage, "No Deed but Memory," 12; Dunaway, *Slavery in the American Mountain South,* 206; Troutman, "Grapevine in the Slave Market," 207; Miller, "Slaves and Southern Catholicism," 151–52; Sparks, "Religion in Amite County," 79.

55. Smith, *Slavery and Plantation Growth,* 519.

Bibliography

ARCHIVAL SOURCES

Department of Archives, Nassau, Bahamas

Duplicate Governor's Despatches

Florida State Archives, Tallahassee, Florida

St. Johns County Probate Records, 1784–1933

Library of Congress, Washington, D.C.

Duncan Clinch Letterbook

National Archives, College Park, Maryland

Record Group 56, General Records of the Department of the Treasury
Record Group 59, Records of the Department of State
Record Group 76, Records of the Boundary and Claims Commissions and Arbitrations
Record Group 206, Records of the Solicitor of the Treasury
Record Group 217, Records of the Accounting Officers of the Department of the Treasury

National Archives, Washington, D.C.

Record Group 15, Records of the Veterans' Administration
Record Group 29, Records of the Bureau of the Census
Record Group 46, Records of the United States Senate
Record Group 94, Records of the Adjutant General's Office
Record Group 127, Records of the United States Marine Corps

New York Historical Society, New York, New York

Buckingham Smith Papers

P. K. Yonge Library of Florida History, Gainesville, Florida

Spanish Land Grants

St. Augustine Historical Society Research Library, St. Augustine, Florida

Burt Papers
Calhoun Putnam Papers
Cathedral Parish Records
City of St. Augustine Papers
Clarke Papers
Marriage Records, 1823–1880, St. Johns County
Minutes and Register of the Trinity Episcopal Church
Negro Passes and Permits
Patriot War Papers and Patriot War Claims
Peck Papers
Report of the Census for Jacksonville, Fernandina, and St. Augustine, Florida, November 1864
St. Johns County Court Cases

St. Johns County Courthouse, St. Augustine, Florida

Deed Books
Judgment Records
Marriage Licenses
Order Books
Wills and Letters of Administration

State Library of Florida, Tallahassee, Florida

Florida Collection

NEWSPAPERS

British and Foreign Anti-Slavery Reporter
Nassau Royal Gazette and Bahama Advertiser
New-Hampshire Sentinel
Pittsburgh Post-Gazette
St. Augustine Ancient City
St. Augustine Florida Herald
St. Augustine Florida Herald & Southern Democrat
St. Augustine News
St. Augustine Tatler
Tarentum (Pennsylvania) Valley News Dispatch

PUBLISHED PRIMARY SOURCES

Abel, Annie Heloise, and Frank J. Klingberg, eds. *A Side-Light on Anglo-American Relations, 1839–1858: Furnished by the Correspondence of Lewis Tappan and Others with the British and Foreign Anti-Slavery Society.* Lancaster, PA: Association for the Study of Negro Life, 1927.

Bryant, William Cullen. *Letters of a Traveller or Notes of Things Seen in Europe and America.* New York: George P. Putnam, 1850.

Carter, Clarence Edwin, ed. *The Territory of Florida, 1821–1824*. Vol. 22 of *The Territorial Papers of the United States.* Washington, DC: Government Printing Office, 1956.

———. *The Territory of Florida, 1834–1839*. Vol. 25 of *The Territorial Papers of the United States.* Washington, DC: Government Printing Office, 1960.

Davis, Cyprian, and Jamie Phelps, eds. *"Stamped with the Image of God": African Americans as God's Image in Black.* New York: Orbis, 2003.

Denham, James M., and Keith L. Huneycutt, eds. *Echoes from a Distant Frontier: The Brown Sisters' Correspondence from Antebellum Florida.* Columbia: University of South Carolina Press, 2004.

Dickins, Asbury, and John W. Forney, eds. *American State Papers: Documents of the Congress of the United States in Relation To Public Lands . . .* Vol. 6. Washington, DC: Gales and Seaton, 1860.

Great Britain, Foreign Office. *British and Foreign State Papers.* Vol. 30. London: James Ridgway and Sons, 1858.

Parry, Clive, ed. *The Consolidated Treaty Series.* Vol. 70. Dobbs Ferry, NY: Oceana, 1969.

Peters, Richard, ed. *The Public Statutes at Large of the United States of America . . .* 8 vols. Boston: Charles C. Little and James Brown, 1845–1867.

Rawick, George P., ed. *Florida Narratives.* Vol. 17 of *The American Slave: A Composite Biography.* Westport, CT: Greenwood Press, 1972.

Verot, Augustin. *A Tract for the Times . . . Being the Substance of a Sermon Preached in the Church of St. Augustine, Florida, on the 4th Day of January 1861 . . .* New edition. New Orleans: Catholic Propagator, 1861.

Walker, Jonathan. *Trial and Imprisonment of Jonathan Walker at Pensacola, Florida for Aiding Slaves to Escape from Bondage . . .* Boston: Antislavery Office, 1846.

White, Geoffrey M., David W. Gegeo, David Akin, and Karen Watson-Gegeo, eds. *The Big Death: Solomon Islanders Remember World War II.* Suva, Fiji: Institute of Pacific Studies, 1988.

Wilson, Clyde N., ed. *The Papers of John C. Calhoun.* Vol. 18. Columbia: University of South Carolina Press, 1989.

Zanca, Kenneth J., ed. and comp. *American Catholics and Slavery: 1789–1866, An Anthology of Primary Documents.* Lantham, MD: University Press of America, 1994.

SECONDARY SOURCES

Alexander, J. H. "The Ambush of Captain John Williams, U.S.M.C.: Failure of the East Florida Invasion 1812–1813." *Florida Historical Quarterly* 56 (January 1978): 280–296.

———. "Swamp Ambush in Florida." *Military History* 14 (March 1998): 38–45.

Aptheker, Herbert. *Abolitionism: A Revolutionary Movement.* Boston: Twayne, 1989.

———. *Negro Slave Revolts in the United States: 1526–1860.* New York: International Publishers, 1939.

Arnade, Charles W. "Raids, Sieges, and International Wars." In *The New History of Florida,* edited by Michael Gannon, 100–116. Gainesville: University Press of Florida, 1996.

Baptist, Edward A. *Creating an Old South: Middle Florida's Plantation Frontier before the Civil War.* Chapel Hill: University of North Carolina Press, 2002.

Bellah, Robert N., Richard Madsen, William M. Sullivan, Ann Swidler, and Steven M. Tipton. *Habits of the Heart: Individualism and Commitment in American Life.* New York: Harper & Row, 1986.

Bennett, Herman L. "Genealogies to a Past: Africa, Ethnicity, and Marriage in Seventeenth-Century Mexico." In *New Studies in the History of American Slavery,* edited by Edward E. Baptist and Stephanie M. H. Camp, 127–147. Athens: University of Georgia Press, 2006.

Bennett, James B. *Religion and the Rise of Jim Crow in New Orleans.* Princeton, NJ: Princeton University Press, 2005.

Berlin, Ira. *Generations of Captivity: A History of African-American Slaves.* Cambridge, MA: Harvard University Press, 2003.

———. *Many Thousands Gone: The First Two Centuries of Slavery in North America.* Cambridge, MA: Harvard University Press, 1998.

Blassingame, John W. *The Slave Community: Plantation Life in the Antebellum South.* New York: Oxford University Press, 1972.

———. *The Slave Community: Plantation Life in the Antebellum South.* Rev. ed. New York: Oxford University Press, 1979.

Blight, David W. *Race and Reunion: The Civil War in American Memory.* Cambridge, MA: Harvard University Press, 2001.

Boles, John B. *Black Southerners, 1619–1869.* Lexington: University Press of Kentucky, 1983.

———. Introduction to *Masters and Slaves in the House of the Lord: Race and Religion in the American South, 1740–1870,* edited by John B. Boles. Lexington: University Press of Kentucky, 1988.

Bolster, Jeffrey. *Black Jacks: African American Seamen in the Age of Sail.* Cambridge, MA: Harvard University Press, 1997.

Bordewich, Fergus M. *Bound for Canaan: The Epic Story of the Underground Railroad: America's First Civil Rights Movement.* New York: HarperCollins, 2005.

Bowman, Charles H., Jr. "Amelia Island and Vicente Pazos of Upper Peru." In *La Republica de las Floridas: Texts and Documents,* compiled by David Bushnell, 43–54. Mexico, D.F.: Pan American Institute of Geography and History, 1986.

Bowser, Frederick P. "Colonial Spanish America." In *Neither Slave Nor Free: The Freedman of African Descent in the Slave Societies of the New World,* edited by David W. Cohen and Jack P. Greene, 19–58. Baltimore: Johns Hopkins University Press, 1972.

Brown, Canter, Jr. "Race Relations in Territorial Florida, 1821–1845." *Florida Historical Quarterly* 73 (January 1995): 287–307.

Brundage, W. Fitzhugh. "Introduction: No Deed but Memory." In *Where These Memories Grow: History, Memory, and Southern Identity,* edited by W. Fitzhugh Brundage, 1–28. Chapel Hill: University of North Carolina Press, 2000.

———. "Le Reveil de la Louisiane: Memory and Acadian Identities." In *Where These Memories Grow: History, Memory, and Southern Identity,* edited by W. Fitzhugh Brundage, 271–298. Chapel Hill: University of North Carolina Press, 2000.

Buker, George E. "The Americanization of St. Augustine." In *The Oldest City: St. Augustine, Saga of Survival,* edited by Jean Parker Waterbury, 151–179. St. Augustine: St. Augustine Historical Society Research Library, 1983.

Bushnell, David. "The Republic of Florida: An Overview." In *La Republica de las Floridas: Texts and Documents,* compiled by David Bushnell, 7–18. Mexico, D.F.: Pan American Institute of Geography and History, 1986.

Childs, Matt D. *The 1812 Aponte Rebellion in Cuba and the Struggle against Atlantic Slavery.* Chapel Hill: University of North Carolina Press, 2006.

Cobley, Alan Gregor. "That Turbulent Soil: Seafarers, the 'Black Atlantic' and Afro-Caribbean Identity." In *Seascapes: Maritime Histories, Littoral Cultures, and Transoceanic Exchanges,* edited by Jerry H. Bentley, Renate Bridenthal, and Kären Wigen, 153–168. Honolulu: University of Hawai'i Press, 2007.

Cohen, Lizabeth. *A Consumers' Republic: The Politics of Mass Consumption in Postwar America.* New York: Random House, 2003.

Colburn, David R. *Racial Change and Community Crisis: St. Augustine, Florida, 1877–1980.* New York: Columbia University Press, 1985.

Craton, Michael. "Loyalists Mainly to Themselves: The 'Black Loyalist' Diaspora to the Bahamas, 1783–c. 1820." In *Working Slavery, Pricing Freedom: Perspectives from the Caribbean, Africa and the African Diaspora,* edited by Verene A. Shepherd, 44–68. Kingston, Jamaica: Ian Randle, 2002.

Craton, Michael, and Gail Saunders. *From the Ending of Slavery to Twenty-First Century.* Vol. 2 of *Islanders in the Stream: A History of the Bahamian People.* Athens: University of Georgia Press, 1998.

Cusick, James G. *The Other War of 1812: The Patriot War and the American Invasion of Spanish East Florida.* Gainesville: University Press of Florida, 2003.

Davis, Cyprian. *The History of Black Catholics in the United States.* New York: Crossroads, 1990.

Davis, David Brion. *Challenging the Boundaries of Slavery.* Cambridge, MA: Harvard University Press, 2003.

Deagan, Kathleen, and Darcie MacMahon. *Fort Mose: Colonial America's Black Fortress of Freedom.* Gainesville: University Press of Florida, 1995.

Denham, James M. *"A Rogue's Paradise": Crime and Punishment in Antebellum Florida, 1821–1861.* Tuscaloosa: The University of Alabama Press, 1997.

Dessens, Nathalie. *Myths of the Plantation Society: Slavery in the American South and the West Indies.* Gainesville: University Press of Florida, 2003.

Dunaway, Wilma A. *Slavery in the American Mountain South.* Cambridge: Cambridge University Press, 2003.

Dunn, Marvin. *Black Miami in the Twentieth Century.* Gainesville: University Press of Florida, 2002.

Dvorak, Katherine L. "After Apocalypse, Moses." In *Masters and Slaves in the House of the Lord: Race and Religion in the American South, 1740–1870,* edited by John B. Boles, 173–191. Lexington: University Press of Kentucky, 1988.

Egerton, Douglas R. *Death or Liberty: African Americans and Revolutionary America.* New York: Oxford University Press, 2009.

———. "Nat Turner in a Hemispheric Context." In *Nat Turner: A Slave Rebellion in History and Memory,* edited by Kenneth S. Greenberg, 134–147. New York: Oxford University Press, 2003.

———. "The Tricolor in Black and White: The French Revolution in Gabriel's Virginia." In *Slavery in the Caribbean Francophone World: Distant Voices, Forgotten Acts, Forged Identities,* edited by Doris Y. Kadesh, 91–105. Athens: University of Georgia Press, 2000.

Franklin, John Hope, and Loren Schweninger. *Runaway Slaves: Rebels on the Plantation.* New York: Oxford University Press, 1999.

Fuller, Herbert Bruce. *The Purchase of Florida: Its History and Diplomacy.* Cleveland: Burrows Brothers, 1906.

Gaddis, John Lewis. *The Cold War: A New History.* New York: Penguin Press, 2005.

———. *Surprise, Security, and the American Experience.* Cambridge, MA: Harvard University Press, 2004.

Gallay, Allan. "Planters and Slaves in the Great Awakening." In *Masters and Slaves in the House of the Lord: Race and Religion in the American South, 1740–1870*, edited by John B. Boles, 19–36. Lexington: University Press of Kentucky, 1988.

Gannon, Michael V. *The Cross in the Sand: The Early Catholic Church in Florida, 1513–1870*. Gainesville: University of Florida Press, 1965.

———. *Florida: A Short History*. Gainesville: University Press of Florida, 1993.

———. *Rebel Bishop: Augustin Verot, Florida's Civil War Prelate*. 1964. Reprint, Gainesville: University Press of Florida, 1997.

Genovese, Eugene. *Roll, Jordan, Roll: The World the Slaves Made*. New York: Random House, 1974.

Glazier, Michael, and Thomas J. Shelley, eds. *The Encyclopedia of American Catholic History*. Collegeville, MN: Liturgical Press, 1997.

González, Luís. *San José de Gracia: Mexican Village in Transition*. Translated by John Upton. Austin: University of Texas Press, 1974.

Gould, Virginia. "In Full Enjoyment of Their Liberty: The Free Women of Color of the Gulf Ports of New Orleans, Mobile, and Pensacola, 1769–1860." PhD diss., Emory University, 1989.

Graham, Thomas. *The Awakening of St. Augustine: The Anderson Family and the Oldest City, 1821–1924*. St. Augustine: St. Augustine Historical Society, 1978.

Greenberg, Kenneth S. "Name, Face, Body." In *Nat Turner: A Slave Rebellion in History and Memory*, edited by Kenneth S. Greenberg, 3–23. New York: Oxford University Press, 2003.

Griffin, Patricia C. "Blue Gold: Andrew Turnbull's New Smyrna Plantation." In *Colonial Plantations and Economy in Florida*, edited by Jane G. Landers, 39–68. Gainesville: University Press of Florida, 2000.

———. "Mullet on the Beach: The Minorcans of Florida, 1768–1788." Special issue, *El Escribano: The St. Augustine Journal of History* 27 (1990).

———. "The Spanish Return: The People-Mix Period 1784–1821." In *The Oldest City: St. Augustine, Saga of Survival*, edited by Jean Parker Waterbury, 125–150. St. Augustine: St. Augustine Historical Society, 1983.

Hahn, Steven. *A Nation Under Our Feet: Black Political Struggles in the Rural South, From Slavery to the Great Migration*. Cambridge, MA: Harvard University Press, 2003.

Hall, Claude H. *Abel Parker Upshur: Conservative Virginian, 1790–1844*. Madison: State Historical Society of Wisconsin, 1964.

Hall, Gwendolyn Midlo. *Social Control in Slave Plantation Societies: A Comparison of St. Domingue and Cuba*. Baltimore: Johns Hopkins University Press, 1971.

Hall, Robert L. "African Religious Retentions in Florida." In *The African American Heritage of Florida*, edited by David R. Colburn and Jane L. Landers, 42–70. Gainesville: University Press of Florida, 1995.

———. "Black and White Christians in Florida, 1822–1861." In *Masters and Slaves in the House of the Lord: Race and Religion in the American South, 1740–1870*, edited by John B. Boles, 81–98. Lexington: University Press of Kentucky, 1988.

Hazouri, Kim. "From Jose Mariano Hernandez to Joseph Martin Hernandez: 1788–1856." Unpublished manuscript. St. Augustine Historical Society Research Library, St. Augustine, Florida.

Hebel, Ianthe Bond. "The Samuel Williams Family." *Journal of the Halifax Historical Society* 2, no. 1 (1952?): 30–31.

Hill, Louise Biles. "George J.F. Clarke, 1774–1836." *Florida Historical Quarterly* 21 (January 1943): 197–253.

Holt, Sharon Ann. "Symbol, Memory, and Service: Resistance and Family Formation in Nineteenth-Century African America." In *Working Toward Freedom: Slave Society and Domestic Economy in the American South,* edited by Larry E. Hudson Jr., 192–210. Rochester: University of Rochester Press, 1994.

Howard, Rosalyn. *Black Seminoles in the Bahamas.* Gainesville: University Press of Florida, 2002.

Jentleson, Bruce W., and Thomas G. Paterson, eds. *Encyclopedia of U.S. Foreign Relations.* New York: Oxford University Press, 1997.

Johnson, Howard. *The Bahamas in Slavery and Freedom.* Kingston, Jamaica: Ian Randle, 1991.

Johnson, Sherry. "The St. Augustine Hurricane of 1811: Disaster and the Question of Political Unrest on the Florida Frontier." *Florida Historical Quarterly* 84 (Summer 2005): 28–56.

Johnson, Whittington B. *Race Relations in the Bahamas, 1784–1834: The Nonviolent Transformation from a Slave to a Free Society.* Fayetteville: University of Arkansas Press, 2000.

Jones, Howard. "The Peculiar Institution and National Honor: The Case of the *Creole* Slave Revolt." *Civil War History* 21 (March 1975): 28–50.

Kapitzke, Robert L. *Religion, Power, and Politics in Colonial St. Augustine.* Gainesville: University Press of Florida, 2001.

Kelly, Joseph. "Charleston's Bishop John England and American Slavery." *New Hibernia Review* 5 (Winter 2001): 48–56.

Kimball, Gregg D. "African, American, and Virginian: The Shaping of Black Memory in Antebellum Virginia, 1790–1860." In *Where These Memories Grow: History, Memory, and Southern Identity,* edited by W. Fitzhugh Brundage, 57–78. Chapel Hill: University of North Carolina Press, 2000.

Klos, George. "Blacks and the Seminole Removal Debate, 1821–1835." In *The African American Heritage of Florida,* edited by David R. Colburn and Jane L. Landers, 128–156. Gainesville: University of Florida Press, 1995.

Kluger, Richard. *Seizing Destiny: How America Grew from Sea to Shining Sea.* New York: Alfred A. Knopf, 2007.

Kolchin, Peter. *American Slavery, 1619–1877.* New York: Hill and Wang, 1993.

Landers, Jane. "Africans and Native Americans on the Spanish Colonial Frontier." In *Beyond Black and Red: African-Native Relations in Colonial Latin America,* edited by Matthew Restall, 53–80. Albuquerque: University of New Mexico Press, 2005.

———. *Black Society in Spanish Florida.* Urbana: University of Illinois Press, 1999.

———. "Black Society in Spanish St. Augustine, 1784–1821." PhD diss., University of Florida, 1988.

———. "The Central African Presence in Spanish Maroon Communities." In *Central Africans and Cultural Transformations in the American Diaspora,* edited by Linda M. Heywood, 227–242. Cambridge: Cambridge University Press, 2002.

———. "Free and Slave." In *The New History of Florida,* edited by Michael Gannon, 167–182. Gainesville: University Press of Florida, 1996.

———. "Traditions of African American Freedom and Community in Spanish Colonial Florida." In *The African American Heritage of Florida,* edited by David R. Colburn and Jane L. Landers, 17–41. Gainesville: University Press of Florida, 1995.

Landers, Jane G. "Acquisition and Loss on a Spanish Frontier: The Free Black Homesteaders of Florida, 1784–1821." In *Against the Odds: Free Blacks in the Slave Societies of the Americas,* edited by Jane G. Landers, 85–101. London: Frank Cass, 1996.

———. "Francisco Xavier Sanchez, *Floridano* Planter and Merchant." In *Colonial Plantations and Economy in Florida,* edited by Jane G. Landers, 83–97. Gainesville: University Press of Florida, 2000.

———. "Free Black Plantations and Economy in Florida." In *Colonial Plantations and Economy in Florida,* edited by Jane G. Landers, 121–135. Gainesville: University Press of Florida, 2000.

———. Introduction to *Colonial Plantations and Economy in Florida.* Gainesville: University Press of Florida, 2000.

Layton, Azza Salama. *International Politics and Civil Rights Policies in the United States, 1941–1960.* Cambridge: Cambridge University Press, 2000.

Lev-Aladgem, Shulamith. "Remembering Forbidden Memories: Community Theatre and the Politics of Memory." *Social Identities* 12 (May 2006): 269–283.

Levine, Lawrence W. *Black Culture and Black Consciousness: Afro-American Folk Thought from Slavery to Freedom.* New York: Oxford University Press, 1977.

Linebaugh, Peter, and Marcus Rediker. *The Many-Sided Hydra: Sailors, Slaves, Commoners, and the Hidden History of the Revolutionary Atlantic.* Boston: Beacon Press, 2000.

Macdougall, Donald V. "Habeas Corpus, Extradition and a Fugitive Slave in Canada." *Slavery & Abolition* 7 (September 1986): 118–128.

Mahon, John K., "Daniel Newnan: A Neglected Figure in Florida History." *Florida Historical Quarterly* 74 (Fall 1995): 148–153.

Mahon, John K., and Brent R. Weisman. "Florida's Seminole and Miccosukee Peoples." In *The New History of Florida,* edited by Michael Gannon, 183–206. Gainesville: University Press of Florida, 1996.

Malone, Ann Patton. *Sweet Chariot: Slave Family and Household Structure in Nineteenth-Century Louisiana.* Chapel Hill: University of North Carolina Press, 2002.

Marotti, Frank, Jr. "Edward M. Wanton and the Settling of Micanopy." *Florida Historical Quarterly* 73 (April 1995): 456–477.

———. "Negotiating Freedom in St. Johns County, Florida, 1812–1862." PhD diss., University of Hawai'i, 2003.

Mathews, Donald G. "Religion and Slavery—The Case of the American South." In *Antislavery, Religion and Reform: Essays in Memory of Roger Anstey,* edited by Christine Bolt and Seymour Drescher, 207–232. Folkestone, England: Wm. Dawson and Son, 1980.

Mattick, Barbara E. "Ministries in Black and White: The Catholic Sisters of St. Augustine, Florida, 1859–1920." PhD diss., Florida State University, 2008.

McDonogh, Gary Wray. *Black and Catholic in Savannah, Georgia.* Knoxville: University of Tennessee Press, 1993.

McNally, Michael J. *Catholicism in South Florida, 1868–1898.* Gainesville: University Presses of Florida, 1982.

Miller, Randall M. "A Church in Cultural Captivity: Some Speculations on Catholic Identity in the Old South." In *Catholics in the Old South: Essays on Church and Culture,* edited by Randall M. Miller and Jon L. Wakelyn, 11–52. Macon, GA: Mercer University Press, 1983.

———. "Slaves and Southern Catholicism." In *Masters and Slaves in the House of the Lord: Race and Religion in the American South, 1740–1870,* edited by John B. Boles, 127–152. Lexington: University Press of Kentucky, 1988.

———. "That Failed Mission: The Catholic Church and Black Catholics in the Old South." In *The Southern Common People: Studies in Nineteenth-Century Social History,* edited by Edward Magdol and Jon L. Wakelyn, 37–54. Westport, CT: Greenwood Press, 1980.

Mills, Gary B. "Piety and Prejudice: A Colored Catholic Community in the Antebellum South." In *Catholics in the Old South: Essays on Church and Culture,* edited by Randall M. Miller and Jon L. Wakelyn, 171–194. Macon, GA: Mercer University Press, 1983.

Mohr, Clarence L. "Slaves and White Churches in Confederate Georgia." In *Masters and*

Slaves in the House of the Lord: Race and Religion in the American South, 1740–1870, edited by John B. Boles, 153–172. Lexington: University Press of Kentucky, 1988.

Monaco, Chris. "Fort Mitchell and the Settlement of the Alachua Country." *Florida Historical Quarterly* 79 (Summer 2000): 1–25.

Morgan, Robert J. *A Whig Embattled: The Presidency under John Tyler.* Lincoln: University of Nebraska Press, 1954.

Norris, David L. "Failure Unfolds: The Loss of Amelia Island." In *La Republica de las Floridas: Texts and Documents,* compiled by David Bushnell, 19–34. Mexico, D.F.: Pan American Institute of Geography and History, 1986.

Panagopoulos, E. P. *New Smyrna: An Eighteenth Century Greek Odyssey.* Gainesville: University of Florida Press, 1966.

Papp, Daniel S., Loch K. Johnson, and John E. Endicott. *American Foreign Policy: History, Politics, and Policy.* New York: Pearson Longman, 2005.

Paquette, Robert L. *Sugar Is Made of Blood: The Conspiracy of La Escalera and the Conflict between Empires over Slavery in Cuba.* Middleton, CT: Wesleyan University Press, 1988.

Parker, Susan R. "The Cattle Trade in East Florida, 1784–1821." In *Colonial Plantations and Economy in Florida,* edited by Jane G. Landers, 150–167. Gainesville: University Press of Florida, 2000.

———. "Success through Diversification: Francis Philip Fatio's New Switzerland Plantation." In *Colonial Plantations and Economy in Florida,* edited by Jane G. Landers, 69–82. Gainesville: University Press of Florida, 2000.

Patrick, Rembert W. *Florida Fiasco: Rampant Rebels on the Georgia-Florida Border, 1810–1815.* Athens: University of Georgia Press, 1954.

Poitrineau, Abel. "Demography and the Political Destiny of Florida during the Second Spanish Period." *Florida Historical Quarterly* 66 (April 1988): 420–443.

Porter, Kenneth W. "Florida Slaves and Free Negroes in the Seminole War, 1835–1842." *Journal of Negro History* 28 (October 1943): 390–421.

———. "John Caesar: Seminole Negro Partisan." *Journal of Negro History* 31 (April 1946): 190–207.

———. *The Negro on the American Frontier.* New York: Arno Press, 1971.

Poyo, Gerald E. "La Republica de las Floridas: The Mexican Connection, 1814–1817." In *La Republica de las Floridas: Texts and Documents,* compiled by David Bushnell, 35–42. Mexico, D.F.: Pan American Institute of Geography and History, 1986.

Pybus, Cassandra. *Epic Journeys to Freedom: Runaway Slaves of the American Revolution and Their Global Quest for Liberty.* Boston: Beacon Press, 2006.

Raboteau, Albert J. *Slave Religion: The "Invisible Institution" in the Antebellum South.* New York: Oxford University Press, 1978.

Rawick, George. *From Sundown to Sunup: The Making of a Black Community.* Westport, CT: Greenwood Press, 1972.

Rice, Madeleine Hook. *American Catholic Opinion in the Slavery Controversy.* Glouster, MA: Peter Smith, 1964.

Riley, Sandra. *Homeword Bound: A History of the Bahama Islands to 1850 with a Definitive Study of Abaco in the American Loyalist Plantation Period.* Miami: Island Research, 1983.

Rivers, Larry Eugene. *Slavery in Florida: Territorial Days to Emancipation.* Gainesville: University Press of Florida, 2000.

Rodríguez, Junius P., ed. *Encyclopedia of Slave Resistance and Rebellion.* Westport, CT: Greenwood Press, 2007.

———. *The Historical Encyclopedia of World Slavery.* Santa Barbara, CA: ABC-CLIO, 1997.

Rugemer, Edward B. "Robert Monroe Harrison, British Abolition, Southern Anglophobia and Texas Annexation." *Slavery & Abolition* 28 (August 2007): 169–191.

Schafer, Daniel L. *Anna Kingsley.* St. Augustine: St. Augustine Historical Society, 1994.

———. *Anna Madgigine Jai Kingsley: African Princess, Florida Slave, Plantation Slaveowner.* Gainesville: University Press of Florida, 2003.

———. "'A Class of People Neither Freemen Nor Slaves': From Spanish to American Race Relations in Florida, 1821–1861." *Journal of Social History* 26 (Spring 1993): 587–609.

———. "Freedom Was as Close as the River: African Americans and the Civil War in Northeast Florida." In *The African American Heritage of Florida,* edited by David R. Colburn and Jane L. Landers, 157–184. Gainesville: University Press of Florida, 1995.

———. "'A Swamp of an Investment'?: Richard Oswald's British East Florida Plantation Experiment." In *Colonial Plantations and Economy in Florida,* edited by Jane G. Landers, 11–38. Gainesville: University Press of Florida, 2000.

———. "U.S. Territory and State." In *The New History of Florida,* edited by Michael Gannon, 207–230. Gainesville: University Press of Florida, 1996.

———. "'Yellow Silk Ferret Tied Round Their Wrists': African Americans in British East Florida, 1763–1784." In *The African American Heritage of Florida,* edited by David R. Colburn and Jane L. Landers, 71–103. Gainesville: University Press of Florida, 1995.

———. "Zephaniah Kingsley's Laurel Grove Plantation, 1803–1813." In *Colonial Plantations and Economy in Florida,* edited by Jane G. Landers, 98–120. Gainesville: University Press of Florida, 2000.

Smail, Daniel Lord. *On Deep History and the Brain.* Berkeley and Los Angeles: University of California Press, 2008.

Smallwood, Stephanie. *Saltwater Slavery: A Middle Passage from Africa to American Diaspora.* Cambridge, MA: Harvard University Press, 2007.

Smith, Julia Floyd. *Slavery and Plantation Growth in Antebellum Florida, 1821–1860.* Gainesville: University of Florida Press, 1973.

Smith, Mark A. "Engineering Slavery: The U.S. Army Corps of Engineers and Slavery at Key West." *Florida Historical Quarterly* 86 (Spring 2008): 498–526.

Smith, Mark M. "Remembering Mary, Shaping Revolt: Reconsidering the Stono Rebellion." *Journal of Southern History* 67 (August 2001): 513–534.

Sparks, Randy J. "Religion in Amite County, Mississippi." In *Masters and Slaves in the House of the Lord: Race and Religion in the American South, 1740–1870,* edited by John B. Boles, 58–80. Lexington: University Press of Kentucky, 1988.

Stevenson, Brenda E. *Life in Black and White: Family and Community in the Slave South.* New York: Oxford University Press, 1996.

Temperly, Howard. *British Antislavery, 1833–1870.* London: Longman, 1972.

Thelen, David. "Memory and American History." *Journal of American History* 75 (March 1989): 1117–1129.

Touchstone, Blake. "Planters and Slave Religion in the Deep South." In *Masters and Slaves in the House of the Lord: Race and Religion in the American South, 1740–1870,* edited by John B. Boles, 99–126. Lexington: University Press of Kentucky, 1988.

Troutman, Phillip. "Grapevine in the Slave Market: African American Geopolitical Literacy and the 1841 *Creole* Revolt." In *The Chattel Principle: Internal Slave Trades in the Americas,* edited by Walter Johnson, 203–233. New Haven, CT: Yale University Press, 2004.

Turley, David M. "'Free Air' and Fugitive Slaves: British Abolitionists Versus Government Over American Fugitives, 1834–1861." In *Anti-slavery, Religion and Reform: Essays in Memory of Roger Anstey,* edited by Christine Bolt and Seymour Drescher, 163–182. Folkestone, England: Wm. Dawson & Son, 1980.

Walker, Daniel E. *No More, No More: Slavery and Cultural Resistance in Havana and New Orleans.* Minneapolis: University of Minnesota Press, 2004.

Wallerstein, Immanuel. "The Construction of Peoplehood: Racism, Nationalism, Ethnicity." In *Race, Nation, Class: Ambiguous Identities,* edited by Etienne Balibar and Immanuel Wallerstein, 71–85. London: Verso, 1991.

Warner, Lee H. *Free Men in An Age of Servitude: Three Centuries of a Black Family.* Lexington: University Press of Kentucky, 1992.

Webber, Thomas L. *Deep Like the Rivers: Education in the Slave Quarter Community, 1831–1865.* New York: W. W. Norton, 1978.

Weber, David J. *The Spanish Frontier in North America.* New Haven, CT: Yale University Press, 1992.

Weigel, George. *Witness to Hope: The Biography of Pope John Paul II.* New York: Harper Perennial, 2005.

Weiss, John McNish. "The Corps of Colonial Marines 1814–16: A Summary." *Immigrants & Minorities* 15 (March 1996): 80–90.

———. *The Merikens: Free Black American Settlers in Trinidad, 1815–1816.* Rev. ed. London: McNish & Weiss, 2002.

White, Deborah Gray. *Ar'n't I a Woman?: Female Slaves in the Plantation South.* Rev. ed. New York: W. W. Norton, 1999.

Wigen, Kären. Introduction to *Seascapes: Maritime Histories, Littoral Cultures, and Transoceanic Exchanges,* edited by Jerry H. Bentley, Renate Bridenthal, and Kären Wigen. Honolulu: University of Hawai'i Press, 2007.

Will, Thomas E. "Weddings on Contested Grounds: Slave Marriage in the Antebellum South." *The Historian* 62 (Fall 1999): 99–118.

Williams, Michael. *Americans and Their Forests: A Historical Geography.* Cambridge: Cambridge University Press, 1989.

Wilson, Gil. "An African American Flight for Freedom." *The Ancient City Geneaologist* 3, no. 1 (1992): 16–18.

Index